Carl C. Yonker

The Rise and Fall of Greater Syria

De Gruyter Contemporary Social Sciences

Volume 1

Carl C. Yonker

The Rise and Fall of Greater Syria

A Political History of the Syrian Social Nationalist Party

DE GRUYTER

ISBN 978-3-11-112174-1
e-ISBN (PDF) 978-3-11-072909-2
e-ISBN (EPUB) 978-3-11-072914-6
ISSN 2747-5689
e-ISSN 2747-5697

Library of Congress Control Number: 2020952340

Bibliographic information published by the Deutsche Nationalbibliothek
The Deutsche Nationalbibliothek lists this publication in the Deutsche Nationalbibliografie; detailed bibliographic data are available on the Internet at http://dnb.dnb.de.

This volume is text- and page-identical with the hardback published in 2021.
Cover image: Syrian Social Nationalist Party gathering in Lebanon, 1 March 1949.

Printing and binding: CPI books GmbH, Leck

www.degruyter.com

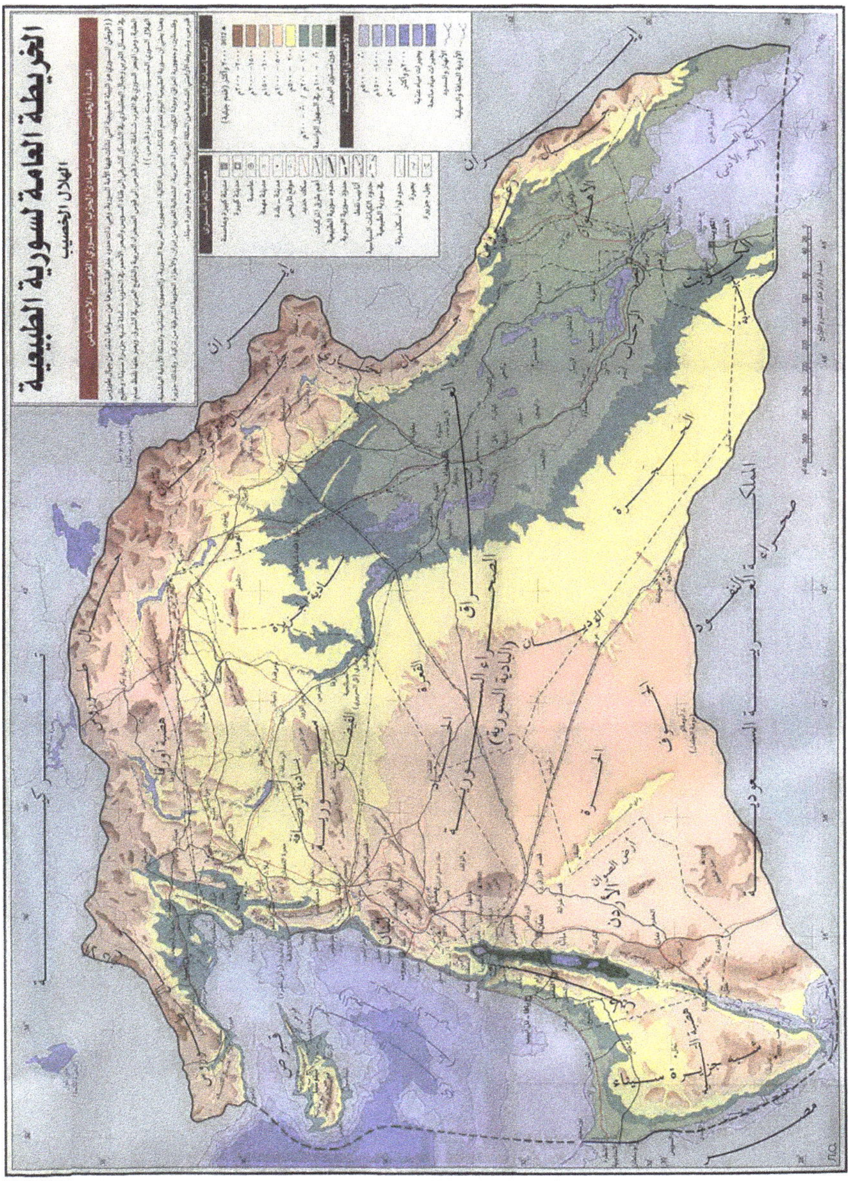

Figure 1: Syrian Social Nationalist Party Map of Greater Syria. (Wikimedia Commons)

Acknowledgments

The English poet John Donne's famous words that "no man is an island," which point to the importance, even necessity, for humans to be in community in order to thrive, are particularly apt as I reflect on the time I dedicated to this project. Were it not for the contributions, guidance, support, and encouragement of my community of family, friends, and colleagues, current and former, I would not have thrived or completed this work. To them, I express my sincere and heartfelt thanks and gratitude for all they have done, while also acknowledging that any shortcomings and mistakes in the study that follow are mine, and mine alone.

This book and the dissertation on which it is based would not exist were it not for the invaluable advice, assistance, encouragement, and contributions of several professors at Tel Aviv University with whom I have worked closely for nearly a decade. Eyal Zisser, my doctoral advisor, provided the initial inspiration for studying the Syrian Social Nationalist Party while I was a graduate student in his Modern History of Lebanon and Syria course. Having planted the seed, he then shepherded my dissertation to completion, offering me valuable guidance, advice, and criticism throughout, ensuring I made steady progress and never lost sight of the larger context of Lebanese and Syrian politics and society. He also helped me secure important funding for my research. Uriya Shavit has been a steadfast source of support, helping me navigate university bureaucracy, advising and assisting me in securing funding, providing me with the opportunity to gain my first teaching experience, and encouraging me every step of the way. Uzi Rabi provided me with an intellectual home at the Moshe Dayan Center and gave me important guidance and recommendations that strengthened the Introduction to this book. Bruce Maddy-Weitzman, who advised my master's thesis, has been a devoted teacher, mentor, colleague, and friend whose door has always been open to me to talk about research, life, and our shared love of baseball. I am deeply grateful to each of them for all they have done and their unceasing encouragement.

Special thanks are due to Michael Reshef, the director of the Arabic Press Archives at the Moshe Dayan Center (MDC), and Marion Gliksberg, the director of the Moshe Dayan Center library, for their assistance in finding and locating archival material and sources for the project. Thanks also to the staffs of the Centre des Archives diplomatiques de Nantes (CADN) and The National Archives at Kew for their assistance in locating relevant files. I would also like to thank the MDC, CADN, and the Palmach Archive for granting me permission to use the photographs that appear in this book. Further, I must thank my friends Andrew Esensten and Chris Solomon, who visited several libraries in the United States to scan

https://doi.org/10.1515/9783110729092-001

important books I was unable to purchase from bookstores in Lebanon, France, and the UK, or find in libraries in Israel.

Throughout the research and writing of this book, many friends and colleagues have willingly listened to me discuss my work, read parts of the manuscript, and offered valuable feedback, insights, support, and encouragement, including Ryan H., Ryan F., Jake, Patrick, Natalie, Ben S., Ben M., Joel, Joyce, Duygu, Rachel, Brandon, Jessie, Or, Roger, Leah, Waleed, Yair, Michael, Gadi, and Tzachi.

At De Gruyter, I would like to thank Gerhard Boomgaarden, the Social Sciences Editorial Director, Tony Mason, the Social Sciences Commissioning Editor, and Michaela Göbels, Content Editor, for acquiring the manuscript and their professionalism in guiding it through the production process.

My greatest debt of gratitude is owed to my family in the United States, United Kingdom, and Israel, first and foremost my wife Sigalit and our son Roi, who was born in the middle of this project. Sigalit lovingly and patiently put up with my absent-mindedness and fretting, keeping me grounded, supporting and encouraging me throughout, providing me feedback, and ensuring I was not consumed by my work. Roi is our greatest source of joy and pride; he inspired me and kept me going. Without their love and support, this book would not exist at all. This work is dedicated to them.

Contents

Part Three: **The Road to a Failed Revolution and Its Aftermath**

Part Four: **Advance and Retreat**

Introduction

On a sun-filled day in the middle of May 1954, an estimated 500 men and women journeyed from Beirut and Latakia to the ruins of Ugarit (Ras Shamra), the ancient port city. The Neolithic era settlement had served as an important center of trade, connecting the lands of modern-day Syria and Iraq to the Eastern Mediterranean kingdoms. The trip's participants were not a disparate group of individuals interested in visiting an archaeological site located several miles north of the Syrian coastal city of Latakia. Instead, all were members of the Syrian Social Nationalist Party (SSNP, *al-Ḥizb al-Sūrī al-Qawmī al-Ijtimāʿī*),[1] established in 1932 by the Greek Orthodox Lebanese intellectual Antun Saʿadeh. Their visit to the ruins of Ugarit, which had come to symbolize an essential cornerstone of the Syrian nation's past and Greater Syria's[2] preeminence, was educational, designed to inspire and shape the Syrian national identity of the trip's participants. The visit's importance was underscored by the presence of party president George ʿAbd al-Masih, who was welcomed by party members lining the hills, standing at attention with the banner of the red tempest (*al-zawbaʿa al-hamrāʾ*) waving above their heads. In his speech, ʿAbd al-Masih extolled the Syrian nation's greatness and urged his listeners to remain steadfast in their struggle to revive

1 Saʿadeh originally named his party the Syrian National Party (*al-Ḥizb al-Sūrī al-Qawmī*, SNP), which was mistranslated by French authorities as Parti Populaire Syrien (PPS). When the party was legalized in Lebanon in April 1944, almost five years after the Lebanese authorities banned its activities, it operated as the National Party (*al-Ḥizb al-Qawmī*, NP) until Saʿadeh, upon his return to Lebanon in March 1947, renamed it the Syrian Social Nationalist Party. For the sake of clarity and continuity, I will refer to the party as the SSNP for the entire period under consideration in this book.

2 The term Greater Syria (*Sūriyya al-Kubra*), also referred to as Natural Syria (*Sūriyya al-Ṭabīʿiyya*) and the Levant (*Bilād al-Shām*), generally denotes a geographic area stretching from the Levant eastward through Mesopotamia. In his own nationalist writings, Saʿadeh preferred to use *Sūriyya al-Kubra* or *Sūriyya al-Ṭabīʿiyya* to describe the geographic territory of the Syrian homeland. While *Bilād al-Shām* is a term commonly used to describe a similar geographic area, it is not one that Saʿadeh himself used and is thus a term this study will not apply in relation to his conception of the geographic territory that constitutes Syria. As articulated in the SSNP's Fifth Basic Principle, "The Syrian homeland is that geographic environment in which the Syrian nation evolved. It has distinct natural boundaries, and extends from the Taurus mountains in the northwest and the Zagros mountains in the northeast to the Suez Canal and the Red Sea in the south, including the Sinai Peninsula and the Gulf of Aqaba, and from the Mediterranean Sea [lit. Syrian Sea, *baḥr al-sūrī*] in the west, including the island of Cyprus, to the arch of the Arabian Desert and the Persian Gulf in the east. This region is known as the Syrian Fertile Crescent (*al-Hilāl al-Sūrī al-Khaṣīb*)." Antun Saʿadeh, *Mabādiʾ al-Ḥizb al-Sūrī al-Qawmī al-Ijtimāʿī wa Ghāyatu* (Beirut: Dār Fikr li-l-Abḥāth wa-l-Nashr, 2011), p. 31.

https://doi.org/10.1515/9783110729092-002

it, always looking forward, not backward. The speech ended with the cries of the party's slogan declaring *"taḥyā Sūriyya wa yaḥyā Sa'adeh"* (Long live Syria and long live Sa'adeh)![3]

The SSNP was established at a time of great social, economic, political, and cultural change in the lands of Greater Syria. The collapse of the Ottoman Empire, the rise of the British and French mandates, the emergence of new national identities and movements, the modernization of society and the establishment of new states in the early part of the twentieth century all contributed to a sense of dislocation and a search for answers.[4] As a young man, Sa'adeh dedicated himself to finding a solution for the "woe" (*al-wail*) that had befallen the Syrian nation, the primary cause of which – he believed – was Syria's loss of national sovereignty. To rectify this situation, he founded the SSNP to "unify the Syrian nation into a sovereign state capable of determining its destiny."[5] He committed his movement to a singular purpose: establishing Greater Syria's complete independence and territorial integrity. The party's rigid secular Syrian nationalist doctrine rejected Lebanese nationalism, Arab nationalism, Communism, and Zionism. It sought to topple the prevailing social and political orders in the lands of Greater Syria, particularly the traditional patrimonial and confessional systems utilized by the social and political elites of Greater Syria to further their power. Indeed, the SSNP's fierce commitment to secularism, embodied in its call for the separation of religion and state and its rejection of sectarianism and religious fanaticism, was a cornerstone of its ideology. To his nascent clandestine nationalist movement, Sa'adeh, a German-language tutor at the American University of Beirut (AUB), recruited young, educated students and faculty at the university and individuals among the intellectual class in greater Beirut. Sa'adeh deemed these two groups the most capable of forcefully challenging and resisting the existing political and social structures of authority in Lebanon – traditional, religious, and mandate.

The social dynamics of the party's ideological and political appeal touched on issues of identity, socioeconomic status, minorities, and youth.[6] The men and women who comprised this emerging, politically conscious group varied in their socio-economic and confessional background, but all were drawn to Sa'adeh's

3 *Al-Bina'*, 26 May 1954.

4 Paul Salem, *Bitter Legacy: Ideology and Politics in the Arab World* (Syracuse: Syracuse University Press, 1994), pp. 3–21.

5 "Risāla ilā Ḥamīd Faranjiyya – Fī Mā Dafa'nī ila Inshā' al-Ḥizb al-Sūrī al-Qawmī," in Antun Sa'adeh, *al-A'māl al-Kāmila, Vol. 2* (Beirut: Sa'ādah Cultural Foundation, 2001), pp. 9–11.

6 For a detailed theoretical discussion on the social dynamics of ideology in the Arab world see Salem, *Bitter Legacy*, pp. 21–30.

ideas and determined to challenge the establishment.[7] The party's ideology provided them with a concrete social identity as Syrians and imbued this Syrian national identity with meaning and purpose. This young, educated middle class would form the nucleus of Saʿadeh's movement, a "radical counter elite"[8] and vanguard tasked with guiding the Syrian nation to its revival, establishing Greater Syria, and changing the course of the Syrian nation's history. The party broadly appealed to minorities and rural populaces throughout Greater Syria as well, crossing confessional and communal boundaries. Its comprehensive, secular pan-Syrian nationalist doctrine offered its adherents a radically secular, non-communal, and supra-national identity that stood in stark contrast to the existing traditional and newly emerging Lebanese and Arab identities. Significantly, the SSNP's ideology did not only provide an answer to the question of identity and inclusion in a new socio-political community, it also offered a path for political engagement and action. Indeed, this radical counter elite would make use various forms of contention to press the SSNP's radical claims against the ruling authorities and rival social and political actors. The types of contention employed – from demonstrations and marches to contesting elections, petitions, individual and collective violence, and armed revolt – varied depending upon the SSNP's strength and political opportunities, such as a decline in repression or the empowerment of its political allies.

To date, the SSNP has received only limited attention from scholars and is rarely, if ever, addressed in the historiography of ideological movements and parties in the broader region. This lack of research is surprising – though understandable to a certain degree[9] – given that despite its failure to attain political power, its relatively small following and the near-constant suppression of its activities, the party has influenced (and continues to do so) both society and politics in Lebanon and Syria. Moreover, given the relative lack of scholarly attention afforded to the study of Syrian nationalism and nationalist movements[10] by historians of the Middle East, a study of the political organization that embodies the Syrian national idea's most explicit expression is even more necessary. This study fills this gap, analyzing the SSNP's formation, development, and po-

---

7 Michael Hudson, *The Precarious Republic: Political Modernization in Lebanon* (Boulder: Westview Press, 1985), p. 169.

8 Hudson, *Precarious Republic*, p. 168.

9 Indeed, after more than eighty years of struggle, the party has yet to realize its ultimate objective, nor does the SSNP seem closer to overcoming the social and political forces that have hindered the movement from its inception.

10 Philip S. Khoury, "Factionalism among Syrian Nationalists during the French Mandate," *International Journal of Middle East Studies* 13, no. 4 (November 1981): p. 441.

litical activities in Lebanon and Syria from its foundation in 1932 to the end of the Lebanese Crisis in 1958 before offering a brief commentary on the party today. Before late 1958, the SSNP was a prominent radical political movement that wielded notable, but by no means decisive, social and political influence in both countries, particularly in the mid-1940s and 1950s, as it pursued its objective of reviving the Syrian nation and its sovereignty over the Syrian nation's historical territory, Greater Syria.[11] After 1958, the party's influence was severely weakened and curtailed, and the party itself experienced significant transformations. Ultimately, it failed to become a mass movement and attain significant political power and influence in Lebanon and Syria.

Through an examination of the SSNP's revolutionary political struggle for national revival (*nahḍa qawmiyya*) in Greater Syria, this study endeavors to provide the most comprehensive and objective historical account to date of this radical nationalist party. To enrich the historical narrative, this book borrows from social movement theory (SMT), using it as a broad theoretical framework or "informative metaphor" to describe, explore, and analyze the SSNP's collective action and contentious politics.[12] This approach is similar to that found in Quintan Wiktorowicz's edited volume *Islamic Activism: A Social Movement Theory Approach*, which explored the contentious politics of "Islamic Activism"[13] to understand its dynamics, process, and organization. As Charles Tilly, one of the scholars who pioneered the study of contentious politics, observed in the book's Forward, most of the studies in Wiktorowicz's volume adopt the following two strategies in appropriating social movement theory: (a) "[borrowing it] as an informative metaphor without insisting on strict correspondence," and (b) "[using it] to pose telling questions about your phenomenon, but not that the answers

11 "al-Khitāb al-Manhājī al-Awal," in Sa'adeh, *al-A'māl al-Kāmila, Vol. 2*, p. 4, and Itamar Rabinovich, *The View from Damascus: State, Political Community and Foreign Relations in Modern and Contemporary Syria* (London: Vallentine Mitchell, 2011), p. 17.

12 Contentious politics, as defined by Tilly and Tarrow, "involves interactions in which actors make claims bearing on other actors' interests, leading to coordinated efforts on behalf of shared interests or programs, in which governments are involved as targets, initiators of claims, or third parties. Contentious politics thus brings together three familiar features of social life: contention, collective action, and politics." Charles Tilly and Sidney Tarrow, *Contentious Politics, 2nd Ed.* (Oxford: Oxford University Press, 2015), p. 7. Also see James Goodman, "Nationalism as a Social Movement," *Oxford Research Encyclopedia of international Studies*, 22 December 2017, accessed 24 October 2020: https://oxfordre.com/internationalstudies/view/10.1093/acrefore/9780190846626.001.0001/acrefore-9780190846626-e-267.

13 Quintan Wiktorowicz, ed., *Islamic Activism: A Social Movement Theory Approach* (Bloomington: Indiana University Press, 2004), p. 2.

would remain the same."[14] It is these two approaches that I adopt in this book in order to understand and analyze the SSNP's political activity and behavior. Thus, within the context of this approach, the book describes, contextualizes, and explores the SSNP's social bases of support, the appeal of its ideology, its contentious politics and use of collective violence, its political behavior, its mobilizing structures, its ideological framing of social and political conflicts, its organization strength, its political opportunities, and the nature of its competition and conflicts with other social and political actors, movements, and organizations. In addition, the book also illustrates the political socialization of SSNP members, particularly the socializing agents of education, peers, the press, the party, and political events, and their role in mobilizing social and political action. By adopting the above approaches, a detailed portrait of the Syrian Social Nationalist Party emerges, shedding new light on the broader social and political histories of Lebanon and Syria.

14 Wiktorowicz, *Islamic Activism*, p. ix.

Imagining Syria: Syrian Nationalism, Greater Syria, and the SSNP

The development and formation of new national and political identities and the establishment of new national and political movements in Greater Syria were accentuated in the aftermath of the Ottoman Empire's collapse. The Ottoman defeat, which also constituted the collapse of a shared Ottoman identity that had hitherto been paramount, provided fertile new ground for new identities and discourses to develop among the now-former Ottoman citizens of Greater Syria. In this milieu, the propagators of three developing and conflicting nationalist ideas – Arab nationalism, Lebanese nationalism, and Syrian nationalism – vied with each other for acceptance. Further, they competed with a plethora of other existing forms of social and political identity – tribal, ethnic, and religious – for adherents.[15] While members of Sunni communities in the region tended to embrace Arab nationalism, an ideology that deemed the region of the Levant to be part of the larger Arab homeland, the Maronite Christian community embraced Lebanese nationalism, holding the territory of Greater Lebanon to be separate from this larger Arab homeland and Syria. Neither Arab nationalist theories espoused by Sunni movements nor Lebanese nationalist notions propagated by Maronite political organizations broadly appealed to minority communities. For some, particularly those from the Greek Orthodox community, Syrian nationalism, which posited the existence of a non-Arab, pre-Islamic Syrian nation, was more appealing.[16]

The idea of a Syrian nation and a Syrian homeland (*waṭan*) was first broached in 1860 by the Maronite Christian intellectual Butrus al-Bustani, "*al-Muʿālim*,"

---

15 Notably, as the scholar Asher Kaufman observed, these three nationalisms developed alongside, and not necessarily in opposition to, each other prior to the First World War. By the end of the Great War and in the immediate aftermath, Syrian national, Arab national and Lebanese national ideas would diverge and distinguish themselves as distinct national conceptions. Asher Kaufman, *Reviving Phoenicia: The Search for Identity in Lebanon* (London: I.B. Tauris, 2004), p. 48.

16 Kamal Salibi, *A House of Many Mansions: The History of Lebanon Reconsidered* (London: I.B. Tauris, 2002), pp. 38–55. This is not to say that there were not members of these minority communities who did not embrace Arab or Lebanese nationalist ideas, nor that there were not members of the Maronite and Sunni communities who embraced Syrian nationalism. For example, one of the founders of the Arab nationalist Baʿth party, Michel ʿAflaq, was a Greek Orthodox Christian and many in the Greek Orthodox community embraced Arab nationalism.

in his publication *Nafīr Sūriyya* (The Clarion of Syria).[17] Published in the wake of the brutal conflict between Druze and Maronites in Mount Lebanon, Bustani appealed for unity and strengthening the bonds among Syria's inhabitants, condemning sectarianism and communalism in its pages.[18] His call for unity was neither political nor a call for national independence, as he remained loyal to the Ottoman political order and did not envision establishing an independent nation.[19] Thus, while Bustani is considered by some to be the "first Syrian nationalist"[20] for urging unity among his fellow countrymen and the love of their homeland, others would later articulate more lucid visions of Syrian nationhood.[21]

Those succeeding Bustani would develop and elucidate more definite notions of Syrian nationalism characterized by ethnicity and geography. Intellectuals in this current advanced the idea that the Syrian nation was ethnically distinct and non-Arab, and that it inhabited a vast geographical territory known as Greater Syria. Among these intellectuals was the French geographer and writer Élisée Reclus who, in 1884, published the ninth volume of his *Nouvelle Géographie Universelle*, in which he drew a distinction between Syrians and Arabs.[22] Several decades later, in the early 1900s, the Jesuit priest Henri Lammens and his student Jacques Tabet argued a distinct, non-Arab Syrian nation had existed from the Phoenicians' time and that this nation had been shaped by, and within, the natural geographic boundaries of Syria.[23] Similarly, Shukri Ghanim and Georges Samné argued that Syrians constituted a distinct nation

---

17 The texts of *Nafīr Sūriyya* are reproduced in both Arabic and English in the following volumes: Butrus al-Bustani, *Nafīr Sūriyya* (Beirut: Dār Fikr li-l-Abḥāth wa-l-Nashr, 1990), and Butrus al-Bustani, *The Clarion of Syria: A Patriot's Call Against the Civil War of 1860*, intro. and trans. Jens Hanssen and Hicham Safieddine (Berkley: University of California Press, 2019).

18 Kamal Salibi, *The Modern History of Lebanon* (New York: Praeger Publishers, 1965), pp. 80–105.

19 Butrus Abu-Manneh, "The Christians between Ottomanism and Syrian Nationalism: The ideas of Butrus al-Bustani," *International Journal of Middle East Studies* 11, no. 3 (May 1980): pp. 287–304, and Rabinovich, *The View from Damascus*, p. 8.

20 Abu-Manneh, "The Ideas of Butrus al-Bustani," p. 294.

21 Bustani would also provide a platform for the spread of the Syrian national idea through *al-Jinan*, a periodical he co-published with his son Salim.

22 Élisée Reclus, *Nouvelle Géographie Universelle: La Terre et Les Hommes*, Vol. IX, *l'Asie Antérieure*, (Paris: Librairie Hachette et Cie., 1884), pp. 5–6.

23 Asher Kaufman, "Henri Lammens and Syrian Nationalism," in *The Origins of Syrian Nationhood: Histories, Pioneers and Identity*, ed. by Adel Beshara (New York: Routledge, 2011), p. 118. See also Henri Lammens, *La Syrie et Son Importance Géographique* (Lourain, 1904); Henri Lammens, *La Syrie: Précis Historique* (Beirut, 1921); and Jacques Tabet, *La Syrie* (Paris, 1920).

and, with France's backing, advocated establishing a secular Greater Syria.[24] Indeed, shortly after the First World War began in 1914, Ghanim and Samné's Paris-based Comité Central Syrien worked to unite all Syrians and sought the independence of a federated Syria (including Palestine and Lebanon) under a French protectorate.[25]

By the end of the First World War, Syrians in the diaspora had established several political organizations calling for Syria's complete independence. In Cairo, Rashid Rida and ʿAbd al-Rahman al-Shahbandar founded the Syrian Union Party (SUP, *Ḥizb al-Ittiḥād al-Sūrī*); in Buenos Aires, Dr. Khalil Saʿadeh, Antun's father, founded the National Democratic Party (NDP, *Ḥizb al-Dimuqratī al-Waṭanī*); in Cairo, Faris Nimr and Yaʿqub Sarruf founded the Syrian Moderates Party (SMP, *Ḥizb al-Sūrī al-Muʿtadil*)[26]; in New York, Georges Khayrallah, Philip K. Hitti, Habib Katibah, and Abraham Rihbany founded the New Syria Party (NSP, *Ḥizb Sūriyya al-Jadida*)[27]; and in the United States, the Syrian National Society was founded. The latter four organizations promoted a similar agenda for establishing a unified, federated, independent Greater Syria with the United States serving as the guarantor of its independence.[28] Further, Khalil's NDP con-

24 Kaufman, *Reviving Phoenicia*, pp. 82–83, and Georges Samné, *La Syrie* (Paris: Éditions Bossard, 1921).

25 "Chronique Syrienne," *Correspondence d'Orient*, 25 November 1917, p. 316, and Eliezer Tauber, *The Arab Movements in World War I* (London: Frank Cass, 1993), p. 210.

26 See No. 455, CADN, SL, 1er Versement, Papiers Georges-Picot, M. LeFevre-Pontalis, Ministre de France en Égypte, à M. Georges-Picot, Haut-Commissaire de la République Française en Syrie et en Arménie, "Parti syrien modéré," Cairo, 26 February 1919, in Antoine Hokayem, Daad Bou Malhab ʿAtallah, and Jean Charaf, eds., *Documents Diplomatiques Français Relatifs à l'Histoire du Liban et de la Syrie à l'Époque du Mandat: 1914–1946, Tome 1* (Paris: L'Harmattan, 2003), pp. 485–487, and No. 459, MAE, SL, M. Nimr, Pour le Parti Modéré Syrien du Caire, à M. Pichon, Ministre des Affaires Étrangères, Cairo, 5 March 1919, in Hokayem et al., *Documents Diplomatiques*, p. 491. Also see Tauber, *The Formation of Modern Iraq and Syria* (London: Frank Cass, 1995), pp. 159–161.

27 No. 451, MAE, SL, Principes de la Nouvelle Ligue Nationale Syrien de New York, New York, February 1919, in Hokayem et al., *Documents Diplomatiques*, p. 481. According to the NSP, the boundaries of Greater Syria extended from the Taurus mountains in the north to the Sinai Peninsula in the south and the Mediterranean Sea in the West to the Euphrates River in East. See Tauber, *The Formation of Modern Iraq and Syria*, p. 147.

28 See, for example, a pamphlet published by the Syrian National Society, penned by Habib Katibah, entitled "Syria for the Syrians under the Guardianship of the United States." In the article, Katibah, like Khalil Saʿadeh, argues that "the Syrians are not a backward people" in need of tutelage nor was military occupation of Syria necessary. Rather, the limited assistance of the United States to help in the country's organization and establishment of basic schools and institutions would be welcome. This "New Syria" would be "a federated union of provinces, each province autonomous within its own borders, yet bonded through one central government into

sidered the separation of religion and state to be one of its foundational principles.[29] However, in time, the Syrian nationalist convictions of many of the figures mentioned above would wane, replaced by greater sympathies for Lebanese and Arab nationalist visions. So, too, would the broader appeal of this current of Syrian nationalism that imagined a distinct, non-Arab Syrian nation and united Greater Syria decline. However, such was not the case for Saʿadeh and his adherents when the SSNP was established in the 1930s.

Saʿadeh's Syrian nationalist convictions developed in South America in the 1920s, where he lived and worked alongside his father to advocate for the Syrian national cause. Like his father, Saʿadeh believed that religious fanaticism lay at the core of the many problems affecting Syrian society and that overcoming it and its deleterious effects were essential if Syrian society was to advance and modernize.[30] Further, through his experiences, particularly his observations of what he considered a unified and effective Zionist movement in contrast to a divided and disorganized Syrian nationalist movement, he came to believe only an organized movement would be capable of bringing about Syria's complete independence. He bluntly lamented that while "Jews from around the world unite to dispossess us of our land, we have yet to see any movement among us towards the type of effective actions urged upon us by leaders who devote their lives in lonely struggle... What can individual effort achieve if it is not made effective by a unified organization or party representing the community?"[31] Having failed to establish two diaspora political organizations, Saʿadeh returned to Lebanon in 1930, determined to spark a nationalist awakening that would carry the Syrian nation to independence and its rightful place among the "living nations."

---

one great nation." Habib Katibah, "Syria for the Syrians under the Guardianship of the United States," *Bulletin of the Syrian National Society* (Boston) 1, no. 9 (28 February 1919): pp. 19–20. Rihbany, in a short booklet entitled *America, Save the Near East*, argued America was best suited for the task, calling for it to "heed the call of those oppressed peoples...." (Rihbany, *America, Save the Near East*, pp. 26, 52, 137).

29 "Min al-Ḥizb al-Dimuqratī al-Waṭanī ila al-Sūriyyin wa-l-Lubnāniyyin wa-l-Falastiniyyin fī al-Mahājir wa-l-Waṭan," in Salim Mujais and Badr el-Hage, *al-Duktūr Khalīl Saʿādah: Sūriyya min al-Ḥarb wa-l-Majāʿa ila Muʾtamar al-Ṣulḥ, al-Mujallad al-Awwal* (Beirut: Muʾassasat Saʿādah li-l-Thaqāfa, 2014), pp. 185–186.

30 See, for example "Irtiqāʾ al-Sharq," in Salim Mujais and Badr el-Hage, *al-Duktūr Khalīl Saʿādah: Mabāḥith ʿUmrāniyya wa Falsafiyya, al-Mujallad al-Rābiʿ* (Beirut: Kutub, 2016), pp. 173–174, and"Kitāb Maftūḥ ila al-Sūriyyin wa-l-Lubnāniyyin wa-l-Falasṭiniyyin," in Mujais and Hage, *Khalīl Saʿādah, Vol. 1*, pp. 148–149.

31 "al-Ṣahyuniyya wa Imtidāduha," in Saʿadeh, *al-Aʿmāl al-Kāmila, Vol. 1*, p. 176.

Back in Lebanon, Saʿadeh would formulate the clearest, and perhaps the most cogent expression[32] of Syrian nationalism in the doctrine of the SSNP. The party's eight basic and five reform principles declared the Syrian nation's existence and described its character, homeland, interests, and mission. His writings outlined the party's comprehensive social objectives, including separating religion and state, establishing a national army, eliminating feudalism, and eliminating the barriers between sects and communities.[33] Other core principles included a firm opposition to French – or any foreign – rule in Syria, a commitment to its territorial integrity and the demand for its complete independence, and secularism, embodied in the call for the separation of religion and state and the rejection of sectarianism and religious fanaticism.

People and territory served as the foundations of Saʿadeh's definition of a nation, which he declared to be "a group of people living a life of unified interests, unified destiny, and unified spiritual-materialist factors in a particular territory that gained through its interactions with this territory, in the course of evolution, characteristics and advantages distinguishing it from other groups."[34] Thus, Saʿadeh asserted that the Syrian nation derived from all the peoples who have inhabited Syria since pre-historic times, except the Jews.[35] Further, these peoples "[have] come to constitute a single society living in a distinguished

32 As will be seen subsequently, Saʿadeh's ideas and principles did not originate with him nor was he unique advocating them. To be sure, Saʿadeh would expand upon these foundational ideas, formulating his own distinctive Syrian nationalist ideology and establishing an organized movement based upon it. Of particular relevance to Saʿadeh's national thought and the SSNP's ideology is the historical development of what Kaufman characterizes as secular non-Arab Syrianism - the idea of a geographically and ethnically distinct "greater Syrian, non-Arab nation." As Kaufman observes, and as will be demonstrated in this work, "[Syrian nationalism] as expressed by [Antun Saʿadeh] can be best understood against the backdrop of this stream…" (Kaufman, *Reviving Phoenicia*, 7, pp. 215–216). Indeed, people and territory (ethnicity and geography) served as the foundations of Saʿadeh's definition of a nation, which he declared to be "a group of people living a life of unified interests, unified destiny, and unified spiritual-materialist factors in a particular territory that gained through its interactions with this territory, in the course of evolution, characteristics and advantages distinguishing it from other groups" (*Nushuʾ al-Umam*, in Saʿadeh, *al-Aʿmāl al-Kāmila, Vol. 3*, p. 147).

33 For more details on the eight basic and five reform principles see Salim Mujais, *The Syrian Social Nationalist Party: Its Ideology and History* (London: Black House Publishing, 2019), pp. 11–66, and Labib Zuwiyya Yamak, *The Syrian Social Nationalist Party: An Ideological Analysis* (Cambridge: Harvard University Press, 1966), pp. 76–100.

34 *Nushuʾ al-Umam*, in Antun Saʿadeh, *al-Aʿmāl al-Kāmila, Vol. 3*, p. 147. See also Maʿin Haddad, *Jadaliyya al-Jughrāfiyā wa-l-Siyāsa* (Beirut: al-Furāt, 2019), pp. 71–138.

35 Saʿadeh, *Mabādiʾ*, pp. 24, 30–31, and "al-Jinsiyyāt al-Sūriyya wa-l-Lubnāniyya wa-l-Filisṭiniyya," in Saʿadeh, *al-Aʿmāl al-Kāmila, Vol. 1*, p. 196.

environment known historically as Syria or the Fertile Crescent."[36] This Syrian nation is separate from an Arab nation, though it is part of and has a mission to the Arab world. In sum, Syria's relationship with the Arab world was political and not national, and Syria was more advanced than the Arab nations.[37]

Saʿadeh's nationalist vision posed a direct challenge to, and differed significantly from, other professed Syrian nationalists. Opposed to his line of thinking were the urban Sunni communities residing along the Lebanese coast and in the Syrian hinterland who embraced a Muslim Arab Syrianism that imagined a unified geographic Syria as a stepping stone towards broader Arab unity.[38] Saʿadeh and the SSNP rejected the religious underpinnings of this type of Syrian nationalism, just as it did that of Lebanese nationalism and Zionism, and dismissed the idea of a single, unified Arab nation. However, these differences did not preclude efforts by Saʿadeh and the party to cooperate with those who embraced differing Syrian nationalist ideas. For example, the party cooperated with the National Bloc (*al-Kutla al-Waṭaniyya*) in Syria and participated in the Second Coastal Conference (*Muʾatamar al-Sāḥil*) in Tripoli, Lebanon, to discuss the reunification of the territories annexed to Mount Lebanon in 1920 with Syria.[39] Despite such efforts, the SSNP's unshakeable commitment to Syria's "complete unity" (*al-waḥda al-shāmila*) tended to complicate matters, and cooperative efforts usually failed to advance the party's agenda due to its unwillingness to compromise on its core demands.

Indeed, any policy or effort that solidified the division of Greater Syria was to be steadfastly opposed by the SSNP. In 1937, in a not-so-veiled swipe at the National Bloc and Lebanese nationalists, Saʿadeh charged that those who embraced religiously inspired national ideas sowed only intellectual and spiritual confusion, helping divide Greater Syria and undo the unity of its life and interests. Adherence to religiously inspired nationalism led directly, he believed, to the perilous political situation that existed at the time as Lebanon and Syria negotiated treaties with France. The establishment of the SSNP, Saʿadeh declared, was a decisive blow against this intellectual and spiritual confusion and those working against the nation's unity. Tensions between the organizations only in-

---

36 Saʿadeh, *Mabādiʾ*, p. 24.

37 "al-ʿUrūba Afalsat," in Saʿadeh, *al-Āʿmāl al-Kāmila, Vol. 8*, pp. 256–258, and "Ḥārabnā al-ʿUrūba al-Wahmiyya li-Nuqīm al-ʿUrūba al-Wāqiʾiya," in Saʿadeh, *al-Āʿmāl al-Kāmila, Vol. 8*, pp. 267–271.

38 On Muslim Arab Syrianism, see Kaufmann, *Reviving Phoenicia*, p. 7.

39 Jan Dayah, *Muḥākamat Anṭūn Saʿādah: Wathāʾiq al-Taḥqīq al-Rasmī* (Beirut: Fajr al-Nahḍa, 2002), p. 174; Meir Zamir, *Lebanon's Quest: The Road to Statehood, 1926–1939* (London: I.B. Tauris, 1997), p. 190; and Firro, *Inventing Lebanon*, pp. 141–143.

tensified. The National Bloc, viewing the SSNP as a political competitor and challenger, suppressed its activities in Syria. The SSNP, likewise, harshly criticized the Bloc, blaming it for losing Alexandretta to Turkey and endangering Syria's sovereignty over the northern Jazira region.[40]

Several years later, in the 1940s, Jordan's King ʿAbdullah articulated his own "Greater Syria" scheme, seeking to create a single kingdom under his authority from the territories of Lebanon, Syria, Jordan, and Mandate Palestine. Saʿadeh, however, eschewed any comparison between the two schemes.[41] Saʿadeh's criticism of ʿAbdullah's plan was restrained, careful not to disparage the idea of Greater Syria but rather the man promoting it, whom Saʿadeh did not consider to be Syrian and, therefore, unqualified to speak on behalf of the Syrian nation.[42] The SSNP would, in late 1946, issue a memorandum condemning ʿAbdullah's Greater Syria scheme as a threat to Syrian and Lebanese independence and its provisions accommodating Jewish settlement in Palestine.[43] Saʿadeh was even less generous towards Iraqi politician Nuri al-Saʿid's "Fertile Crescent" plan,[44] arguing it was nothing more than a thinly veiled effort by Arab nationalists to take control of Syria and dictate its future, a notion that violated one of his most fundamental tenets: Syrian's complete sovereignty over their destiny. The SSNP's opposition to the Greater Syria and Fertile Crescent schemes of Hashemite Jordan and Iraq would continue throughout the 1950s, but this opposition did not preclude finding other matters of common interest on which they could cooperate.

---

40 *Oriente Moderno*, 18.3, March 1938, p. 118; *Oriente Moderno*, 18.4, April 1938, p. 159; *Oriente Moderno*, 18.6, June 1938, pp. 294–296; Jurayj, *Min al-Juʿbat, Vol. 4*, pp. 171–185; "Nidāʾ Zaʿīm," in Saʿadeh, *al-Aʿmāl al-Kāmila, Vol. 2*, p. 363; "Iʿtiqālāt Dimashq," in Saʿadeh, *al-Aʿmāl al-Kāmila, Vol. 3*, pp. 172–174; "al-Siyāsa al-Sirriyya," in Saʿadeh, *al-Aʿmāl al-Kāmila, Vol. 3*, pp. 251–252; and "Siyāsa al-Baṭsh fī al-Shām," in Saʿadeh, *al-Aʿmāl al-Kāmila, Vol. 3*, pp. 217–219.

41 Adel Beshara, "Saʿadeh and the Greater Syria Scheme," in *Antun Saʿadeh: The Man and His Thought: An Anthology*, ed. by Adel Beshara (Reading: Ithaca Press, 2007), pp. 121, 128–132.

42 The scholars Stephen H. Longrigg and Yehoshua Porath allege the party made overtures to ʿAbdullah to cooperate with him and promote his plan in the early 1940s, but little evidence supports this claim. Beshara, "Saʿadeh and the Greater Syria Scheme," pp. 132–134; Stephen H. Longrigg, *Syria and Lebanon under the French Mandate* (London: Oxford University Press, 1958), p. 352; and Yehoshua Porath, "Abdullah's Greater Syria Programme," *Middle Eastern Studies* 20, no. 2 (April 1984): p. 185.

43 *Mashrūʿ Sūriyya al-Kubra* (Beirut: al-Ḥizb al-Qawmī, ʿUmdat al-Idhāʿa, 1946).

44 On Nuri al-Saʿid's plan see Yehoshua Porath, "Nuri al-Saʿid's Arab Unity Programme," *Middle Eastern Studies* 20, no. 4 (October 1984): pp. 76–98.

The SSNP in Popular Discourse

The SSNP's rejection of the existing Syrian and Lebanese social and political orders provoked mostly negative responses among those interested in maintaining the status quo and advancing a different ideological or political program. The popular discourse that emerged from the mid-1930s onward tended to characterize the party as a group of misguided ideologues and the servants of foreign powers who threatened Lebanese independence, the Arab nation, and public order. At the forefront of establishing this discourse were French Mandate authorities and the Lebanese government, followed by Lebanese and Syrian politicians, religious leaders, and political organizations.

As the preeminent authority in Lebanon before 1943, the French sought to keep political activity and discourse, particularly that which undermined French rule, under its firm control and watchful eye. Often acting in concert with the Lebanese government, the French used the security establishment to infiltrate, gather intelligence, monitor and subvert the movements it deemed a threat to public order and internal security, foremost among which were the SSNP and the Communist Party. Closely related to their security operations was using the legal system to bring cases against the SSNP, detain members, grant or withhold licenses recognizing the party as a legal political entity, approve or deny applications for public demonstrations, and legalize the publication of the SSNP's newspapers. Together, these measures were designed to curb the party's activity and limit its ability to spread its message in the public sphere and develop a mass following.

Another popular, albeit less coercive though no less confrontational, method to counter the message and activities of the SSNP was through the local press, often done with the tacit approval of government authorities.[45] Mandate authorities did little to counter the developing narrative, regardless of its validity or merit, that the party had relations with a foreign power, threatened the security of the state, and was "fascistically-inclined." Such a narrative helped the French counter their Italian and German rivals' activities in the Levant in the 1930s and 1940s. Rival parties, movements, and confessional groups used their platforms to publish articles disparaging the SSNP, portraying it as the lackey of foreign

45 Jan Dayah, *Saʿādah wa-l-Naziya* (Beirut: Fajr al-Nahḍa, 1994), pp. 49–59; and Götz Nordbruch, *Nazism in Syria and Lebanon: The Ambivalence of the German Option, 1933–1945* (New York: Routledge, 2009), pp. 42–43, 154.

powers and foreign imperialism.[46] *Ittihad al-Lubnani* considered the party's objective of securing a position in the Lebanese administration to be "absurd" and "ridiculous." At the same time, the Greek Catholic newspaper *al-Masa'* characterized the SSNP as "an association of children that want to direct the destiny of the country," and the Jesuit periodical *al-Bashir* similarly deemed it a "party of juveniles." Other newspapers suggested a foreign power had financially supported the SSNP and aided its establishment and activities; in 1935, for example, *al-Masa'* and *al-Bilad* unequivocally accused the German Consul in Beirut of helping the party.[47]

Further contributing to the anti-SSNP narrative were the leaders of Lebanon's larger religious communities who worked to dampen the party's appeal among the faithful. Maronite and Jesuit clergymen sought to portray the SSNP as the enemy of God and the Lebanese state. In 1935, a Maronite priest authored a pamphlet with the Maronite Patriarch's blessing entitled "A Conspiracy Against Religion and Country: The Syrian National Party" (*Mu'āmara ʿalā al-Dīn wa-l-Waṭan: al-Ḥizb al-Sūrī al-Qawmī*). The pamphlet essentially declared that embracing the SSNP's nationalist doctrine was tantamount to the betrayal of the Maronite Church and blasphemy against God, as SSNP doctrine contravened God's law and the teachings of the Church.[48] The Jesuit establishment, ardent supporters of Lebanese nationalism, frequently attacked the party and were among the most vociferous groups in opposing the SSNP, urging the banning of SSNP newspapers and suppressing its activities.[49] Opposition to the party based on religious arguments also arose in the Druze community. In 1944, for example, several Druze sheikhs called for the ex-communication of their coreligionists who belonged to the SSNP, a demand that influenced some Druze to resign their membership.[50] The SSNP typically responded to religious leaders' attacks with calls for the clergymen to concern themselves with religious affairs

---

46 CADN 471, Cabinet Politique 1183, Beyrouth, 29 November 1935, and CADN 471, Beyrouth, "Revue de la Presse Libanaise et Syrienne," 29 November 1935.

47 CADN 471, Cabinet Politique 1183, Beyrouth, 29 November 1935, and CADN 471, Beyrouth, "Revue de la Presse Libanaise et Syrienne," 29 November 1935.

48 For a reproduction of the pamphlet and an analysis of the relationship between the Maronite Church and the SSNP, see Salim Mujais, *Anṭūn Saʿādah wa-l-Iklīrūs al-Mārūnī* (Beirut: 1993). Also ʿAbdallah Qubrusi, *ʿAbd Allah Qubruṣī Yatadhakkar, Vol. 1* (Beirut: Mu'assasat Fikr li-l-Abḥāth wa-l-Nashr, 1982), pp. 205–207.

49 Salim Mujais, *Antoun Saadeh, A Biography – Volume II: Years of the French Mandate* (Beirut: Kutub, 2009), p. 252.

50 CADN 2118, Services Politique, Poste de Merdjayoun, No. 149/ME/28, Bulletin D'Informations Hebdomadaires no. 43, 29 December 1944, and Yusri Hazran, *The Druze Community and the Lebanese State: Between Confrontation and Reconciliation* (New York: Routledge, 2014), p. 61.

only and stay out of politics, echoing the party's reform principle demanding a separation of religion and state.

The party had fierce rivalries with three other ideological political organizations: the Kata'ib, the Communists, and the Baʿth. The Lebanese nationalist Kata'ib, led by Pierre Gemayel, was an overwhelmingly Maronite movement seeking to preserve an independent and sovereign Lebanon and Lebanon's unique, distinct "Phoenician" identity. Championing its faith and the Lebanese nation (its slogan was "God, Nation, Family"), it strongly opposed Syrian and Arab nationalism and, thus, considered the SSNP a threat to Lebanon. The Communist Party also fiercely disagreed with the SSNP and frequently attacked it as a "fascist" movement aligned with Nazi Germany and Fascist Italy. The Lebanese Communist Party deemed it, for example, "Hitler's henchmen in Lebanon" in its official daily *Sawt al-Shaʿb*.[51] Following the war, while not hesitating to declare the party "fascist," the communists continued to depict the party as a tool of foreign imperialism and a threat to Lebanon and Syria.

Just as the SSNP's rejection of Lebanese nationalism and communism incited staunch opposition, so too did the party's rejection of Arab nationalism and the notion of a single Arab nation. This rejection led Arab nationalists to brand the party as "the enemy of Arabism," limiting the SSNP's appeal among Sunni Muslims. In 1961, Baʿth Party founder Michel ʿAflaq described the SSNP to journalist Patrick Seale as "an extreme right-wing movement" and a movement that had "aborted and lost itself in an unhealthy romanticism."[52] Even Arab nationalist intellectuals who had initially engaged the party in a genuine, civil manner, or had formerly embraced Syrian nationalist principals, eventually turned on Saʿadeh and the SSNP. Foremost among its detractors was Satiʿ al-Husri.[53]

---

51 *Sawt al-Shaʿb*, 8 July 1944.

52 Patrick Seale, *The Struggle for Syria: A Study of Post-War Arab Politics, 1945–1958* (London: I.B. Tauris, 1986), p. 68.

53 In his study entitled *al-ʿUrūba bayna Duʿātihā wa Muʿāriḍīha*, Husri wrote: "The Arab world has not seen until now a party that can compete with the SSNP for the quality of its propaganda, which influences reason as well as the emotions, and for the strength of its organization, which is as efficient on the surface as it is underground." However, in the mid–1950s after the party spitefully attacked him, describing his views – and those of Arab nationalists in general – as bankrupt and worthless. In response, Husri denounced the SSNP, attacking its ideology as "half–baked nationalism" (*al-qawmiyya al-iʿtibāṭiyya*) and offering a staunch defense of Arabism. Satiʿ al-Husri, *al-ʿUrūba bayna Duʿātihā wa Muʿāriḍīha* (Beirut: 1951), p. 59, and Satiʿ al-Husri, *Difāʿ ʿan al-ʿUrūba* (Beirut: 1956). Others, like Habib Katibah, an early Syrian nationalist whose sympathies had since shifted toward Arab nationalism, referred to the SSNP as a "fascistically inclined party," imitating Italian Fascists and German National Socialists in organization, leadership, propaganda, symbolism, and ideology. Katibah also characterized the SSNP's ideol-

To be sure, the party and its supporters countered this popular discourse. Most importantly, the negative discourse did not dissuade some Lebanese politicians – who sought to co-opt the SSNP's support for their political aims – from tolerating the party's activities to a certain extent or from reaching accommodations with it. This tactic to garner the SSNP's support – and subvert its program in the process frequently – was employed by several different leading Lebanese political figures. This political bargaining and selective alliance making would come to be a defining feature of the party's relations with such figures – and, by extension, the Lebanese government – throughout its history.

ogy as "fascistic," but later contradicts himself, acknowledging that the party's ideology is not based on "racialism." He notes that the party "[takes] a realistic view of nationalism that is based on community of interest, the result of a long chain of historical events that unified the people living in the same land – be what may their racial or ethnic origin." Habib Ibrahim Katibah, *The New Spirit in Arab Lands* (New York, 1940), pp. 70–72.

Comparing Radical Rivals: The Communists, the Baʿth, and the Kataʾib

As noted, the SSNP had three primary "radical" rivals between the 1930s and 1950s that championed contending alternative ideological visions and territorial claims, and with which the SSNP vied for adherents and supporters: the Communists, the Baʿth, and the Kataʾib. Like the SSNP, each movement, in its way, constituted highly organized and disciplined opposition movements that challenged the status quo and the traditional social and political leadership in Lebanon and Syria. To better understand the SSNP's socio-political position in Lebanon and Syria, a brief comparative overview of its three radical rivals follows below, describing each's social bases of support and tracing the course of each's political activity and influence.

The Communists

The Communist Party of Syria and Lebanon (CPSL) was formed in the mid-1920s out of the merger of the Lebanese People's Party, founded by the Lebanese intellectual and writer Yusuf Yazbek, and the Spartacus Group, an Armenian Bolshevik party. In the mid-1940s, the party separated into Lebanese and Syrian organizations led by Farajallah Helou, a Maronite from Hosrayel, and Khaled Bakdash, a Kurd from Damascus, respectively. By 1947, the Communist Party had an estimated 20,000 members in Lebanon and 15,000 members in Syria; these numbers would precipitously decline over the next decade and do not include communist sympathizers in various peace movements and labor unions.[54]

Like the SSNP, the Communist Party sought to transform the existing social and political order in Lebanon and Syria, its secular ideology appealing to individuals of varied socio-economic and confessional backgrounds and minority groups. Socio-economically, most Communist Party members and leaders in Lebanon hailed from the middle and upper classes, including intellectuals, doctors, lawyers, teachers, students, and professors. In contrast, the minority of its membership hailed from the lower and working classes, including peasants, laborers, and tradesmen. The same was true in Syria, where the Communist Party

54 Hanna Batatu, *Syria's Peasantry, the Descendants of Its Lesser Rural Notables, and Their Politics* (Princeton: Princeton University Press, 1999), p. 120. Other estimates put party membership in Lebanon at 10,000. See Suleiman, *Political Parties in Lebanon*, p. 74.

struggled to attract mass support among rural peasants, the working class, and army officers and were more successful in attracting followers from the educated and urban middle and upper classes.[55] Though it had cross-sectarian appeal, minorities like the Armenians in Lebanon and Syria and the Kurds in Syria were particularly attracted to the Communist Party, while other minority groups like the Greek Orthodox and ʿAlawis were less so.[56]

The Lebanese and Syrian Communist organizations, like the SSNP, would see their political influence and appeal marginalized by the end of the 1950s, eclipsed by the socialism and pan-Arabism of Egypt's Gamal ʿAbd al-Nasser and the Baʿth. Its public activities would be tolerated to a certain degree, and with exceptions,[57] until the early 1950s in Lebanon, at which time, the Lebanese government's pro-Western and anti-Communist orientation relegated it to the margins of the political opposition and the Lebanese Sûreté Générale targeted it. Communist candidates would contest Lebanese parliamentary elections in 1947, 1951, 1953, and 1957, but none would secure a seat in the Chamber of Deputies, its candidates' share of votes dwindling significantly over time.[58] In Syria, the Communist Party's political influence would remain negligible until 1954, when its political standing improved following Adib al-Shishakli's demise. For the next four years, its political influence would expand as its leader Khaled Bakdash was elected to Syria's parliament, and it allied with the Baʿth to purge Syria of the SSNP, their shared rival. The enhanced political influence and standing of Syria's Communist Party would be fleeting, its gains erased by Egypt and Syria's union in 1958 as Communist opposition to the unity agreement and the broader appeal of Nasser and the Baʿth's Arab socialism marginalized it.

---

55 Seale, *The Struggle for Syria*, p. 179. In the 1930s and 1940s, the party gained a rural following in among Kurds in the Hasaka Governorate (formerly Jazira Governorate), several ʿAlawi and Greek Orthodox villages in Tartus Governorate, and Greek Orthodox villages in the Hama, Homs, and Rif Dimashq Governorates. These communities would largely abandon the Communist party by the 1950s, at which point it succeeded gaining support among Sunni Arab peasants in Idlib and Deir el-Zour. See Batatu, *Syria's Peasantry*, pp. 119–120.

56 Rabinovich, *The View from Damascus*, p. 137.

57 For example, its activities were curtailed following the outbreak of the Second World War in 1939 and following the outbreak of war in Palestine in 1948.

58 Hudson, *Precarious Republic*, p. 180, and Suleiman, *Political Parties in Lebanon*, pp. 68–70.

The Ba'th

The Ba'th Party was officially established on 7 April 1947 in Damascus by the Syrians Michel 'Aflaq, a Greek Orthodox Christian, and Salah al-Din al-Bitar, a Sunni Muslim, but its roots lay in the early political activism of its founders that began in the 1930s and early 1940s. The Ba'th, from its founding, was a revolutionary secular Arab nationalist movement dedicated to three tenets: Unity, Freedom, and Socialism. The Ba'th's regional branch in Lebanon was established in 1949 by a handful of students at the American University of Beirut, including Iraqis, Syrians, and Jordanians, though the Ba'th's ideology had already been spread in Nabatieh, a city in southern Lebanon.[59] While the Ba'th's following in Syria would grow significantly, particularly after its merger with Akram al-Hawrani's Arab Socialist Party in the early 1950s, its membership in Lebanon would remain relatively small, attracting a following of several thousand.[60]

In both Lebanon and Syria, the Ba'th would begin as a predominately urban movement attracting members from the educated middle and upper classes, including secondary and university students, school teachers and professors, doctors, lawyers, and civil servants, who found its messages of Arab nationalism and socialism appealing. In Syria, the merger with Hawrani's party changed its composition, bringing the Ba'th a rural following of peasants and lower-class workers that had previously been absent. In the early 1950s, it would also attract a following among Syrian army officers, an arena of potential support fiercely contested by the SSNP. In Lebanon, a similar transformation took place following the 1956 Suez Crisis as it began to expand its base of support beyond the intellectual elite to the masses, thereby enhancing its political standing. The Ba'th in Lebanon was incredibly successful in eroding the Lebanese Communist Party's influence in Tripoli, Saida, Tyre, and Nabatieh, which had previously been considered Communist strongholds.[61] In both countries, the Ba'th would predominately appeal to Sunni Muslims and Greek Orthodox Christians, but it also successfully attracted members from the Druze, Isma'ili, and 'Alawi communities.[62]

---

59 Fayez 'Ilm al-Din al-Qays, *Ḥizb al-Ba'th al-'Arabī al-Ishtirākī, Vol. 1* (Beirut: Dār al-Fārābī, 2017), Loc. 334, Kindle.

60 Hudson, *Precarious Republic*, p. 199, and Batatu, *Syria's Peasantry*, p. 136.

61 Hudson, *Precarious Republic*, pp. 198–199. By 1965, the Ba'th had an estimated 3,000 members in Lebanon.

62 Batatu, *Syria's Peasantry*, pp. 142–143, and Rabinovich, *The View from Damascus*, pp. 127–128.

The Ba'th's political influence in Lebanon would be minimal. In 1957, one Ba'thist candidate, a physician from Tripoli, would contest the Lebanese parliamentary elections that year, but not win a seat. The following year, amid the tensions of the 1958 crisis, the Ba'th, as a member of the opposition, would fight against Chamoun and his government, its members participating in fighting in Tripoli, Saida, and Baalbek.[63] In Syria, as will be seen later, the Ba'th's influence would expand greatly following the downfall of Adib al-Shishakli in 1954, securing 22 seats in the subsequent elections.[64] The following year, it would join with the Communists and supporters in the Syrian army to drive the SSNP from Syria's political scene. With the UAR's establishment in 1958, it would marginalize the Syrian Communist Party and end their short-lived alliance to rid Syria of their familiar rival, the SSNP.

The Kata'ib

Founded in late 1936 by Pierre Gemayel as a youth movement, and, later, a political party dedicated to preserving Lebanon's independence, the state's institutions, and its Lebanese identity rooted in its Phoenician past, the Christian community, and its relationship with France.[65] It was on these matters that the Kata'ib-SSNP conflict was overwhelmingly based. A predominately Maronite political movement, it had an estimated following of 22,000 by 1939, a number that would more than double by 1960 to around 50,000 adherents, including Greek Catholics and some Shi'i Muslims. It had little appeal to Greek Orthodox, Druze, and Sunni communities. Though it draws followers from different classes, the "middle class merchants, small businessmen, and professionals predominate." [66]

Dissolved by official decree a year after its establishment, the Kata'ib were legalized in 1943, acknowledging the youth movement's contribution to the struggle for Lebanon's independence. Though not an official political party, its first candidate would run for parliament in 1945; he lost, in part, due to the SSNP's support for his opponent. Three Kata'ib members would be elected in 1951, but it would only secure a single seat in the 1953 and 1957 elections.[67] However, the Kata'ib's representation in parliament does not accurately reflect its

63 al-Qays, *Ḥizb al-Ba'th*, loc. 371.
64 Seale, *The Struggle for Syria*, pp. 176–178.
65 Rabinovich, *The View from Damascus*, p. 131.
66 Suleiman, *Political Parties in Lebanon*, pp. 234, 240–241.
67 Suleiman, *Political Parties in Lebanon*, pp. 234–235.

overall political influence. Though a predominately Maronite organization, by 1958, it had established itself throughout all of Lebanon, though its core strength would be centered in Mount Lebanon, and it was instrumental in supporting Chamoun's government in the 1958 crisis.

The SSNP in Academic Discourse

The party remains relatively unfamiliar to Western academics, researchers, and policymakers still today. Few scholarly works about the party have appeared in English. Indeed, to date, existing critical scholarly literature on the SSNP is scarce and tends to limit itself to recounting the same central narrative of events from the party's history. Most prevalent are shorter accounts of the SSNP that appear as either whole chapters or parts of chapters in books on particular episodes in the SSNP's history.[68] Works on Lebanese and Syrian political parties and history,[69] studies on Syrian nationalism,[70] and analyses of Saʿadeh's life and intellectual thought mention the party to some extent.[71] The latter of these works, particularly those on Saʿadeh's life and thought, cannot necessarily be categorized as historical studies on the SSNP as they address the party and its history to a limited degree. This tendency toward the episodic and tangential discussion of the party is regrettable. It has frequently, though not always, resulted in the perpetuation of misconceptions and misstatements regarding the party and its ideology and a lack of serious detailed and nuanced analysis regarding the party's ideology and activities. For example, Patrick Seale disparaged both the party and its founder, referring to Saʿadeh's nationalist thought as "mumbo-jumbo."[72] Others have uncritically perpetuated analyses that overem-

---

68 For notable works of this type, see Beshara, *Outright Assassination*; Beshara, *Lebanon*; Ghassan al-Khalidi, *al-Ḥizb al-Qawmī wa-Qaḍīyat al-Mālkī: Ḥaqīqa am Ittihām* (Beirut: Dār wa Maktabat al-Turāth al-Adabī, 1999); Ghassan al-Khalidi, *al-Ḥizb al-Qawmī wa-l-Thawra al-Thāniyya 1961–1962, al-Inqilāb wa-l-Muhākamāt, Vol. 1* (Beirut: Dār wa Maktabat al-Turāth al-Adabī, 2003); and Ghassan al-Khalidi, *Saʿādah wa-l-Thawra al-Awwalī* (Beirut: Dār wa Maktabat al-Turāth al-Adabī, 1997).

69 See, for example Suleiman, *Political Parties in Lebanon*, pp. 91–119; Hudson, *Precarious Republic*, pp. 171–175; Seale, *The Struggle for Syria*; Andrew Rathmell, *Secret War in the Middle East: The Covert Struggle for Syria, 1949–1961* (London: I.B. Tauris, 2014); Itamar Rabinovich, *The War for Lebanon* (Cornell: Cornell University Press, 1986), pp. 60–88; Zisser, *Lebanon*, pp. 176–190; and Eyal Zisser, "The Syrian Phoenix – The Revival of the Syrian Social National Party in Syria," *Die Welt des Islams* 47, no. 2 (2007).

70 Adel Beshara, *Syrian Nationalism: An Inquiry into the Political Thought of Antun Sa'adeh, Second Edition* (Melbourne: IPhoenix Publishing, 2011); Salem, *Bitter Legacy*, pp. 239–259; and Pipes, *Greater Syria*.

71 See, for example Adel Beshara, ed., *Antun Sa'adeh: The Man and His Thought: An Anthology* (Reading: Ithaca Press, 2007) and Adel Beshara, *The Intellectual Legacy of Antun Sa'adeh: Philosophy, Culture and Society, Vol. 1* (Beirut: Kutub, 2017). Numerous works on Antun Saʿadeh's life, thought, and leadership of the SSNP, cited throughout this study, have been published in Arabic.

72 Seale, *The Struggle for Syria*, p. 243.

phasize and overstate European fascism's influence on Saʿadeh and the party's ideology. Also problematic is the tendency in current scholarship to equate Saʿadeh with the party he founded, which overlooks internal disagreements and debates and ignores the fact that Saʿadeh was absent from Lebanon and Syria for almost a decade, a period in which he had minimal contact with the party he founded and led.[73]

The earliest scholarly works on the SSNP were Ph.D. dissertations published by Sethian and Makdisi in 1946 and 1960.[74] Both provide helpful insights on the SSNP's first years, overviews of the party's central ideological positions, and reasons for the party's failure to inspire Geographic Syria's unification. Makdisi, for example, argues that the party provided the newly politicized youth in Syria and Lebanon with appealing, clearly articulated principles for comprehensive national renewal and reform but failed to win broad appeal due to its "dictatorial [internal] organization," its rigid rejection of Arabism, and "the haziness of its economic concepts," ultimately resulting in the party "[missing]the opportunity to become one of the most constructive elements in the Arab nationalist movement." While much of their analyses remain relevant, they nevertheless require updating and expansion considering the quantity of new primary sources and scholarly works now available.

A similar critique can be made of Labib Yamak's concise 1966 monograph *The Syrian Social Nationalist Party: An Ideological Analysis*, which remains one of the most critical studies on the party available in English. However, as its title suggests, Yamak – a former SSNP member and deputy minister of information – focused his study on analyzing the party's ideology, providing only a brief account of key moments in the SSNP's history from its formation until 1962. While it remains an important study for researchers, for all its academic merits, the study is tinged with the author's disillusionment of his experience as a party member having fallen sway to Saʿadeh's charisma and ideas.

Several years after Yamak's monograph was published, scholars Michael Suleiman and Michael Hudson published studies on Lebanese political parties and

---

73 Just as this study seeks to separate the SSNP from Saʿadeh the man, Mujais takes a similar approach, only with the opposite, corresponding intention, to separate "the understanding of [Saʿadeh] the man from the idiosyncrasies of the history of the political organization." Salim Mujais, *Antoun Saadeh, A Biography – Volume I: The Youth Years* (Beirut: Kutub, 2004), p. 11.
74 R.D. Sethian, "The Syrian National Party," Ph.D. Dissertation, University of Michigan, 1946, and Nadim K. Makdisi, "The Syrian National Party: A Case Study of the First Inroads of National Socialism in the Arab World," Ph.D. Dissertation, American University of Beirut, 1960.

political modernization, respectively.[75] Suleiman's treatment of the SSNP is more substantial than Hudson's, but both offer concise, measured analyses of the party and its objectives. Hudson ultimately concludes, however, that "[to] talk with the brilliant young recruits of the [SSNP]… is to confront thwarted idealism twisted into a doctrine of total escape."[76] Given the broader focus of both studies regarding Lebanon's political environment, each serves as an excellent source that contextualizes the SSNP and its political program within Lebanon's body politic.

After Hudson's study, little was written about the SSNP until the late 1980s and early 1990s until the publication of Daniel Pipes' journal article "Radical Politics and the Syrian Social Nationalist Party" and his book *Greater Syria: The History of Ambition.* As previous scholars had done, Pipes broadly outlined the party's ideology, social bases of support, and radical political activity from its inception through the Lebanese Civil War. While providing a much-needed update on the party's activities since the early 1960s, Pipes also advanced several questionable arguments and poorly cited assertions.[77] Around this time, Haytham Kader (the pen name of Salim Mujais) published his *The Syrian Social Nationalist Party: Its Ideology and Early History,* which, like Yamak's work, outlines the SSNP's ideology while providing a short overview of the party's early history. Kader's analysis lacks depth due to its brevity, an issue he recently resolved with the 2019 publication (under his name) of *The Syrian Social Nationalist Party: Its Ideology and History.* This study is greatly expanded and more thoroughly researched, but its examination concludes in 1949 with Saʿadeh's execution, a frustratingly common cut-off point for works on the party.

Kader's and Pipes' works on the party and Greater Syria were followed by Paul Salem's examination of ideology and politics in the Arab world. A substantial part of Salem's work was dedicated to analyzing regional nationalisms, including the SSNP's Syrian nationalism. Like Pipes and others before him, Salem sought to emphasize the SSNP's "fascist" characteristics and the influence of racialist, nationalist, and fascist ideology on Saʿadeh's thought and, by extension, the SSNP's ideology. However, this prevailing line of argument was over-

---

75 See Suleiman, *Political Parties in Lebanon*, pp. 91–119, and Hudson, *Precarious Republic*, pp. 171–175.

76 Hudson, *Precarious Republic*, p. 169.

77 For example, Pipes alleged the SSNP's was involved in the Marine Barracks bombing and attempted to assassinate a Libyan diplomat in Beirut but did not cite any sources that could verify his claims. Some of these assertions were maintained in his book.

stated[78] and ignored a substantial body of evidence that more convincingly grounds Saʿadeh's thought not in Europe's foreign soils but within the Levant and the Syrian-Lebanese diaspora in South America.[79]

---

78 As Zisser notes, "It goes without saying that the character [i.e. fascist character] of the [SSNP] has been the focus of scholarly debate ever since its founding at the beginning of the 1930s, and certainly since the 1940, when it became a significant political power in Syria and Lebanon. The [SSNP] is discussed more than any other political party…" (Eyal Zisser, "Memoirs Do Not Deceive: Syrians Confront Fascism and Nazism—as Reflected in the Memoirs of Syrian Political Leaders and Intellectuals," in *Arab Responses to Fascism and Nazism: Attraction and Repulsion*, ed. Israel Gershoni (Austin: University of Texas Press, 2014), p. 78) The French and the party's opponents, as will be seen, labeled the party as fascist, but there has been little serious scholarly engagement with the issue until recently. The late German scholar Christoph Schumann, whose works focused on the development of radical nationalism and radical nationalist organizations in Syria and Lebanon between 1930 and 1958, including the SSNP, added more nuance to the debate. Addressing the "fascist" label often ascribed to the party, Schumann noted that the SSNP was among several radical nationalist organizations that arose in the Levant whose symbols and organization resembled that of European fascist movements, often leading to the accusation that these parties were "the servants of the Axis powers in the Levant." By this measure of style and organization, including the party's emphasis on symbols, exaltation of youth, and tendency toward authoritarian and charismatic leadership, the SSNP was arguably fascistic; this was not the case regarding the party's ideology and aims. (For typological description of fascism, see Stanley G. Payne, *A History of Fascism, 1914–1945* (New York: Routledge, 1995), p. 7) Schumann's argument was further expanded upon by Götz Nordbruch in his study Nazism in Syria and Lebanon. Nordbruch demonstrates a far more "ambivalent" reception to Nazi advances by Lebanese and Syrians than previously thought. Indeed, the SSNP's response to Italy and Germany, like those of other Lebanese and Syrians must be seen in the context of seeking independence from France. The desire to be rid of the Mandate, rather than any true affinity for Fascism or National Socialism, was paramount. See Christoph Schumann, "The experience of organized nationalism: radical discourse and political socialization in Syria and Lebanon, 1930–1958," in *From the Syrian Land to the States of Syria and Lebanon*, eds. Thomas Philipp and Christoph Schumann (Beirut: Orient-Institute, 2004), p. 344; Christoph Schumann, "Symbolische Aneignungen. Antun Sa'adas Radikalnationalismus in der Epoche des Faschismus," in *Blind für die Geschichte? Arabische Begegnungen mit dem Nationalsozialismus*, eds. G. Höpp, P. Wien, R. Wildan-Gel (Berlin: Hans Schiler Verlag, 2004), pp. 178–180; Peter Wien, "Arabs and Fascism: Empirical and Theoretical Perspectives," *Die Welt des Islams* 52, no. 1 (January 2012): pp. 331–350; and Götz Nordbuch, "A Challenge to the Local Order: Reactions to Nazism in the Syrian and Lebanese Press," in *Arab Responses to Fascism and Nazism: Attraction*, ed. Israel Gershoni (Austin: University of Texas Press, 2014), pp. 35–54.

79 In his works, Beshara convincingly grounded Saʿadeh's political and intellectual thought in the South American diaspora of the early 1920s, which would serve as a foundation for the SSNP's ideology. This line of argument was further developed by the German scholar Christoph Schumann in his journal article on Syrian nationalism in Latin America between the World Wars in which he compared the national thought of Saʿadeh and his father, Khalil, who was himself a widely-respected Syrian nationalist activist and intellectual. Christoph Schumann, "National-

The prevailing academic discourse on the party began to be challenged in the late 1990s by the Australian-Lebanese scholar Adel Beshara. To date, however, no scholar has matched Beshara's output and efforts to shine a scholarly light on Saʿadeh and the party, publishing at least eight books in English on topics related to Saʿadeh, the SSNP, and Syrian nationalism, including separate studies on the two most seminal events in the SSNP's history – Saʿadeh's trial and execution in 1949 and the failed coup in Lebanon on the eve of 1962.[80] While the works mentioned above contain substantive overviews of the party's history, they still fall short of constituting a definitive study on the movement. To date, the most comprehensive overviews and analyses of the SSNP's early history are Mujais' 2019 book mentioned above and Ahmad Salim Ahmad's *Ḥizb al-Sūrī al-Qawmī al-Ijtimāʿī, 1932–1962: Dirāsa Tārīkhīya*, published in 2014. Ahmad's book situates the SSNP within its social and political contexts in Lebanon and Syria while also adding valuable observations on the broader geopolitical situation in which the SSNP operated. Unlike Mujais' work, Ahmad's covers the party's early history until its failed coup in January 1962. Nevertheless, it still falls short in assessing the party's development, social and political mobilization methods, and political behavior.

In contrast, the present study builds on these past works using original, previously unused source material published in Arabic and French to provide the most detailed and comprehensive scholarly account of the party's early history to date in the English language.

---

ism, Diaspora and 'Civilisational Mission': The Case of Syrian Nationalism in Latin America between World War I and World War II," *Nations and Nationalism* 10, no. 4 (October 2004).

80 Excluding previously mentioned studies edited or authored by Beshara, see *Outright Assassination*; *Lebanon*; and *Fayez Sayegh: The Party Years, 1938–1947* (London: Black House Publishing, 2019).

Organization of the Book

The study presented herein is a political history of the SSNP, providing a detailed analytical account of the movement's formation, development, and political activities in Lebanon and Syria. It is based on a qualitative and historiographical examination of primary and secondary textual sources in Arabic, French, and English. It draws on the vast corpus of literature produced by the SSNP and its adherents throughout its history, including personal (e.g., memoirs,[81] articles, and speeches) and official (e.g., newspapers, leaflets, and booklets) publications. It also draws on archival records in France, Great Britain, and, to a lesser extent, the United States, on published documentary collections, on relevant Lebanese, Syrian and international newspapers, and the relevant secondary literature.

The study describes the party's social bases of support, elaborates on its contentious politics and the forms of contention it employed, explores the dynamics of its relations with Lebanese and Syrian social and political authorities and actors, and describes its ultimate failure to transform into a mass movement and attain political power in either country. In focusing on the SSNP's political behavior, this study necessarily, but regrettably, excludes to a great degree any serious treatment of the party's cultural activities, which were integral to its overall program of national revival. The study only engages with the party's ideology if immediately relevant to the political events being discussed. It is organized chronologically in four parts, each with three chapters, dividing the SSNP's early history into four periods, concluding with an epilogue addressing the present state of the party:

Part One, "A New Generation," examines the development of Antun Saʿadeh's political thought in the 1920s and his first attempts at political organization and activism in the South American *mahjar*. It then examines the first six years of the SSNP's existence, from its inception in the winter of 1932 until Saʿadeh's exile from Lebanon in the summer of 1938. It first explores its initial clandestine beginnings, focusing on its recruitment methods, ideological and organ-

81 Following Schumann's general guidelines "for the historical analysis of autobiographical material," this study will both cross-check and compare the representation of facts and events in the autobiographies used with other sources and autobiographies; address the way in which both the life experience of the author and the period in which he writes influence his representation of the past; and, finally, the author's socialization, i.e. radicalization. Christoph Schumann, "The Generation of Broad Expectations: Nationalism, Education, and Autobiography in Syria and Lebanon, 1930–1958," *Die Welt des Islams* 41, no. 2 (July 2001): p. 177.

izational development, and geographic expansion through Lebanon and Syria's urban and rural centers. It then continues with an examination of the SSNP's first three years of open political activity following its discovery by French authorities in November 1935, ending in the summer of 1938 when Saʿadeh leaves Lebanon.

Part Two, "The War Years," details the party's activity in the *mahjar* and Syria and Lebanon from the beginning of Saʿadeh's de facto exile until the end of the War in Europe in May 1945. The first five years until Lebanon's independence in 1943 would be characterized by an intense confrontation with the French that would take a heavy toll on the party. The beleaguered party would find a respite in its relationship with the Lebanese government in 1943, but its accommodationist policies would facilitate a striking internal transformation in both the party and its ideology to which Saʿadeh would strenuously object.

Part Three, "The Road to Revolution and its Aftermath," details a tumultuous and transformative period in the party's history, beginning with the period preceding and immediately following Saʿadeh's return to Lebanon in March 1947. This period was characterized by internal party conflict, and renewed confrontation with Lebanese authorities as the party provocatively reiterated that Lebanon was merely part of the Syrian nation, rather than distinct from it, and was highly critical of the Lebanese government's conduct in the 1948 Arab-Israeli War. The confrontation reached its apogee in the SSNP's failed "social nationalist revolution" and Saʿadeh's subsequent execution in the summer of 1949, after which the party was outlawed in Lebanon and forced to move the center of its activities to neighboring Damascus.

Part Four, "Advance and Retreat," addresses how the SSNP acted to shape the emerging regional and domestic orders in a manner that was more in line with its ideological vision in the 1950s. In 1952, the party reemerged on the Lebanese political scene and, thanks to its cooperative relations with President Camille Chamoun, it re-organized and advanced its agenda in a way it had been unable to previously. However, this brief period of influence in Lebanon declined rapidly in the aftermath of the 1958 crisis, as the SSNP and those allied with Chamoun found themselves marginalized in Fuad Chehab's new government. In Syria, where the party had been headquartered since the late summer of 1949, the SSNP worked to further consolidate its influence in government and the armed forces under Shishakli's regime. Following Shishakli's resignation, the party lacked popular appeal, and poor decision-making led it into open conflict with its increasingly powerful rivals, the Baʿth and the communists. In the end, the bitter, often violent struggle between the party and its rivals in Syria resulted in its demise and retreat from the Syrian public sphere.

The **Epilogue, "The Rise of Factionalism,"** offers an analysis of the SSNP in the six decades that have since passed, detailing its failure to transform into a mass movement and expand its political influence in Lebanon and Syria. Particular attention is given to the party's struggle to overcome internal division and factionalism and its efforts to support the Baʿthist regime of Bashar al-Asad in the ongoing civil war in Syria.

Part One: **A New Generation**

1 Nationalist Formation: Antun Saʿadeh in the South American *Mahjar*

In February 1921, Antun, together with his siblings Edward, Salim, and Grace, left their uncle in Springer, New Mexico, and traveled to São Paulo, Brazil, where they were reunited with their father, Khalil. The siblings had emigrated from Shuwayr in late 1919 or early 1920,[1] traveling first to Marseilles, France, and then to the United States, arriving at Ellis Island in New York on 28 March 1920 before continuing to Springer.[2] Saʿadeh and his younger siblings had endured the years of hardship and suffering brought about by the famine, deprivation, and oppression visited upon Greater Syria under the rule of Cemal Pasha and experienced firsthand the tumult and uncertainty brought about by the end of Ottoman rule. The experience, Antun would later recall, prompted him to reflect on the state of the Syrian nation and ask, "what was it that brought all this woe on my people?"[3] It was not, however, until he arrived in São Paolo at the young age of seventeen that he became openly engaged and active in the Syrian national cause, first assisting his father in the publication of *al-Jarida* (São Paolo, 1920–1923) – the newspaper co-founded by Khalil – as an editor, writer, and printer. Over the following five years, the two worked together closely to oppose French colonial rule and the territorial division of Geographic Syria and promote the Syrian national cause among their compatriots in the South American diaspora.

When Antun arrived in Brazil, the Syrian diaspora community in South America was ever more divided, polarized over French rule and its military occupation of Syria and Lebanon, and the establishment of Greater Lebanon. The São Paolo-based, pro-French *Jāmiʿat al-Nahḍa al-Lubnāniyya*, established in 1914, championed France's role in Syria and Lebanon and supported France's establishment of an 'independent' Greater Lebanon, while the São Paolo-based, pro-French Comité Patriotique Syrien-Libanais supported a unified, federal Syria that included Lebanon. Anti-French political associations and periodicals,

1 There is disagreement regarding the exact date Saʿadeh and his siblings left Lebanon. Saʿadeh himself recalled leaving in early 1920, as does one of the early members of the party, Jibran Jurayj, while one of Saʿadeh's biographers, Salim Mujais, suggests they left in late 1919. See "Risāla ila Ḥamīd Faranjiyya," in Saʿadeh, *al-Aʿmāl al-Kāmila, Vol. 2*, p. 9; Jibran Jurayj, *Min al-Juʿbat: Marwiyyāt, Mustanadāt wa Adabiyyāt ʿan al-Ḥizb al-Sūrī al-Qawmī al-Ijtimāʿī, Vol. 1* (Beirut: 1985), 18; and Mujais, *Saadeh, Vol. 1*, p. 141.

2 Mujais, *Saadeh, Vol. 1*, pp. 142–145.

3 "Risāla ila Ḥamīd Faranjiyya," in Saʿadeh, *al-Aʿmāl al-Kāmila, Vol. 2*, pp. 9–11.

https://doi.org/10.1515/9783110729092-003

such as Khalil's, opposed the establishment of Greater Lebanon and France's mandate. Meanwhile, France continued to implement its divide and rule policy in Syria and Lebanon, consolidating its grip over its new territories. Having already declared the 'independence' of Greater Lebanon and divided it into four sanjaks in September 1920, the French also established the state of Aleppo, the state of Damascus, and the territory of the 'Alawis in the fall of 1920 and granted autonomy to Jabal Druze in March 1922, essentially partitioning the Syrian hinterland into areas that reinforced sectarian and communal divisions.[4] In time, France would alter these administrative divisions as needed to ensure its authority over the territories under its mandate.[5] French policies encountered resistance from some locals in certain areas, particularly in the coastal region inhabited by the 'Alawis and in the northern region around Aleppo.[6] However, armed opposition to French forces was unsustainable and did not pose a serious threat to France's pacification of the territories, ultimately achieved in 1921.[7]

After several months of working with his father, Antun penned his first article on Syrian national issues for *al-Jarida*. He would contribute five other articles directly addressing national issues and only several others on different subjects until the newspaper ceased publication in early 1923.[8] Together, the essays constitute the first explicit expressions of themes and ideas that would pervade Antun's nationalist discourse for the remainder of his life and serve as the bedrock for his unique conceptualization and articulation of Syrian nationhood and Syrian nationalist ideology. His nationalist discourse was developed under his father's watchful eye and tutelage and borrowed heavily, though not entirely, from Khalil's foundational nationalist convictions. Differences of opinion would develop between the two, but, at the time, Khalil and Antun were inseparable partners in the Syrian national struggle, and their writings reflected their shared concerns regarding the state of the Syrian nation and its future. As editors and contributors, they filled the pages of *al-Jarida* with articles voicing opposition to Greater Syria's territorial division and criticizing French colonial rule, and critiques of Lebanese particularism and the dismal state of the Syrian nation and the national movement.

4 Longrigg, *Syria and Lebanon*, pp. 117–118.
5 Longrigg, *Syria and Lebanon*, pp. 123–132.
6 Longrigg, *Syria and Lebanon*, pp. 118–123, and Philip Khoury, *Syria and the French Mandate: The Politics of Arab Nationalism, 1920–1945* (Princeton: Princeton University Press, 1987), pp. 99–110.
7 Khoury, *Syria*, p. 99.
8 Mujais, *Saadeh, Vol. 1*, p. 176.

Like his father,[9] Antun maintained that 'religious fanaticism' was a curse plaguing the Syrian nation and the source of its woes while asserting other calamities would befall the nation should Syrians fail to address it.[10] Not only was religious fanaticism and division the source of the nation's woes, but the calamities of French occupation and "Zionist oppression" (*al-iḍṭihād al-ṣahyūnī*) were the reward for it and an obstacle to Syria's independence and advancement, preventing it from taking its place among the "living nations" (*al-umam al-ḥayā*). Using similar language as his father, Antun likened religious intolerance to disease and a "cancer eating away at its [the Syrian nation's] flesh and bones."[11] Yet, the Syrian nation remained consumed by religious intolerance, and his fellow countrymen seemed to not care about the threats facing their nation, preferring instead to argue amongst themselves over trivial matters. The "idle state of the people," characterized by ignorance and a general lack of concern, worried Antun and his father, who questioned how long Syrians would remain silent under French rule and divided as a people.[12]

To shake the nation out of its "idle state," Antun and Khalil believed a patriotic spirit needed to be kindled among their fellow countrymen. For Antun, the absence of patriotism (*waṭaniyya*) was an underlying reason for a nation's underdevelopment and decay. In contrast, the presence of patriotism was an underlying reason for a people's advancement (*sirr taqaddum al-shuʿūb huwa al-waṭaniyya. wa ʿadam wujūd al-waṭaniyya huwa sirr taʾakhkhur wa inḥiṭāṭ al-umam*).[13] Therefore, Syria's lack of progress and independence was due to a lack of patriotic sentiment within society, and patriotism, thus, was the foundation upon which Syria must depend if it hoped to gain independence and advance.[14] Antun hoped that a new sense of patriotism, together with a growing awareness of the tyranny of French colonial rule, would inspire Syrians in the *mahjar* to aid their brethren in the homeland and spark "a true revival"

9 "al-Taʿṣṣub al-Dīnī fī al-Sharq," in Mujais and Hage, *Khalīl Saʿādah, Vol. 4*, pp. 146–161, and "Hayatnā al-Waṭaniyya," in Salim Mujais and Badr el-Hage, *al-Duktūr Khalīl Saʿādah: Sūriyya wa-l-Intidāb al-Faransiyya, Vol. 2* (Beirut: Muʾassasat Saʿādah li-l-Thaqāfa, 2014), p. 111.

10 "al-Sūriyyūn wa al-Istiqlāl," in Saʿadeh, *al-Aʿmāl al-Kāmila, Vol. 1*, pp. 11–13.

11 "al-Sūriyyūn wa al-Istiqlāl," in Saʿadeh, *al-Aʿmāl al-Kāmila, Vol. 1*, p. 13.

12 See, for example, Khalil's plea for unity and for the nation to awaken to the dangers confronting it: "Hayatnā al-Waṭaniyya," in Mujais and Hage, *Khalīl Saʿādah, Vol. 2*, p. 114.

13 "al-Waṭaniyya," in Saʿadeh, *al-Aʿmāl al-Kāmila, Vol. 1*, pp. 3–4.

14 Antun stated, "No nation can hope for independence and progress except through patriotism. There is no independence without patriotism, and no progress without independence" (*lā amal li-ayya umma kānit bi-l-istiqlāl wa al-irtiqāʾ ilā ʿan ṭarīq al-waṭaniyya. Fa-lā istiqlāl bidūn waṭaniyya, wa lā irtiqāʾ bidūn istiqlāl*). "al-Waṭaniyya," in Saʿadeh, *al-Aʿmāl al-Kāmila, Vol. 1*, p. 3.

(*nahda ḥaqīqiyya*). Neither had yet to occur, a situation Antun believed resulted from Syrians prioritizing economic concerns and success over the national cause's success.[15]

Syrians' failure to appreciate the national cause's importance raised Antun's ire, particularly since some of these same individuals tended to portray themselves as dedicated nationalists sacrificing for the cause. Antun panned their hypocrisy and lamented the dire and disorganized state of the Syrian national movement.[16] In his estimation, Syrian political activism in the diaspora had not moved beyond giving speeches and sending protest cables to the League of Nations, which were of limited effect or entirely useless. In the homeland, the opposition had failed to confront French rule effectively. Organized action was needed if Syrian independence was to be achieved and recognized.[17] This action would require Syrians everywhere to stand with determination, prepared to make the necessary sacrifices to obtain their rights, and free themselves from colonial rule. Indeed, love and jealousy for one's country and acknowledging and sharing in the sorrows of its suffering would not suffice in securing Syria's freedom.[18]

Antun's legitimate criticism of the effectiveness of Syrian political activism on behalf of the national cause and the general lack of concrete, organized action notwithstanding, his reproach was somewhat hypocritical. He had only just become politically engaged, and his activism was and would be until at least 1925, limited to writing articles and publishing periodicals rather than undertaking the organized, sacrificial political activity he was demanding his fellows engage.[19] Moreover, his criticism was dismissive of Syrian nationalists' efforts, such as those of his father, to bring about Syrian independence and confront the French colonial rule, even dismissing armed attempts to do so. To be sure, all these efforts failed, but not for lack of determination and willingness

---

15 "al-Waṭaniyya," in Sa'adeh, *al-A'māl al-Kāmila, Vol. 1*, p. 4.

16 "al-Waṭaniyya," in Sa'adeh, *al-A'māl al-Kāmila, Vol. 1*, pp. 3–4.

17 "Āmāl al-Waṭan," in Sa'adeh, *al-A'māl al-Kāmila, Vol. 1*, p. 1.

18 "Āmāl al-Waṭan," in Sa'adeh, *al-A'māl al-Kāmila, Vol. 1*, p. 2.

19 Antun and his father were members of the Freemason Star of Syria Lodge in São Paulo, his father even serving as the Syrian Lodge's president between 1924 and 1926. (Mujais, *Saadeh, Vol. 1*, 185) Antun, and perhaps his father as well, believed the lodge could serve as an organization that promoted the national cause. However, both ultimately resigned their membership in the lodge in May 1926 over the lodge's reluctance to engage in political activism, a decision both respected and understood. For Khalil's resignation letter see "Istiqāla min al-Māsuniyya," in Mujais and Hage, *Khalīl Sa'ādah, Vol. 2*, pp. 402–404. For Antun's resignation letter see "Ilā 'Maḥfil Najmat Sūriyya' al-Māsunī – Kitāb Istiqāla," in Sa'adeh, *al-A'māl al-Kāmila, Vol. 1*, pp. 203–206.

to struggle for the nation. Thus, while correctly recognizing the need for organized action beyond speeches and letters of protest, he himself only heeded his advice several years later, suggesting his harsh criticism reflected more the zealousness of youth than an entirely objective analysis of the national situation.

In addition to lamenting the dismal state of the nation and the national movement, Antun also addressed the territorial division of Geographic Syria, mainly Lebanese independence. Like his father, Antun believed in the unity of Geographic Syria and that all its constituent territories – Lebanon, Palestine, and Syria – should be united in one independent state.[20] Though it is unclear if Antun accepted his father's position that such a state should be in the form of a federal union comprised of the three territories, it is evident that Antun believed Lebanon was an integral part of Geographic Syria and that he considered the Lebanese and Syrians to be one people. Yet, according to Antun, many Lebanese mistakenly had come to believe Lebanon's separation from Syria was advantageous, fearing that union with Syria would mean losing their rights and privileges, thereby enslaving them and making them a colony of a foreign state, i.e., Syria.[21] Khalil expressed concern that certain "factions" among the Lebanese spoke of Syrians as though they were strangers and foreigners, suggesting a lack of a common bond or any relation between Syrians and Lebanese.[22] These beliefs, however, were misguided. Syria, Antun asserted, had no intention of robbing Lebanese of their rights, nor was there any reason why Lebanon and Syria should not be united. Indeed, a united Lebanon and Syria would be even stronger and more formidable than if they were separate entities, with a vast territory and army capable of thwarting French colonial designs.[23] Yet, many

20 "al-Waḥda al-Sūriyya wa Makhāwif al-Lubnāniyyin," in Saʿadeh, *al-Aʿmāl al-Kāmila, Vol. 1*, pp. 5–7. Antun and his father continued to reiterate this position on the unity of Geographic Syria, again asserting that there was no difference between Lebanese and Syrians or Syrians and Palestinians and that the three parts of Geographic Syria – Lebanon, Palestine, and Syria – are part of a whole body that must be united in solidarity and committed to pursuing a singular purpose. France's administrative division of the Syrian nation into multiple states with multiple nationalities had only caused great damage. See "al-Jinsiyyāt al-Surriya wa-l-Lubnāniyya wa-l-Filisṭiniyya," in Saʿadeh, *al-Aʿmāl al-Kāmila, Vol. 1*, p. 196.

21 Many Lebanese, according to Antun, viewed Syria as an "ogre that wants to swallow them up or a monster who wants prey upon them." "al-Waḥda al-Sūriyya wa Makhāwif al-Lubnāniyyin," in Saʿadeh, *al-Aʿmāl al-Kāmila, Vol. 1*, p. 5.

22 "Idighām Lubnān fī Sūriyā," in Mujais and Hage, *Khalīl Saʿādah, Vol. 2*, p. 248.

23 "al-Waḥda al-Sūriyya wa Makhāwif al-Lubnāniyyin," in Saʿadeh, *al-Aʿmāl al-Kāmila, Vol. 1*, p. 6. Also, Antun would conclude the article expressing a similar sentiment: "Are they and the Syrians not one people? I am not one of those who deny Lebanon's suitability for independence, but I believe that Lebanon and Syria as one state is better since a unified people in a unified

Lebanese (predominately Maronite Christians) had been convinced that Greater Lebanon, separate and independent from Syria, was strong and formidable. However, many Lebanese had failed to realize that their "independence" was beholden to French colonial interests and, thus, that Lebanon was not truly independent.

For years, Khalil had sought to convince the Lebanese that the road leading to their true independence first passed through Syria, which they had failed to support in the struggle for independence, particularly during the battle at Maysalun. Only by joining with the Syrians could they remove France's yoke from their necks.[24] Expanding on his father's critique, Antun criticized Lebanese and Syrians who welcomed French rule and believed France intended to rebuild Lebanon and Syria, arguing that they had deluded themselves and failed to understand that their entreaties before Mandate authorities only harmed the national cause.[25] Yet, it was not just the Lebanese who had misunderstood French ambitions. Syrians who had also initially shown the French hospitality and respect had done so as well, mistakenly thinking France had come to liberate them when it had come, in reality, to enslave them forever.[26] According to Antun, France, "the goddess of freedom and the savior of the weak," had done nothing for Syria except to divide its territory, defeat the Syrian national movement, and imprison nationalist leaders. What then, Antun asked, has France and its High Commissioner, the "tyrant" (*ṭāghiyya*) Henri Gouraud, done to help move Syria closer to freedom and independence?[27]

Antun and Khalil did not mince their criticisms of France, denouncing its unjust and 'tyrannical' colonial rule in Lebanon and Syria. Instead of bringing freedom and independence, France, whom they mockingly referred to as "the mother of freedom and democracy" (*um al-ḥurriyya wa al-dimuqrāṭiyya*)[28] and "the affectionate mother" (*al-um al-ḥanūn*),[29] had instead enslaved them and instituted its oppressive colonial rule. Even more contemptuous, though failing to abide by its noble ideals, France nevertheless felt comfortable lecturing Syrians and Lebanese on freedom and "France's honorable traditions."[30] Antun and

state is indivisible." "al-Waḥda al-Sūriyya wa Makhāwif al-Lubnāniyyin," in Saʿadeh, *al-Aʿmāl al-Kāmila, Vol. 1,* p. 7.

24 "Idighām Lubnān fī Sūriyā," in Mujais and Hage, *Khalīl Saʿādah, Vol. 2,* pp. 248–249.

25 "Gouraud wa Sūriyya," in Saʿadeh, *al-Aʿmāl al-Kāmila, Vol. 1,* p. 9.

26 "al-Imbarāṭūriyya al-Ifaransiyya al-Sharqiyya," in Saʿadeh, *al-Aʿmāl al-Kāmila, Vol. 1,* p. 15.

27 "Gouraud wa Sūriyya," in Saʿadeh, *al-Aʿmāl al-Kāmila, Vol. 1,* p. 10.

28 "Āmāl al-Waṭan," in Saʿadeh, *al-Aʿmāl al-Kāmila, Vol. 1,* p. 1.

29 "Idighām Lubnān fī Sūriyā," in Mujais and Hage, *Khalīl Saʿādah, Vol. 2,* p. 247.

30 "Muʿāraḍa al-Intidāb al-Faransī Jarīma," in Mujais and Hage, *Khalīl Saʿādah, Vol. 2,* p. 143.

Khalil understood that France was driven to build an empire that would rival that of Great Britain's and that Syria was one of the prized possessions of the French colonial project, underscoring why France intended "to remain in Syria forever."[31] Syrians, Antun observed, eventually understood this after experiencing the defeat at Maysalun and enduring France's unjust and despotic colonial policies under Gouraud. Moreover, for Antun and Khalil, France's policy reflected its understanding that a unified Greater Syria posed a clear threat to its colonial interests. Having realized these points, Antun believed the time was right for Syrians to rise and destroy France's colonial aspirations, thereby ending its unjust and tyrannical rule and building on its ruins monuments of independence and "councils of freedom, brotherhood, and equality."[32]

Besides his determined opposition to the French mandate, Antun identified another threat to Syria's independence that was, in his estimation, just as grave, or only slightly less so, as French colonialism: Zionism.[33] Though Syrians were mindful of the terrible consequences were the Zionists to succeed in Palestine, Antun feared they had not fully grasped the immanency of the Zionist threat, just as they had failed and been late to understand the danger of French colonialism. Antun remarked, "It is strange that Syrians do not care about these imminent threats as they are ignorant of their reality, completely aloof and obsessed with arguing with one another for no reason."[34] Instead, Syrians must confront Zionism in the same manner as French colonialism: they must unite and be prepared to make sacrifices to attain their freedom and independence.[35]

Despite his urgent pleas for sacrifice and action to bring about Syria's independence, Antun himself, over the coming years, seemed disengaged from the national cause. He continued to assist his father with publishing *al-Jarida* until it ceased publication in the spring of 1923 and then helped Khalil revive *al-Majalla* (1923–1925) as a monthly periodical in São Paulo, only contributing a handful of articles to the national cause during its two years in circulation.[36] Only then, in 1925, would Antun begin to engage in what could be characterized

31 "al-Imbarāṭūriyya al-Ifaransiyya al-Sharqiyya," in Saʿadeh, *al-Aʿmāl al-Kāmila, Vol. 1*, p. 14, and "Tafkīk Sūriyā," in Mujais and Hage, *Khalīl Saʿādah, Vol. 2*, p. 74.

32 "al-Imbarāṭūriyya al-Ifaransiyya al-Sharqiyya," in Saʿadeh, *al-Aʿmāl al-Kāmila, Vol. 1*, p. 17.

33 "al-Sūriyyūn wa al-Istiqlāl," in Saʿadeh, *al-Aʿmāl al-Kāmila, Vol. 1*, p. 11.

34 "al-Sūriyyūn wa al-Istiqlāl," in Saʿadeh, *al-Aʿmāl al-Kāmila, Vol. 1*, p. 12.

35 "al-Sūriyyūn wa al-Istiqlāl," in Saʿadeh, *al-Aʿmāl al-Kāmila, Vol. 1*, p. 13.

36 See, for example, "Dhikrā al-Waṭan wa al-Ahal" and "al-ʿAuda ilā Maḥajja al-Ṣawāb Khaṭwa Jadīda naḥwa al-Fallāḥ," in Saʿadeh, *al-Aʿmāl al-Kāmila, Vol. 1*, pp. 43–45, 81–88.

as "organized political activity" on behalf of the Syrian cause beyond his membership in the local Freemason Syrian Lodge in São Paulo.[37]

The continuing lack of an influential and effective organized national movement actively opposing French rule and working to secure Greater Syria's independence weighed on Antun's mind. In February 1925, in response to a lecture given by a Zionist activist visiting Brazil, Antun penned a warning, once again, of the "Zionist threat" to Syria, which he referred to as "the greatest danger to our nation and society."[38] Pointing to what he considered the Zionist movement's success and effective organization, he argued that only a similarly effective organization following a disciplined plan would turn back Zionist gains in Palestine. Syrians' inability to develop an opposing disciplined plan and organized movement was nothing less than a national failure, which had left the Syrian nation exposed to this grave danger. Few Syrians had grasped the threat and taken action to defend the nation, leaving those who urged such actions alone in their struggle. This situation must change, argued Antun, calling on all Syrians to join parties and organizations so that their efforts would be more effective and yield more significant results.[39] In time, Antun's calls for organization and action became more emboldened and insistent as he sought to shake his compatriots out of their complacency.

Not all was lost, however, for the Syrian national cause. In early April 1925, Lord Arthur Balfour arrived in Damascus, where widespread organized popular demonstrations greeted him, the hollering masses condemning the man who had declared Britain's support for establishing a Jewish national home in Palestine.[40] For Antun, the angry demonstrations against Balfour were "the first glimmer of hope" for the Syrian nation and the national cause.[41] However, he tempered his enthusiasm by downplaying and characterizing the protests as "the least Syria, or any other nation, could do"[42] on behalf of their nation. Antun urged his fellow Syrians to establish secret and public parties and organizations, relying on "organized force" (*al-quwwa al-munaẓẓama*) to save the nation, as history has proven this to be the most effective method for preserving a nation's rights and independence.[43] Of the two, Antun believed secret political organizations were

---

37 Ahmad Asfahani, *Mafhum al-Ḥizb 'inda Sa'ādah (Beirut: al-Furāt li-l-Nashr wa-l-Tawzī',* *2016)*, p. 39.

38 "al-Ṣahyuniyya wa Imtidāduha," in Sa'adeh, *al-A'māl al-Kāmila, Vol. 1*, pp. 173–178.

39 "al-Ṣahyuniyya wa Imtidāduha," in Sa'adeh, *al-A'māl al-Kāmila, Vol. 1*, pp. 175–176.

40 Khoury, *Syria*, pp. 142–143, and Longrigg, *Syria and Lebanon*, p. 151.

41 "Sūriyya Tujāha Balfour," in Sa'adeh, *al-A'māl al-Kāmila, Vol. 1*, p. 190.

42 "Sūriyya Tujāha Balfour," in Sa'adeh, *al-A'māl al-Kāmila, Vol. 1*, p. 190.

43 "Sūriyya Tujāha Balfour," in Sa'adeh, *al-A'māl al-Kāmila, Vol. 1*, p. 192.

more effective (*man aladhīna yaʿtaqidūn bi-taʾthīr al-jamiʿiyyāt al-siyāsiyya al-sir-riyya*).[44] In particular, the young Syrians had a responsibility to fulfill their duty to the homeland, noting the youth have carried out the most significant revolutions in history, understanding and grasping the reality in which they lived.[45] These three elements – secrecy, organization, and youth – were central to the success of revolutions and political movements in Antun's assessment and would serve as essential guides when he established the SSNP in the early 1930s.

Antun, too, was, at last, moved to act and, together with six friends and intellectuals from the Syrian community in São Paolo, he formed a secret political movement dedicated to establishing an independent, secular Syrian state called the Organization of Syrian Youth Fighters (OSYF, *Jamʿiyyat al-Shabība al-Sūriyya al-Fidāʾiyya*).[46] However, disagreements over whether or not it should be a secret organization or publicize its existence and engage in public political activities[47] resulted in Antun abandoning the group. The organization's name was ultimately changed to the Syrian Patriotic League (SPL, *al-Rābiṭa al-Waṭaniyya al-Sūriyya*), and it spoke openly of "national actions" (*al-aʿmāl al-waṭaniyya*) and "national jihad" (*al-jihād al-waṭanī*).[48] Several years later, when reflecting on this initial attempt to establish a secret political organization, Antun criticized his former associates' "love of appearances" and their useless and ineffectual political activities. However, he did not specify the types of political actions he believed ineffective.[49]

Despite his frustrating initial foray organizing a political movement, Antun continued to urge his fellow countrymen to change the status quo and effectively advance the national cause. In a June 1925 article, he decried the damage caused by France's division of Greater Syria into multiple states with multiple nationalities. He urged the formation of a mass movement throughout Syria to move the Syrian nation towards true independence, stating that "the Syrian nation alone must defend its rights and security."[50] The following month, in an article entitled "Revolution of the East," Antun criticized "the West" for portraying "every national renaissance in any part of the East aimed at achieving freedom and inde-

44 "Sūriyya Tujāha Balfour," in Saʿadeh, *al-Aʿmāl al-Kāmila, Vol. 1*, p. 190.
45 "Sūriyya Tujāha Balfour," in Saʿadeh, *al-Aʿmāl al-Kāmila, Vol. 1*, p. 193.
46 Nawaf Hardan, *Saʿādah fī al-Mahjar, Vol. 1* (Beirut: Dār Fikr li-l-Abḥāth wa-l-Nashr, 1989), p. 143.
47 Hardan, *Saʿādah fī al-Mahjar*, p. 144.
48 "Ilā Sulymān Yusuf ʿAzzām," in Saʿadeh, *al-Aʿmāl al-Kāmila, Vol. 9*, p. 1.
49 "Ilā Sulymān Yusuf ʿAzzām," in Saʿadeh, *al-Aʿmāl al-Kāmila, Vol. 9*, p. 1.
50 "al-Jinsiyyāt al-Surriya wa-l-Lubnāniyya wa-l-Filisṭiniyya," in Saʿadeh, *al-Aʿmāl al-Kāmila, Vol. 1*, p. 198.

pendence as a barbaric movement threatening the civilization who banner Europe carries."[51] Antun argued that the East could not afford to wait for the West to treat it fairly and grant it its rights but must, instead, rely on force to defend and obtain them, as only the use of force can rid the East of European colonialism.[52] Calling for "a general revolution in the East," he urged those in the East, including Syrians, Egyptians, Chinese, and Indians, to act without delay "as the prolonging of the colonial order means the perpetuation of the order of humiliation, servitude, and suffering."[53] Antun's hopes for a revolt in Syria would soon be realized as a popular revolt against French rule spread throughout Syria over the following months.

The outbreak of the Great Syrian Revolt[54] in the summer of 1925 south of Damascus in the Jabal Druze united Syria's diverse population in common cause to end France's colonial project in Greater Syria and obtain its independence and undo its partitioning into separate states.[55] What began as a local uprising transformed into a broad-based national mass movement that crossed sectarian, communal, and urban-rural cleavages in Syrian society. The French ultimately defeated the revolt in 1927 after a brutal and destructive military campaign.[56] Many Syrian expatriates in the *mahjar* were keenly interested and engaged in events transpiring in the homeland. These expatriates sought to contribute to the national cause from abroad, whether "through the formation of relief committees that collected donations for those affected by the uprising in Syria and parts of Lebanon" or through newspapers and journals, actively participating in and attempting shape views and ideas regarding the revolt.[57] Antun and his father, unsurprisingly, were among those who added their voices to the growing chorus of anti-French condemnations and support for the rebel cause.

Following France's indiscriminate shelling and bombing of rebels and civilians in southern Damascus in October 1925, which allegedly killed more than

---

51 "Thawrat al-Sharq," in Sa'adeh, *al-A'māl al-Kāmila, Vol. 1,* p. 199.
52 "Thawrat al-Sharq," in Sa'adeh, *al-A'māl al-Kāmila, Vol. 1,* p. 202.
53 "Thawrat al-Sharq," in Sa'adeh, *al-A'māl al-Kāmila, Vol. 1,* p. 202.
54 For more details on the Great Syrian Revolt see Michael Provence, *The Great Syrian Revolt and the Rise of Arab Nationalism* (Austin: University of Texas Press, 2005); Khoury, *Syria,* pp. 168–218; and, Longrigg, *Syria and Lebanon,* pp. 148–181.
55 Provence, *The Great Syrian Revolt,* p. 22.
56 Provence, *The Great Syrian Revolt,* p. 26.
57 Reem Bailony, "Transnationalism and the Syrian Migrant Public: The Case of the 1925 Syrian Revolt," in *Mashriq & Mahjar* 1, no. 1 (2013): pp. 14, 17.

1,400 people,[58] Khalil penned a harshly-worded letter of protest to the League of Nations castigating France's "cruel behavior."[59] Meanwhile, Antun delivered a similar note of protest to the French Embassy in São Paolo in November 1925, condemning France and demanding an end to its mandate in Syria.[60] According to France's Ambassador to Brazil, Antun claimed the protest statement had been signed by hundreds of Syrians and delivered to the Pope, the League of Nations, and the press across South and North America, England, France, and Italy. Other local Lebanese and Syrians sent letters and held public demonstrations condemning France's military campaign as unjust and a contravention of international law. However, the French Ambassador sought to assure the Quai d'Orsay that these demonstrations and protests, citing members of the Syrian-Lebanese community, did not genuinely represent Syrian and Lebanese opinion in Brazil regarding France and its governance of Syria and Lebanon. Indeed, the Ambassador stressed that the local community was divided along sectarian lines, with Muslims and Greek Orthodox generally being hostile to the French, while Maronites supported them.[61]

Beyond this November 1925 letter and Antun's membership, until May 1926, in the local Freemason Syrian lodge, through which he attempted to effect political change, little is known regarding his political activism on behalf of the national cause until the end of 1926. According to Antun himself, his engagement in political activities outside of the Lodge occupied an increasing amount of his time and, together with the Lodge's decision to remain apolitical, compelled him to resign his membership as a Freemason.[62] By November 1926, several members of the Syrian Patriotic League who sympathized with Antun approached him to convince him to resume his SPL activities and transform the organization from within it.[63] Acceding to their entreaties and pledges of support, Antun agreed

58 According to Khoury, the Damascus Municipality claimed 1,416 killed, among whom were 336 women and children, while France claimed only 150 "civilian casualties." See Khoury, *Syria*, pp. 177–178.

59 Maria del Mar Logroña Narbona, "Development of Nationalist Identities in French Syria and Lebanon: A Transnational Dialogue with Arab Immigrants to Argentina and Brazil" (Ph.D. diss., University of California-Santa Barbara, 2007), p. 114.

60 CADN, M.A.E., "Manifestations politiques de Syriens et Libanais résidant au Brésil," Conty to S.E. Monsieur le Ministre des Affaires Etrangeres, no. 293, 16 November 1925, reproduced in Mutaniyus Yusuf Ibrahim, *Anṭūn Saʿādah wa-l-Niẓām al-Lubnānī* (Beirut: al-Jāmiʿa al-Lubnāniyya, 2016), pp. 861–863.

61 Ibrahim, *Anṭūn Saʿādah*, pp. 861–863.

62 "Ilā 'Maḥfil Najmat Sūriyya' al-Māsunī – Kitāb Istiqāla," in Saʿadeh, *al-Aʿmāl al-Kāmila, Vol. 1*, pp. 203–206.

63 "Ilā Sulymān Yusuf ʿAzzām," in Saʿadeh, *al-Aʿmāl al-Kāmila, Vol. 9*, pp. 1–2.

to deliver a speech at an official SPL gathering on 23 November. However, it became evident to Antun at the meeting that he and his supporters were in the minority, most of the SPL's members remaining opposed to him and his views, thereby rendering any effort of his to transform the League futile from the start.[64] Frustrated by this, Antun officially resigned his membership from the SPL, ending his hitherto ambiguous relationship with it. Yet, all was not lost; his speech appealed to some attendees and, within weeks, Antun and his new group of supporters established the Party of Free Syrians (PFS, *Ḥizb al-Aḥrār al-Sūriyyin).*[65] The PFS's political platform consisted of five principles:

1. The Syrian nation is sovereign over itself
2. The unification of Syria within its geographical borders
3. Separation of religion and state
4. Fight against communalism/sectarianism (*mukāfaḥa al-ṭāʾifiyya*)
5. The use of force to win the rights of the Syrian nation and attain its objectives

Antun claimed that his new party quickly gained the support of many within the community, its membership surpassing that of the SPL, emboldening him to expand its influence through collaborative partnerships with other Syrian diaspora parties that shared similar values. Based on a connection established by his father, Antun sent a letter to Suleiman Yusuf ʿAzam, a Syrian nationalist activist and member of the New Syria Party (NSP, *Ḥizb al-Sūriyā al-Jadīd*)[66] in the United States, proposing they cooperate and coordinate their nationalist activities. Both parties championed Syria's right to self-determination and were determined to end France's occupation of Lebanon and Syria and achieve independence and statehood. Moreover, both supported the ongoing rebellion against France, even though "the revolt teetered on [the edge of] collapse."[67] However, the attempted merger and cooperative efforts failed to materialize, leaving Antun frustrated and dejected, and, by 1928, the PFS had been disbanded.[68]

Troubled by his failure to form a political organization, Antun also concluded that political activism and organization in the *mahjar* were doomed to fail as

64 "Ilā Sulymān Yusuf ʿAzzām," in Saʿadeh, *al-Aʿmāl al-Kāmila, Vol. 9,* p. 2.
65 "Ilā Sulymān Yusuf ʿAzzām," in Saʿadeh, *al-Aʿmāl al-Kāmila, Vol. 9,* p. 2, and Hardan, *Saʿādah fī al-Mahjar, Vol. 1,* pp. 145–149.
66 For details on the NSP's activities in the United States during the period of the Great Syrian Revolt, see Hani J. Bawardi, *The Making of Arab Americans: From Syrian Nationalism to U.S. Citizenship* (Austin: University of Texas Press, 2015), pp. 119–158.
67 Khoury, *Syria*, p. 203.
68 Asfahani, *Mafhum al-Ḥizb*, p. 55.

it is crushed under the weight of local concerns, as the connection to the homeland and desire for action waned from abroad.[69] In contrast, only in the homeland could the national cause hope to progress, and the struggle for Syrian independence be advanced. Influenced by his new outlook, Antun ceased his political activity in Brazil, dedicating himself to his teaching duties at the National College of Arts and Science while longing to return home and end his sojourn in the *mahjar*.[70] Adding to Antun's general discontent was his brother's tragic death and a strained relationship with his father due to Khalil's membership in the SPL and his agreeing to edit its periodical *al-Rabita*.[71] By early 1930, Antun had decided to return home, and, in July, he returned to Lebanon carrying the experience of his years abroad and early nationalist education with him and, within a few years, began his political activities anew.

---

69 Beshara, *Syrian Nationalism*, p. 68.
70 Mujais, *Saadeh, Vol. 1*, pp. 186–187.
71 Mujais, *Saadeh, Vol. 1*, pp. 187–189, and Beshara, *Khalil Sa'adeh*, pp. 147–148. The two reconciled before Antun left Brazil in 1930. Until his death in April 1934, Khalil would belong to the SPL society, serving as the editor for, and contributing articles to, *al-Rabita*. Though he, unlike Antun, eschewed joining an organized political movement in his later years, he remained a dedicated nationalist activist, intellectual, and scholar who championed Syria's independence and denounced French colonialism. Antun, in a tribute to his father published in *al-Rabita*, praised his father's steadfastness and commitment to the Syrian diaspora community and his service and dedication to the national cause. Khalil's patriotism and devotion were a model to be followed and Antun, to honor his father, dedicated himself to walking in Khalil's path. "Nidā' ilā al-Jāliyya al-Sūriyya fī al-Brāzīl," in Sa'adeh, *al-A'māl al-Kāmila, Vol. 1*, pp. 488–493.

2 Establishing a Nationalist Movement

Saʿadeh returned to Lebanon in the summer of 1930, eager to engage in political activity but unsure of where to begin. There he reacquainted himself with the land and people he had been absent from for a decade, but only briefly. In the fall, he moved to Damascus, where he gained employment as an English-language instructor at the Scientific College (*al-Jāmiʿa al-ʿIlmiyya*) and worked as a journalist, contributing several articles to the Damascene dailies *Alif Baʾ*, *al-Qabas*, and *al-Yawm*. While in Damascus, Saʿadeh attempted to cultivate relationships with National Bloc members, including one of his father's old acquaintances, Jamil Mardam. However, his efforts came to naught as he struggled to find common ground with a party that, in his assessment, perpetuated the rule of Syria's old social urban elite.[1] After several months in Damascus, in May 1931, Antun made his first public foray into national affairs since his return in the form of an open letter to former British Prime Minister Lloyd George, who had recently been honored at a Zionist association banquet in London. Published in *Alif Baʾ*, the letter excoriated George's support for Zionism and British policies in Mandate Palestine, argued for Syria's territorial unity, and defined Syria's national rights in a secular manner.[2] As he had previously, Saʿadeh asserted that Palestine was southern Syria, inseparable from the rest of the Syrian homeland and, to undermine Jewish and Islamic claims to Syria, argued that a secular Syrian nation predating Judaism and Islam existed.

In Damascus, Saʿadeh's frustration with the political situation in both Syria and Lebanon intensified.[3] He believed that the traditional leaders, clergy, urban notables, and colonial authorities controlled the social and political systems. Political parties formed around ideas and principles did not exist and, instead, were organized around personal ties of loyalty or religion, not doctrine. Returning to Beirut, Saʿadeh secured a position teaching German at AUB thanks to the assistance of Bayard Dodge, the university's president. The job allowed him to engage in dialogue with students and faculty colleagues whom he deemed the most capable of forcefully challenging and resisting the existing political and social structures of authority in Lebanon and Syria, engaging them in dialogue on various intellectual topics, particularly those related to national issues. AUB and its surrounding environs thus served as a base from which he began to recruit

1 Jan Dayah, *Muḥākamat Anṭūn Saʿādah: Wathāʾiq al-Taḥqīq al-Rasmī* (Beirut: Fajr al-Nahḍa, 2002), p. 174.

2 "Radd ʿalā Lloyd George," in Saʿadeh, *al-Aʿmāl al-Kāmila, Vol. 1*, pp. 241–244.

3 Asfahani, *Mafhūm al-Ḥizb*, p. 72.

https://doi.org/10.1515/9783110729092-004

individuals from among the populace he viewed as the ideal core and foundation for his movement: the emerging young, educated middle class. The young men and women who comprised this emerging, politically conscious middle class varied in their socio-economic and confessional background, but all were drawn to Saʿadeh's ideas and determination to challenge the establishment. They would form the national movement's nucleus, a new enlightened social class (*ṭabaqa mutanawwira*), an elite vanguard, tasked with guiding the Syrian nation to its revival and establishing Greater Syria.

2.1 Beginnings: Clandestine Organization and Recruitment

After years of discussion and preparation, the twenty-eight-year-old Saʿadeh established the SSNP in the fall of 1932 with five other individuals, including Jamil Sawaya, Fuʾad Haddad, and George ʿAbd al-Masih, intending to be a movement and political organization that would struggle to "break the grip of the *zuʿama aqṭāb* and undo the hold of the confessional system over Lebanon's political destiny."[4] Then known as the National Party (*al-Ḥizb al-Qawmī*), it was commonly referred to by its members by its Arabic initials "*ḥaq*."[5] Saʿadeh was determined, as he had been in South America, to safeguard his movement by maintaining its clandestineness and building it around a core membership of honorable youths (*ʿunṣur al-shabāb al-nazīh*) dedicated to its radical program of political and social transformation by keeping them detached from the pernicious influence of the traditional "politics of notables."[6] The ideological education of its members was paramount. Thus, the party's activities primarily consisted of small gatherings and individual meetings to discuss doctrine and matters related to the national cause, held in places around Beirut and Choueir such as at the Haddad family restaurant (owned by Fuʾad's father Gerges) and AUB (from which it

4 Firro, *Inventing Lebanon*, p. 127.
5 Jibran Jurayj, *Min al-Juʿbat: Marwiyyāt, Mustanadāt wa Adabiyyāt ʿan al-Ḥizb al-Sūrī al-Qawmī al-Ijtimāʿī, Vol. 1* (Beirut: 1985), p. 91.
6 "Risāla ila Ḥamīd Faranjiyya," in Saʿadeh, *al-Aʿmāl al-Kāmila, Vol. 2*, p. 10. On the "politics of notables," see, for example, Keith D. Watenpaugh, "Middle-Class Modernity and the Persistence of the Politics of Notables in Inter-War Syria," *International Journal for Middle East Studies* 35 (2003): pp. 257–286; James L. Gelvin, "The 'Politics of Notables' Forty Years After," Middle East Studies Association Bulletin 40, no. 1 (June 2006): pp. 19–29; Philip S. Khoury, *Urban Notables and Arab Nationalism: The Politics of Damascus 1860–1920* (Cambridge: Cambridge University Press, 1983); and Albert Hourani, "Ottoman Reform and the Politics of Notables," in *Beginnings of Modernization in the Middle East: The Nineteenth Century*, ed. William R. Polk and Richard L. Chambers (Chicago: University of Chicago Press, 1968), pp. 41–68.

drew almost all of its early recruits).[7] The party's eight basic and five reform principles, as well as a statement of the party's aim, were written on a notebook page and passed around from member to member.[8] The party's principles declared the existence of the Syrian nation and described its character, homeland, interests, and mission, and outlined its comprehensive social objectives, including separating religion and state, establishing a national army, eliminating feudalism eliminating the barriers between sects and communities. Besides declaring the primacy of the Syrian nation and its interests, the party's reform principles directly challenged the existing social and political orders in Lebanon and Syria, seeking to replace them with a new order or system (*niẓām*) (see Tab. 1).

---

7 Jurayj, *Min al-Juʿbat, Vol. 1,* pp. 47–48.
8 Asfahani, *Mafhūm al-Ḥizb,* p. 76, and Jurayj, *Min al-Juʿbat, Vol. 1,* p. 121.

Tab. 1. Basic and Reform principles of the SSNP as set out in 1932. The English text of the principles is taken from Mujais (2009), *Saadeh, Vol. 2*, pp. 72–73.

Basic Principles	Reform Principles
1. Syria is for the Syrians and the Syrians are a complete nation.	1. Separation of religion and state.
2. The Syrian cause is an integral national cause distinct from any other cause	2. Debarring the clergy from interference in political and judicial matters.
3. The Syrian cause is the cause of the Syrian nation and the Syrian homeland	3. Removal of the barriers between the various sects and confessions.
4. The Syrian nation is the product of the ethnic unity of the Syrian people developed throughout history.	4. The abolition of feudalism, the organization of the national economy based on the production and the protection of the rights of labor and the interests of the nation and state.
5. The Syrian homeland is that geographic environment in which the Syrian nation evolved. It has distinct natural boundaries and extends from the Taurus range in the north to the Suez Canal in the south and includes the Sinai Peninsula and the gulf of Aqaba, and from the Syrian sea in the west to the shores of the Tigris in the east.	5. Formation of strong armed forces that will be effective in determining the destiny of the country and the nation.
6. The Syrian nation is one society.	
7. The Syrian nationalist movement derives its inspiration from the talents of the Syrian nation and its cultural-political national history.	
8. Syria's interest supersedes every other interest.	

Though the SSNP's early activities were limited to building the party's organizational structure and educating its few members in the doctrine of the renaissance (*al-ʿaqīda al-nahḍawiyya*), Saʿadeh did take advantage of opportunities to articulate several of the party's fundamental tenets in public forums. In December 1932, he delivered a lecture at AUB to *al-ʿUrwa al-Wuthqā* (The Unbreakable Bond Society) on the role of education in promoting national unity and countering challenges to this unity, specifically ethnic and religious doctrines that hinder progress. The following month, he delivered another lecture in Beirut to the *Nādī al-Filasṭīnī* (Palestine Club) in which he called on Syrians to organize to defeat the Zionist threat and, in an indirect manner, articulated the party's principles.[9] In addition to these talks, Saʿadeh succeeded in generating his opportunity to publicize the party's social and political thought, reissuing *al-Majalla* as a monthly periodical in March 1933. Aiming to educate its readers, Saʿadeh also hoped to publish the newspaper in both Lebanon and Brazil to strengthen the ties between homeland and the diaspora. However, due to financial difficulties, only four issues were printed before the paper ceased publication in June 1933, putting a quick end to Saʿadeh's endeavor to use the press to disseminate the party's nationalist doctrine.

The new movement grew slowly as informal recruitment efforts focused on individuals in the immediate social circles of those who had already joined, and, by the end of its first year of activity, the party had only fifteen adherents.[10] Secrecy paramount, recruitment built upon strong personal relationships and private discussions; this served to safeguard against infiltration but hindered the spread of the party's nationalist doctrine. Moreover, Saʿadeh's identity remained guarded from potential recruits who were only exposed to the party's ideology, ascribed to an unnamed university instructor. However, this guardedness and secrecy did not concern Saʿadeh much as he believed his movement's strength was found not in numbers but its principles.[11] Throughout that year, Saʿadeh recruited four new members, including Raja Hawali, one of his German-language students, Anis Sawaya, a friend and classmate from Choueir, Muhamad Ghandur, a doctor from Beirut with whom he had lived in Damascus, and Faris Salameh from Roumieh-Metn, whose home served as a meeting place for intellectuals and clubs. Hawali convinced three of his friends to join the movement: Bahij al-Khuri al-Maqdisi, his cousin and an engineer, Anis Qasatali, a tradesman, and Sami Qurban. Qurban, in turn, recruited two of his close friends and classmates, Rafiq Marush and Amir al-Lubnan. Fu'ad Haddad, one of the party's first members, recruited two of his friends with whom he had formed a bond through athletic clubs, Victor Asad and Iliya Rubiz from Ras Beirut, as well as Musa Suleiman, a preparatory school teacher.[12] Suleiman, in turn, recruited his friend and former classmate, ʿAbdallah Qubrusi, a Beirut lawyer originally from Koura.[13] Members studied the party's doctrine while gathered around tables in cafes and restaurants, drawn to its call for revolution against the forces of reac-

9 Mujais, *Saadeh, Vol. 2*, pp. 69–72.

10 Jurayj, *Min al-Juʿbat, Vol. 1*, p. 63, and "Ilā Ghassan Tueni," in Saʿadeh, *al-Aʿmāl al-Kāmila, Vol. 11*, p. 98.

11 *Al-Zawbaʿa*, 15 June 1943.

12 Jurayj, *Min al-Juʿbat, Vol. 1*, pp. 71–73, 78–79, 84–85.

13 Jurayj, *Min al-Juʿbat, Vol. 1*, pp. 81, 152.

tion and colonialism in their society and the intellectual aura of their comprehensive discussions on culture, literature, and history.

Despite its small number of adherents, the party's message slowly spread through the Beirut neighborhoods of Ashrafiyyeh, Ras Beirut, and Ayn Marissa. Its message also reached to the villages of Beit Meri, Roumieh, and Broumana (where ʿAbd al-Masih, Faris Habib, and Rashid Abu Fadl oversaw party activities, respectively) in the predominately Christian Metn District, and to the predominately Sunni Tripoli District and predominately Greek Orthodox Koura District (where Iliya Rubiz oversaw party expansion).[14] By the summer of 1934, when classes had ended for the year, the party had added another fifteen members to its ranks, most of whom were undergraduates at AUB, including its 30th member Neʿmeh Thabit, an economics and political science student who joined in July.[15] Among the others who joined the party were Jibran Jurayj from Koura, Rafiq al-Halibi from Bshamoun, and Halibi's family friend Shafiq al-Shartuni.[16] On holiday, students hailing from other parts of the country returned home, carrying the party's message with them and busying themselves with learning the movement's doctrine, solidifying their convictions that Natural Syria was a complete nation that needed to be freed and united, and educating themselves in its rich cultural, social and political heritage. Saʿadeh returned to Choueir, where he passed his time resting and reading in his *ʿirzāl* (tree hut), receiving party members for discussions, and reflecting on his father's recent death.[17]

Around this time, the growing yet small party began to develop the movement's emblems, symbols, and rituals that would express and represent its core ideas. At Saʿadeh's request, Bahij al-Maqdisi designed two tempest-shaped symbols (*zawbaʿa*), one with three points and a second with four points.[18] Maqdisi's four-pointed design raised the concern of several members who worried it too closely resembled the Nazi swastika, an association they scorned and desired to avoid, and therefore voiced their preference for the more distinct looking three-pointed symbol. Saʿadeh did not share their concern. Instead, he main-

14 Jurayj, *Min al-Juʿbat, Vol. 1,* pp. 97–99.

15 Yamak, *SSNP,* p. 55, and Jurayj, *Min al-Juʿbat, Vol. 1,* pp. 104, 113–114.

16 Jurayj, *Min al-Juʿbat, Vol. 1,* pp. 107–108.

17 Mujais, *Saadeh, Vol. 2,* pp. 83–85; and Jurayj, *Min al-Juʿbat, Vol. 1,* pp. 115–116, 132; and "Nidāʾ ilā al-Jāliyya al-Sūriyya fī al-Barāzīl," in Saʿadeh, *al-Aʿmāl al-Kāmila, Vol. 1,* pp. 488–493.

18 The party maintains the four-pointed design was inspired by combining the cross, the symbol of Christianity, and the crescent, the symbol of Islam, into one as an expression of the party's secularism and anti-sectarianism. Others point to its similarities with the Nazi swastika and assert this to be the primary source of inspiration for the SSNP's symbol and evidence of the party's fascist leanings. The comparison continues to be made today.

tained, the four-pointed *zawbaʿa* was not a "broken cross" like the swastika, as it differed from the latter's rigidity with its flowing design that suggested movement and advancement, hinted at national renaissance and revolution, symbolized national unity, and embodied the party's four principles: duty, freedom, discipline, and power.[19] However, in the end, and quite rapidly, those who had voiced their concerns were proven correct as the party's critics and opponents drew a direct comparison between the two symbols to discredit the party.

By late 1934, the party had more than doubled in size, numbering some sixty-three members. In the following months, "the movement extended its domain beyond the university and schools to the districts of Beirut, the villages of Mount Lebanon, and Damascus."[20] However, AUB remained the most important source of recruits for the party, providing adherents with a conducive environment to interact and converse with friends, classmates, and colleagues consistently and securely. The party was also successful in attracting new members from among the students, graduates, and staff of the Suq al-Gharb school in the predominately Greek Catholic and Greek Orthodox Aley District, several of whom returned to their home villages where they spread the party's doctrine, including Rafiq al-Ayubi who went to Koura and Elias Habush who returned to Machghara in Bekaa el-Gharbi.[21] Recruitment continued to be driven by personal connections and conversations between friends on Lebanon's political situation, leading to propositions to join the party in its bid for national revival. Within the SSNP, education in the party's creed and Syrian culture and history aimed to further the creation of new Syrians who were fully aware of their nation's rich heritage and history.

As more party branches were established, at the urging of several members, a formal party constitution was written that included the party's main principles, a member's pledge of allegiance, and, notably, called for creating a party militia.[22] Discussions over the constitution, particularly the promise of loyalty, did lead to some debate. ʿAbd al-Masih and Sawaya voiced their concerns over the centralization of power in Saʿadeh's hands, even attempting to walk out of the discussion before being stopped by Haddad.[23] In the end, they dropped their objections and agreed to a revised loyalty pledge and constitutional text that, in theory, curtailed the powers of the leader by establishing separate legislative

19 Jurayj, *Min al-Juʿbat, Vol. 1*, pp. 116–118; Mujais, *Saadeh, Vol. 2*, p. 105; and Qubrusi, *Yatadhakkar, Vol. 1*, p. 30.

20 "Ilā Ghassan Tueni," in Saʿadeh, *al-Aʿmāl al-Kāmila, Vol. 11*, p. 98.

21 Jurayj, *Min al-Juʿbat, Vol. 1*, p. 126.

22 Yamak, *SSNP*, p. 55.

23 Jurayj, *Min al-Juʿbat, Vol. 1*, p. 144.

and executive authorities. The party's membership continued to expand as new branches and cells were established throughout Lebanon and Syria, and its organizational structure also developed and matured.[24] The party leadership dedicated much of its energies to managing its growth, focusing on internal party affairs, finances, and activities.

In December 1934, the party's *Majlis al-ʿUmud* (Council of Deputies) held its first administrative meeting at Thabit's home; though Thabit was the Council's head, Saʿadeh oversaw the meeting's agenda and affairs.[25] Qubrusi, serving as the deputy for information, was tasked with establishing an infrastructure to disseminate the party's propaganda and publications within the party and to the broader public.[26] Qubrusi formed a committee comprised of party members who had excelled and were well-versed in the worlds of journalism, literature, and politics, including Maʿmun Ayas, Salah Labaki, and Fu'ad Suleiman.[27] However, the committee failed to function correctly, its meetings dissolving into intense quarreling among its members that required Saʿadeh to intervene and reestablish order by disbanding it and reassigning its members to other roles.[28] The party also needed to rebuild its presence at AUB after many of its members graduated. Saʿadeh and several members who had yet to graduate led the new recruitment drive. Their efforts bore fruit, enlisting individuals such as George Hakim, George Haddad, and Fu'ad Abu ʿAjram, who would serve essential roles in the party.[29]

---

24 Yamak, *SSNP*, p. 56.

25 Mujais, *Saadeh, Vol. 2*, p. 99; Qubrusi, *Yatadhakkar, Vol. 1*, p. 33; and Jurayj, *Min al-Juʿbat, Vol. 1*, pp. 177–180.

26 Qubrusi, *Yatadhakkar, Vol. 1*, p. 41.

27 Ayas, a Sunni, had graduated from AUB in 1932, after which he spent a year in Cairo before returning to Beirut in early 1934 where he joined the party thanks to his friend Sami Qurban. Early, in his role as the party's Director of Information, Ayas was responsible for articulating the SSNP's earliest slogans: "*taḥyā Sūriyya wa yaḥyā Saʿadeh*" and "*Abnāʾ al–Ḥayāt*" (Children of Life). The latter slogan, borrowed from Gibran Khalil Gibran, was used to refer to SSNP members. Labaki, born in 1906 in São Paulo to a prominent Maronite family and raised in Mount Lebanon's Metn district, was a practicing lawyer and well–respected poet who learned of the party through both his relative Emil Dabbas and his close friend, the artist Yusuf al-Huwayek; Qubrusi had recruited the latter. Suleiman, a Greek Orthodox Christian from Koura, was also a poet and writer who joined the party at around the same time. See Jurayj, *Min al-Juʿbat, Vol. 1*, pp. 106–107, 181–184, 199–200; Jurayj, *Min al-Juʿbat: Marwiyyāt, Mustanadāt wa Adabiyyāt ʿan al-Ḥizb al-Sūrī al-Qawmī al-Ijtimāʿī, Vol. 3* (Beirut: 1988), pp. 24–25; and, George Faris, *Fuʾād Sulaymān bayn al-Waṭaniyya wa-l-Qawmiyya* (Beirut: Khāṣ Lubnān, 2011).

28 "al-Nazʿa al-Fardiyya fī Shaʿbnā," in Saʿadeh, *al-Aʿmāl al-Kāmila, Vol. 6*, p. 157.

29 Jurayj, *Min al-Juʿbat, Vol. 1*, pp. 185–190.

In the spring of 1935, the party's following continued to increase as it solidified its existing branches. It established new ones throughout Lebanon and Syria, including in Metn's Jdeidah and Jal al-Dib, along the coast south of Beirut in Burj al-Barajneh, Harat Hereik, Choueifat, Bshamoun, in south Lebanon's Saida and Jezzine, in the Shouf's Deir al-Qamr, and Syria's Tartus governorate in Safita.[30] Its existence still a closely guarded secret, recruitment remained dependent on the personal networks of its members, whose casual conversations on national politics with trusted friends tested the interest and suitability of their interlocutors, leading to a proposition to join the SSNP. Saʿadeh also maintained the party's secrecy by establishing covers to expand membership and activities by creating a front company. After years of using his own home or that of the Haddad family for meetings, Saʿadeh rented an apartment to serve as the office for a trading company (*sharika tijāriyya)* that had been established by Fu'ad Mufarrej, an academic at AUB who had previously served as an advisor to King Faysal in Damascus and joined the party earlier that year.[31] The office provided space for meetings while also serving as cover for collecting membership dues.

On 1 June 1935, the SSNP held its first sizeable general meeting at the Thabit family manor in Beirut's Bir Hassan district, whose enclosed grounds ensured privacy and could accommodate the several hundred attendees from the SSNP's central and regional leadership.[32] Committed to safeguarding the meeting's secrecy, guests arrived discreetly at Thabit's home to avoid raising neighbors or the authorities' suspicion. After Qubrusi reviewed the party's activities and several poems had been read, including one by Salah Labaki, Saʿadeh ascended the dais to speak, dressed in the party's official uniform of "charcoal pants and a white shirt with the party emblem on the right side of the chest and a wide waist sash."[33] Saʿadeh offered the crowd an ardent, resolute, and comprehensive defense of the party's core principles and strategies, the goals of which were to bring about authentic social and political change in Greater Syria. Only action and organization could achieve such a radical transformation.

Casting a vision of a glorious future for the Syrian nation, Saʿadeh declared that "we have repudiated by our actions [the SSNP's establishment] the judgment of history and begun our true history, the history of freedom, duty, organization, and power, the history of the Syrian Nationalist Party, the true history of

---

30 Jurayj, *Min al-Juʿbat, Vol. 1*, pp. 217–219, 227–235, 252.

31 Jurayj, *Min al-Juʿbat, Vol. 1*, pp. 202, 275, 279–280, and *Oriente Moderno*, 15.12, December 1935, p. 633.

32 Mujais, *Saadeh, Vol. 2*, p. 99; *al-Zawbaʿa*, 1 June 1942; and Jurayj, *Min al-Juʿbat, Vol. 1*, pp. 289–296.

33 Mujais, *Saadeh, Vol. 2*, p. 99.

the Syrian nation."[34] The party, thus, "is not a mere society or group... [but] an idea and a movement that embraces the life of a nation in its entirety. It is the revival of a nation that some thought to have collapsed forever [...], the rise of a great nation."[35] Indeed, the aim of the party's struggle was a lofty one (*gharaḍ asmā*): to make the Syrian nation the sole actor exercising sovereignty over the entirety of its people and territory. By joining the SSNP, party members liberated themselves from "foreign hegemony and outside elements" (*al-taḥarrur min al-siyāda al-ajnabiyya wa-l-ʿawāmil al-khārijiyya*). They rejected the existing social and political orders that had hindered the nation's advancement and independence and dedicated themselves to the lofty aim of reviving the nation through concrete action and creating facts on the ground, as "history does not record hopes and intentions."[36]

In contrast, the party advanced the nation's social unity and strengthened it, increasing its ability to attain its independence. Saʿadeh was confident that the forces of revival would be victorious over the forces of reaction because of the SSNP's organization, power, and principles. Through their actions as an organized force, Saʿadeh declared, the SSNP "will change the history of the Near East" and end the era of foreign conquests and interference. Concluding his remarks, Saʿadeh painted an evocative picture of a rising nation, stating:

> "A day will soon come when the world will witness a new sight and a momentous event: men clothed with black sashes on gray cloths, their sharpened bayonets shimmering above their heads, walking behind the banners of the red tempest carried by the giants of the army. The forest of bayonets will advance in ordered ranks, and the will of the Syrian nation will not be repelled."[37]

In its entirety, the speech was a harsh indictment of the existing social and political order and a revolutionary call to bring about its end. Notably, given the continued emphasis on the two themes of power and organization throughout the speech, Saʿadeh felt compelled to deny the party's system was an imitation or bore any similarities to the fascist and national socialist systems, but was an original Syrian system built upon the needs of the Syrian people and designed to benefit it.[38] Moreover, Saʿadeh warned party members of "falling victim" to recently intensified Italian and German propaganda, which posed a threat to inde-

34 "al-Khiṭāb al-Manhājī al-Awwal [1/6/1935]," in Saʿadeh, *al-Aʿmāl al-Kāmila*, *Vol. 2*, p. 3.
35 "al-Khiṭāb al-Manhājī al-Awwal [1/6/1935]," in Saʿadeh, *al-Aʿmāl al-Kāmila*, *Vol. 2*, p. 4.
36 "al-Khiṭāb al-Manhājī al-Awwal [1/6/1935]," in Saʿadeh, *al-Aʿmāl al-Kāmila*, *Vol. 2*, pp. 4–5.
37 "al-Khiṭāb al-Manhājī al-Awwal [1/6/1935]," in Saʿadeh, *al-Aʿmāl al-Kāmila*, *Vol. 2*, pp. 7–8.
38 "al-Khiṭāb al-Manhājī al-Awwal [1/6/1935]," in Saʿadeh, *al-Aʿmāl al-Kāmila*, *Vol. 2*, p. 6.

pendent and free Syrian thought and promoted social chaos.[39] The importance of Saʿadeh's speech and the general meeting of 1 June 1935 cannot be understated, as it came to be considered a seminal event in the party's history that Saʿadeh would consistently reference, urging members to consult the speech's text should questions regarding the party's doctrine arise. Thus, the address came to serve the role of an ideological signpost against which members could judge future decisions and policies' legitimacy.[40] In the months that followed the meeting, the party's ranks significantly expanded as knowledge of its existence spread.

As it was still summer break, the party recruited but a few students at AUB and the National University in Aley.[41] Throughout Beirut, however, the story differed, as the party added new members, including students, recent graduates, and professionals residing in areas like Ras Beirut and Choueifat.[42] These new members, many of whom hailed from other parts of Lebanon and Syria, had come to the city to study or work, at which point they were exposed to the party's doctrine. In turn, these new members enabled the party to spread its ideology even further through their relationship networks and ongoing ties to their places of origin. The party also expanded its presence throughout villages in Mount Lebanon, specifically in Metn, Aley, and Shouf districts, in the Bekaa Governorate's Bekaa el-Gharbi district, in North Lebanon's Koura and Tripoli districts, and in South Lebanon's Jezzine district. Outside of Lebanon, the party expanded its following in Syria, predominately in Damascus and Tartus, and in Palestine, in Haifa, Jaffa, and Jerusalem.[43] Of note, Rafiq al-Halibi and Asaf Abu Marad immigrated to West Africa and Mexico, respectively, where they each established party branches and undertook activities on behalf of the party.[44] By October, the party's following had enlarged to an estimated 2,000 – 3,000 members, at least half of whom were centered in Beirut.

2.2 Discovery: The Beginning of Open Struggle

By the middle of October 1935, intelligence reports on the SSNP began to appear as its increased following left it more vulnerable to infiltration by French and

---

39 "al-Khiṭāb al-Manhājī al-Awwal [1/6/1935]," in Saʿadeh, *al-Aʿmāl al-Kāmila, Vol. 2*, pp. 7 – 8.
40 *al-Zawbaʿa*, 1 June 1942.
41 Jurayj, *Min al-Juʿbat, Vol. 1*, pp. 299 – 300.
42 Jurayj, *Min al-Juʿbat, Vol. 1*, pp. 301 – 308.
43 Jurayj, *Min al-Juʿbat, Vol. 1*, pp. 333 – 384.
44 Jurayj, *Min al-Juʿbat, Vol. 1*, pp. 323 – 324.

Lebanese intelligence services. At that time, the Mayor of Beirut, Salim Niqala, began receiving reports from an informant he had ordered to join the party and gather intelligence. Having succeeded in infiltrating the party, the informant filed several reports on the party's activities gleaned from his observations and conversations with Saʿadeh and other party members over the following weeks. These reports, and others prepared for the Delegate of the High Commissioner for the Republic of Lebanon, Pierre Lafond, were circulated among local government and security officials, including High Commissioner Damien de Martel and the head of the Sûreté Générale's *(al-Amn al-ʿĀmm*, General Security) Department of Investigations, Farid Chehab.

One report provided a brief but detailed overview of important party officials, including lawyers, educators, merchants, and the taxi drivers union's head. The report also included translations of the party's principles, a questionnaire for prospective members, the party oath of allegiance, and observations on the party's efforts to recruit members from among the youth, police, gendarmerie, and government officials.[45] Other reports, including one based on a conversation between an informant and Saʿadeh, noted the party comprised 2,000 – 3,000 adherents. Beyond Beirut and its environs, party branches had been established in Mount Lebanon, Tripoli, Zahlé, Machghara, Merdjayoun, and Saida.[46] Another report described information shared by Shafiq al-Shartuni, the party member responsible for distributing the Trading Company's shares, with Niqala's informant during a conversation between the two at Thabit's home.[47] Shartuni spoke open-

45 CADN 2395, Beyrouth, Le délégué du Haut–Commissaire à Comte de Martel, "Agitation Nationaliste," 28 October 1935.

46 See CADN 2395, Beyrouth, Le délégué du Haut-Commissaire à Comte de Martel, "Agitation Nationaliste," 4 November 1935; CADN 2395, Saida, "Feuille de Renseignements: L'Association 'Osbat Wotan Kaoumi,'" 9 November 1935; CADN 2395, "Renseignements au sujet agitation nationaliste," 15 November 1935; Ahmad Asfahani and Yumna ʿAsaili, eds., *Fī Khidmat al-Waṭan: Mukhtārāt min al-Wathāʾiq al-Khaṣṣa li-l-Amīr Farīd Shihāb* (Beirut: Kutub, 2005), pp. 116 – 121; and, Ahmad Asfahani, ed., *Anṭūn Saʿādah wa-l-Ḥizb al-Sūrī al-Qawmī al-Ijtimāʿī fī Awrāq al-Amīr Farīd Shihāb al-Mudīr al-ʿĀmm li-l-Amn al-ʿĀmm al-Lubnānī* (Beirut: Kutub, 2006), pp. 15 – 20. Interestingly, the SSNP's branch in Saida, according to the French, had been formed by Adel Ossieran, a Shiite Muslim who ultimately became a well-known and popular Lebanese politician, together with Shafiq Lutfi and Nur el-Juhari, both Sunni lawyers. The branch had several other Sunni members whose professions ranged from secondary school teachers to bakers and a secretary at the Chamber of Commerce. CADN 2395, Saida, "Feuille de Renseignements: L'Association 'Osbat Wotan Kaoumi,'" 9 November 1935.

47 CADN 2395, "Renseignements au sujet agitation nationaliste," 15 November 1935, and Asfahani, *Anṭūn Saʿādah*, pp. 19 – 20. There is a discrepancy between the original French translation of the report and the reproduction of the original Arabic-language report in Asfahani's book regarding the number of shares in the Trading Company. According to Chehab's report, Shartuni

ly with the informant about the Trading Company, which the SSNP used as a front for its activities, and specified that the party had 3,000 members in Beirut and 3,000 members elsewhere, including a branch in Damascus.[48]

Perhaps of greatest concern to Lebanese and French authorities were Saʿadeh's discussions with the informant regarding establishing weapons and ammunition caches for the party's militia and his revelation that the party counted several military and police officers among its ranks, including Lebanese Army officers and the Assistant Commissioner of Beirut's police force, Asad al-Ayubi.[49] According to the report, Saʿadeh sought the informant's advice on the types of weapons and ammunition the party should acquire, their availability, and the best method of smuggling them into Lebanon. He also asked the informant to provide him with details regarding French weapons depots and the informant's opinion about whether the types of weapons used by Lebanese soldiers, once seized, would be sufficient to arm the party militia.[50] Also, Saʿadeh's admission that an unspecified number of military and police officers were party members confirmed French suspicions that the SSNP was recruiting members from among these security services, which the French considered a threatening and destabilizing phenomenon.

The potential threat the secret party posed to public security and order was no doubt assessed to be more acute, given the prevailing political environment in Lebanon and Syria. Indeed, "the Lebanese political system was in turmoil... focused on the elections, with political figures and the public disregarding the dramatic international and regional events taking place – Italy's invasion of Ethiopia and national uprisings in Egypt and Syria."[51] Given the situation and based on the intelligence it had gathered, French authorities assessed it was necessary to act against the party. Early in the morning of 16 November 1935, security forces conducted a sweeping arrest and detention operation, taking Saʿadeh and other party officials into custody at their homes and transferring them to the Sûreté Générale's headquarters for interrogation; further searches of party mem-

---

states the company has only 5,000 shares valued at five Syrian pounds each, while the French report states that Shartuni said the company has 10,000 shares valued at five Syrian pounds each. The informant in both reports is the only one who uses the number 10,000, though it is unclear where he got this number from.

48 CADN 2395, "Renseignements au sujet agitation nationaliste," 15 November 1935.

49 Ayubi joined the party in the spring of 1935. CADN 2395, Beyrouth, Le délégué du Haut-Commissaire à Comte de Martel, "Agitation Nationaliste," 4 November 1935; Asfahani, *Anṭūn Saʿādah*, pp. 15–16; and Qubrusi, *Yatadhakkar, Vol. 1*, p. 59.

50 Asfahani, *Anṭūn Saʿādah*, pp. 15–16.

51 Zamir, *Lebanon's Quest*, p. 175.

bers' homes that morning resulted in the seizure of important party documents and weapons.[52] In dispatches to the Quai d'Orsay, the High Commissioner's office updated the French government on Saʿadeh's clandestine 3,000-member organization organized similarly, in its assessment, as the German Nazi party (lit. "formations hitlériennes") and threatened the security of the state.[53] Following the party's discovery, the informant continued to provide Niqala with internal party documents and, on his orders, began meeting with French authorities to better coordinate efforts against the party.[54]

The SSNP's aims were now public, provoking a broad array of reactions. Most were antagonistic, plagued with conjecture and unsubstantiated accusations. The public now understood that the party had operated in secret and sought to unify Greater Syria, remove religious leaders' influence from politics, and carry out broad social and political reforms.[55] In general, the Lebanese press provided comprehensive coverage of the affair, publishing articles on the arrested individuals and the party's aims, while at the same time trying to downplay its importance.[56] *Ittihad al-Lubnani* considered the party's objective of securing a position in the Lebanese administration to be "absurd" and "ridiculous." At the same time, the Greek Catholic newspaper *al-Masaʾ* characterized the SSNP as "an association of children that wants to direct the destiny of the country."[57] Other newspapers suggested a foreign power had financially supported the SSNP and aided its establishment and activities; *al-Masaʾ* and *al-Bilad* unequivocally accused the German Consul in Beirut of supporting the party.[58] The German Consul denied all accusations claiming Germany had a relationship or collaborated with the SSNP, exchanging several letters with the High Commissioner demanding the French intervene to stop the publication of facetious alle-

52 CADN 2395, Sûreté Générale, "Information No. 3188," N.D.; *The Palestine Post*, 21 November 1935; and CADN 471, Beyrouth, "Bulletin d'Information,"29 November 1935.

53 See MAE, Cabinet Politique 1150, Beyrouth, HC to MAE, "découverte d'une organization politique clandestine," 22 November 1935, and MAE, Télégramme No. 637, Beyrouth, 16 November 1935, reproduced in Ibrahim, *Anṭūn Saʿādah wa-l-Nidhām al-Lubnanī*, pp. 877–879.

54 Asfahani, *Anṭūn Saʿādah*, pp. 21–22.

55 *The Palestine Post*, 21 November 1935

56 CADN 471, Cabinet Politique 1183, Beyrouth, 29 November 1935, and CADN 471, Beyrouth, "Revue de la Presse Libanaise et Syrienne," 29 November 1935.

57 CADN 471, Cabinet Politique 1183, Beyrouth, 29 November 1935, and CADN 471, Beyrouth, "Revue de la Presse Libanaise et Syrienne," 29 November 1935.

58 CADN 471, Cabinet Politique 1183, Beyrouth, 29 November 1935, and CADN 471, Beyrouth, "Revue de la Presse Libanaise et Syrienne," 29 November 1935.

gations and repudiate them.[59] After sanctimoniously opining on the openly liberal environment in which the Lebanese and Syrian press operated and noting their freedom to form and express their opinions without government interference, the High Commissioner's office agreed to reprimand the relevant publishers.[60]

Despite the widespread detention of its members, its opponents' determined efforts to delegitimize it, and growing frustration within the party, the SSNP did push back. In a statement published in *Filastin* and other newspapers, an SSNP member clarified the party's aims, denouncing the French mandate and criticizing those who accused the party of working for anything other than the betterment of Greater Syria. Further, noting that the SSNP, like other movements, was established and organized in secret to improve its chances of success, the unnamed *qawmī* (nationalist) denied the party had "any material relations with or was subservient to the Nazis or the Fascists or the Communists" and stated that the party acted independently to achieve its aims.[61]

As the investigation continued, French and Lebanese authorities made further arrests and implemented legal measures to negate any challenge the party may pose. Having noted the SSNP's significant presence on AUB's campus, where it had successfully recruited many members from among students and staff, the French focused on disrupting its networks there.[62] In early December, three SSNP members on AUB's faculty were arrested by French authorities and interrogated regarding the SSNP's alleged foreign ties. The three denied all accusations and asserted the party sought to secure national independence through peaceful means. Indeed, after weeks of investigation, French authorities failed to find any incriminating evidence that suggested or proved the party had any formal ties to a foreign power.[63] However, the lack of evidence did little to end speculation among a few segments of the Lebanese press that the hand of a foreign power was behind the party's organization.[64]

---

59 For copies of the documents see Jan Dayah, *Saʿādah wa-l-Nāziyya* (Beirut: Fajr al-Nahḍa, 1994), pp. 50–59.

60 Dayah, *Saʿādah wa-l-Nāziyya*, pp. 56–57.

61 *Filastin*, 27 November 1935.

62 MAE, Cabinet Politique 1186 Beyrouth, HC to MAE, "découverte d'une organization politique clandestine/Note A/S Association Nationale Syrien," 29 November 1935, reproduced in Ibrahim, *Anṭūn Saʿādah wa-l-Nidhām al-Lubnanī*, pp. 880–884.

63 *The Palestine Post*, 10 December 1935.

64 Moreover, newspapers like *Ittihad al-Lubnani*, *Sawt al-Ahrar*, and *Rakib* generally dismissed the aims of the party – "a chimera that is certainly unrealizable" – and the ability of its members to attain them – "youths incapable of fomenting revolution." CADN 471, Cabinet Politique 1212, 26 December 1935.

In early January 1936, charges were officially filed against several SSNP officials, though Saʿadeh, Thabit, and Zaki Naqqash were the only ones who remained in custody.[65] Their trial was postponed until the conclusion of the upcoming presidential elections, the first since 1931, which had consumed the Lebanese public and Mandate authorities' attention. The French were particularly keen on securing the victory of a candidate who would safeguard France's interests in the country and thus worked to bolster the Maronite community while simultaneously impede the efforts of Syrian nationalists and the Muslim community.[66] Following the election of Emile Eddé on 20 January, the delayed legal proceedings began before a joint French-Lebanese tribunal with Hamid Frangieh, a friend of Salah Labaki's, representing the defendants.

In his testimony before the court, Saʿadeh admitted to establishing the clandestine party but denied charges that his party posed a threat to the Lebanese state and the Mandate, offering a robust defense of the party's doctrine and aims.[67] The proceedings were widely covered in the Beirut press, their articles providing a platform for the party's principles to be disseminated among a broader audience than had it remained a covert organization. Newspapers like *al-Nahar* noted the accused's courage and calm while defending the party and their actions before the court; *Le Jour* dismissed talk of the party's young, educated members being a "dangerous generation" that threatened the country's future.[68] After only four days of hearings, the trial was over, and the defendants were found guilty, sentenced, and fined. Saʿadeh was sentenced to six months in prison and fined 25 Syrian pounds, while Ayubi, Qubrusi, Naqqash, and Thabit were each sentenced to suspended one-month prison terms and fined 25 Syrian pounds. Almost two dozen other party members received suspended two-week prison sentences, while several others were acquitted.[69] Given the seriousness of the charges, the punishment was considerably light, "[representing] the obligatory minimum under the prevailing laws and [reflecting] the leniency of the court."[70]

While Saʿadeh and the others served their prison terms, the party remained publicly active under Labaki and Thabit's leadership, recruiting new members

65 Mujais, *Saadeh, Vol. 2*, p. 118.
66 Zamir, *Lebanon's Quest*, p. 183.
67 CADN 2395, Sûreté Générale, Beyrouth, "Information No. 230," 26 January 1936.
68 CADN 471, Cabinet Politique 142, Beyrouth, "Revue de la Presse Libanaise et Syrienne," 31 January 1936.
69 *Mirat al-Sharq*, 30 January 1936, and CADN 2395, Sûreté Générale, Beyrouth, "Information No. 266: Sûreté Beyrouth/Affaire Parti National Syrien," 28 January 1936.
70 Mujais, *Saadeh, Vol. 2*, p. 123.

and promoting Syrian-Lebanese unity. A French intelligence report noted in early February 1936 that the party, though momentarily hindered by the court proceedings, had increased its activities due to the events transpiring in Syria, where public unrest against the French, fueled by the expulsion of nationalist leaders, had resulted in a state of emergency, the deaths of more than a dozen protestors, and the detainment of over three thousand.[71] Party representatives, including Christian, Muslim (three of whom were female), and Druze members, traveled throughout Mount Lebanon to recruit new members and enjoyed some success, particularly in Metn and the Shouf.[72] This party activity lasted until the middle of March 1936 when the French took action against any group agitating for Syrian unity and ordered the party's dissolution.[73] Yet, despite the concerted efforts of French and Lebanese authorities, aided by the party's opponents in the press, to suppress its activities and weaken its appeal, there were still those in the Lebanese establishment who defended the SSNP as a legitimate political actor and who viewed it as a potential ally and source of political support.

Michel Zakkur, the editor of *al-Maʿrad* and member of Beshara al-Khuri's Constitutional Bloc (*al-Kutla al-Dustūriyya*),[74] publicly defended the party in the pages of his newspaper despite his disagreement with the SSNP's principles. Zakkur went so far as to publish a special edition dedicated to the party, its principles, and its cultural and political thought, featuring articles written by Neʿmeh Thabit, Salah Labaki, Maʾmun Ayas, ʿAbdallah Qubrusi, and Fuʾad Suleiman.[75] Zakkur wrote that while "we do not share the same principles as the SSNP... we must admit that the causes that gave birth to this group and allowed it to develop among the youth are the very same ones that for fifteen years have

---

71 CADN 2158, "Renseignement," N.D., and Zamir, *Lebanon's Quest*, p. 184.

72 CADN 472, "Bulletin d'Information No. 9 – allant du 21 au 28 février 1936," N.D.

73 *The Palestine Post*, 24 March 1936, and TNA, FO 406/74, Cairo, Enclosure in No. 104, "Memorandum respecting the Pan-Islamic Arab Movement," 28 March 1936.

74 Khuri established the Constitutional Bloc in 1934, championing Lebanon's complete independence and the end of the Mandate. Other notable members of the Bloc were Hamid Frangieh, Saʿadeh's lawyer at the time, and Camille Chamoun, Lebanon's future prime minister who would frequently ally with the SSNP. Its main rival was the National Bloc of Emile Eddé, a fellow Maronite and Khuri's personal rival. As Hudson observes, "The National Bloc and the Constitutional Bloc were the organization manifestations of the rivalry between [the two]." Hudson, *Precarious Republic*, pp. 136–137.

75 See *al-Maʿrad*, 25 February 1936. Months later, when Saʿadeh was arrested for a second time in June 1936, Zakkur visited him and implored him to change the party's ideology in a way that made it more Lebanese. Zakkur also urged the government to ease its pressure on the party and recognize it as a legitimate Lebanese political party. See "al-Nidhām," in Saʿadeh, *al-Aʿmāl al-Kāmila, Vol. 2*, p. 65.

been eating away at Lebanese convictions and weakening their strength." Indeed, Zakkur continued, "...it was because of their disappointment with the decline of the Lebanese cause that many young people turned away from it. They had found that independence was only an illusion, national dignity, a dream, and the constitution, a delusion." Nevertheless, Zakkur praised and expressed his respect for the SSNP's two great strengths: its firm convictions and its organization.[76] This sentiment – disagreement mixed with respect and implicit acknowledgment of the party's rightful place within Lebanon's political culture – would be a defining feature of the party's relations with a Lebanese political establishment that overwhelmingly didn't share its aims.

At the time, the widespread demonstrations and general strike in Syria encouraged and organized by the National Bloc and League of National Action had provided the party with an opportunity for cooperation with Lebanon's urban Sunni community in Beirut and Tripoli.[77] Many Sunnis from Beirut and Tripoli embraced Arab nationalist calls for Syrian unity and sympathized with the protestors in the Syrian hinterland, demanding France grant Syria its independence and calling for national unity. Though Mandate authorities initially suppressed demonstrations, the National Bloc-led general strike had succeeded in convincing the French to alter their approach and open treaty negotiations by the beginning of March.[78] To that end, the SSNP was invited to participate in the Second Coastal Conference (*Muʾtamar al-Sāḥil*) that brought together several dozen Lebanese proponents of Arabism and Syrianism, predominately from the Sunni Muslim community but also Lebanese Christians, who sought the reunification of the territories annexed to Mount Lebanon in 1920 with the Syrian hinterland.[79]

Held at the Beirut home of Salim Ali Salam on 10 March 1936, a week after de Martel and the National Bloc agreed to negotiate, an SSNP delegation including Salah Labaki and Maʿmun Ayas joined the proceedings. Labaki delivered a speech in which he asserted some fifteen thousand Lebanese youths were demanding Lebanon's unity with Syria as an expression of their discontent with "being separated from their nation."[80] Following the day-long conference,

---

76 CADN 471, Cabinet Politique, Beyrouth, "Revue de la Presse Libanaise et Syrienne," 6 March 1936.

77 Khoury, *Syria*, pp. 457–464.

78 Hourani, *Syria and Lebanon*, p. 199, and Khoury, *Syria*, pp. 464–468.

79 Zamir, *Lebanon's Quest*, p. 190, and Firro, *Inventing Lebanon*, pp. 141–143.

80 CADN 413, Cabinet Politique, Beyrouth, Dossier Unite Syrienne – Congrès du Littorel, Information no. 861, 11 March 1936; Hassan Hallaq, *Muʾatamar al-Sāḥil wa-l-Aqḍiya al-Arbaʿa 1936*

party members sent telegrams to newspapers and politicians supporting Labaki's demand to rejoin all Lebanon with Syria.[81] However, Labaki and the SSNP's demand for Syria's complete unity (*al-waḥda al-shāmila*) differed from that of the others in attendance, who sought only the reunification of Lebanon's predominately Sunni areas with the hinterland and viewed this type of Syrian unity as a stepping-stone to more comprehensive Arab unity. The latter constituted the Conference's official position, expressed in a statement released at the end of the proceedings. Regardless, the demands for complete unity and total independence (*al-istiqlāl al-tam*) worried Lebanese Christians, predominately Maronites, and many French officials who believed it would be detrimental to France's interests and position in Lebanon.[82] Labaki's statement, in particular, was taken as an insult to the Lebanese government by some Beirut youths, most likely Maronite, who demonstrated their anger by destroying a statue honoring Labaki's father in Baabda.[83] However, of greater importance was the ultimate failure of the SSNP delegation to galvanize support for the party or establish a foundation for broader cooperation with Lebanon's Sunni community while at the conference.

Accusations of the party's alleged ties to a foreign power continued to be raised. In early April 1936, *al-Rabita* began a campaign against the SSNP, attempting to depict it as the creation and "instrument of Italian Fascism." Following Italy's invasion of Abyssinia in October 1935, concern over Italy's designs in Lebanon and Syria grew among French and Lebanese authorities. Of particular concern were Italy's efforts to undermine the Mandate through propaganda and its developing relationship with the Maronite community.[84] The paper alleged that a Lebanese-Italian intermediary named Yusuf Huwayak, together with Emir Shakib Arslan, a known sympathizer of Italy, had facilitated the establishment of the SSNP on behalf of the Italians and that the party and Arslan were

(Beirut: 1983), p. 28; and Ahmad Salim Ahmad, *Ḥizb al-Sūrī al-Qawmī al-Ijtimāʿī, 1932–1962: Dirāsa Tārīkhīya* (Beirut: Dār wa Maktabat al-Turāth al-Adabī, 2014), pp. 84–86.

81 CADN 2158, "Renseignements no. 65," 9 March 1936. For copies of the several of the telegrams sent to the High Commissioner's office, see CADN 413, Cabinet Politique, Beyrouth, Télégramme 954 (11/3/1936), Télégramme 955 (11/3/1936), Télégramme 956 (11/3/1936), Télégramme 925 (9/3/1936), and Télégramme 869 à 873 (6/3/1936).

82 Zamir, *Lebanon's Quest*, p. 185.

83 CADN 2158, "Renseignements no. 65," 9 March 1936.

84 Raghid El-Solh, *Lebanon and Arabism: National Identity and State Formation* (London: I.B. Tauris, 2004), pp. 11–12; Zamir, *Lebanon's Quest*, pp. 89–92; and Nir Arielli, *Fascist Italy and the Middle East, 1933–40* (New York: Palgrave Macmillan, 2010), pp. 22,37, 73–74.

the recipients of Italian financial support.[85] Huwayak, a respected artist and the nephew of Maronite Patriarch Elias al-Huwayak, had become a supporter of the SSNP through Labaki, but his connection to Arslan and Arslan's relationship with the SSNP was unsubstantiated.[86] While Arslan's ties to Italy were known, *al-Rabita's* accusation that he facilitated contacts between the Italians and the SSNP was merely grist for the rumor mill.[87] Adding further intrigue to *al-Rabita*'s assertions of an Italian connection with the SSNP, a Sûreté informant claimed that Saʿadeh had organized a group of twenty young party members to be sent for military training in light weapons and tactics by the Italians in Abyssinia before his arrest in November. These individuals were to form the party militia's nucleus, which would help the SSNP secure its objectives.[88] Yet, as with other allegations, no evidence was provided to substantiate the claim, nor would any subsequently appear.

85 CADN 471, Cabinet Politique, Beyrouth, "Revue de la Presse Libanaise et Syrienne," 17 April 1936, and CADN 471, Cabinet Politique, Beyrouth, "Revue de la Presse Libanaise et Syrienne," 24 April 1936.

86 Endnote 201 in Mujais, *Saadeh, Vol. 2*, p. 164.

87 Arslan allegedly encouraged his coreligionists in the Shouf to join the SSNP according to a report provided to the Sûreté Générale by an informant, who cited a letter Arslan had allegedly written to his friends in Lebanon. The informant, however, was unable to provide a copy of the letter to his handlers. See CADN 2158, Baabda, "Renseignements," 20 April 1936, and CADN 2158, Baabda, "Renseignements," 22 April 1936.

88 CADN 2158, Baabda, "Renseignements," 20 April 1936.

3 Freedom Proves Fleeting

On 12 May 1936, Saʿadeh was released from prison, a cause for celebration among the party faithful and a source of dismay among its opponents. Party members held small demonstrations and festivities celebrating his release in locales throughout Mount Lebanon, where they lit celebratory bonfires and set off fireworks.[1] The smaller celebrations, however, were not what Saʿadeh had wanted or hoped for upon his release. Months earlier, he had expressed his desire for the party to use the day of his release to publicly demonstrate its strength by holding mass demonstrations that would capture the public and the authorities' attention and attract new members to its ranks.[2] The SSNP's central leadership disagreed, fearing such large gatherings would provoke a hostile response that would seriously harm the party. Though Saʿadeh ultimately concurred with their view, he later regretted that the party had not taken advantage of the moment as the decision to hold smaller gatherings did little to deter French and Lebanese efforts to suppress any public manifestation of party activity whatsoever.[3]

From district administrators to village elders, authorities threatened party members with prosecution if they demonstrated in celebration of Saʿadeh's release, tried to dissuade them from holding any planned events, and urged members to abandon the party altogether.[4] The Police, Sûreté Générale, Gendarmerie Libanaise, and Guards Champetres (Rural Guards) rigorously observed party activities, placed party members under strict surveillance, and worked to extinguish any celebratory fires and suppress public gatherings.[5] Some were arrested

1 CADN 472, Delegation du Haut Commissariat, Beyrouth, "Bulletin d'Information, No. 20, allant du 8 au 15 Mai 1936," 15 May 1936; CADN 2158, Gendarmerie Libanaise/Compagnie du Mont-Liban/Section de Beit-Eddine/Caracol de Baakline/No. 2/4, Baakline, "Le Sergent à pied Farid Saab a Mr. le Cdt de Section Beit-Eddine," 12 May 1936; and CADN 2158, Jdeide, No. 143, "Le Caimacam du Matten a Monsieur L'Administrateur du Mont Liban," 12 May 1936.

2 Dayah, *Muḥākamat*, p. 202, and "Khiṭāb al-Zaʿīm fī Awwal Mars 1938," in Saʿadeh, *al-Aʿmāl al-Kāmila, Vol. 3,* p. 190.

3 "Khiṭāb al-Zaʿīm fī Awwal Mars 1938," in Saʿadeh, *al-Aʿmāl al-Kāmila, Vol. 3,* p. 190, and "Ilā Asaf Abu Murad," in Saʿadeh, *al-Aʿmāl al-Kāmila, Vol. 9,* p. 9.

4 See, for example CADN 2158, "Rapport du Pt. de Broumana a/s de l'incident du 12 mai 1936," 15 May 1936, and CADN 2158, Le Conseiller Administratif du Mont Liban a Monsieur le Delegue du Haut Commissaire, No. 82, Beyrouth, "P.P.S," 18 May 1936.

5 See, for example CADN 2158, No. 85, Caza du Metn, "Renseignements sur le P.P.S.," 22 May 1936, and CADN 2158, Jdeide, No. 143, "Le Caimacam du Matten a Monsieur L'Administrateur du Mont Liban," 12 May 1936.

https://doi.org/10.1515/9783110729092-005

for holding demonstrations, including 15 members of the party in Zahlé; the Gendarmerie also detained a large group of SSNP members attempting to travel to Beirut from villages in Mount Lebanon to hold a massive march.[6]

At the time of Saʿadeh's release, the debate over ongoing Franco-Lebanese and Franco-Syrian treaty negotiations intensified in the Levant. In Lebanon, the Francophile Lebanese president Emile Eddé sought to establish a broad consensus with his political rivals, particularly Beshara al-Khuri and the Maronite Patriarch, to silence opposition to the French. In Syria, the National Bloc had been leading negotiations, and talks had resumed in early June in Paris after France's new government led by socialist Prime Minister Léon Blum assumed office. Saʿadeh, concerned by the news coming out of Paris regarding the negotiations, wrote to Shukri al-Quwatli, then the National Bloc's vice president overseeing its internal affairs. Saʿadeh's concern centered on discussions over national economic and political issues related to Syria and Lebanon's "common interests" (*al-maṣāliḥ al-mushtaraka*) and requested Quwatli's clarification on the matter.[7] The SSNP also published a memorandum expressing its concerns and declaring its opposition to the Franco-Syrian treaty negotiations, which it believed were ultimately aimed at confirming the status quo rather than establishing Syria's complete independence and sovereignty. The "Blue Memorandum" ("*al-Balāgh al-Azraq*") lambasted the empowerment of "separatists" and the separation of the Lebanese question from the Syrian issue, emphasizing the unity of the Syrian cause and Lebanon's importance to it. Rather than promote national political and economic unity or true independence, the current negotiations undertaken by Syrian leaders, specifically the National Bloc, only perpetuated Greater Syria's division, dire economic conditions, and continued lack of sovereignty.[8]

The party's renewed outspokenness and activity following Saʿadeh's release displeased Eddé's government and supporters of Lebanese separatism. The most vocal opposition to the party was found in the pages of the periodical *al-Masaʾ* and the opinions of its editor ʿArif al-Ghurayb. In an intense and sustained hostile campaign, *al-Masaʾ* branded the SSNP lackeys of a foreign government and suggested the party was losing adherents.[9] Taking exception to the near-constant

6 *The Palestine Post*, 28 May 1936, and CADN 2158, Bikfaya, "Le Caimacam du Matten a Monsieur L'Administrateur du Mont Liban," 19 May 1936.
7 "Ilā Nāʾib Raʾīs al-Kutla al-Waṭaniyya," in Saʿadeh, *al-Aʿmāl al-Kāmila*, *Vol. 9*, p. 11.
8 "al-Balāgh al-Azraq," in Saʿadeh, *al-Aʿmāl al-Kāmila*, *Vol. 2*, pp. 31–36.
9 CADN 472, Cabinet Politique, Beyrouth, "Revue de la Presse Libanaise et Syrienne," 8 May 1936; CADN 472, Cabinet Politique, Beyrouth, "Revue de la Presse Libanaise et Syrienne," 12 June 1936; CADN 472, Cabinet Politique, Beyrouth, "Revue de la Presse Libanaise et Syrienne,"

disparagement, several party members decided to intimidate Ghurayb in hopes of getting him, and his paper, to stop their criticism. Following him to his home one day in June, several party members forced open the door to his apartment and physically assaulted him. Ghurayb was not the only journalist attacked. Other SSNP members attempted to burn down the offices of *al-Rabita*, and allegedly devised plans to assassinate the newspaper's owner, Ibrahim Haddad.[10] Like *al-Masa'*, *al-Rabita*'s editors had also suggested the party was losing adherents and had sharply criticized it for not participating in the Palestinian uprising against the British Mandate.[11]

While the violent opposition to Franco-Lebanese and Franco-Syrian treaty negotiations raised the ire of Lebanese and French authorities, the security services became more intent on suppressing the party after discovering a copy of an SSNP "Emergency Decree." The decree, found in possession of George Haddad, called for the establishment of a temporary higher council to oversee party affairs and acts of civil disobedience in the event of Saʿadeh's arrest. According to the authorities, the decree was proof that Saʿadeh had reconstituted the party they had ordered disbanded, providing them with enough justification to arrest Saʿadeh and other party members.

On the orders of Chief of Police Asad al-Bustani, approximately 15 officers with the Sûreté Générale led by Farid Chehab raided the Ras Beirut home where Saʿadeh was staying, at which point a standoff ensued between the security forces and armed SSNP members assigned to protect Saʿadeh. A short time passed before Saʿadeh emerged from his room and warned Chehab that his forced entry into the home was illegal. Chehab and his forces temporarily retreated and surrounded the house. They were subsequently encircled by armed SSNP reinforcements, raising the tension of the standoff even higher. Saʿadeh, fearing the French military intervention, surrendered and was taken to court where he was deposed.[12] In addition to Saʿadeh, several other party members were arrested and charged with assaulting Ghurayb, attempting to burn down the printing press of *al-Rabita*, and establishing a secret political organization.[13] Eddé also

19 June 1936; and CADN 472, Cabinet Politique, Beyrouth, "Revue de la Presse Libanaise et Syrienne," 26 June 1936.

10 CADN 2395, Republique Libanaise, Beyrouth, No. 73/P, "Le Premier President de la Cour De Cassation à Monseiur le Delegue du Haut Commissaire," 19 July 1937.

11 CADN 472, Cabinet Politique, Beyrouth, "Revue de la Presse Libanaise et Syrienne," 19 June 1936.

12 "Mudhakkirat al-Ḥizb al-Sūrī al-Qawmī al-Ijtimāʿī ilā al-ʿUṣbat al-Umamiyya Sana 1936," in Saʿadeh, *al-Aʿmāl al-Kāmila, Vol. 6*, pp. 555–557.

13 *Al-Difaʿ*, 9 July 1936.

put pressure on the party and other political organizations by creating the Bureau d'Investigation, a central office for investigating the illegal meetings of prohibited and dissolved organizations with direct and unfettered access to all documents from various security organizations. The investigation into Ghurayb's assault allegedly uncovered a "terrorist committee" within the SSNP tasked with intimidating or attacking the party's opponents; President Eddé and Secretary of State Dr. Ayub Tabet reportedly appeared on a list of "marked persons."[14]

The party remained undeterred despite Sa'adeh's arrest, increased surveillance of its activities, pressure campaigns urging members to abandon the party, and widespread detentions of party adherents by security forces. Great attention was given to the party's alleged ties to Italy, a focus that reflected France's prioritization of gathering intelligence on ongoing Italian propaganda activities in Syria and Lebanon, including press and radio broadcasts on Radio Bari, and Italy's funding of local schools and hospitals.[15] Feeding this concern, several Beirut-based newspapers known for their opposition to the SSNP published evidence they claimed proved earlier allegations that Italy had financed the party through Yusuf al-Huwayak.

According to the party, the allegations and the *al-Masa'* campaign were driven by Aziz al-Hashim, the head of the Republican Independence Party (RIP, *Ḥizb al-Istiqlāl al-Jumhūrī*),[16] who joined the SSNP in 1935 but whom the party quickly came to believe was a French informant trying to sow internal discord to weaken the movement.[17] When the allegations of the party's ties to Italy appeared in May, they had raised some party members' concern, notably prompting a party delegation from Zahlé, which included Sa'id al-Aql,[18] to visit Sa'adeh in

14 *The Palestine Post*, 10 July 1936.

15 CADN 472, Cabinet Politique 855, Beyrouth, HC to MAE, "Activité Italienne dans les territoires sous mandate," 18 August 1936.

16 On the Republican Independence Party, see Jurayj, *Min al-Ju'bat, Vol. 1*, pp. 273–274, and Adil al-Sulh, *Ḥizb al-Istiqlāl al-Jumhūrī: Min al-Muqāwama li-Waṭaniyya Ayām al-Intidāb al-Faransī* (Beirut: Dār al-Ṭalī'a li-l-Tibā'a wa-l-Nashr, 1970).

17 "Wafāh Khā'in Jāsūs – al-Shaykh 'Azīz al-Hāshim," in Sa'adeh, *al-A'māl al-Kāmila, Vol. 6*, pp. 246–251. The accusations appear in an article Sa'adeh wrote when Hashim passed away in 1942. Sa'adeh, then living in Argentina, penned a stinging rejoinder in *al-Zawba'a* to several articles that had appeared in the Syrian–Lebanese press in the Americas praising Hashim's noble character and contribution to the national struggle. Sa'adeh, however, viewed him as nothing more than a traitor and spy who had sold out the national cause to the French, acts that Sa'adeh would neither forgive nor forget.

18 Aql would be counted among the most prominent writers to have joined the SSNP in its early years, joining the likes of Salah Labaki, Fu'ad Suleiman, Yusuf al-Khal, and Rushdi Ma'aluf. Little is known on Aql's time and activity in the SSNP during the 1930s and Aql subsequently, and until his death, would deny having ever been associated with it despite evidence to the contrary.

his home in the hope of finding answers to their questions. Sa'adeh met with the delegation and instructed Salah Labaki to arrange a meeting between the party members from Zahlé and Hashim. Hashim refused to meet them, leading Aql and the others to conclude he had fabricated the allegations against the party and Sa'adeh.[19]

Subsequently, during the investigation, Huwayak, Sa'adeh, and Hashim were deposed on the party's alleged relations with Fascist Italy. While Huwayak and Sa'adeh denied all the allegations, Hashim maintained the opposite, contradicting them.[20] In his deposition, Hashim suggested he had helped conceal evidence of the relationship, asserting that Sa'adeh had asked him to assure Huwayak and the Italian Consul that all incriminating evidence had been secured.[21] The contradictory testimony was enough for newspapers like *al-Nahar* and *Sawt al-Ahrar* to tell their readers that nothing had been proven. However, *al-Bilad* and *al-Masa'* dug in, seizing on Hashim's testimony and previous statements by Huwayak expressing sympathy for Fascist Italy and his claims he was intermediary between the party and the Italians.[22] The Italian Ambassador denied the accusations leveled against his country by Lebanese papers and filed a formal complaint with the High Commissioner.[23] By the end of the investigation in early September 1936, investigators had failed to substantiate Hashim's and others' allegations the party had collaborated with a foreign entity.[24] Whether this outcome was due partially or entirely to Italian political pressure on Mandate authorities, which in turn pressured the Lebanese government, is

---

Aql's literary talent greatly impressed Sa'adeh, who first heard of the poet through party members who alerted him to Aql's first play, *Bint Yiftāḥ* (Japheth's Daughter), in the middle of 1935. Sa'adeh would encourage Aql to seek inspiration in Syria's history and myths. These Syrian themes would appear in Aql's subsequent work, the epic-poem *Qadmus*, which he completed in 1937. Soon, however, Aql, like Labaki and others, would drift away from the party's Syrian nationalism and embrace Lebanese nationalist views rooted in a Phoenician past and promulgated by Charles Corm. On Aql, Sa'adeh, and the SSNP, see Antun Sa'adeh, *al-Ṣirā' al-Fikrī fī al-Adab al-Sūrī, 12th ed.* (Beirut: Sa'ādah Cultural Foundation, 2013), pp. 57–76; Salameh, *Language, Memory, and Identity*, pp. 132–135, and *al-Nahar*, 6 December 2014.

19 "Wafāh Khā'in Jāsūs," in Sa'adeh, *al-A'māl al-Kāmila, Vol. 6*, pp. 246–251.

20 "Wafāh Khā'in Jāsūs," in Sa'adeh, *al-A'māl al-Kāmila, Vol. 6*, pp. 246–251; *The Palestine Post*, 9 September 1936; and CADN 473, Cabinet Politique, Beyrouth, "Revue de la Presse Libanaise et Syrienne," 4 September 1936.

21 Mujais, *Saadeh, Vol. 2*, p. 144.

22 CADN 473, Cabinet Politique, Beyrouth, "Revue de la Presse Libanaise et Syrienne," 4 September 1936.

23 Mujais, *Saadeh, Vol. 2*, p. 145.

24 CADN 473, Cabinet Politique, Beyrouth, "Revue de la Presse Libanaise et Syrienne," 11 September 1936.

not known, but was altogether irrelevant to the legal fate of Saʿadeh and other detained party members, who remained incarcerated.

Despite the investigation, and with Saʿadeh in prison, the SSNP continued its activities under Thabit and Ayas' direction, focusing on treaty negotiations. In August 1936, the party petitioned the League of Nations on matters related to the unity of Geographic Syria, expressing its continuing opposition to any Franco-Lebanese or Franco-Syrian treaty that would ultimately preserve its division. Further, their petition assessed the Mandate territories' prevailing economic and political situation, the source of the pervading sense of discontent among both Lebanese and Syrians.[25] Threatened by the prospect of solidifying the partition of Geographic Syria into separate, independent states, the party's 21-page memorandum suggested a compromise solution: the establishment of a federalist system in Syrian territories governed by the Mandate.[26]

The idea for such a scheme was not new or unique but was one that had been embraced by several Syrian nationalists, including by Antun's father Khalil, at the end of World War I. Grounded in the party's conviction that the peoples inhabiting Geographic Syria were one nation bound together through "geographic, economic, social, cultural and historical factors," a federalist system provided the best opportunity for avoiding the harmful effects of division and "the actualization of Syrian nationhood." However, the federalist system was not the SSNP's ultimate objective, which viewed it as a step toward the complete unity of Greater Syria. However, the recommendations detailed in the August memorandum failed to resonate among the broader public or sway the opinions of those in power who were more inclined to consolidating the separation of Lebanon and Syria into two distinct states, albeit while maintaining a special relationship. Seeking to strengthen opposition to proposed treaties with the French, the party found allies among the Sunni community, primarily in Tripoli, for whom the idea of Syrian unity still resonated. In further protest of the treaty negotiations, the SSNP participated in a massive and violent demonstration with the League for National Action in Tripoli against Lebanese Prime Minister

25 "Mudhakkirat al-Ḥizb al-Sūrī al-Qawmī al-Ijtimāʿī ilā al-ʿUṣbat al-Umamiyya Sana 1936," in Saʿadeh, *al-Aʿmāl al-Kāmila, Vol. 6*, p. 558. For the petition's text, see "Petition: Note of the Syrian National Party to the League of Nations," in *Commission Permanente des Mandats* (CPM), Tome 37, C.P.M. 1964, *Petitions Relating to Syria*, 4 November 1937, United Nations Archives (UNA). For the League of Nations' response, see Jibran Jurayj, *Min al-Juʿbat: Marwiyyāt, Mustanadāt wa Adabiyyāt ʿan al-Ḥizb al-Sūrī al-Qawmī al-Ijtimāʿī, Vol. 4* (Beirut: 1993), pp. 71–77.
26 UNA, C.P.M. 1964, pp. 15–17.

Khayr al-Din al-Ahdab, who was visiting the city to promote the negotiations that September.[27]

The efforts of the French and Lebanese security forces took their toll on the party. The temporary leadership council (comprised of Labaki, Thabit, Ayas, and two others) responsible for leading the party in Saʿadeh's absence was functioning as intended, organizing civil disobedience throughout the Mandate territories, and demanding the release of all SSNP detainees, freedom of speech and assembly, and the legalization of the political parties.[28] However, the temporary council's activities were severely hampered when Labaki was arrested, and Thabit was forced into hiding as the Sûreté targeted the party's leadership to weaken and impede its activities.[29] Indeed, in early September, a Sûreté report argued the SSNP was in disarray, a direct result of the Sûreté's suppressive measures against the radical movement. Financially, the report suggested the SSNP suffered from a general lack of funds and received only small, ineffectual contributions that were used to support their imprisoned comrades' legal defense and general needs. Internally, according to the Sûreté, a significant number of party members were no longer attending gatherings. Druze members, who were considered one of the party's pillars, were increasingly disgruntled to the extent that some were leaving the party, and Labaki was reportedly searching for the right time to abandon the party as well.[30] At least sixty members remained in custody, further disrupting the party, awaiting trial in al-Raml Prison on various charges ranging from illegally gathering, attempted assassination, and attempted arson.[31]

In early October, the SSNP dispatched a letter to French Prime Minister Blum protesting the local French authorities' persecution of the party, decrying "the brutal and inhumane treatment" of its "political detainees."[32] According to Thabit and Labaki, the letter's signatories, proceedings against the detainees had dragged on for four months, and their ill-treatment had led to the deterioration of several prisoners' health. They hoped that Blum, the head of the socialist-led Popular Front government, would be far more sympathetic to their plight and

27 Zamir, *Lebanon's Quest*, p. 206.

28 "Marsūm al-Ṭawāriʾ," in Saʿadeh, *al-Aʿmāl al-Kāmila, Vol. 2*, pp. 37–38, and Endnote 199 in Mujais, *Saadeh, Vol. 2*, p. 163.

29 "Mudhakkirat al-Ḥizb al-Sūrī al-Qawmī al-Ijtimāʿī," in Saʿadeh, *al-Aʿmāl al-Kāmila, Vol. 6*, p. 558.

30 CADN 2395, Sûreté Générale, Beyrouth, "Information No. 3272: A/S Parti Populaire Syrien," 12 September 1936.

31 *The Palestine Post*, 12 October 1936.

32 CADN 2395, Sûreté Générale, Beyrouth, "Information No. 3577: A/S Parti Populaire Syrien," 2 October 1936.

therefore intervene on their behalf as an act of goodwill. Their hopes were misplaced as party members continued to be arrested by Mandate authorities.[33] Moreover, the letter's authors found it ironic that their party was persecuted for espousing the same beliefs about Syrian unity that others in Syria and Lebanon advocated while the others were not.[34] However, while the SSNP may have borne the brunt of French and Lebanese efforts to curtail opposition to Franco-Lebanese treaty negotiations, de Martel and Eddé did pursue a broader policy that sought "to allay Muslim fears of the treaty and to weaken and isolate Syria's supporters on the coast [i.e., Tripoli]."[35]

3.1 Freedom and Confrontation

Eddé's government signed the Franco-Lebanese treaty on 13 November, provoking a passionate response that devolved only several days later into riots and confessional violence between Maronites and Sunnis.[36] Eddé's supporters, particularly those from the Maronite community, rejoiced at the treaty's conclusion and openly celebrated the recognition of Lebanon's borders. Others, predominately Sunni Muslims in Beirut and Tripoli who still hoped for Greater Syria's unity, in contrast, viewed the treaty formalizing Lebanon's borders and status as a separate entity as the death knell for their aspirations. The rising intensity of the confessional violence, which required the French military to forcefully intervene to restore order, raised the concerns of Sunni and Maronite leaders who, fearing its "[escalation] into "civil war,"" pleaded for their fellow countrymen to end the violence.[37] Though the violence ultimately abated, the effects of the confessional conflict were far-reaching, including the establishment of two confessional paramilitary movements, the Maronite, Lebanese nationalist Kata'ib (Pha-

33 CADN 2395, Direction de la Police, Compte-Rendu, "Parti Populaire Syrien," 20 October 1936.

34 The party had voiced the same criticism in its 12 August petition to the League of Nations, stating: "The authorities never [recognized] such parties until they had acquired sufficient strength and popular backing dangerous enough to cause serious trouble. A few months ago the members of the Syrian Delegation now at Paris, were considered by authorities as a set of riotous mob-leaders endangering public security, as termed by the several manifests issued by the High Commissioner during the last troubles in Syria." UNA, C.P.M. 1964, p. 13.

35 Zamir, *Lebanon's Quest*, p. 205.

36 Firro, *Inventing Lebanon*, pp. 149–150, and Zamir, *Lebanon's Quest*, p. 210.

37 Firro, *Inventing Lebanon*, p. 149.

langes Libanaises)[38] and the Sunni, Arab nationalist Najjadeh (The Helpers),[39] both of which were vociferously opposed to the SSNP and posed organizational, ideological, and political challenges to it.

The SSNP remained on the sidelines, issuing pleas for restraint and urging Lebanese not to engage in sectarian-inspired violence, including publishing articles penned by Saʿadeh and Labaki in *al-Nahar* and *al-Jumhur.* In his article in *al-Nahar,* published on the day he was released from jail, Saʿadeh praised the party's steadfastness and restraint amid "this dangerous situation." According to Saʿadeh, the nation stood at a crossroads between its rise or decline, and it was incumbent upon the party to remain united and not entangle itself in the violence.[40] Saʿadeh argued that the events revealed that the SSNP was the only organized movement working for the nation's advancement and dignity while the forces of reaction and sectarianism promoted barbarism, hatred, and regression. In *al-Jumhur,* Saʿadeh decried what he viewed as the weaponization and exploitation of the slogans "Independence of Lebanon" and "Syrian unity" by corrupt politicians and sectarian religious leaders. He urged readers to stop sacrificing their lives for narrow individual or sectarian interests and instead do so for the national interest.[41] In an article titled "Consequences" (*al-Natāʾij*), Labaki, then serving as head of the party's political bureau, lamented "the bloody incidents in Beirut," noting the party viewed them as regrettable and did not see what positive result they could bring about, reiterating that the homeland (*al-waṭan*) belonged to all sects.[42] For the party, the confessional violence was nothing more than a futile, misguided expression of opposition to the treaty signed by Eddé.

Though Saʿadeh had ostensibly been released from prison after accepting Eddé's demand to acknowledge the legitimacy of the Lebanese state, Saʿadeh

---

38 On the Kata'ib, see Suleiman, *Political Parties in Lebanon*, pp. 232–249; Hudson, *Precarious Republic*, pp. 142–146; John P. Entelis, "Party Transformation in Lebanon: Al-Kata'ib as a Case Study," *Middle Eastern Studies* 9, no. 3 (October 1973): pp. 325–340; and John P. Entelis, *Pluralism and Party Transformation in Lebanon: Al-Kata'ib, 1936–1970* (Leidan: Brill, 1974).

39 The Najjadeh movement was formed out of the Muslim scout youth movement and was established in November 1936, though its formal inauguration only took place a year later in November 1937. On the Najjadeh, see Suleiman, *Political Parties in Lebanon*, pp. 201–213, and Hudson, *Precarious Republic*, pp. 175–178.

40 "Nidāʾ ilā al-Qawmiyyun bi-Munāsiba al-Fitna al-Diniyya," in Saʿadeh, *al-Aʿmāl al-Kāmila, Vol. 2*, pp. 54–55.

41 "Dam al–Ghawghāʾ," in Saʿadeh, *al-Aʿmāl al-Kāmila, Vol. 2*, pp. 56–57.

42 "al-Natāʾij," in Jurayj, *Min al-Juʿbat, Vol. 3*, pp. 16–18. Notably, Labaki avoided using the terms "Lebanon" and "Syria" in his article, speaking only of the "homeland," a term that could be interpreted in any way that suited a reader.

wasted little time explaining his interpretation of the terms of their arrangement. In short, the party's political platform remained unchanged, and the party reaffirmed its commitment to the content of the June 1936 Blue Memorandum, which adamantly expressed the SSNP's opposition to the proposed treaties and Greater Syria's division. Saʿadeh acknowledged the challenge confronting the party with "Syria divided into internationally recognized regions" and understood the need to develop a plan that would effectively advance its agenda. To do so, Saʿadeh suggested that while all party branches in Lebanon, Syria, Palestine, and Jordan would work for the same objective, each would pursue a political program specific to its needs and local realities in a manner that did not endanger the safety of the movement.[43]

In December 1936, Saʿadeh, together with a small entourage, traveled to Syria's Tartus Governorate, located in the southern part of Syria's predominantly ʿAlawi coastal region. There they visited party branches and held several private and public meetings in different towns.[44] Over the preceding year, the SSNP had established itself in the ʿAlawi locales of Latakia, Banyas, Tartus, Safita, Marmarita, and Tel Kalkh, where they recruited some youths and educated professionals, including several journalists, a dentist, and the son of a ʿAlawi mufti.[45] Beset by internal tribal, religious, and geographic divisions and rivalries, ʿAlawis were also politically divided between those advocating for maintaining or even expanding the ʿAlawi region's autonomy and those promoting its integration into the rest of Syria.[46] The party's secularism, opposition to Arabism, respect and advocacy for workers and peasants, and support for Syrian unity resonated among individual members of the ʿAlawi elite, particularly those seeking to better integrate their community into the broader fabric of Syria's society and politics.[47] Saʿadeh touched upon these themes in the speeches he delivered while visiting Safita and Tel Kalkh.

In Safita, on an overcast and rainy day, excited party members and supporters gathered in the town square to hear Saʿadeh speak, welcoming him by declaring their fealty to him – their Zaʾīm – and dedication to Syria.[48] Saʿadeh empha-

---

43 "Kalimat al-Zaʿīm ithra khurujihu min al-Sijn li-l-Marra al-Thāniyya," in Saʿadeh, *al-Aʿmāl al-Kāmila, Vol. 2,* pp. 366–367.

44 Jurayj, *Min al-Juʿbat, Vol. 3,* p. 22.

45 Jibran Jurayj, *Min al-Juʿbat: Marwiyyāt, Mustanadāt wa Adabiyyāt ʿan al-Ḥizb al-Sūrī al-Qawmī al-Ijtimāʿī, Vol. 2* (Beirut: 1986), pp. 202–203.

46 Khoury, *Syria,* p. 523. Khoury also writes about the parallel process that was also taking place at the time among the Druze population in Jabal Druze. Khoury, *Syria,* pp. 515–519.

47 Khoury, *Syria,* p. 525.

48 Jurayj, *Min al-Juʿbat, Vol. 3,* p. 24.

sized the characteristics that distinguished the SSNP from other political movements. According to him, the party had moved beyond making mere assertions of national unity to actually build the foundations for such unity after identifying the people and the nation's actual needs and interests.[49] Seeking to transform Syria into "a living nation" and to serve that nation by addressing its needs and promoting its interests, the SSNP, Saʿadeh asserted, had overcome within itself the societal divisions wrought by religious fanaticism and was the only force in society not working for a particular sect or group, but rather for the advancement of all of Syria's communities.[50] The party sought to liberate the persecuted peasants, workers, and the population at large from "the reactionary forces" (*al-rajaʿiyya*) seeking to perpetuate the status quo in which their rights were denied or infringed. The SSNP would struggle to secure these rights and Syria's territorial integrity and sovereignty because advancing the nation's interest was its sole, "sacred" pursuit.[51]

Saʿadeh reiterated his message the following day in Tel Kalkh. There, Saʿadeh used the traditional welcome he received from the villagers – a welcome party of sword-wielding horsemen – not only to express his respect and admiration for the tradition's historical and social importance but to emphasize the importance of such a tradition to Syria's national identity. Indeed, the SSNP sought to bring together all of Syria's groups (*al-ʿaṣabiyyāt*) "to form one personality [*shakhṣiyya waḥida*], the personality of the Syrian nation."[52] Moreover, lest his audience fear the loss of their identity and traditions, Saʿadeh suggested that the figurative "joining of these tribal swords to the Syrian national movement does not diminish their exploits, but only adds to their splendor and sharpness,"[53] thereby claiming the ʿAlawis and their traditions to be an integral part of Syria's social and cultural fabric and history. This message of integration enhanced the party's standing among the ʿAlawi community. Ultimately, the SSNP was "to have a lasting impact" on the ʿAlawi community and "promoted in different ways the process of [ʿAlawi] integration into Syria."[54]

Returning to Lebanon, Saʿadeh continued his efforts to rally support for the party and openly challenge the Lebanese government and French authorities. In early 1937, the SSNP planned private meetings and public rallies throughout Leb-

---

49 "Khiṭāb al-Zaʿīm fī Sāfītā," in Saʿadeh, *al-Aʿmāl al-Kāmila, Vol. 2*, pp. 59–63.
50 "Khiṭāb al-Zaʿīm fī Sāfītā," in Saʿadeh, *al-Aʿmāl al-Kāmila, Vol. 2*, pp. 60.
51 "Khiṭāb al-Zaʿīm fī Sāfītā," in Saʿadeh, *al-Aʿmāl al-Kāmila, Vol. 2*, pp. 62–63.
52 "Min Khiṭāb al-Zaʿīm fī Talkalkh," in Saʿadeh, *al-Aʿmāl al-Kāmila, Vol. 2*, p. 64.
53 "Min Khiṭāb al-Zaʿīm fī Talkalkh," in Saʿadeh, *al-Aʿmāl al-Kāmila, Vol. 2*, p. 64.
54 Khoury, *Syria*, p. 525. Khoury also applied the analysis to the Syrian army, an institution that would also have a lasting impact on the ʿAlawi community.

anon to demonstrate its strength, relevance, and commitment to its struggle, despite authorities' efforts to curtail its activities. The first of the planned events took place on 9 January 1937 in Baakline, a Druze town in Mount Lebanon's Shouf district, consisting of several small meetings and speeches. The party leadership, based on the advice of Labaki, the political bureau's head, and Kamal Abu Kamal, the party's general secretary in the Shouf region, had decided not to hold any large public gatherings there based on the assessment that such gatherings would provoke unnecessary confrontations with government authorities.[55] Indeed, Saʿadeh and his entourage were briefly delayed on their journey when police diverted them to a meeting with Nadhim al-Akari, the district administrator, who sought to convince Saʿadeh – to no avail – to abandon his plans altogether.[56]

Several days later, Saʿadeh returned to the northern part of the Shouf district to the majority Druze town of Ammatour to hold a large public gathering with the party faithful from the area.[57] Despite the cold, rainy weather and further warnings from the district administrator to abandon their plans, party members gathered in the town's square to hear Saʿadeh's afternoon speech. Local authorities dispatched approximately 50 police officers to the gathering to maintain public order and disrupt the meeting if needed. However, their ability to control the situation was adeptly neutralized by the party, which welcomed the police into their midst, ushering them to the audience's front, effectively surrounding them. Other, more discreet, gatherings were held in other areas where the party's following was robust, including Beirut's Mar Elias.[58]

In addition to party gatherings, the SSNP focused on disseminating its views on matters related to Syria's territorial integrity, particularly regarding the regions of Alexandretta and Palestine. The party vociferously protested Turkish efforts to separate the district of Alexandretta from Syria under the pretext that a significant Turk population lived in the region.[59] The party even offered to put its

55 Jurayj, *Min al-Juʿbat, Vol. 3*, pp. 71–72.

56 Jurayj, *Min al-Juʿbat, Vol. 3*, p. 72.

57 For more details on the events in Baakline and Ammatour see Jurayj, *Min al-Juʿbat, Vol. 3*, pp. 71–96.

58 CADN 2395, Sûreté Générale, Beyrouth, Information No. 159, "Surete Beyrouth," 11 January 1937.

59 According to a 1936 report by the French High Commission, the estimated total population of the district of Alexandretta was 220,000. Turks comprised 39 %, ʿAlawis 28 %, Armenians 11 %, Sunni Arabs 10 %, Christians 8 %, and Jews, Kurds, and Circassians 4 % of the local population. Thus, "[although] Turkish speakers formed the largest single community, the Arabic speaker… were numerically larger than the Turks." See Roberta Micallef, "Hatay Joins the Motherland,"

members at the Mandate's disposal to repel any Turkish military action in Alexandretta to ensure it remained Syrian territory.[60] The status of the Sanjak had been negotiated between France and Turkey in the early 1920s. Subsequent agreements had all seemingly favored Turkey rather than Syria, including the decision to grant Alexandretta internal independence in January 1937, a further step towards Turkish annexation. Despite the Syrian protests, France did not alter its Alexandretta policy.[61] The SSNP blamed the failure to influence French policy on Syria's government; it accused the government, then-headed by the National Bloc, of capitulating, ceding Syria's sovereignty, and failing to defend the nation's interests. The party also argued that Syrians were "fed up with the intellectual sterility and political paralysis that pervades the positions of traditional politicians who are in control."[62] The National Bloc chaffed at the criticism, regardless of the validity of its merit.[63]

While focused on external issues, the party also tended to internal organization matters. In late January 1937, under Saʿadeh's direction, the party amended the constitution it had adopted in 1934. Saʿadeh was keen to stress that while the organization and discipline outlined in the constitution had helped it survive tremendous persecution, they were neither an end nor the source of the party's strength. Instead, the party's strength and success were grounded in and sprang forth from its doctrine and organization.[64] Thus, the first three articles of the revised party constitution expressed the party's aim – the complete independence and sovereignty of the Syrian nation – and its fundamental and reform principles; the remaining eleven articles addressed the party's institutions and executive and legislative authorities within the party. Significantly, the revised constitution expanded the party's central organization, establishing a second council called the *Majlis al-Aʿlā* (Higher Council) in addition to the existing Council of Deputies.[65] The Higher Council was tasked with consulting and advising the leader as needed on matters of great importance to the party and was initially

---

in *State Frontiers: Borders and Boundaries in the Middle East*, ed. Inga Brandell (London: I.B. Tauris, 2006), p. 144.

60 "Mudhakkirat al-Ḥizb al-Sūrī al-Qawmī ilā Jamʿiyya al-Umam," in Saʿadeh, *al-Aʿmāl al-Kāmila, Vol. 2*, p. 58; "Mudhakkirat al-Ḥizb al-Sūrī al-Qawmī ilā al-Mafūḍ al-Sāmī bi-Sha'n Sanjaq al-Iskandarūna," in Saʿadeh, *al-Aʿmāl al-Kāmila, Vol. 2*, p. 69; and *Oriente Moderno*, 17.2, February 1937, p. 101.

61 Yamak, *SSNP*, pp. 57–58.

62 "al-Bilād al-Suriyya Sayudafaʿa ʿan Salāmatihā Jaysh Sūrī Lā Jaysh Turkī," in Saʿadeh, *al-Aʿmāl al-Kāmila, Vol. 2*, p. 97.

63 Mujais, *Saadeh, Vol. 2*, p. 179.

64 "al-Niẓām," in Saʿadeh, *al-Aʿmāl al-Kāmila, Vol. 2*, pp. 66–68.

65 "Dustūr al-Ḥizb al-Sūrī al-Qawmī," in Saʿadeh, *al-Aʿmāl al-Kāmila, Vol. 2*, pp. 75–80.

headed by Fakhri Maʿaluf. Higher Council members included ʿAbd al-Masih, Thabit, Ayas, Qubrusi, Kamal Abu Kamal and Maʿaruf Saʿab; Thabit quickly replaced Maʿaluf as its head.[66] Further constitutional decrees issued by Saʿadeh elaborated on the administrative authorities of the *Munafidhiyyāt* (Administrative Regions) (including collecting funds, directing local propaganda campaigns, and overseeing military training for the party's militia) and established representative councils in the *Mudīriyyāt* (Local Branches) to advise local administrators.[67]

The formalization of the party's constitution and its institutions responded to the needs of a growing movement whose membership and geographic reach had expanded despite the pressures exerted upon it by its opponents. In Lebanon, the party consolidated its presence in Beirut, in Mount Lebanon's Metn, Aley, and Shouf districts, in the Bekaa's Bekaa el-Gharbi and Zahlé districts, and North Lebanon's Akkar, Zghorta, Tripoli, and Koura districts. In Syria, the party had succeeded in establishing itself in Damascus, Homs, Hama, Aleppo, Deir el-Zour, Latakia, and Tartus. Among those who joined the party in Syria were Akram al-Hawrani and the brothers Adib and Salah al-Shishakli. All would eventually play essential roles in shaping Syria's future, though not as members of the SSNP. The party's presence in South Lebanon and Palestine, where its activities were limited to Tyre and Haifa, respectively, was not as strong.[68] The party's following among Lebanese and Syrian diaspora communities abroad had also grown over the preceding year, and the party established four official branches, including in Mexico, the Gold Coast (West Africa, today Ghana), and Cairo.[69]

The party's growth abroad led to the establishing of an executive bureau, the Office of Cross-Border Affairs (*Maktab ʿAbr al-Ḥudūd*), responsible for handling party branches and members' affairs in the *mahjar*. However, it was also a practical measure taken to resolve an internal problem by distancing the party from the activities of Fuʾad Mufarrej, one of the SSNP's founding members, then in exile in America. Mufarrej had undertaken activities in the party's name that SSNP's leaders considered suspect and, to avoid confusion and controversy, declared any activities he undertook while abroad were personal and not in the

66 Jurayj, *Min al-Juʿbat, Vol. 3*, pp. 121–122.
67 "Marsūm 2: Muʾassasa al-Munafidhiyyāt" and "Marsūm 3: Muʾassasa al-Mudīriyyāt," in Saʿadeh, *al-Aʿmāl al-Kāmila, Vol. 2*, pp. 82–86.
68 Jurayj, *Min al-Juʿbat, Vol. 2*, pp. 177–222.
69 Jurayj, *Min al-Juʿbat, Vol. 2*, pp. 223–226.

name of the party.[70] In time, the office of Cross-Border Affairs would come to play a vital role in maintaining ties between the homeland and the diaspora as the party expanded its presence overseas. Yet, the party's increasingly public posture was setting it on a collision course with Lebanese authorities, which would soon come to a breaking point in the early spring of 1937.

On 21 February 1937, several hundred SSNP members[71] from Beirut and its surrounding environs gathered in Bikfaya, a small mountain town in Metn with beautiful views of the Mediterranean Sea. In the town's main square in front of the Hotel Continental, they gathered to hear Saʿadeh and others deliver speeches, boldly waving the party's flag and shouting nationalist slogans decrying Lebanese separatism. While assembled, a contingent of lightly-armed Lebanese gendarmes was dispatched by Metn's administrator to break up the gathering – by force if necessary.[72] Refusing an order to disband, SSNP members scuffled with the advancing Lebanese gendarmes before reaching an agreement to disperse peacefully. The deal did not hold, and clashes between SSNP members and the Lebanese gendarmerie ensued in which several party members and gendarmes were injured. The party subsequently transformed the incident into one of the most important days in its history.

Following the incident, Saʿadeh went into hiding in Beirut to plan the party's response to the clash, while the Lebanese government opened an investigation into the incident and began detaining party members. Newspapers like *al-Bashir* urged a harsh official reaction, demanding the Lebanese government defend the country instead of continuing to indulge and be lenient with a party the editors argued acted against Lebanon and its existence.[73] From his Beirut hideout, Saʿadeh traveled to party strongholds and held several secret meetings with

70 "Bayān Ḥaqīqiyya min al-Ḥizb al-Sūrī al-Qawmī," in Saʿadeh, *al-Aʿmāl al-Kāmila, Vol. 2*, p. 104, and Jurayj, *Min al-Juʿbat, Vol. 2*, p. 226.

71 Estimates on the number of participants range from 200 to 400. See Mujais, *Saadeh, Vol. 2*, p. 188, and CADN 2395, Republique Libanaise/Gendarmerie/Inspection/Compagnie du Mont–Liban, Baabda, No. 77/2, "Rapport du Chef de Bataillon Ayrault sur une reunion du parti populaire syrien à Bikfaya," 22 February 1937.

72 *Oriente Moderno*, 17.4, April 1937, p. 177; Qubrusi, *Yatadhakkar, Vol. 1*, p. 191; George ʿAbd al–Masih, *Ayyām Qawmiyya: Min ʿAmāṭūr ilā al-Iskandarūn* (Beirut: al-Rukn li-l-Ṭibāʿa wa-l-Nashr, 2004), pp. 73–75; and Jurayj, *Min al-Juʿbat, Vol. 3*, pp. 159–168. Mujais suggests there were 250 gendarmes present, but a Gendarmerie report states only 25 officers were initially present before an unknown number of reinforcements were dispatched. See Mujais, *Saadeh, Vol. 2*, p. 188, and CADN 2395, Republique Libanaise/Gendarmerie/Inspection/Compagnie du Mont–Liban, Baabda, No. 77/2, "Rapport du Chef de Bataillon Ayrault sur une reunion du parti populaire syrien à Bikfaya," 22 February 1937.

73 *Oriente Moderno*, 17.4, April 1937, p. 177.

party cadres. Nonetheless, for all Saʿadeh's efforts to maintain secrecy and the operational security of the party's plans, the SSNP was so deeply infiltrated by informants that its new plans quickly came to light. Indeed, the Sûreté was aware party leaders had met on 23 February and made plans for an even more massive, better-organized demonstration in the Shouf than had occurred in Bikfaya, urging every precaution be taken to ensure the demonstration's success and suggesting party members come armed.[74]

Marking his birthday in hiding on 1 March, Saʿadeh issued a memorandum in which he defended the party from the charges leveled against it and questioned the legitimacy of the Lebanese government, which he argued was behaving in a tyrannical manner by limiting the civil and political rights of Lebanese. Saʿadeh declared Lebanon to be a "fundamentally corrupt entity" if it did not exist for the benefit of all Lebanese citizens, including those who espoused differing views. Decrying the unjust persecution of Syrian nationalists whose only crime was being concerned for the nation's future, Saʿadeh argued that the party did not aim to destroy Lebanon but eliminate the conditions of sectarianism, traditionalism, and colonial rule that led to its establishment as a nation in the first place.[75] The memorandum was published a week later on 9 March in the Damascene daily *al-Ayyam*, and party members, some of whom were subsequently arrested, distributed the statements throughout Lebanon.[76]

The *bayān* provoked an immediate controversy, and Lebanese authorities looked to arrest Saʿadeh once again. On the day it was published, Saʿadeh, together with ʿAbd al-Masih and Widad Nassif, attempted to leave Lebanon unnoticed following a meeting in Aley. En route to Damascus, they were forced to turn back at a gendarmerie checkpoint at Chtaura in the Bekaa. As they made their way back to Beirut, they encountered another checkpoint. Saʿadeh and ʿAbd al-Masih abandoned the vehicle, evading detention, but Nassif was arrested. Hours later, however, Saʿadeh voluntarily handed himself over to the police in exchange for her release.[77] The Lebanese authorities promptly ordered the

---

74 CADN 2395, Sûreté Générale, Beyrouth, Information No. 1006, "Surete Beyrouth: Activite du PPS," N.D.

75 "Bayān al-Ḥizb al-Sūrī al-Qawmī ilā al-Raʾy al-ʿĀm wa-l-Tārīkh," in Saʿadeh, *al-Aʿmāl al-Kāmila, Vol. 2*, pp. 105 – 109.

76 CADN 2395, Sûreté Générale, Beyrouth, Information No. 1314, "A/S: tracts du P.P.S.," 11 March 1937, and CADN 2395, Sûreté Générale, Beyrouth, Information No. 1311, "Surete Tripoli, 10 – 3 – 37: Parti Populaire Syrien," 11 March 1937.

77 On Saʿadeh's arrest see CADN 2395, Gendarmerie Libanaise, Beyrouth, Inspection No. 9I/C.G., "Renseignements: Parti Populaire Syrien," 9 March 1937, and Jurayj, *Min al-Juʿbat, Vol. 3*, pp. 185 – 189.

SSNP disbanded and placed Sa'adeh on trial; Sa'adeh pleaded not guilty to the charges.[78] Some in Lebanon and Syria condemned Sa'adeh's arrest and the Lebanese government's crackdown on the party, but some suffered retribution for defending the party: Syrian authorities suspended the Damascus newspaper *al-Jazira* for its pro-SSNP editorials.[79]

Arrests of SSNP members continued through April and early May. The party decried the persecution it was enduring, which, it argued, was the result of the Lebanese government's mistaken assessment that the party posed a threat to public order and feared the party might have electoral success in certain areas. The SSNP issued several official statements demanding the Lebanese government end the illegal detention of party members, conclude legal proceedings against the group, and free Sa'adeh. They continued to argue that the party was not the enemy of the country.[80] Eddé and Ahdab bargained with Sa'adeh for his release. They sought his support for their coalition in the upcoming election to overcome the Khuri-led Constitutional Bloc and the opposition, so they offered to release him from prison in exchange for the SSNP's political support. Suggesting such a bargain was difficult to justify given the content of Sa'adeh's 1 March memorandum in which he had decried the "tyranny" of Eddé's government.[81]

Eddé and Ahdab could not easily ally themselves with a man who opposed Lebanese unity and had been charged with provoking political unrest without "absolving" their new ally to a certain extent. It was thus resolved – the two sides having reached an understanding – that the charges would be dismissed on a technicality,[82] and Sa'adeh would clarify his and the party's attitude toward foreign propaganda and influence, French rule, and national unity before the Beirut Magistrate, George Murad. In his discussions with Murad, Sa'adeh dismissed claims of foreign influence and training as mere rumors, argued that the party fought against foreign propaganda, and declared France a friendly power with whom the SSNP advocated strong relations because of France's importance to securing Lebanon's national interests.[83] On 10 May, the Beirut court dismissed charges against Sa'adeh for seditious speech and, following addition-

78 *The Palestine Post*, 10, 21 March 1937.

79 *The Palestine Post*, 10 March 1937, and *Oriente Moderno*, 17.4, April 1937, p. 178.

80 *Oriente Moderno*, 17.4, April 1937, p. 178, and *Oriente Moderno*, 17.5, May 1937, p. 231.

81 "Bayān al-Ḥizb al-Sūrī al-Qawmī ilā al-Ra'y al-'Ām wa-l-Tārīkh," in Sa'adeh, *al-A'māl al-Kāmila, Vol. 2*, pp. 105–109.

82 Jurayj, *Min al-Ju'bat, Vol. 3*, p. 222, and Qubrusi, *Yatadhakkar, Vol. 1*, p. 190.

83 "Au Juge d'Instruction Mourad" and "Ilā al-Qāḍī al-Taḥqīq Murād," in Sa'adeh, *al-A'māl al-Kāmila, Vol. 9*, pp. 25–28.

al questioning three days later, Saʿadeh and dozens of other party members were released from Baabda prison.[84]

3.2 From Détente to Exile

The agreement between Eddé and Saʿadeh inaugurated a period of rapprochement between the party and the Lebanese government that, while tenuous and exceedingly vulnerable to collapse, would last until early the following year and allow the party to strengthen its ranks relatively free from harassment. After his release, Saʿadeh praised the Lebanese judiciary for fulfilling its duty and praised party adherents for their steadfastness. The latter had adhered to the SSNP's principles despite the hardships they had faced and, vindicated by the investigation's conclusion, Saʿadeh urged them to continue their work on behalf of the Syrian nation and its betterment.[85] Saʿadeh held additional meetings with Eddé and Ahdab to assuage their concerns regarding his commitment to the understanding they had reached. At Ahdab's request, Saʿadeh met with High Commissioner de Martel's general secretary on 24 May for discussions regarding the party, its ideology, and its political positions to ease any French misgivings regarding the arrangement and lessen tensions between the party and Mandate authorities.[86] Despite the appearance of mutual benefit, Saʿadeh's bargain with Eddé and Ahdab did have a cost beyond what the agreement demanded.

After months of deliberation, Salah Labaki resigned his membership from the SSNP in June 1937.[87] Labaki had grown increasingly frustrated with Saʿadeh and the decisions he had taken. Foremost among these was Saʿadeh's agreement with Eddé, which Labaki considered a mistake. Instead of aligning the party with the political figure responsible for the party's persecution, Labaki had urged Saʿadeh to find common ground with the Khuri-led opposition. Further angering Labaki was his belief that Saʿadeh had gone back on his word regarding the party's participation in the upcoming parliamentary elections. According to Labaki, Saʿadeh had stated the party would participate in the elections and promised

84 *Oriente Moderno*, 17.6, June 1937, p. 290.
85 "Ḥadīth al-Zaʿīm ilā Jarīda al-Nahār," in Saʿadeh, *al-Aʿmāl al-Kāmila, Vol. 2*, p. 111, and "Kalimat al-Zaʿīm ithra Khurujihu min Sijn al-Raml li-l-Mara al-Thālatha," in Saʿadeh, *al-Aʿmāl al-Kāmila, Vol. 2*, p. 110.
86 For the secretary's summary and analysis of his meeting with Saʿadeh, see Jurayj, *Min al-Juʿbat, Vol. 3*, pp. 706–709. His dispatch to Ministry of Foreign Affairs also included Saʿadeh's letter to Judge Murad.
87 *Oriente Moderno*, 17.8, August 1937, p. 374.

Labaki that he would be one of the party's candidates. But Saʿadeh later decided the party would not participate, negating Labaki's potential electoral bid. For Labaki, the decision reflected what he and others had begun to consider Saʿadeh's growing authoritarian leadership tendencies, which had already severely curtailed the party leadership's influence, effectively reducing them to rubber stamps for his decisions and to serving a merely ceremonial function in contravention of the party's constitution.[88] Labaki's resignation deprived the party of a key leader who had helped shoulder the burden of guiding the party as its president while Saʿadeh was in prison and who, since he hailed from a respected and notable Maronite family, served as a bridge between the radical political movement and the Lebanese political establishment.[89]

Despite the internal debate, the party's attention remained focused on countering Greater Syria's territorial division, particularly Palestine and Alexandretta. The publication of the Peel Commission report on 7 July 1937 was the culmination of a British investigation into the causes of the unrest and general strike that arose the preceding year in Mandate Palestine. Despite its firm ideological conviction that Palestine was an integral part of Greater Syria and its genuine commitment to the Palestinian issue, the SSNP had given only its discreet support for the Arab revolt there. Its hesitant backing for the uprising owed mostly to the political strain it was under in Lebanon and to Saʿadeh's disdain for those leading the revolt, which he considered a disorganized and ineffective uprising. Headed by Lord William Peel, the British Royal Commission, as it was officially known, recommended ending the Mandate and partitioning the territory to ease tensions between Arabs and Jews. The SSNP, which submitted an official memorandum to the Commission in January recommending Palestine's reunification with Syria, rejected the findings entirely.[90] The party argued the partition plan

---

88 On the affair and Labaki's letter of resignation, see Jurayj, *Min al-Juʿbat, Vol. 3*, pp. 271–276.
89 Shortly after Labaki resigned his membership, he published his first notable collection of poems in a publication titled *Urjūḥat al-Qamar* (The Moon's Cradle). In time, he would come to embrace Lebanese nationalist convictions and his writings – poetry and prose – would express themes related to Phoenician mythology and the land of Mount Lebanon, rooting his conception of Lebanon's national identity in a pre-Islamic and pre-Arab past. Ironically, Labaki would ultimately become a member of Eddé's National Bloc, with whom Saʿadeh's alliance had been a source of frustration that contributed to Labaki's decision to leave the SSNP. As will be seen, Labaki's change of heart did not entirely sour his views on the party: in 1955, following Adnan Malki's assassination, Labaki would come to the defense of Saʿadeh's widow and party leader ʿIsam al-Mahayri, urging the Syrian regime to cease their persecution of them and the party. See Franck Salameh, *Language, Memory, and Identity in the Middle East: The Case for Lebanon* (Lanham: Lexington Books, 2010), pp. 134–135.
90 *The Palestine Post*, 21 January 1937.

only benefited the Jewish community to the Arab populace's detriment, characterized as Syrians residing in southern Syria. The memorandum further denied any Jewish historical rights in Palestine and rejected the legal legitimacy of Jewish claims to Palestine grounded in religious doctrine and the Balfour Declaration.[91] Despite its steadfast defense of the Palestinian cause, the party, particularly Saʿadeh, remained frustrated – and increasingly so – with the Palestinian leadership, particularly the Mufti Hajj Amin al-Husseini, and the reactive, disorganized, incoherent, and ineffective strategy and rebellious campaign being waged against what he considered an organized and cohesive Zionist movement.[92]

Regarding Alexandretta's independence, the SSNP urged the National Bloc and the Syrian government to press for Syrian sovereignty over the district while also working to mobilize party members for a campaign to defend Syria's northern borderlands.[93] Relations between the National Bloc and the SSNP had been strained for much of the preceding year. This was due in no small part to the National Bloc's efforts to undermine the SSNP's by portraying the party as a sectarian movement, thwarting its recruitment efforts, encouraging members – Sunni members in Hama and Homs, for example – to abandon the party and to promote allegations of the party's collaboration with an unnamed foreign power.[94] The SSNP had fueled the dispute, criticizing the National Bloc's inaction on Alexandretta and its accommodationist policies vis-à-vis the Mandate and portraying the Bloc as a party of the traditional elite and reactionaries who were responsible for selling Syria's sovereignty and independence to foreign rulers.[95] In an aggressive step, the SSNP, together with the Syrian-Lebanese Communist Party, worked to destroy confidence in the Bloc-led government and French authorities by organizing demonstrations and encouraging a general atmosphere of lawlessness in protest to the rising prices of flour and bread. Their efforts came to naught as the government quickly alleviated the crisis by suppressing public demonstrations and importing a large quantity of duty-free flour and targeting its distribution in lower-income areas.[96] SSNP members

91 "Mudhakkirat al-Ḥizb al-Sūrī al-Qawmī al-Ijtimāʿī ilā al-ʿUṣbat al-Umamiyya wa al-Umam al-Mutamaddina," in Saʿadeh, *al-Aʿmāl al-Kāmila, Vol. 2*, pp. 133–137.
92 "Thawrat Filasṭīn," in Saʿadeh, *al-Aʿmāl al-Kāmila, Vol. 2*, pp. 187–188.
93 *The Palestine Post*, 19 July 1937.
94 Mujais, *Saadeh, Vol. 2*, p. 236, and Qubrusi, *Yatadhakkar, Vol. 1*, pp. 194–195.
95 See, for example "Shaq al-Ṭarīq li-Taḥyā Sūriyya," in Saʿadeh, *al-Aʿmāl al-Kāmila, Vol. 2*, pp. 124–132.
96 *The Palestine Post*, 1 August 1937.

who had publicly demonstrated were arrested but quickly released.[97] Despite this, Saʿadeh sought to forge a mutually beneficial relationship between the party and the Bloc to advance the national interest, even holding several meetings with Jamil Mardam to promote cooperation in the summer and early fall of 1937, but to no avail.[98]

As the October 1937 parliamentary elections in Lebanon neared, the party's tenuous arrangement with Eddé appeared on the verge of collapse. In September, Lebanese police had raided a secret party meeting held in a private home in Beirut's Achrafieh neighborhood, arresting two-hundred people and seizing light weapons and documents. In an official statement, the party leadership declared that the meeting had taken place without its approval. All but eleven were quickly released, and those who remained in custody were accused of seditious speech.[99] The incident, as well as the government's increasing pressure on the SSNP to publicly support government electoral lists or suffer the consequences, confirmed to the party that the government had done little to curb its hostility toward it as stipulated by their May agreement. However, the SSNP had not necessarily upheld its side of the agreement either. The party had refrained from giving its outspoken backing to the government and, while welcoming the opportunity the coming elections presented for breaking the political paralysis gripping Lebanon, had also criticized the government, albeit mildly, as weak and ineffective.

Nevertheless, Saʿadeh demanded the government drop all outstanding charges against party members, cease harassing the party, and grant the party a license to publish a newspaper before publicly supporting Eddé and the government. Eddé, then under significant opposition pressure from the now French-supported Khuri and his Constitutional Bloc, acceded to Saʿadeh's demands. Saʿadeh, in turn, gave his public endorsement of the government's candidates. In the end, a French-brokered agreement between Eddé and Khuri divided the Chamber of Deputies between the government and the Constitutional Bloc, allotting 37 seats to the former and 26 seats to the latter, rendering the elections a mere formality with a foregone conclusion and the SSNP's role insignificant.[100]

Of far greater consequence than the election results was the party's success in obtaining a license to publish a newspaper. The newspaper provided the party with a platform to promulgate its agenda for the first time, and its talented editorial committee was comprised of the SSNP's most esteemed intellectuals, in-

---

97 *Oriente Moderno*, 17.9, September 1937, p. 443.
98 Mujais, *Saadeh, Vol. 2*, pp. 237–238.
99 *Oriente Moderno*, 17.10, October 1937, p. 510.
100 Zamir, *Lebanon's Quest*, pp. 228–231, and Mujais, *Saadeh, Vol. 2*, p. 229.

cluding Fu'ad Suleiman and Yusuf al-Khal.[101] Both men would contribute numerous articles to *al-Nahda* while it was in print. The first edition of the daily was published 14 October 1937, wherein the paper's editors promised its readers that it was not just another paper but one that aimed to advance the nation's material and spiritual well-being and renaissance.[102] The party did not hesitate to embrace the opportunity to advance its agenda, as *al-Nahda* urged the government to work with the SSNP to implement the party's reform program to promote Lebanon's development.[103] The paper also pressed the party's positions on Alexandretta and Palestine, blasting both the Syrian government and Palestinian leadership's policies.[104] Further, the newspaper sustained its criticism of Syria and Lebanon's treaties with France and the National Bloc policies in Syria.[105]

The arrangement with Eddé also enabled the party to weather the political storm brought about by the Lebanese government's dissolution of all paramilitary movements several weeks after the elections and emerge relatively unscathed as *al-Nahda* continued publication and party activities proceeded unimpeded. Based on the recommendation of the Sûreté Générale, the Lebanese nationalist Kata'ib and White Shirts (*Qumṣān al-Bayḍā'*) movements, and the Arab nationalist Najjadeh, were ordered to disband to maintain public order and avoid confessional conflicts, both of which threatened national unity.[106] The order infuriated the groups, their members taking to the streets in protest, and raised the ire of the Maronite religious establishment and the groups' supporters in the parlia-

101 The son of a Protestant pastor, al-Khal was born in a small village in Syria's Homs Governate. He spent his early childhood in the town of Mhardeh in Syria's Hama Governorate, where his father oversaw a local congregation, before moving with his family to Tripoli in 1928. He joined the party in the summer of 1934 shortly after he had graduated high school and begun working for several local Tripoli-based newspapers as a writer. He would go on to have a prolific career as a poet, helping found the influential *Shi'r* poetry magazine in the late 1950s.

102 *Al-Nahda*, 14 October 1937. For detailed studies on *al-Nahda* and its content see Jihad al-'Aql, *Ṣiḥāfat al-Ḥaraka al-Qawmiyya al-Ijtimā'iyya fī-l-Waṭan wa-l-Mahjar, 1933–1949, Vol. 1* (Beirut: al-Furāt, 2004), pp. 117–273, and Jihad al-'Aql, *al-Iltizām fī Jarīdatay 'al-Naḥḍa' wa 'Sūriyā al-Jadīda'* (Beirut: al-Furāt, 2002), pp. 15–60.

103 "Mawqif al-Ḥizb al-Sūrī al-Qawmī," in Sa'adeh, *al-A'māl al-Kāmila, Vol. 2*, pp. 197–199.

104 "Liwā' al-Iskandirūn," in Sa'adeh, *al-A'māl al-Kāmila, Vol. 2*, pp. 208–210, and "Thawrat Filasṭīn," in Sa'adeh, *al-A'māl al-Kāmila, Vol. 2*, pp. 133–137.

105 "al-Ma'āhada al-Sūriyya–al-Faransiyya," in Sa'adeh, *al-A'māl al-Kāmila, Vol. 2*, pp. 245–246; "al-Ma'āhadatān al-Sūriyya al-Faransiyya – al-Lubnāniyya al-Faransiyya," in Sa'adeh, *al-A'māl al-Kāmila, Vol. 2*, pp. 185–186; "Mushākil Dawla al-Shām – al-Ḥizbiyya qabl al-Qawmiyya," in Sa'adeh, *al-A'māl al-Kāmila, Vol. 2*, pp. 162–163; and, "Siyāsa al-Ḥukūma al-Kutlawiyya," in Sa'adeh, *al-A'māl al-Kāmila, Vol. 2*, pp. 172–173.

106 Zamir, *Lebanon's Quest*, pp. 233–235.

ment, who decried the persecution of "young Lebanese patriots."[107] At least one demonstration by the Kata'ib, held on the anniversary of its founding on 21 November, devolved into violence and required the intervention of security forces, who arrested one hundred demonstrators.[108]

The SSNP's immediate response to the 21 November incidents, echoing that of the previous year, came several days later in an interview with Saʿadeh published in *al-Nahda.* While Saʿadeh wished a speedy recovery to those injured, including Kata'ib leader Pierre Gemayel, he bemoaned the violence and the rise of sectarian parties seeking only to keep the nation fragmented in chaos through their embrace of religious fanaticism. In an appeal to his Syrian nationalist followers, Saʿadeh urged them to be patient and not become enmeshed in the sectarian fighting. The formation of these sectarian groups, he argued, was done in reaction to the SSNP. They sought only to frustrate the party's aim to eliminate sectarianism and unite a religiously fragmented nation behind the doctrine of Syrian nationalism (*huwa izāla al-madhhabiyyāt wa-l-naʿarāt al-dīniyya wa tawḥīd al-umma al-mujazzā warāʾa al-adyān fī aqīda wāḥida hiyya al-aqīda al-qawmiyya*).[109] Over the following weeks, Saʿadeh detailed the party's position in a series of articles that analyzed the recently banned movements and the public and parliamentary debate over the government's decision and defended the party from several political attacks from parliamentarians and Maronite religious leaders.[110]

In a two-part article, Saʿadeh provided his readers with a concise analysis of the Najjadeh, Kata'ib, and White Shirts, detailing each's establishment, aims, and connections to members of parliament (MPs) and the Maronite and Sunni religious establishments. Saʿadeh noted that MP Muhi al-Din al-Nasuli, who was calling on the government to establish a national scout movement, had been a key leader of the Muslim Scouts (*al-Kashshāf al-Muslim*) and had helped transform it into a sectarian youth movement, the Najjadeh, to support his political objectives. Regarding the White Shirts, the youth movement of the Lebanese Union Party (LUP, *al-Waḥda al-Lubnāniyya*) whose founding had been endorsed

---

107 Zamir, *Lebanon's Quest*, p. 235; Mujais, *Saadeh, Vol. 2*, pp. 232–234; and Jurayj, *Min al-Juʿbat, Vol. 4*, pp. 21–27.

108 CADN 477, Cabinet Militaire, Beyrouth, "Bulletin d'Information: Période du 15 au 21 Novembre 1937," 29 November 1937; CADN 477, Cabinet Politique 1100, Beyrouth, "Revue de la Presse Libanaise et Syrienne," 24 November 1937; and CADN 477, Cabinet Politique 1152, HC to MAE, "La dissolution des associations paramilitaires et la question des Balillas," 7 December 1937.

109 "Nidāʾ al-Zaʿīm ilā al-Qawmiyyīn," in Saʿadeh, *al-Aʿmāl al-Kāmila, Vol. 2*, pp. 279–281.

110 Ibrahim, *Anṭūn Saʿādah wa-l-Nidhām al-Lubnanī*, pp. 338–341.

by Eddé,[111] Saʿadeh argued that MP Tawfiq ʿAwad had stated they had only been founded to confront the SSNP and promote a thinly-veiled, narrow sectarian Maronite political agenda. Likewise, Saʿadeh argued the Kataʾib was formed solely to promote Maronite sectarian interests but frequently clashed with the LUP, reflecting and perpetuating the division and rivalry between their respective patrons in the Maronite religious establishment and supporters in the broader Maronite community.[112]

Regarding the parliamentary and public debates on the law, Saʿadeh criticized those who defended the now-dissolved organizations and warned that the real problem lay not with their dissolution but their formation, as they had done nothing but encourage religious fanaticism and sectarian hatred.[113] He also defended the party against calls for the government to resume its campaign of repression against the SSNP instead of persecuting "Lebanese organizations" by some parliament members, including his former lawyer Hamid Frangieh, and the Maronite Patriarch, Antun Butrus Arida. Saʿadeh decried what he characterized as Frangieh's disingenuous condemnation of the party he had once defended and Frangieh's attempt to depict the SSNP as subservient "foreign wills" (*irādāt ajnabiyya*). At the same time, he openly praised France's role in "preserving Lebanon."[114] Like Frangieh, Patriarch Arida, in a sermon he gave in early December, lamented that the Lebanese government had not done enough to suppress the Syrian-Lebanese Communist Party and the SSNP. According to Arida, both were working to undermine Lebanese independence and propagate "evil principles" that threatened religion, the nation, and general morality among the Lebanese youth with foreign support. Patriarch Arida's effort to paint the SSNP as the enemy of God and Lebanon was not new, as a Maronite priest had authored a pamphlet with his blessing the previous year that essentially declared that embracing the SSNP's nationalist doctrine was tantamount to the betrayal of the Maronite Church and blasphemy against God.[115] Saʿadeh responded by reiterating his and the party's conviction that religious leaders such as Arida should not meddle in state affairs as their interference only hindered the work of

---

111 Zamir, *Lebanon's Quest*, p. 233.

112 "ʿArḍ Sarīʿ li-l-Aḥzāb al-Siyāsiyya al-Munḥalla fī al-Jumhūriyyaā al-Lubnāniyya (1 and 2)," in Saʿadeh, *al-Aʿmāl al-Kāmila, Vol. 2*, pp. 322–330.

113 "Qaḍiyya al-Aḥzāb al-Babghāʾiyya fī al-Majlis (1–11)," in Saʿadeh, *al-Aʿmāl al-Kāmila, Vol. 2*, pp. 284–321.

114 Zamir, *Lebanon's Quest*, pp. 303–306.

115 For a reproduction of the pamphlet and an analysis of the relationship between the Maronite Church and the SSNP, see Salim Mujais, *Anṭūn Saʿādah wa-l-Iklīrūs al-Mārūnī* (Beirut: 1993). Also see Qubrusi, *Yatadhakkar, Vol. 1*, pp. 205–207.

qualified individuals and perpetuated social and political backwardness, national disunity, and inequality.[116] Ignoring their appeals, while still monitoring and collecting intelligence through its network of informants, the government refrained from obstructing the SSNP's activities, allowing it to conduct its affairs freely and strengthen and enlarge its ranks.

Advancing its aims for Syria's national revival, party branches throughout Lebanon and Syria held regular meetings to conduct party business and indoctrinate members in its ideology and Syria's cultural and social history. Branches also disseminated party propaganda and recruited new members to its ranks, mainly targeting secondary and university students in Beirut and its surrounding environs. The party consolidated its presence in Lebanon's central and northern districts and Syria's coastal regions while also successfully expanding its presence and activities in south Lebanon and further afar in Iraq, Mexico, and the Gold Coast.[117] The party's presence in Iraq, Mexico, and the Gold Coast, as in other locales outside Lebanon and Syria, was established by party members – businessmen, teachers, physicians – who had emigrated from Lebanon and Syria to work abroad in their respective fields and trades.[118] Despite these gains, the state of the party's finances, which were limited and dependent upon membership dues, remained a constraint on the party's plans to advance its agenda. Its financial limitations notwithstanding, the party prioritized arming and training its members and increased its expenditures to establish a provisional army commanded by a well-trained officer corps.[119]

Due in part to the dismal state of its financial affairs, as well as out of a motivation to deepen its ties to and grow its following among the Lebanese-Syrian mahjar, Saʿadeh published a message to émigrés describing the current state of national affairs and inviting them to participate in the work of national revival. In the article, Saʿadeh repeated his assessment that the policies of so-called "nationalist" parties, like the National Bloc, only advanced the traditional elite's interests and perpetuated religious leaders' interference in social and political affairs, and failed to advance national unity. In contrast, the SSNP promoted national unity and social, political, and economic principles that would transform Syria into a living nation. The differences between these two competing nationalist visions could not be reconciled and, according to Saʿadeh, "the fate of the nation and the homeland is dependent upon the outcome of this violent in-

116 "al-Radd ʿalā Khitāb al-Baṭriyark al-Mārūnī," in Saʿadeh, *al-Aʿmāl al-Kāmila, Vol. 2*, pp. 339–361.
117 Jurayj, *Min al-Juʿbat, Vol. 4*, pp. 155–202, 311–328.
118 Jurayj, *Min al-Juʿbat, Vol. 4*, pp. 202.
119 "Abṭāl wa Abṭāl," in Saʿadeh, *al-Aʿmāl al-Kāmila, Vol. 4*, p. 55.

ternal war" (*maṣīr al-umma wa-l-waṭan muʿallaq ʿalā natīja hadhihī al-ḥarb al-dākhiliyya al-ʿanīfa*). He called on Syrians in the diaspora to participate in this struggle between light and darkness, life and tradition, renaissance and indolence, and order and chaos, and to not ignore the struggle in the homeland. Indeed, they should strengthen their links to the homeland and help, including with their finances, to advance the work of national revival.[120]

Evermore emboldened and outspoken, the SSNP prepared to mark Saʿadeh's birthday with several large gatherings in Syria and Lebanon. Celebrations the previous two years had been more subdued, taking place while Saʿadeh was either in hiding or in prison and under threat of severe government repression. This year, however, Saʿadeh was a free man, and the party was on generally amicable terms with the government and Mandate authorities, though this had been tested of late with de Martel's ordering of the suspension of *al-Nahda* for eight days for publishing articles that "endangered international relations."[121] Aware of the party's plans, and concerned that the large gatherings would transform into massive street demonstrations, the Lebanese Interior Minister met with Saʿadeh, who pledged the celebrations would remain small and not incite disorder.[122] In the afternoon of 1 March, Saʿadeh delivered a speech at Thabit's Beirut home as party members gathered in their local branches throughout Lebanon and Syria to read the speech's text, published as a 29-page pamphlet and delivered to party branches beforehand.[123]

In a rousing speech, Saʿadeh asserted that the great trials and tribulations that the SSNP had passed through were "an indication of its unbridled strength, ability to survive, and superiority in the violent conflict between it and the forces working to kill the nation for their own sake." These forces were the proponents of the "Arab cause" and "Lebanese cause," whose embrace of these religiously-inspired national ideas had sowed only intellectual and spiritual confusion, helped divide Greater Syria and undo the unity of its life and interests, leading directly to the current perilous political situation. The establishment of the SSNP, Saʿadeh declared, was a decisive blow against this intellectual and spiritual confusion and those working against the nation's unity. The party had consolidated its institutions, expelled traitors and opportunists from among its ranks, and withstood attempts to curb its activities, all of which fed a growing sense of con-

120 "Nidāʾ Zaʿīm al-Nahḍa al-Qawmiyya ilā al-Sūriyyīn ʿabr al-Ḥudūd," in Saʿadeh, *al-Aʿmāl al-Kāmila, Vol. 2*, pp. 362–365.

121 Al-ʿAql, *Ṣiḥāfat, Vol. 1*, pp. 138–142, and "Qarār 62 – bi-Taʿaṭīl Jarīda al-Nahḍa fī Bayrūt," in Saʿadeh, *al-Aʿmāl al-Kāmila, Vol. 3*, pp. 170–171.

122 Mujais, *Saadeh, Vol. 2*, p. 305.

123 Mujais, *Saadeh, Vol. 2*, p. 305.

fidence that it would be victorious in its struggle.[124] Saʿadeh's assessment of the state and strength of the movement was, perhaps, a bit overgenerous, particularly considering the party remained deeply infiltrated by informants. Nor did the speech's provocative content advance the spirit of détente between the party and the Lebanese government or please party opponents in Lebanon and Syria.

In the weeks that followed, the party clashed with the Jesuit establishment in Lebanon and intensified its criticism of the National Bloc in Syria. Editorials in *al-Nahda* accused the Jesuits of fomenting a propaganda campaign against the SSNP, spreading false rumors of internal division in articles published in *al-Bayraq*, *Le Jour*, and *al-Bashir*. Furthermore, *al-Nahda* editorials chided the Jesuits' reactionary position calling on the Lebanese government to confront the SSNP, arguing that the call for the government to suppress the freedom of political expression by Lebanese would establish a dangerous precedent and denouncing the Jesuits as a foreign institution opposed to Syrian nationalism and the nationalist renaissance.[125] At the same time, tensions continued to mount between the SSNP and the National Bloc as it worked to suppress SSNP activities in Syria. In response, the SSNP harshly criticized the Bloc's policies and actions in the pages of *al-Nahda*, blaming the Bloc for losing Alexandretta, endangering Syria's sovereignty over the northern Jazira region, and stifling criticism through oppressive policies, including arresting opposition members.[126]

The party's determined challenge and outspoken criticism of Lebanon's government and the socio-political situation only pushed its delicate arrangement with Lebanon's rulers to the breaking point. Its activities more heavily scrutinized, and with pressure against the party mounting, the SSNP's Higher Council urged Saʿadeh to leave Lebanon for a brief period until the authorities' renewed campaign against the party had subsided.[127] Saʿadeh, who had already been considering a trip abroad to raise awareness of the national cause and build the party in the *mahjar* by recruiting new members and securing financial support for its activities in the homeland, concurred with their assessment and left Leb-

124 "Khiṭāb al-Zaʿīm fī Awal Māris," in Saʿadeh, *al-Aʿmāl al-Kāmila, Vol. 3*, pp. 175–196.

125 "Fashal al-Maḥāwalāt al-Rajʿiyya li-Qatl al-Rūḥiyya al-Qawmiyya," in Saʿadeh, *al-Aʿmāl al-Kāmila, Vol. 3*, pp. 197–199, and "al-Shaʿb al-Lubnānī wa Jamʿiyya al-Jazwīt," in Saʿadeh, *al-Aʿmāl al-Kāmila, Vol. 3*, pp. 225–227.

126 *Oriente Moderno*, 18.3, March 1938, p. 118, *Oriente Moderno*, 18.4, April 1938, p. 159; *Oriente Moderno*, 18.6, June 1938, pp. 294–296; Jurayj, *Min al-Juʿbat, Vol. 4*, pp. 171–185; "Nidāʾ Zaʿīm," in Saʿadeh, *al-Aʿmāl al-Kāmila, Vol. 2*, p. 363; "Iʿtiqālāt Dimashq," in Saʿadeh, *al-Aʿmāl al-Kāmila, Vol. 3*, pp. 172–174; "al-Siyāsa al-Sirriyya," in Saʿadeh, *al-Aʿmāl al-Kāmila, Vol. 3*, pp. 251–252; and "Siyāsa al-Baṭsh fī al-Shām," in Saʿadeh, *al-Aʿmāl al-Kāmila, Vol. 3*, pp. 217–219.

127 Beshara, *Syrian Nationalism*, pp. 77–78.

anon on 11 June.[128] At the time of his departure, he could not have imagined that the journey he was embarking upon would develop into nearly a decade of exile.

128 Mujais, *Saadeh, Vol. 2*, pp. 311–312, and Kader, *SSNP*, p. 93.

Part Two: **The War Years**

4 Those Who Have Departed and Those Who Have Remained

The letter from Bashir Fakhuri's family implored French authorities to release the young man arrested for his alleged membership in the SSNP. The letter noted that Fakhuri, who recently completed his pharmacy studies in Geneva, had been duped into accepting the SSNP's doctrine out of a mistaken belief that doing so would be in his country's service. According to his family, he realized his error in judgment was due to "youthful enthusiasm," and he had abandoned the party. The remainder of their letter emphasized the family's long-standing pro-French views in the hopes that their supplications would lead to his release; their petition was to no avail.[1] The Fakhuri family's letter would not be the only one sent by families of SSNP activists requesting their relatives' release.[2] Indeed, hundreds of SSNP members would be arrested and held without trial in internment camps throughout Lebanon during World War II. The common accusations included threatening the security of the state and distributing pro-German and pro-Italian propaganda.[3]

---

1 On the Fakhuri affair, see CADN 2395, Secretariat d'Etat, No. 671/S, "Requête presentée par la famille Fakhoury a/s affaire Béchir Fakhoury," 4 October 1939, and CADN 2395, Guillotin (Justice Militaire) a Commandant la Gendarmerie Libaniase, "Note au sujet du nomme Bechir Fakhoury," 11 October 1939.

2 See, for example, a letter from the Bayan family of Tripoli: CADN 2395, Tripoli, No. 3220, "a le General Arlabosse, Delegue du Haut–Commissaire," 24 February 1941.

3 The French detained large numbers not only of SSNP activists, but other "nationalists" – Arab and Lebanese – and held them in internment camps (lit. "concentration camps" (camps de concentration)) and prisons, including Mieh Mieh, al-Raml, and Rashaya. See, for example CADN 2396, Sûreté Générale de Tripoli, No. 1594/C.E., Tripoli, "Suspects à interner," 12 September 1942; CADN 2396, Cabinet Militaire, No. 3,693/CM, Beyrouth, "Note pour Monsieur le Directeur de la Sûreté Générale," 27 July 1942. For allegations of the SSNP threatening the security of the state and its members distributing pro–Axis propaganda see, for example: CADN 2396, Gendarmerie Libanaise, Compagnie de la Bekaa, Section de Chtaura, Poste de Kab Elias, No. 18, Kab Elias, "Rapport du Sergent à cheval Elias Haddad du poste de Kab Elias," 17 January 1942; and CADN 2396, Direction Sûreté Générale aux Armées, Beyrouth, Bulletin d'information spéciale No. 768/C.E., "Sûreté Baalbeck – Activités du P.P.S.," 29 June 1942. Several SSNP leaders recalled their time of imprisonment in the early 1940s in their memoirs. See, for example ʿAbdallah Saʿadeh, *Awrāq Qawmiyya: Mudhakkirāt ʿAbdallah Saʿādah* (Beirut: 1987), p. 31; Masʿad Hajal, *Lam Ubaddil... wa Lan: al-Mujallad al-Awwal* (Beirut: 2018), pp. 60 – 64; ʿAbdallah Qubrusi, *ʿAbd Allah Qubruṣī Yatadhakkar, Vol. 2* (Beirut: Muʾassasat Fikr li-l-Abḥāth wa-l-Nashr, 1982), pp. 70 – 74, 94 – 98; Ibrahim Yammut, *al-Ḥaṣād al-Murr – Qiṣṣat Tafattut Qiyādat Ḥizb wa Tamāsuk ʿAqīda* (Beirut: Dār al-Rukn, 1993), pp. 74 – 117; and Jibran Jurayj, *Haqāʾiq ʿan al-Istiqlāl: Ayyām Rāshayā* (Beirut: Dār Amwāj Lubnān, 2000).

https://doi.org/10.1515/9783110729092-006

Throughout World War II, France's policy in the Levant was characterized by its high degree of continuity as it sought to preserve its "historic" role in the region. France's pre-war policy of containment vis-à-vis nationalist movements in its colonial territories, which had succeeded in curtailing the SSNP's activities and growth, became more interventionist and confrontational with the outbreak of war in Europe. Nationalist movements' pre-war activity, particularly that of movements clamoring for independence and liberation, was tolerated to a certain degree. Now no such tolerance could be extended to these same movements as doing so would, in the French view, undermine its authority and thus damage its war effort. This policy was even maintained by the pro-Axis Vichy regime of Marshal Philippe Pétain and its successor, the Free French government of Charles de Gaulle, both of which refused to cede France's colonial rule over Lebanon and Syria.

Through it all, the SSNP was considered a threat to France's authority in Lebanon and Syria. Though Saʿadeh and the SSNP vigorously protested otherwise, emphasizing the party bore no hostility towards France (or any country for that matter), its raison d'être of promoting national independence and sovereignty was inimical to France's policy and national interest. While the confrontation with France would take a heavy toll on the party, Saʿadeh's absence in de facto exile would also impact the party. Saʿadeh had left Lebanon to establish the party's organization abroad and secure the Syrian-Lebanese diaspora community's financial and moral support for the SSNP. By 1942, contact between the exiled Saʿadeh and the party virtually ceased and would not be restored until after World War II. This situation left the beleaguered party leadership in Lebanon and Syria to conduct party affairs and determine its policies. Isolation from Saʿadeh would, in the end, result in a striking internal transformation in both the party and its ideology, to which he strongly objected. This chapter and those that follow in Part Two trace these developments, detailing the party's activity in the *mahjar* and Syria and Lebanon until the end of the War in Europe in May 1945.

4.1 Exile

In June 1938, *Le Jour* reported that authorities had revived their investigations into the party and that Saʿadeh was on the run.[4] Indeed, shortly after Saʿadeh

4 *Le Jour*, 17 June 1938; CADN 2396, Services Spéciaux du Levant, Poste de Tripoli, Tripoli, "Renseignements recueillis relatifs au P.P.S. dans le Koura," 5 March 1942.

had left Lebanon, French authorities initiated a widespread campaign of arrests, suspended the publication of the SSNP's newspaper *al-Nahda*, and raided the party's Beirut offices, confiscating files.[5] Having left Lebanon, Saʿadeh made his way first to Transjordan before traveling on to Palestine and Cyprus, where he arrived at the end of June. While in Cyprus, Saʿadeh planned to go onward to the Americas in August. Changing his mind, he went instead to Rome, where he would remain until October.

In Rome, Saʿadeh contacted Italian authorities. The Italian government had no problem with his presence in the country and put the Italian diplomatic courier service at his disposal to communicate securely with the party in Lebanon and Syria. The authorities also offered graduate scholarships for SSNP students to study at Italian universities.[6] Few other details are known regarding the broader extent of his contacts with Italian government officials, the nature of their discussions, and any further understandings reached between them. From Italy, Saʿadeh traveled to Berlin, visiting the party branch established there by students in 1937. In addition to meeting with SSNP members, Saʿadeh also met with German officials on Middle Eastern affairs and lectured on the SSNP's doctrine and aims at Humboldt University.[7] Little is known about the extent of Saʿadeh's contacts with the German government and the nature of any discussions. Regardless, the time Saʿadeh spent in Italy and Germany would bring the party no benefit. Instead, it would prove harmful to the SSNP's interests, as France and the party's opponents in Lebanon and Syria would use it to pillory the party and brand it a threat.

As war loomed in Europe, France implemented new security measures. Surveillance of foreign nationals increased, and French military courts were granted the power to try Lebanese and Syrian citizens accused of security-related offenses.[8] These measures augmented France's ongoing efforts, begun in March 1938, to reinforce its military capabilities in Lebanon in preparation for the outbreak of war. Despite the heightened state of alert, the SSNP's Higher Council proceeded with plans to hold a secret general conference of party leaders to deliberate its activities considering recent developments and Saʿadeh's absence. The meeting, overseen by new Higher Council president Neʿmeh Thabit, was held at the end of

---

5 Jurayj, *Min al-Juʿbat, Vol. 4*, pp. 225, 226, 250 – 262,

6 Mujais, *SSNP*, pp. 150 – 151.

7 Mujais, *SSNP*, p. 152.

8 Zamir, *Lebanon's Quest*, p. 236. Also see "39. German Propaganda in Syria," British Consulate, Damascus, 9 December 1938, MacKereth to FO, in Michael G. Fry and Itamar Rabinovich (eds.), *Despatches from Damascus: Gilbert MacKereth and British Policy in the Levant* (Tel Aviv: Dayan Center, 1985), pp. 199 – 201.

September at the party's Beirut headquarters. Though the leadership had sought to maintain the meeting's secrecy, its date and time were known to Lebanese and French authorities, who ordered the Lebanese police to raid and disperse the gathering. Several party leaders were arrested and detained, and, according to a report in the pro-French *L'Orient*, documents seized in the raid suggested that the SSNP, on Saʿadeh's orders, was preparing to cause trouble for the Mandate in the event of the outbreak of a world war.[9]

Saʿadeh's presence in Italy and Germany only added to suspicions that the party posed a threat to French authority and enabled the party's opponents to brand it as fascist and an ally of the Axis powers. On the former point, the French assessment was correct. Saʿadeh, indeed, sought to pressure France to end its mandate and believed that pursuing a dialogue with Germany and Italy would induce the French to compromise with the party and its demands. Saʿadeh, however, was willing to work with any country that would support Greater Syria's independence and subsequently would make formal overtures also to France, Britain, and Spain. Articles in the Greek Catholic *al-Masa'* and Jesuit *al-Bashir* accused the SSNP of receiving financial and material support from an unnamed foreign country (i.e., Italy or Germany) and sought to stir up trouble in Lebanon and Syria. As had happened before, assailants once again attacked and beat the editor of *al-Masa'*, and police arrested six SSNP members in response, though the party denied any involvement and asserted authorities were unjustly persecuting the party.[10]

By November, Saʿadeh had left Europe for Brazil, first traveling to West Africa and stopping in Dakar, where he met Khalid Adib and Asad al-Ashqar, who oversaw the party's activities there. Though Saʿadeh knew Adib from Beirut, he had never met Ashqar; Saʿadeh knew of him as having funded the publication of his *Nushu al-Umam* and contributed articles to the party's newspaper *al-Nahda*.[11] Ashqar, a Lebanese Maronite, was an influential figure in the diaspora community and had used his position to promulgate the SSNP's ideology to which he was fervently devoted. Adib, on the other hand, had joined the party in its early days in Lebanon and served an essential role in the party's leadership as deputy director of the party's internal affairs. He had recently moved to West Africa, where he had connected with Ashqar. Saʿadeh hoped both men would help him establish and build the party's organization in the Americas and spread its

9 Jurayj, *Min al-Juʿbat, Vol. 4*, pp. 277–288, and *Oriente Moderno*, 18.10, October 1938, p. 550.
10 *The Palestine Post*, 25 October 1938, and *Oriente Moderno*, 18.11, November 1938, p. 606.
11 Jurayj, *Min al-Juʿbat, Vol. 4*, pp. 313–314, and Salim Mujais, *Antoun Saadeh: A Biography – Volume 3: Years of Exile* (Beirut: Kutub, 2018), pp. 20–21.

ideas through the Syrian-Lebanese communities.[12] By the time they had arrived in Brazil at the end of November 1938, the party had established branches in Germany and West Africa, as well as in Martinique, the United States, Cuba, and Mexico. The party's branch in Mexico was its most important overseas branch, and Saʿadeh had made it a priority to visit.[13]

Upon arriving in Brazil, one of the first tasks Saʿadeh set himself to was editing a second, expanded edition of the treatise on the party's principles and objectives with explanations. Among the notable additions and clarifications were two significant points. One was the dismissal of the notion that Syrian unity constituted a step toward a broader goal of Arab unity, as Arab unity would weaken Syria's independence and sovereignty. The second was the unequivocal opposition to Jewish immigration to any part of Natural Syria, and the declaration that Jewish ideals were contrary to Syrian ideals and, therefore, Jews were not part of the Syrian nation nor could they be assimilated to it, unlike other communities like the Armenians, Kurds, and Circassians.[14] Regarding the former, Saʿadeh clarified the SSNP supported cooperative efforts among Arab nations and establishing diplomatic alliances with other Arab nations, falling well short of the notions of unity promulgated by the proponents of Arab nationalism. Regarding the latter, having declared Jews to be "incompatible" with the Syrian nation, Saʿadeh emphasized that "Syrian nationalists must repel with all their power the immigration of these people [to Greater Syria]."[15]

By March 1939, the three had made enough progress in establishing themselves in São Paulo that they were able to launch the party's new weekly newspaper *Suriyya al-Jadida*. The periodical provided the party with an important platform from which it could propagate its ideology, aims, and news of the party's exploits in Syria to the Syrian-Lebanese *mahjar* communities in the Americas. In his early articles, Saʿadeh focused on recent political developments in Syria. Addressing the collapse of the National Bloc, Saʿadeh criticized the Bloc and its many failures, namely its blind pursuit of a treaty with France at any

12 Mujais, *Saadeh, Vol. 3*, p. 21. A French report alleged that it was, in fact, Nazi Germany that had ordered Saʿadeh to establish party branches in the Americas. The allegation was baseless and demonstrably untrue but complemented general efforts by the French to portray Saʿadeh and the SSNP as the lackeys of foreign European powers. CADN 2395, Sûreté Beyrouth, Beyrouth, Information 242, "Antoine Saadé," 11 January 1939.

13 Jurayj, *Min al-Juʿbat, Vol. 4*, pp. 311–328. On the significance of the party's branch in Mexico specifically, see Jurayj, *Min al-Juʿbat, Vol. 4*, pp. 317–328, 418–420, and "Ilā Munafidh 'Āmm Farʿ al-Meksīk," in Saʿadeh, *al-Aʿmāl al-Kāmila, Vol. 9*, pp. 59–60.

14 Mujais, *Saadeh, Vol. 3*, pp. 23–25.

15 Mujais, *Saadeh, Vol. 3*, pp. 25–26.

cost, its capitulations to Turkey regarding the District of Alexandretta, and its divisive domestic policies that had alienated Kurds, ʿAlawis, and Druze.[16] To be sure, the effects of the Bloc's domestic policies were exacerbated by the new high commissioner Gabriel Puaux who, reversing his predecessor de Martel's policy, implemented a "divide and rule" policy that encouraged separatism among Syria's minorities in Jabal Druze, the ʿAlawi region, and the Jazira.[17]

No sooner had *Suriyya al-Jadida* appeared than opposition to its publication and Saʿadeh's political activity started. Within weeks, Brazilian authorities arrested Saʿadeh, Ashqar, and Adib based on allegations they were foreign agents working on behalf of Nazi Germany and Fascist Italy. France requested their extradition, but Brazilian authorities balked, unconvinced of the accusations' veracity after a month-long investigation.[18] After five weeks of detention, the three were released and, per a Brazilian request, left the country for Argentina before their visas expired to avoid dealing with the French extradition request.[19] Just six months after arriving in the country, they hastily departed, leaving their organizational work in disarray. Saʿadeh would come to blame his arrest on his deputies Adib and Ashqar, who, having been informed Brazilian authorities wanted to arrest Saʿadeh, failed to warn him. Moreover, when questioned by Brazilian police at the paper's printing press, they voluntarily led them to where Saʿadeh was staying.[20] Adib and Ashqar's poor judgment led Saʿadeh to assign

---

16 "al-Ḥāla al-Siyāsiyya fī al-Shām," in Saʿadeh, *al-Aʿmāl al-Kāmila, Vol.* 3, pp. 313–318; "Aqalliyāt – Lā Aqalliyāt," in Saʿadeh, *al-Aʿmāl al-Kāmila, Vol.* 3, pp. 320–323; "Fashal al-Muʿāhada wa Tafakkuk al-Wiḥda al-Sūriyya al-Kutlawiyya," in Saʿadeh, *al-Aʿmāl al-Kāmila, Vol.* 3, pp. 329–337; and "Tafakkuk al-Kutla al-Nihāʾī wa Iʿtizāl Mardam," in Saʿadeh, *al-Aʿmāl al-Kāmila, Vol.* 3, pp. 350–353.

17 See "43. Deteriorating Situation in Syria," British Consulate, Damascus, 22 March 1939, MacKereth to Baxter, in Fry and Rabinovich, *Despatches from Damascus*, pp. 207–210, and "44. Deteriorating Situation in Syria," British Consulate, Damascus, 31 March 1939, MacKereth to Baxter, in Fry and Rabinovich, *Despatches from Damascus*, pp. 210–211.

18 While it is unclear who made the accusations to Brazilian authorities that prompted their investigation into the matter, it is clear the French were promulgating this accusation against the party in general. Indeed, a Sûreté report from January 1939 declared that "the Nazis had charged Saʿadeh with establishing SSNP branches in Brazil among the youth of the Syrian–Lebanese colony." CADN 2395, Section de la Sûreté Générale, Beyrouth, Information 242, "Antoine Saade," 11 January 1939.

19 "Ilā Ibrahim Tannous," in Saʿadeh, *al-Aʿmāl al-Kāmila, Vol.* 9, pp. 105–108.

20 Mujais, *Saadeh, Vol. 3*, p. 36, and "Ilā Ibrahim Tannous," in Saʿadeh, *al-Aʿmāl al-Kāmila, Vol.* 9, pp. 296–297.

them to different roles in the party as a reprimand; Ashqar notably replaced Fakhri Maʿaluf as the head of the party's overseas directorate.[21]

Pressure on the party from French and Lebanese authorities intensified after the Fall of 1938, forcing the party to operate in a predominately clandestine manner, severely curtailing its public activity. The SSNP, however, continued to distribute its propaganda to recruit new members, particularly around AUB.[22] SSNP students at AUB were among the most active of the party's branches. Under the leadership of Maʿaluf and Fayez Sayegh, the students' branch had worked throughout the school year to build a student association called the "Syrian Society" based on the model of *al-ʿUrwa al-Wūthqā*, an Arab nationalist society.[23] Meanwhile, party directorates continued to oversee the party's limited clandestine activities, managing internal affairs, financial matters, propaganda distribution, and military training.[24] While the party in the homeland concerned itself with day-to-day concerns, Saʿadeh attempted to articulate the party's political strategy vis-à-vis France and Britain on the one hand and Germany and Italy on the other.

Grounded in the principles of *realpolitik*, Saʿadeh formulated a pragmatic strategy that would govern the party's international relations and advance the cause of Greater Syria's independence. Saʿadeh concluded the most effective way of inducing the French and British to negotiate any change in their policies in Lebanon, Syria, and Palestine would be to approach Germany and Italy and use the threat of aligning and cooperating with France and Britain's rivals to exert pressure. The rub was approaching Germany and Italy in a manner that did not provoke outright opposition or impede reaching an understanding with either the French or British. Indeed, Saʿadeh's primary concern was and would remain to reach an accord with France. However logical and understandable, this approach was significantly flawed as it was grounded in four incorrect assumptions. First, Saʿadeh overestimated the party's strength, influence, and appeal within the Lebanese and Syrian society and politics. Second, he incorrectly believed that the party was able and well-positioned to effect a meaningful

---

21 Ashqar would leave Argentina in July 1939 and make is way back to Beirut, while Adib would remain with Saʿadeh until the following summer in 1940, when Saʿadeh expelled him from the party. "Ilā Munafidh ʿĀmm al-Meksīk," in Saʿadeh, *al-Aʿmāl al-Kāmila, Vol. 9*, pp. 289–290, and "Ṭarad Khālid Adīb min al-Ḥizb al-Sūrī al-Qawmī," in Saʿadeh, *al-Aʿmāl al-Kāmila, Vol. 4*, p. 81.

22 Jurayj, *Min al-Juʿbat, Vol. 4*, pp. 421–423, 425, and CADN 2395, Sûreté Beyrouth, Beyrouth, Information 2124, "Sûreté Beyrouth: a/s. Activité du Parti Populaire Syrien," 24 March 1939.

23 Jurayj, *Min al-Juʿbat, Vol. 4*, pp. 456–457.

24 On the SSNP's activity in Lebanon and Syria during this period, see Jurayj, *Min al-Juʿbat, Vol. 4*, pp. 435–440, 462–476.

change in French policy. Third, he underestimated France's resolve to maintain its colonial system and overestimated France's willingness to reach any understanding that would ultimately erode its authority. Fourth, Saʿadeh failed to understand the counterproductive nature of any move toward Germany and Italy; the party was consistently portrayed as the lackeys of France's enemies, and France had demonstrated it would not tolerate any overtures by local actors to its enemies. Instead, the party would have been better served by initially approaching the British and the Americans. To be sure, the SSNP presented a formidable challenge to French authorities, but it was far from being a broadly supported mass movement or capable of forcing a wholesale transformation in French policy.[25]

However, political developments in the Levant did not provide Saʿadeh the opportunity to blunt his harsh criticism of France and its policies. While maintaining the SSNP sought reconciliation with France, Saʿadeh openly acknowledged the conflict between the two was deeply rooted in almost irreconcilable conflicting interests. In articles published throughout the summer of 1939, Saʿadeh criticized French policies towards the SSNP and detailed the party's struggle against French authorities. He noted French security services had intensified their efforts to suppress the party, tirelessly recruiting more informants inside the party to gather intelligence and raiding party officials' homes, deeming the situation "alarming." At the same time, Saʿadeh dismissed criticism of his visits to Rome and Berlin as mere French propaganda, the aim of which was to justify the party's persecution, and rejected France preconditioning any negotiations on abolishing the party's fifth reform principle and disbanding its militia.[26] Saʿadeh also addressed France's relinquishment of Alexandretta to Turkey, which outraged Syrian nationalists and sparked massive protests and demonstrations. Saʿadeh deemed the loss of Alexandretta an act of aggression against Syria, lamenting Syria's "fractured, paralyzed" state and the National Bloc's

---

25 A French intelligence report from the fall of 1940 estimated the SSNP had 5,000 – 6,000 members in Syria and Lebanon, calling larger estimates of 10,000, 20,000, or even 70,000 adherents to be exaggerated. See CADN 2395, Le Délégué-Adjoint du Haut-Commissaire, Conseiller Administratif du Mont-Liban, Beyrouth, No. 194, "A.S. Parti Populaire Syrien (PPS)," 18 September 1940.

26 See "Dawāʾir al-Amn al-ʿĀmm Tulāḥiq al-Qawmiyyīn," in Saʿadeh, *al-Aʿmāl al-Kāmila, Vol. 3*, p. 369; "Khaṭar al-Iṣṭidām bayn al-Ḥizb al-Sūrī al-Qawmī wa-l-Sulṭa," in Saʿadeh, *al-Aʿmāl al-Kāmila, Vol. 3*, pp. 370 – 372; "Mawqif Zaʿīm al-Ḥizb al-Sūrī al-Qawmī wa Mawqif Faransa," in Saʿadeh, *al-Aʿmāl al-Kāmila, Vol. 3*, pp. 377 – 382; "al-Khaṭar al-Muqbil Masʾūliyya Faransa," in Saʿadeh, *al-Aʿmāl al-Kāmila, Vol. 3*, pp. 393 – 396; and "Niṭāq min al-Ḥadīd wa-l-Nār," in Saʿadeh, *al-Aʿmāl al-Kāmila, Vol. 3*, pp. 408 – 412.

woeful leadership.[27] However, it would not be the SSNP's vocal opposition to French policies that would provoke Mandate authorities' harsh reaction. Instead, it was the outbreak of war in Europe.

4.2 Under Pressure: The Mandate Cracks Down on the SSNP

Following the German invasion of Poland in September 1939, France declared a state of emergency in Lebanon and Syria, tightening its military control over its Mandate territories, censoring the press, and banning public gatherings from listening to German Arabic-language radio broadcasts.[28] Several weeks later, on 21 September, High Commissioner Puaux suspended the Lebanese constitution, dissolved the government, and appointed Emile Eddé as the nominal head of state while the mandate authority assumed full control over governance.[29] The state of emergency profoundly affected the party as "French mandatory authorities claimed that the urgency of the situation necessitated the dissolution of the SSNP along with several other political organizations judged to be favorable to the enemies of France."[30] Asserting the party was associated with France's enemies and deeming it a threat to public order, the SSNP was banned in October 1939, and French authorities implemented various security measures, from mass arrests to spreading disinformation, to undermine the party.

The arrests of SSNP members had begun shortly after Germany's invasion of Poland. Among the first to be detained was George ʿAbd al-Masih, who had in late August, according to a Sûreté report, spoken publicly in Beit Meri in favor of German victory. He also allegedly commented on the presence of some 70 SSNP members in Germany who kept the party apprised of developments in the country and offered advice regarding the party's policy in the event of hostilities between Germany and France. Such statements provoked a mostly negative response from authorities and the populace.[31] The attempts to link the party to Germany did not end there. In early October, the French accused Saʿadeh and another party member, Daoud Mujais, of "directing propaganda via the Arab sec-

27 "al-Muʿāhadatān bayn Faransa wa Turkiyya," in Saʿadeh, *al-Aʿmāl al-Kāmila, Vol. 3*, pp. 397–400.

28 "49. Political Report, Syria, No. 24," British Consulate, Damascus, 29 September 1939, MacKereth to FO, in Fry and Rabinovich, *Despatches from Damascus*, pp. 219–221.

29 Zamir, *Lebanon's Quest*, p. 239, and Ziadeh, *Syria and Lebanon*, p. 62.

30 Beshara, *Lebanon*, p. 35.

31 CADN 2395, Direction de la Sûreté Générale, Beyrouth, Information 6416, "Sûreté Beyrouth: a/s. Activité Pro Allemande," 20 August 1939, and Jurayj, *Min al-Juʿbat, Vol. 4*, p. 519.

tion of Radio Berlin" from Germany, but both were, in fact, thousands of miles away in Argentina and Mexico, respectively.[32] The accusation, which was also repeated by the British (who amusingly referred to Saʿadeh as a "Lebanese Falangist"), was disinformation propagated by the French who were well-aware Saʿadeh was in South America.[33] The French also accused the party of promoting pro-German views in the Shouf, particularly among the Druze populace in Baakline.[34] By the end of October, accusations of SSNP pro-German activity had given way to a widespread detention campaign targeting ranking SSNP leaders in Lebanon and Syria. Those arrested were placed in internment camps without trial on charges of subversive activity and conspiracy against internal security.[35] Thabit, Qubrusi, ʿAbd al-Masih, Adib Qaddura, and Victor Asad were among the first senior party officials to be arrested.[36]

Thabit's arrest had been particularly demoralizing as it was the result of a severe misjudgment. French authorities had sent Thabit a letter inviting him to negotiate an understanding between them and the party. Despite several party leaders warning it was likely a trick to get Thabit to turn himself in, he decided otherwise, believing the invitation to have been extended in good faith. Upon his arrival, he was arrested, proving the others had been correct in their assessment.[37] While Thabit and the others were held in a French military prison in Beirut, other wanted senior officials, including Maʿmum Ayas, Fakhri Maʿaluf, and Jibran Jurayj, were on the run and had, in the meantime, succeeded in evading arrest, seeking refuge in North Lebanon in the remote areas of Koura District, particularly in the environs of the Greek Orthodox village Btaaboura.[38]

---

32 CADN 2395, Haut-Commissariat, Cabinet Militaire, Beyrouth, No. 261-S, "Note relative à l'activité du parti populaire syrien et de lag ligue d'action nationale," 12 October 1939, and Mujais, *SSNP*, p. 158.

33 "49. Political Report, Syria, No. 24," British Consulate, Damascus, 29 September 1939, MacKereth to FO, in Fry and Rabinovich, *Despatches from Damascus*, p. 220, and CADN 2395, Section de la Sûreté Générale, Beyrouth, Information 242, "Antoine Saade," 11 January 1939.

34 CADN 2395, Haut-Commissariat, Cabinet Politique, Beyrouth, Note, "Activite du parti populaire syrien et de la ligue d'action nationale," 14 September 1939, and CADN 2395, Haut-Commissariat, Cabinet Militaire, Beyrouth, No. 261-S, "Note relative à l'activité du parti populaire syrien et de la ligue d'action nationale," 12 October 1939.

35 Jurayj, *Min al-Juʿbat, Vol. 4*, pp. 519–522.

36 CADN 2395, Commandement Supérieur des Troupes du Levant, Etat Major, 1st Bureau, Justice Militaire, No. 9538/JM, "Affaire du P.P.S.," 27 October 1939.

37 "al-Ḥāla al-Siyāsiyya fī al-Waṭan – ʿAwda ilā al-Laʿba al-Qadīma," in Saʿadeh, *al-Aʿmāl al-Kāmila, Vol. 4*, pp. 199–203.

38 Jurayj, *Min al-Juʿbat, Vol. 4*, pp. 524, 536–545, and Jibran Jurayj, *Maʿa Anṭūn Saʿādah, Vol. 3* (Beirut: Ḥuqūq al-Ṭabʿa wa-l-Nashr Maḥfūẓa li-l-Muʾallif, 1979), pp. 30–31.

The party did its best to defend itself from the French campaign, appealing to the public for support. On 8 December, it issued a statement declaring the French had no grounds on which to charge any SSNP members with crimes against the state or put them on trial. Party detainees were praised for being resolute and forthright under the authorities' intense questioning. Though in Argentina, Saʿadeh was well-informed of the party's suppression and defended the SSNP's actions to the diaspora community in the Americas. In *Suriyya al-Jadida*, Saʿadeh praised the party's steadfastness in the face of French security measures, pointing out it had endured a wave of arrests, heavy surveillance, and a sustained disinformation campaign portraying the SSNP as the servants of a foreign state.[39] He also penned a blistering attack against Syrian leaders whom he deemed "French slaves," ridiculing their misguided declarations of support for France and their surrender to a colonial power that had betrayed them. These "charlatans" were not true leaders of the national cause, and he reiterated the party's primary demand: French and British recognition of Syria's right to self-determination and respect for its national sovereignty.[40]

French authorities did not hesitate to extend the reach of their campaign against the party to Argentina. In November 1939, Puaux contacted the French Ambassador in Buenos Aires to obtain information on Saʿadeh's activities there, informing him that Saʿadeh was a subversive leader wanted by the French military, accused of collaborating with enemy powers.[41] Initially, Puaux's request only alerted their French diplomatic counterparts in Buenos Aires regarding Saʿadeh's significance. The practical – and harmful – effect of the alert would manifest itself in the spring of 1940 when Saʿadeh applied to renew his travel documents at the French mission in Buenos Aires. Saʿadeh had intended to travel to Mexico to visit the party's branch there, as it was considered the party's most important center overseas.[42] Aware that Saʿadeh was a wanted man, the French ambassador cabled Beirut "seeking guidance on how to handle the request." In Beirut, French authorities responded that Saʿadeh's travel documents should and would not be renewed, as doing so would have aided and abetted his

39 "Iʿtiqāl Arkān Qawmiyyīn," in Saʿadeh, *al-Aʿmāl al-Kāmila, Vol.* 3, pp. 432–433, and "Jihādān wa Qiyādatān," in Saʿadeh, *al-Aʿmāl al-Kāmila, Vol.* 3, pp. 434–438.

40 "Jihādān wa Qiyādatān," in Saʿadeh, *al-Aʿmāl al-Kāmila, Vol.* 3, pp. 434–438, and "Nos Formula Interesantes Declaraciones Antún Saadeh, el Jefe del Partido Nacionalista Sirio," in Saʿadeh, *al-Aʿmāl al-Kāmila, Vol.* 3, pp. 439–442.

41 Mujais, *Saadeh, Vol. 3*, pp. 59–62.

42 "Ilā al-Amīn 'Asaf Abi Murad," in Saʿadeh, *al-Aʿmāl al-Kāmila, Vol. 9*, p. 223, and Jurayj, *Min al-Juʿbat, Vol. 4*, pp. 600–605.

and the SSNP's subversive efforts to weaken the Mandate's authority.[43] Khalid Adib's passport was also revoked, and Sa'adeh would remain stuck in Argentina for another seven years until the Spring of 1947.

43 "Ilā Ibrahim Tannous," in Sa'adeh, *al-A'māl al-Kāmila*, *Vol.* 9, p. 271, and Mujais, *SSNP*, pp. 158–159.

5 Tightening the Noose: Life Under Vichy

Following France's fall to German forces in May 1940, French forces in Lebanon and Syria pledged their allegiance to the new Nazi-aligned Vichy regime headed by Marshal Philippe Pétain. The SSNP hoped the Vichy regime would be more lenient and accommodating toward the party, but time would prove otherwise. Though France's fall was a critical development in the war in Europe, it was less so in the Levant. French authorities continued to govern the mandate territories in a manner consistent with existing French policy. A French report published in early June expressed hope that the security measures – increased surveillance, increased arrests, and interdicting foreign radio broadcasts – implemented against pro-Axis individuals and nationalist groups, including the SSNP, would weaken the appeal of "hostile propaganda."[1] Over the previous month, the enhanced surveillance of the SSNP had observed notable party activities, both overt and covert, in locales like Broummana, Beit Meri, Ammatour, and Rachaya.[2] French reports also named SSNP adherents or sympathizers who allegedly harbored pro-Nazi views, maintained contacts with local German or Italian consular officials, or had "Nazi tendencies."[3] In Ammatour, a stronghold of the SSNP in the Shouf, the Services Spéciaux arrested the party's local director, Masud ʿAbd al-Samad, dealing a severe blow to the party and its Druze adherents in the area.[4]

The summer of 1940 was a period of renewed SSNP activity throughout Lebanon and Syria. The party made its presence known through public statements, distributing propaganda, and organizing impromptu public gatherings in cities like Beirut, Damascus, and Aleppo. SSNP members continued to be arrested and imprisoned as French authorities remained wary of tolerating nationalist-re-

1 CADN 2135, Haut-Commissariat, Délégation du HC No. 11, "Résume des Evenements Politiques," 2 June 1940.

2 CADN 2135, Services Spéciaux du Levant, Poste de Merdjayoun, No. 569/MCR/28, Merdjayoun, Bulletin Hebdomadaire d'information, No. 21, 20 May 1940, and CADN 2395, Délégation du Haut-Commissariat, Le Délégué Adjoint du Haut-Commissaire, Conseiller Administratif du Mont-Liban, Baabda, No. 78, "a.s. activité du Parti Populaire Syrien dans la région de Beit-Méri et de Broummana," 18 May 1940.

3 See, for example, CADN 2135, Services Spéciaux du Levant, Poste de Merdjayoun, No. 658/MCR/28, Merdjayoun, Bulletin Hebdomadaire d'information, No. 23, 3 June 1940.

4 CADN 2135, Services Spéciaux du Levant, Poste de Merdjayoun, No. 658/MCR/28, Merdjayoun, Bulletin Hebdomadaire d'information, No. 23, 3 June 1940, and CADN 2135, Services Spéciaux du Levant, Poste de Merdjayoun, No. 719/MCR/28, Merdjayoun, Bulletin Hebdomadaire d'information, No. 25, 17 June 1940.

https://doi.org/10.1515/9783110729092-007

lated activities, expressions of anti-French or anti-Mandate views, and the spreading of German, Italian, or Russian propaganda. French authorities followed the SSNP's renewed activities, and administrative and security officials readied themselves to suppress the party's activities when ordered to do so.[5] Lebanese authorities explored ways to assist the French in their mission. In late June, a secret letter from the advisor to the Lebanese Secretary of State to French administrators suggested that local Lebanese administrative authorities and the Lebanese Gendarmerie should serve an enhanced role in combatting subversive groups, particularly the SSNP. The enhanced role of local authorities would, the advisor argued, augment the efforts of the French High Commission and Army, improving their overall effectiveness.[6]

In Beirut, the party pushed back against narratives critical of Saʿadeh and the party by distributing Saʿadeh's photograph throughout the city's neighborhoods, plastering them on as many walls as possible. Though done at night, many of the party members were under surveillance and subsequently arrested, preventing further distribution of the propaganda.[7] Elsewhere, the party's branch in Koura thwarted a visit of the high commissioner to the area. In Damascus, Victor Asad oversaw the distribution of party propaganda in the city and other Syrian cities to remind the people of the party's existence.[8] In another internal document, the Council of Deputies announced the party's intention to hold several general meetings in different locales. Every precaution was to be taken to ensure French authorities would not become privy to the gatherings and maintain the speakers' and participants' security. The clandestine meetings,

---

5 See, for example, the suggestion of the French Governor of the Colonies to the Administrative Councilor in the Bekaa to provide an updated and detailed list of SSNP members in the area in preparation for their eventual arrest: CADN 2395, Le Gouverneur des Colonies Schoeffler à Monsieur le Conseiller Administratif pour la Békaa, 22 June 1940. Also see, CADN 2395, Cabinet Politique, Haut-Commissariat, Beyrouth, No. 6312, Puaux à Le Conseiller Auprès du Secretaire d'Etat du Gouvernement Libanais, "Ouverture d'une mission d'information sur le Parti Populaire Syrien et la Ligue d'Action Nationale," 14 June 1940; CADN 2395, Cabinet Politique, Schoeffler à Puaux, 21 June 1940; CADN 2395, Cabinet Politique, Commandement Superieur des Troupes du Levant, No. 883/23, Caillault à M. l'Ambassadeur de France, Haut-Commissaire (Cabinet Militaire), 1 June 1940; and CADN 2395, Services Spéciaux du Levant, Poste de Baalbek, Baalbek, No. 365/S.S.S., Gacon à Le Conseiller Administratif de la Bekaa, "a/s Sécurité du Territoire," 5 June 1940.

6 CADN 2395, Secret, No. 2665, "Note pour Messieurs les Conseillers Administratifs," 27 June 1940.

7 Jurayj, *Min al-Juʿbat, Vol. 4*, p. 659, and CADN 2395, Commandement des Polices Libanaises, Beyrouth, " Rapport sur le placardage dans la ville de Beyrouth, Pendant la nuit du 12 au 13 Juillet 1940," 13 July 1940.

8 Jurayj, *Min al-Juʿbat, Vol. 4*, pp. 659–660.

planned for the beginning of August, would inaugurate a period of renewed and intense party activity.[9] In turn, it would provoke a severe response from French and Lebanese authorities.

Figure 2: Poster of Antun Saʿadeh distributed by Syrian Social Nationalist Party members in July 1940. It reads "Saʿadeh... they await [your] arrival." (Affiche de Antoun Saadé – MAE, Centre des Archives diplomatiques de Nantes, 1SL/1 V Beyrouth 2395)

9 Jurayj, *Min al-Juʿbat, Vol. 4*, pp. 660–666.

As planned, in early August, four general meetings were held throughout Lebanon: in Btaaboura and Afsadik, Choueifat, and Machghara. In the Shouf and Metn districts, the SSNP distributed propaganda circulars urging party members to liberate the country and be prepared for any eventuality.[10] Alerted to the meetings, French and Lebanese authorities responded swiftly and aggressively. The Gendarmerie quickly dispersed the demonstrations, party members were detained, and the circulars confiscated.[11] In Machghara, an estimated 50 to 60 SSNP members gathered in the afternoon of 1 August outside the town to hear a speech by young Shiʿi party member ʿAbdallah Mehsene. The Gendarmerie dispersed the demonstration, arresting some 23 party members; Mehsene, who escaped detention, turned himself in several days later.[12] The SSNP intended to hold meetings in other locales such as Baakline, but these meetings did not occur due to concerns the French already knew of the planned events. Indeed, a Services Spéciaux report noted that SSNP activity had yet to manifest itself in areas where it had previously operated, suggesting the aggressive security measures had achieved their desired effect.[13]

The swift and aggressive response of French authorities to the party's activities in early August foreshadowed the storm that descended upon it in the weeks that followed. On 18 August, Beirut police intensified their patrols and increased the number of officers in the city in response to orders to prevent any public manifestation by the SSNP.[14] The new measures were implemented to ensure any SSNP response to the French Military Tribunal's forthcoming proceedings

---

10 Jurayj, *Min al-Juʿbat, Vol. 4*, pp. 667–669.

11 CADN 2395, Gendarmerie Libanaise, Commandement, Beyrouth, No. 496/CG., "Renseignements," 2 August 1940, and CADN 2395, République Libanaise, Le Secrétaire d'Etat à Monsieur le Délégué du Haut-Commissaire, No. 259/SE., "a/s Parti Populaire Syrien," 6 August 1940. For a list of those detained see CADN 2395, Gendarmerie Libanaise, Commandement, Beyrouth, "Suite à Bulletin de Renseignements No. 496/CG," 2 August 1940.

12 CADN 2395, Délégation du H.C.F. Auprès de la République Libanaise, Le Conseiller Administratif de la Bekaa, Zahle, No. 652/C.A.B., "Information," 2 August 1940; CADN 2395, Services Spéciaux du Levant, Poste de Baalbek, Baalbek, No. 516/5.S.S., "Information: a/s activité du Parti Populaire Syrien," 3 August 1940; CADN 2395, Délégation du H.C.F. Auprès de la République Libanaise, Le Conseiller Administratif de la Bekaa, Zahle, No. 660/C.A.B., "Information," 5 August 1940; and CADN 2395, Cabinet Politique, La Délégué du Haut-Commissaire à Puaux, "Lettre P.P.S.," September 1940.

13 CADN 2135, Services Spéciaux du Levant, Poste de Merdjayoun, No. 974/MCR/28, Merdjayoun, Bulletin Hebdomadaire d'information, No. 32, 5 August 1940, and Jurayj, *Min al-Juʿbat, Vol. 4*, p. 668.

14 CADN 2395, Commandement des Polices Libanaises, Beyrouth, No. 3,362/CP, "Service d'Ordre du Dimanche," 17 August 1940, and CADN 2395, Commissariat Central de Beyrouth, Beyrouth, No. 2,706, "Compte-Rendu," 18 August 1940.

would be quickly quelled. However, when the military tribunal issued verdicts against almost four dozen Lebanese and Syrian party members several days later on charges they threatened public order and security, the party's response was notably absent. While some of those convicted were already imprisoned, including Thabit and ʿAbd al-Masih, others were on the run, including Jurayj, Ayas, Ashqar, and Qubrusi. With its leaders detained or in hiding, the party was ill-equipped and ill-positioned to respond. The situation would only deteriorate further as, by the end of the month, Lebanese police managed to arrest all those convicted by the tribunal.[15]

Nevertheless, those tasked to fill the detained party officials' roles made a concerted effort to raise party members' morale. They appealed for the wider public's support to dampen the French security campaign's effects, which proved difficult. French measures against the party had failed to provoke sympathy among the masses, and French authorities showed no intention of easing their pressure on the party.[16] In a propaganda tract published 28 August, Kamal Abu Kamal, the new president of the Council of Deputies, denounced Ayas and other Council members' arrests, arguing the French had gone back on their word to reach an amicable arrangement that would reduce tensions between the two sides. The tract also reassured party members that the leadership remained in control of its "holy cause" and recalled the words of Saʿadeh's 1 June 1935 speech, declaring that the day was coming when the nation would walk behind the banners of the red tempest.[17] The Lebanese Gendarmerie arrested Kamal in the forest near Bshamoun just days after its publication.[18]

From early September, intelligence reports noted the initial positive effects of security measures, including arrests and harsh sentencing imposed on SSNP

---

15 For a list of those condemned by the French military tribunal and their sentences see CADN 2395, Commandant Superieur des Troupes du Levant, Etat-Major-1 Bureau, Justice Militaire, 22 August 1940, and CADN 2395, Police Judiciare, Beyrouth, No. 4551/PJ, "Rapport Special," 27 August 1940. Also see, Jurayj, *Min al-Juʿbat, Vol. 4*, pp. 678–680.

16 CADN 2395, Haut-Commissariat, Conseiller Administratif Liban Sud, Saida, No. 322, "a/s P.P.S.," 11 September 1940.

17 CADN 2395, Le Délégué-adjoint du Haut-Commissaire, Conseiller Administratif du Mont-Liban, Mont Liban, No. 188, "Information," 7 September 1940.

18 CADN 2135, Haut-Commissariat, Délégation du HC, No. 19, "Resume des Evenements Politiques," 23 September 1940; CADN 2395, Gendarmerie Libanaise, Commandement, Beyrouth, No. 674/C.G., "Renseignements," 9 September 1940; and CADN 2395, Ministère de l'Intérieur, Secrétaire d'Etat a Monsieur le Délègue du Haut-Commissaire, Beyrouth, No. 1828, "Lettre no. 314," 3 September 1940.

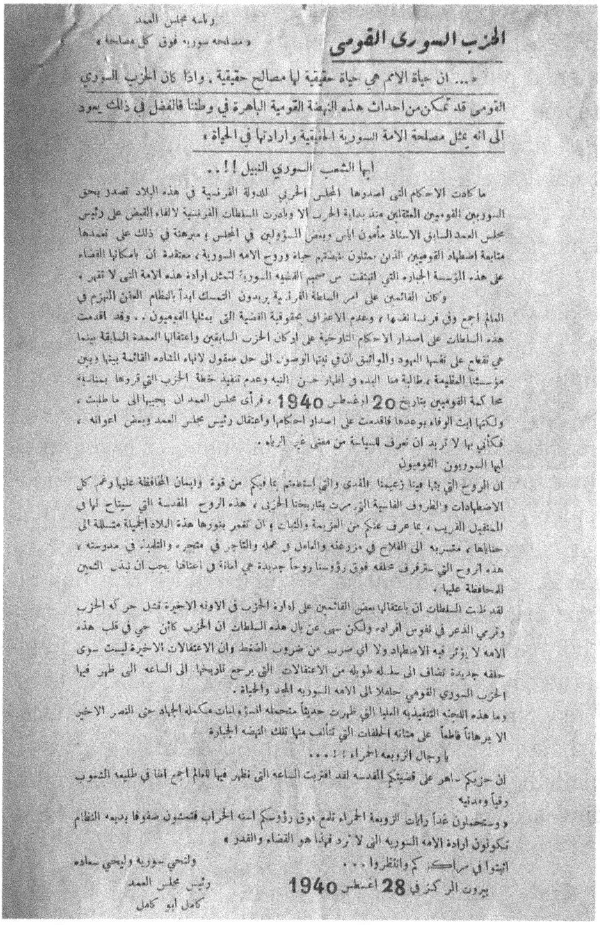

وزعامة مجلس العمد
«ومصلحة سورية فوق كل مصلحة»

الحزب السوري القومي

«... ان حياة الامم هي حياة حقيقية لها مصالح حقيقية . واذا كان الحزب السوري
القومي قد تمكن من احداث هذه النهضة القومية الباهرة في وطننا فالفضل في ذلك يعود
الى انه يمثل مصلحة الامة السورية الحقيقية وارادتها في الحياة»

ايها الشعب السوري النبيل !!..

ما كادت الاحكام التي اصدرها المجلس الحربي للدولة الفرنسية في هذه البلاد تصدر بحق
السوريين القوميين المعتقلين منذ بداية الحرب الا وبادرت السلطات الفرنسية لالقاء القبض على رئيس
مجلس العمد السابق الاستاذ مأمون اياس وبعض المسؤولين في المجلس ، مبرهنة في ذلك على تعمدها
متابعة اضطهاد القوميين الذين يمثلون بمجموعهم حياة وروح الامة السورية ، معتقدة ان بامكانها القضاء
على هذه المؤسسة الجبارة التي انبثقت من صميم القضية السورية لتمثل ارادة هذه الامة التي لا تقهر .
وكان القائمين على امر السلطة الفرنسية يريدون التمسك ابداً بالنظام العتيق المنهزم في
العالم اجمع وفي فرنسا نفسها ، وعدم الاعتراف بحقوقية القضية التي يمثلها القوميون . . وقد اقدمت
هذه السلطات على اصدار الاحكام التاريخية على اركان الحزب السابقين واعتقالها العمدة السابقة بينما
هي تقطع على نفسها العهود والمواثيق ان في نيتها الوصول الى حل معقول لانهاء المشادة القائمة بينها وبين
مؤسستنا العظيمة ، طالبة منا البدء في اظهار حسن النية وعدم تنفيذ خطة الحزب التي قررها بمناسبة
محاكمة القوميين بتاريخ 20 اغسطس 1940 ، فرأى مجلس العمد ان يجيبها الى ما طلبت ،
ولكنها ابت الوفاء بوعدها فاقدمت على اصدار احكامها واعتقال رئيس مجلس العمد وبعض اعوانه ،
فكأني بها لا تريد ان تعرف للسياسة من معنى غير الرياء .
ايها السوريون القوميون
ان الروح التي بثها فينا زعيمنا الفذ والتي استطعتم بما فيكم من قوة وايمان المحافظة عليها رغم كل
الاضطهادات والظروف القاسية التي مرت بتاريخنا الحزبي ، هذه الروح المقدسة التي سيتاح لها في
المستقبل القريب ، بما عرف عنكم من العزيمة والثبات ، ان تغمر بنورها هذه البلاد الجميلة متسللة الى
حناياها ، متسربة الى الفلاح في مزرعته والعامل في عمله والتاجر في متجره والتلميذ في مدرسته ،
هذه الروح التي سترفرف خلفه فوق رؤوسنا روحاً جديدة هي امانة في اعناقنا يجب ان نبذل الثمين
للمحافظة عليها .
لقد ظنت السلطات ان باعتقالها بعض القائمين على ادارة الحزب في الاونة الاخيرة تشل حركة الحزب
وترمي الذعر في نفوس افراده ولكن سهى عن بال هذه السلطات ان الحزب كائن حي في قلب هذه
الامة لا يؤثر فيه الاضطهاد ولا اي ضرب من ضروب الضغط وان الاعتقالات الاخيرة ليست سوى
حلقة جديدة تضاف الى سلسلة طويلة من الاعتقالات التي يرجع تاريخها الى الساعة التي ظهر فيها
الحزب السوري القومي حاملا الى الامة السورية المجد والحياة .
وما هذه اللجنة التنفيذية العليا التي ظهرت حديثاً متحملة المسؤوليات مكملة الجهاد حتى النصر الاخير
الا برهاناً قاطعاً على متانة الحلقات التي تتألف منها تلك النهضة الجبارة
يا رجال الزوبعة الحمراء !!...
ان حزبكم ساهر على قضيتكم المقدسة لقد اقتربت الساعة التي نظهر فيها للعالم اجمع اننا في طليعة الشعوب
رقياً ومدنية
وستحملون غداً رايات الزوبعة الحمراء تلمع فوق رؤوسكم اسنة الحراب فتمشون صفوفاً بديعة النظام
تكونون ارادة الامة السورية التي لا ترد فهذا هو القضاء والقدر »
اثبتوا في مراكزكم وانتظروا ...

ولتحي سورية وليحي سعاده
رئيس مجلس العمد
كامل ابو كامل

بيروت المركز في 28 اغسطس 1940

Figure 3: A statement by the head of the Syrian Social Nationalist Party's Council of Deputies, Kamal Abu Kamal, protesting the arrest and legal proceedings against party members by Mandate authorities in August 1940. (Déclaration PPS du 28 août 1940 – MAE, Centre des Archives diplomatiques de Nantes, 1SL/1 V Beyrouth 2395)

members by the military tribunal.[19] Indeed, the French had succeeded in arresting the party's leaders and their subsequent replacements very quickly (one

19 CADN 2135, Services Spéciaux du Levant, Poste de Merdjayoun, No. 1019/MCR/28, Merdjayoun, Bulletin Hebdomadaire d'information, No. 34, 19 August 1940; CADN 2135, Services Spéciaux du Levant, Poste de Merdjayoun, No. 1070/MCR/28, Merdjayoun, Bulletin Hebdomadaire

party official was arrested just two days after assuming his office), effectively decimating the party leadership and hampering the party's ability to function.[20] Perhaps the most profound effect the arrests had on the SSNP was forcing it to decentralize its leadership structure to ensure its survival, devolving power to multiple local leaders. Nevertheless, despite the crackdown, the party's activities did not cease as it distributed tracts protesting the military tribunal's verdicts, attacking French authorities, urging party members to remain steadfast, and calling for protests. For example, on 1 October, Lebanese police in Beirut seized approximately 4,000 SSNP tracts, arresting nine individuals preparing to distribute them. The leaflet called on Syrians and Lebanese to protest SSNP members' arrests and the punitive campaign against the party. The text reaffirmed that the party would remain steadfast in its fight with the knowledge that its victory was inevitable and appealed to High Commissioner Puaux to end the injustice.[21] Another five individuals were arrested for distributing propaganda in Mount Lebanon, but some tracts managed to be distributed in other locales.[22]

5.1 Disconnected

Mostly unaware of recent developments regarding the party, Saʿadeh sent a letter to the French ambassador in Argentina proposing the SSNP and French engage in dialogue to reach an understanding that would enable the two sides to work together "to serve the common interests of Syria and France."[23] Saʿadeh stressed to the Ambassador that the SSNP was "a purely Syrian and independent organization… [seeking] to restore national sovereignty…. Accordingly, the [SSNP] was not created to be hostile to any foreign power, France, or any other, or to serve

d'information, No. 36, 2 September 1940; CADN 2395, Le Délégué-adjoint du Haut-Commissaire, Conseiller Administratif du Mont-Liban, Beyrouth, No. 194, "A.S. Parti Populaire Syrien (PPS)," 18 September 1940; and CADN 2135, Services Spéciaux du Levant, Poste de Merdjayoun, No. 1177/MCR/28, Merdjayoun, Bulletin Hebdomadaire d'information, No. 38, 16 September 1940.

20 Jurayj, *Min al-Juʿbat, Vol. 4*, pp. 715–717.

21 CADN 2395, Haut-Commissariat, Services Spéciaux du Levant, Poste de Tripoli, Tripoli, No. 662/SS, "Traduction d'un tract du P.P.S.," 10 October 1940.

22 CADN 2135, Haut-Commissariat, Délégation du HC, No. 20, "Resume des Evenements Politiques," 7 October 1940; CADN 2395, Commandant des Polices Libanaises, Le Chef d'Escadron Picard, Beyrouth, "Bulletin de Renseignement," 1 October 1940; CADN 2395, Gendarmerie Libanaise, Commandement, Beyrouth, No. 617/C.G., "Renseignements," 2 October 1940; and CADN 2395, Gendarmerie Libanaise, Commandement, Beyrouth, No. 619/C.G., "Renseignements," 3 October 1940.

23 Mujais, *Saadeh, Vol. 3*, p. 93.

the particular interests of any foreign power."[24] Saʿadeh further argued that the SSNP had not initiated any action against France, but had only responded in defense "to the measures adopted against it," and had repeatedly made overtures towards France to reach an understanding.[25]

The French ambassador, who had dismissed Saʿadeh's relevance months earlier when asked to provide information on his activities to Puaux,[26] now judged him to be important. He cabled Puaux, positively relating the contents of Saʿadeh's letter. Puaux replied that, while he was interested in achieving an understanding with the organization, the SSNP must first demonstrate its loyalty to France. Despite the cordial exchange, no further action appears to have been taken to advance the dialogue. Regardless, the likelihood of any agreeable arrangement between the SSNP and the French was a chimera: France would not accept an agreement that eroded its position in the Levant nor the growth of any true national independence movement; the SSNP, a radical nationalist movement dedicated to achieving independence, did not have the power, means, and influence to effect a significant change in French policy. Put another way, the gap between the French and the SSNP was wide and unbridgeable, considering each's aims starkly opposed those of the other.

By the end of the year, the war and French security measures completely impeded communications between Saʿadeh and the party in Lebanon and Syria. The party welcomed the end of Puaux's tenure as high commissioner and the arrival of his replacement, General Henri Dentz, in late December 1940. Unlike his predecessor, Dentz was known to have taken a conciliatory approach in his meetings with local political and religious leaders.[27] His style signaled a possible change in French policy and for the party, in particular, suggested he may be more open to hearing appeals for the release of detained SSNP political prisoners. No such change, however, was imminent.

In the spring of 1941, Saʿadeh published an article in *al-Zawbaʿa* warning Syrians to not repeat the past mistakes by eagerly accepting support from a foreign power without safeguarding Syrian sovereignty. He opposed endorsing Nazi Germany's declaration of support for the independence of "Arab peoples," singling out Shakib Arslan, a known supporter of Germany, for particular criticism.[28] Arslan, Saʿadeh argued, was repeating the same mistake Shukri Ghanem and oth-

24 Mujais, *Saadeh, Vol. 3*, p. 93.
25 Mujais, *Saadeh, Vol. 3*, p. 93–94.
26 Mujais, *Saadeh, Vol. 3*, p. 92.
27 CADN 2135, Haut-Commissariat, Délégation du HC, No. 1, "Resume des Evenements Politiques," 14 January 1941.
28 "Takrār al-Aghlāṭ al-Māḍiyya," in Saʿadeh, *al-Aʿmāl al-Kāmila, Vol. 4*, pp. 143–145.

ers had made during World War I when they readily endorsed the promises of independence from the Entente, and instead received colonial rule in the form of the mandate. Saʿadeh urged Syrians to understand Axis propaganda for what it was – a political tool to win support rather than a genuine expression of support for Syrian independence – and not let it govern decision-making.[29] Unconvinced and undeterred, Arslan would continue to promote a political alliance with the Axis Powers and promote his Arab nationalist vision, leading Saʿadeh, amid his campaign to discredit Arslan, to call him "the agent of German propaganda in the Arab World."[30] Saʿadeh's warnings, however, failed to reach his followers in the homeland, some of whom continued to distribute pro-Axis propaganda and stray from the party's official policy of neutrality.

Though Saʿadeh's primary focus remained organizing and managing the party's affairs in the Americas, he followed events transpiring back home closely.[31] In mid-April, Saʿadeh published a stinging critique of France's suppression of any nationalist sentiment and the security measures it had taken to stifle the SSNP, particularly the lengths to which the Sûreté Générale went to arrest party members. He stated, "The French authorities exhausted every trick regarding the SSNP, [having] even resorted to the tricks of deceit and treachery...," recalling how the French had deceived Thabit by inviting him to negotiate an understanding with them in the Fall of 1939.[32]

While Saʿadeh criticized French policies from South America, Thabit's sister Claudia led the effort in Lebanon to obtain the release of detained SSNP members. Appealing directly to General Dentz, her efforts came at a convenient time. Dentz, ever more concerned by the possibility of a Free French and British invasion, explored options for bolstering the ranks of his significantly outnumbered forces, including arming the very nationalists he and his predecessors had worked to contain, including the SSNP.[33] "The British, already troubled by the

---

29 Saʿadeh would return to this theme at the beginning of June when he called on Syrians to unite behind the SSNP which was struggling to ensure that the results of any confrontation between the Axis and Allies in the Levant would, first and foremost, serve the national interest of Syria rather than the interests of a foreign power, whichever one it may be. See "Sūriyya wa al-Irādāt al-Ajnabiyya," in Saʿadeh, *al-Aʿmāl al-Kāmila, Vol. 4*, pp. 218–221.

30 "Laʿbat al-Muʾtamar al-ʿArabī," in Saʿadeh, *al-Aʿmāl al-Kāmila, Vol. 4*, pp. 172–176, and "Sūriyya wa-l-Irādāt al-Ajnabiyya," in Saʿadeh, *al-Aʿmāl al-Kāmila, Vol. 4*, pp. 218–221.

31 In April and May, Saʿadeh made trips to Pergamino, Tucumán, Santiago, and Córdoba in Argentina to deliver lectures and attended to organizational matters. See "al-Zaʿīm fī Pergamino," in Saʿadeh, *al-Aʿmāl al-Kāmila, Vol. 4*, pp. 207–212, and Mujais, *Saadeh, Vol. 3*, pp. 127–131.

32 "al-Ḥāla al-Siyāsiyya fī al-Waṭan – ʿAwda ilā al-Laʿba al-Qadīma," in Saʿadeh, *al-Aʿmāl al-Kāmila, Vol. 4*, pp. 199–203.

33 Nordbruch, *Nazism in Lebanon and Syria*, pp. 100–101.

pro-Axis leanings of Arab nationalists in Egypt, Iraq, and Palestine, considered the Vichy administration in Syria and Lebanon as a hostile entity."[34] Nevertheless, the British sought to avoid armed conflict with the Vichy forces and warned Dentz to not place the mandate territories at the Axis Powers' disposal. Their hand was forced, however, following two significant events. In early April, the pro-Axis Rashid ʿAli al-Gaylani seized power in a coup in Iraq. Then, the following month, under orders from Vichy authorities in Paris and contrary to his wishes, Dentz granted Germany the use of Syrian airfields and territory to support Iraqi forces battling British counterattacks. More concerned than ever by Germany's penetration into Syria and Lebanon, British and Free French forces quickly intervened, launching their joint invasion on 8 June 1941.[35]

5.2 "The Mandate Continues": The Free French and the SSNP

The British-Free French campaign, overseen principally by British general Edward Spears and nominally by Free French leader Charles de Gaulle, lasted until 14 July, when an armistice was signed following Beirut's fall to an Australian brigade.[36] In the early days of the war, the Germans offered to provide Dentz and Vichy forces with air support, but Dentz turned their offer down. Seeking to shore up popular support for Vichy forces, Dentz and Pétain personally appealed to the local population. Their call resonated with the Najjadeh and Kata'ib, and the two movements took practical, but limited, steps to cooperate with the French in the wake of the British bombing campaign in Beirut, which had forced many of the city's residents to flee to the mountains.[37] Though initially hesitant to do so, Dentz decided to release SSNP members on the condition they join the effort to repel the British-Free French military advance. Their release occurred three days after the outbreak of fighting, and the officers and soldiers tasked with arming SSNP fighters refused to do so. Unarmed and shunned, the SSNP did not participate in the fight that ended in the defeat of Vichy forces. Regardless, within months, the Free French returned most of the previously detained

34 Rogan, *The Arabs*, p. 241.
35 Rogan, *The Arabs*, p. 241, and Ziadeh, *Syria and Lebanon*, p. 63.
36 For a detailed account of the Free French and British military campaign see Henri de Wailly, *Invasion Syria 1941: Churchill and De Gaulle's Forgotten War* (London: I.B. Tauris, 2016), and James Barr, *A Line in the Sand: The Anglo-French Struggle for the Middle East, 1914–1948* (New York: W.W. Norton & Company, 2012), Chapters 16 and 17.
37 CADN 2135, Haut-Commissariat, Délégation du HC, No. 12, "Resume des Evenements Politiques," 26 June 1941.

SSNP members to prison in Mieh Mieh, the fortress of Rachaya, and Tripoli.[38] General Catroux made appeals of his own, issuing a statement declaring that the Free French had come to put an end to the mandate and usher in Lebanon and Syria's independence.[39] Catroux's declaration, however, was carefully worded and contained a significant caveat: Lebanese and Syrian independence would be guaranteed by bilateral treaties whose foundations were in the treaties proposed by the French in the 1930s that effectively enshrined France's dominance in the guise of a negotiated agreement. The British, too, supported Syria and Lebanon's independence but were careful to acknowledge France's "special position" in the Levant so as not to challenge their ally. For de Gaulle and the Free French, Britain's acknowledgment of France's "special position" was more salient than British declarations of support for independence, and it conducted itself in a manner consistent with its agenda of reasserting the authority of the mandate.

With the arrival of the British and Free French, the SSNP set about convincing the new authorities it posed no threat to public security. From Argentina, and with no way to communicate with his followers in the homeland, Saʿadeh provided his general assessment of events back home. In several articles in *al-Zawbaʿa*, Saʿadeh dismissed as worthless pro-independence proclamations made by the British and Free French (and the Germans and Italians) and criticized his fellow countrymen who praised and over-enthusiastically welcomed them. While British declarations may have been more sincere, French statements suggesting Syria and Lebanon's independence be based on the treaties of 1936 – which the French had never ratified – cast doubt over their sincerity in negotiating independence and a fair and just treaty.[40]

To Saʿadeh, whether declarations of support were sincere was not the issue. Saʿadeh argued there was "no such thing as true or false political promises" (*lā yūjad fī al-siyāsa wuʿūd ṣādiqa wa wuʿūd kadhāba*), only legally binding written agreements between parties; anything less was rhetoric.[41] National independence and sovereignty, according to Saʿadeh, could only be secured by the will of the nation and could not be determined, granted, or bestowed by an external

38 Mujais, *SSNP*, p. 172.
39 Ziadeh, *Syria and Lebanon*, p. 65.
40 Charles de Gaulle is reported to have declared that "the Mandate continues" upon his arrival in Beirut at the end of July, brusquely dismissing any notion the Free French had committed themselves to Lebanon and Syria's independence. Quoted in de Wailly, *Invasion Syria 1941*, p. 315.
41 "Istiqlāl al-Sūrī al-Mawʿūd wa Qīmat al-Taṣrīḥāt," in Saʿadeh, *al-Aʿmāl al-Kāmila*, *Vol.* 4, pp. 265–269.

party. To further support his argument casting doubt on French sincerity, he observed that Catroux and de Gaulle had so far taken no steps to suggest that the end of the Mandate was coming. Indeed, they had allowed former Vichy-loyalists in the bureaucracy, armed forces, and security services to retain their positions so the mandate's institutions could continue to function as they had previously.[42]

The only significant change brought about by recent events was, in Saʿadeh's assessment, Britain's enhanced influence and status in Lebanon and Syria at France's expense. This development in the long-established rivalry between the two countries could undermine the British and Free French alliance to fight the Axis powers. Concluding it unlikely the Free French would change its policy vis-à-vis the party and his return to the homeland, Saʿadeh decided to pursue contacts with the British. He charged William Bahliss, who had recently assumed the editorial duties of *Suriyya al-Jadida*, with this responsibility.[43] Accepting Saʿadeh's charge, Bahliss sent an intermediary to convey the SSNP's message to the British that the party was ready to engage with them regarding independence, the question of Palestine, and the party's principles and policies. The British response was positive but exceptionally restrained. The possibility of a meeting between Saʿadeh and the British ambassador in Argentina was discussed, but Saʿadeh sought assurances that any such meeting or discussion with the British would be done without French knowledge. The preliminary discussion led nowhere; prioritizing the war effort in Europe against the Axis Powers, Britain preferred not to unnecessarily antagonize their Free French allies by extending its influence in the Levant.[44] At the same time, Saʿadeh sought dia-

---

42 "al-Naẓra al-Qawmiyya ʿalā al-Ḥawādith al-Ḥarbiyya wa-l-Siyāsiyya al-Akhīra," in Saʿadeh, *al-Aʿmāl al-Kāmila, Vol.* 4, pp. 243–256, and "Istiqlāl Sūriyya ʿalā ḍawʾ al-Ḥawādith al-Siyāsiyya al-Akhīra," in Saʿadeh, *al-Aʿmāl al-Kāmila, Vol.* 4, pp. 257–264.

43 The newspapers previous editors, the Bunduqi brothers, had, contrary to Saʿadeh's directives, shifted the periodical's neutral editorial position on the War decidedly toward the Axis. Saʿadeh's efforts to reign in their pro–Axis declarations culminated in Bahliss's appointment. However, only several months after Bahliss had taken over responsibilities of *Suriyya al-Jadida*, Brazilian authorities banned the publication of all foreign language periodicals in August 1941, causing the cessation of *Suriyya al-Jadida*'s publication. See Mujais, *Saadeh, Vol. 3*, pp. 121–125; "Ilā William Bahliss," in Saʿadeh, *al-Aʿmāl al-Kāmila, Vol.* 9, pp. 4–8, 18, 68–71; "Ilā Ibrahim Tannous," in Saʿadeh, *al-Aʿmāl al-Kāmila, Vol.* 9, pp. 9–11; and "Ilā George Bunduqi," in Saʿadeh, *al-Aʿmāl al-Kāmila, Vol.* 9, pp. 16–17.

44 Zisser, *Lebanon*, pp. 26–28; "Ilā William Bahliss," in Saʿadeh, *al-Aʿmāl al-Kāmila, Vol.* 10, pp. 141–143, 147–149, 160–164, 168–172.

logue with Germany and Franco's Spanish State, but these overtures also failed to move beyond preliminary exchanges.[45]

While Saʿadeh's entreaties failed to yield positive results, the continued mass detention of party activists, as well as growing frustration over the party's ideological direction, strained its effectiveness and cohesiveness. The French campaign to detain, arraign, and sentence SSNP members continued well into the new year. The party's requests that the British intercede and secure low-ranking party members' release went unanswered.[46] The Free French kept a watchful eye on many SSNP members' activity, and, in early 1942, prioritized information and intelligence collection on the party's activities, a task that fell on the Sûreté to do so prudently and cautiously.[47] Lists of party members including information regarding their residence, profession, and religion were compiled, as were reports dividing individuals into three groups: (1) those to be immediately arrested, (2) those to be arrested, but less urgently, and (3) individuals to be placed under surveillance by the security services, particularly in the case of any security incidents. The intelligence was collected from diverse sources, including previous lists of SSNP members prepared by Vichy authorities and information indirectly obtained from the British, corroborated by other sources.[48]

45 Bahliss was also tasked with managing discussions with the Germans at the same time as he managed discussions with the British: "Ilā William Bahliss," in Saʿadeh, *al-Aʿmāl al-Kāmila, Vol.* 10, pp. 168–172. Discussions with Spanish authorities had been initiated through the party's branch in the Canary Islands and its leader there, Sassin Hanna Sassin. Through Sassin, Saʿadeh had exchanged letters with the head of Spain's Bureau of Near Eastern Affairs in September 1940. The initial exchange had not led anywhere, but Saʿadeh had instructed Sassin to push Spain on the matter, which he did in the fall of 1941. However, by January 1942, the exchange had ceased with no results to show. See Mujais, *Saadeh, Vol. 3*, pp. 131–136; "Ilā Sassin Hanna Sassin," in Saʿadeh, *al-Aʿmāl al-Kāmila, Vol.* 9, pp. 91–92, 181–182, 309–310, 329–330.
46 Mujais, *SSNP*, p. 172.
47 CADN 2396, Beyrouth, 118/SP, Ph. David to le-Chef de la Sûreté Générale, 7 March 1942, and CADN 2396, Section Sûreté Générale aux Armées, Beyrouth, Information No. 307, "Activite du PPS," 21 March 1942.
48 See, for example, the following reports on the SSNP throughout Lebanon in early 1942: CADN 2396, Conseiller Administratif Liban Sud, Saida, No. 172, 10 January 1942; CADN 2396, Services Spéciaux du Levant, Poste de Baalbeck, Baalbeck, No. 372/I.S.S., 8 February 1942; and CADN 2396, Delegation Générale de la France Libre au Levant, Beyrouth, No. 111/S.P., 5 March 1942. According to French documentation, the British also compiled their own lists of SSNP members, at least in south Lebanon. See, for example, a snippet of a report mentioning SSNP members to be arrested in Merdjayoun and Rachaya el Fokhar: CADN 2396, Cabinet Politique, Saida, No. 548, 22 April 1942.

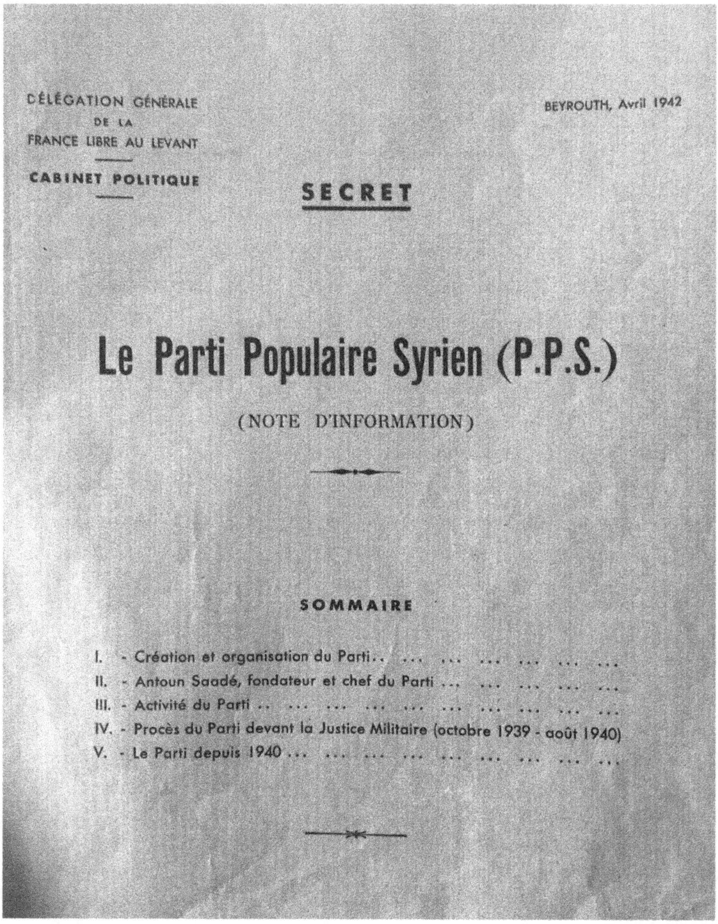
DÉLÉGATION GÉNÉRALE
DE LA
FRANCE LIBRE AU LEVANT

CABINET POLITIQUE

BEYROUTH, Avril 1942

SECRET

Le Parti Populaire Syrien (P.P.S.)

(NOTE D'INFORMATION)

SOMMAIRE

I. - Création et organisation du Parti .. ..
II. - Antoun Saadé, fondateur et chef du Parti ... ...
III. - Activité du Parti .. ..
IV. - Procès du Parti devant la Justice Militaire (octobre 1939 - août 1940)
V. - Le Parti depuis 1940 ... ...

Figure 4: A secret report on the SSNP prepared by General Delegation of the Free French in the Levant for the French government in April 1942. (Lettre de sûreté générale de avril 1942 – MAE, Centre des Archives diplomatiques de Nantes, 1SL/1 V Beyrouth 2396)

While some SSNP members continued to evade arrest or even escape the internment camps where they were being held, others were less fortunate.[49] In December 1941, three SSNP officials – Abu Kamal, Jurayj, and Ayas – were indicted again by the French military tribunal on three charges: (1) working to subvert the

49 CADN 2396, Gendarmerie Libanaise, No. 334/C.G., Beyrouth, "Commandant a le Chef du Gouvernement," 14 October 1941.

security of the state; (2) membership in and helping reestablish a dissolved organization; and (3) distributing foreign propaganda whose content was against state interests.[50] The French alleged the accused sought to foment a rebellion against the Mandate, establish an armed militia, and distribute propaganda calling for a revolt, demonstrations, and subversive activities. The indictments also listed several security incidents involving the SSNP between 1938 and 1940 to strengthen the authorities' argument that the party was, indeed, a subversive movement that needed to be curtailed. Party members on the run or under surveillance were arraigned on similar charges of subversive activities, including arms smuggling, and sentenced to 10 to 20 years in prison and an equal period of exile.[51] The measures were taken against the party "dampened any apparent militant activities for most of 1942"[52] but did not eradicate them.

Indeed, the party continued to show signs of life in early 1942. Leaflets distributed throughout Rachaya el-Fokhar, Hasbaya, and Merdjayoun in January 1942 urged party members to remain vigilant in the face of France's military rule. The text declared the party's victory was assured despite the dark and trying period they were enduring.[53] In early February, SSNP activists held meetings in the village of Btaboura at Jurayj and Qubrusi's homes. The town, whose populace was mostly sympathetic to the party, had become a refuge of sorts for the SSNP, a fact well-known to French authorities. Alerted to the meetings of some two dozen activists, including those who had previously been sentenced by the military tribunal in absentia, a gendarmerie detachment launched an operation to disrupt the meetings and arrest the attendees. While they succeeded in surrounding the village and capturing several members, Jurayj, Qubrusi, and ʿAbd al-Masih – who had been released from their previous detention – again evaded arrest, leaving before the town was completely cordoned off.[54] In addition, French authorities were concerned that an estimated 400 SSNP members, according to their assessment, had managed to gain employment (or "in-

---

50 Jurayj, *Maʿa Anṭūn Saʿādah, Vol. 3*, p. 39.

51 Jurayj, *Maʿa Anṭūn Saʿādah, Vol. 3*, pp. 38–47, and CADN 2162, Services Spéciaux du Levant, Poste de Merdjayoun, No. 579/ME/30, "Information: a/s de Fouad Abou Ayache," 23 December 1941.

52 Mujais, *SSNP*, p. 172.

53 CADN 2118, Services Spéciaux, Poste de Merdjayoun, No. 82/ME/28, Bulletin D'Informations no. 19, 18 January 1942; and CADN 2162, Services Spéciaux du Levant, Poste de Merdjayoun, No. 27/ME/30, "Information: Tracts P.P.S.," 10 January 1942; and CADN 2396, Services Spéciaux du Levant, Poste de Chtaura, No. 115/Z.R./22, Information, 31 January 1942.

54 CADN 2396, Delegation Generale de la France Libre au Levant, No. 47/SP, Beyrouth, "Copie d'un rapport de la Gendarmerie sur l'activité du P.P.S. dans la region d'Amioun," 14 February 1942.

filtrate" as the French characterized it) in a variety of public-sector fields, including the gendarmerie, the fire services, and the post office.[55]

Though concerned by nationalist political activity, to the extent of ordering all political parties' dissolution in March 1942,[56] French authorities were much more perturbed by any expression of support for the Axis. Thus, the continued pro-Axis pronouncements of several SSNP members only provoked the ire of French authorities and did no service to the party's cause. In March, for example, a radio message delivered by Karim Azkul, the SSNP's Director of Information who had studied in Germany and was known for his pro-German tendencies, was denounced for its alleged pro-Axis views. In April, Alfred Abu Samara, an SSNP member and journalist in Merdjayoun, was arrested by the Sûreté Générale and sent to Mieh Mieh prison on charges of distributing pro-Axis propaganda.[57] French authorities also accused SSNP members of exploiting an accidental explosion in Beirut's port to spread disinformation and cause alarm. One of the alleged rumors spread by party activists was that a German submarine had destroyed three transport ships and a unit of Allied soldiers; the rumor supposedly proof that the Axis fleet was prepared to launch a coordinated attack on the port involving Syrian, Italian, and German forces. The rumors, which the French believed were being spread to weaken support for the Allied cause and enhance the party's morale, did manage to cause some panic among the populace.[58]

These SSNP activities only served to strengthen the resolve of French authorities. The Sûreté and the Services Spéciaux held numerous meetings with their British counterparts, the British Security Mission (BSM) and the British Field Security Service (FSS), to discuss measures to be taken against persons of interest whom they deemed a threat to public order.[59] By the fall of 1942, the Sûreté Générale had succeeded in arresting and imprisoning three other key SSNP leaders

55 CADN 2396, Beyrouth, Information, 26 March 1942.

56 CADN 2162, Direction Sûreté Générale aux Armées, Beyrouth, Information No. 363, "La dissolution des partis politique," 27 March 1942.

57 CADN 2396, Direction Sûreté Générale aux Armées, Beyrouth, Information No. 440/C.E., "Karim Azkoul," 31 March 1942, and CADN 2118, Services Spéciaux, Poste de Merdjayoun, No. 118/ME/28, Bulletin D'Informations no. 29, 24 April 1942.

58 CADN 2162, Direction Sûreté Générale aux Armées, Beyrouth, Information No. 863/C.E., "Activite du P.P.S.," 21 April 1942.

59 CADN 2396, Services Spéciaux du Levant, Poste de Baalbeck, Baalbeck, No. 538/S.S., "Cauro to Conseiller Administratif de la Békaa à Zahle," 25 April 1942.

who had evaded capture until then: Qubrusi, ʿAbdallah Saʿadeh, and Masʿad Hajal.[60]

60 CADN 2396, Cabinet Militaire, No. 3,693/CM, Beyrouth, "Note pour Monsieur le Directeur de la Sûreté Générale," 27 July 1942, and CADN 2396, Services Spéciaux du Levant, Poste de Tripoli, Tripoli, "Information," 31 July 1942; CADN 2396, Sûreté Générale de la France Libre au Levant, Sûreté Générale, No. 647, "Arrestation de members du P.P.S.," 11 May 1942; Saʿadeh, *Awrāq Qawmiyya*, p. 31; Hajal, *Lam Ubaddil...*, pp. 60–64; and Qubrusi, *Yatadhakkar, Vol. 2*, pp. 70–74.

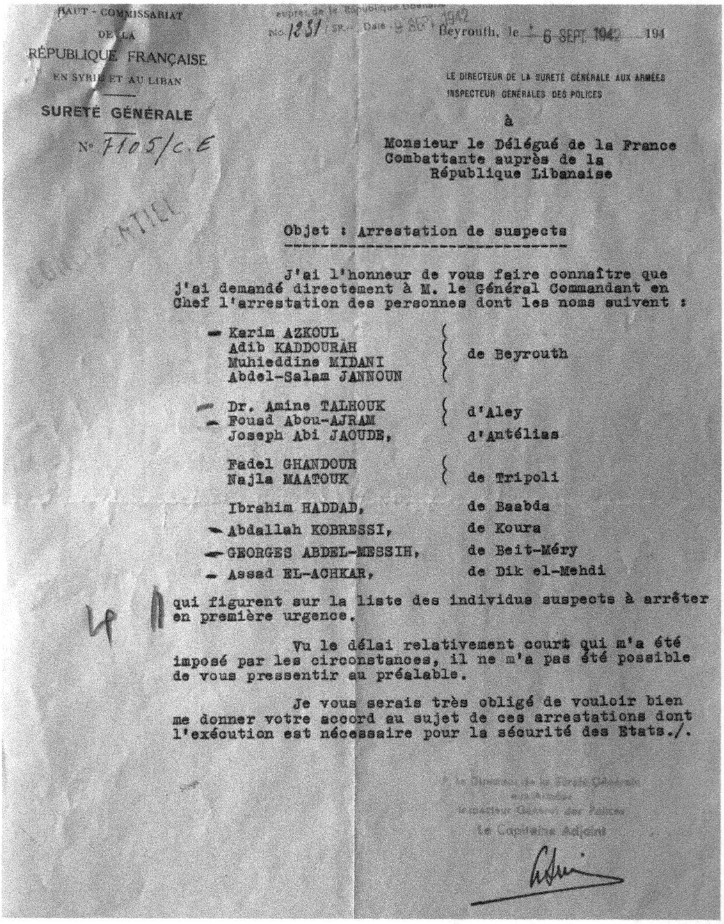

HAUT - COMMISSARIAT
DE LA
RÉPUBLIQUE FRANÇAISE
EN SYRIE ET AU LIBAN

SURETÉ GÉNÉRALE

N° 7105/C.E

No 1231 / SP. Date 9 SEPT 1942

Beyrouth, le 6 SEPT 1942 194

LE DIRECTEUR DE LA SURETÉ GÉNÉRALE AUX ARMÉES
INSPECTEUR GÉNÉRALES DES POLICES

à

Monsieur le Délégué de la France
Combattante auprès de la
République Libanaise

Objet : Arrestation de suspects

J'ai l'honneur de vous faire connaître que j'ai demandé directement à M. le Général Commandant en Chef l'arrestation des personnes dont les noms suivent :

Karim AZKOUL Adib KADDOURAH Muhieddine MIDANI Abdel-Salam JANNOUN	de Beyrouth
Dr. Amine TALHOUK Fouad Abou-AJRAM	d'Aley
Joseph Abi JAOUDE,	d'Antélias
Fadel GHANDOUR Najla MAATOUK	de Tripoli
Ibrahim HADDAD,	de Baabda
Abdallah KOBRESSI,	de Koura
GEORGES ABDEL-MESSIH,	de Beit-Méry
Assad EL-ACHKAR,	de Dik el-Mehdi

qui figurent sur la liste des individus suspects à arrêter en première urgence.

Vu le délai relativement court qui m'a été imposé par les circonstances, il ne m'a pas été possible de vous pressentir au préalable.

Je vous serais très obligé de vouloir bien me donner votre accord au sujet de ces arrestations dont l'exécution est nécessaire pour la sécurité des Etats./.

Figure 5: Letter from the Director of the Sûreté Générale reporting he had ordered the arrest of more than a dozen leading Syrian Social Nationalist Party officials. Their arrests were an urgent matter “necessary for the security of the state.” (Lettre de sûreté générale de septembre 1942 – MAE, Centre des Archives diplomatiques de Nantes, 1SL/1 V Beyrouth 2396)

6 The Early Days of Independence

By the summer of 1943, the French had reinstated a nominal constitution in Lebanon and allowed for parliamentary elections to be held. In doing so, France hoped that they "would be able to claim greater British support for [their] demands" and could also "conclude treaties with the newly-elected governments which would ensure France's future standing in the Levant."[1] General elections were held in late August. Lebanon was divided into five voting districts, and the resulting parliament was relatively evenly split between pro-British and pro-French representatives.[2] The British and French would trade accusations of election meddling but quickly turned their attention to getting their preferred candidate elected president. Ultimately, both would support Beshara al-Khuri's candidacy though he was neither's preferred or first choice. Of more significant consequence to the British and French were Khuri's efforts to encourage Sunni notables to reach a power-sharing agreement between Lebanon's Christian and Muslim communities. The result of Khuri's discussions with Riad al-Sulh in September 1943 became known as the National Pact, which became "the genuine, solid cornerstone of the state structure of independent Lebanon."[3] Furthermore, it enshrined Khuri and Sulh's shared vision of a "Lebanon of all [its] communities" and "provided the Lebanese with a common framework of authority… but also preserved the division between the communities…."[4]

France's continued commitment to maintaining its status in the Levant conflicted with the Khuri and Sulh's vision for Lebanon's future. In early October, Khuri and Sulh met with Delegate General Jean Helleu, who had replaced Catroux several months earlier, to press the French into transferring authority over 'common interests' – such as "the ports, airports, broadcasting stations, government buildings and economic authorities"[5] – to the Lebanese government, while leaving security-related matters aside. Helleu argued no such transfer of authority could take place so long as the mandate remained in effect but suggested that some control might be transferred in the context of a bilateral treaty between the two countries. Sulh and Khuri rejected the proposition, view-

1 Zisser, *Lebanon*, p. 38.

2 For detailed analyses of the 1943 election, see Zisser, *Lebanon*, pp. 41–56, and El-Solh, *Lebanon and Arabism*, pp. 195–211.

3 Zisser, *Lebanon*, p. 56. For more on the National Pact, see Basim al-Jisr, *Mīthāq 1943: Li-mādhā Kāna wa Li-mādhā Saqaṭa* (Beirut: Dar al-Nahār li-l-Nashr, 1997) and Seale, *The Struggle for Arab Independence*, pp. 498–509.

4 Zisser, *Lebanon* pp. 57–58.

5 Zisser, *Lebanon*, p. 69.

https://doi.org/10.1515/9783110729092-008

ing French demands for any settlement ensuring France's "special status" to be unacceptable.[6] Frustrated by French intransigence, and with Helleu in Algiers for consultations with the Free French Committee, the Lebanese government "decided to take a series of immediate and unilateral measures, mostly of a symbolic kind, meant to demonstrate the independent status of their country." Proposed measures included amending the constitution to annul provisions granting certain authorities to France.[7] Having considered the Lebanese government's proposed constitutional amendments, Helleu and the Free French issued a statement from Algiers declaring any revisions to the constitution invalid, which tacitly amounted to France's refusal to cede any authority whatsoever. Instead, the French doubled-down and insisted the Franco-Lebanese treaty of 1936 be ratified.[8]

The Lebanese government promptly responded to the French declaration. Khuri ordered the newly elected Chamber of Deputies to convene early on 8 November to consider amending the constitution. Despite French warnings reserving France's right to respond as it saw fit to the passage of any amendments and efforts, including enlisting Eddé to convince deputies not to attend the session so that a quorum was not reached, the Chamber convened and amended the constitution, removing any mention of the French mandate and clauses that upheld French authority. The stage for a confrontation was set and, upon his return to Beirut, Helleu aggressively worked to undo the Chamber's actions. In the early morning hours of 11 November, "French armed forces raided the residences of senior government figures and arrested them."[9] The detainees, who included Sulh, Khuri, Chamoun, and Taqla, were sent to the fortress at Rachaya and detained together with SSNP officials and other political prisoners who had been held there for several years. In addition to the arrests, Helleu suspended the constitution, dissolved the Chamber, dismissed the president and his cabinet, and appointed Eddé as president.

Helleu's measures infuriated Britain's representative in the Levant, General Edward Spears, who pushed for the British to declare martial law and restore order. Spears' eagerness to confront the French was rebuffed by his superiors, who feared – correctly – a confrontation with the French in the Levant would threaten the joint war effort in Europe. Eddé, meanwhile, worked to form a new government but found the going tough. Many Lebanese notables, regardless of the religious community from which they hailed, refused to support Eddé and

6 Zisser, *Lebanon*, pp. 69–70
7 Zisser, *Lebanon*, p. 70, and Ziadeh, *Syria and Lebanon*, p. 75.
8 Zisser, *Lebanon*, pp. 70–71, and Ziadeh, *Syria and Lebanon*, p. 75.
9 Zisser, *Lebanon*, p. 74.

the French. Even Maronite notables who had traditionally been supportive of France, withdrew their support. Leading figures in the Maronite Church, including Patriarch ʿArida and Beirut's Archbishop Ignace Mubarak, vociferously criticized the French; their declarations were added to those of the Sunni Mufti of Lebanon and leading figures in the Shiʿi and Druze communities, including Sabri Hamadeh and Majid Arslan. Hamadeh and Arslan, together with Habib Abu Shahla, had evaded arrest and fled to the village of Bshamoun in the Shouf. There they declared themselves the legitimate government and began organizing opposition to the French. Demonstrations, protests, and a general strike took place throughout the country as resentment grew. The Kataʾib and Najjadeh organized demonstrations and distributed anti-French propaganda, while the SSNP, for its part, provided armed protection for the opposition government in Bshamoun and moral support for imprisoned Lebanese leaders.[10]

As the crisis threatened to devolve further, Catroux was sent from Algiers to find a solution. Arriving on 16 November, he took immediate steps to calm the situation and reverse Helleu's actions. Notably, he ordered the withdrawal of a French army unit comprised of Senegalese troops sent to Bshamoun to arrest several opposition leaders. The group had been confronted near the village of ʿAynab by armed volunteers, including several SSNP members, who engaged them in battle. One volunteer, SSNP member Saʿid Fakhr al-Din, was killed in the firefight before Catroux's withdrawal orders reached the front and calmed the situation. Though Catroux's order was more influential in ending the fighting than the armed resistance of the Lebanese volunteers, the battle subsequently "became an element in the evolving myth of the Lebanese independence struggle."[11] Indeed, Arslan and, later, Khuri, would recognize Fakhr al-Din's heroism and honor his sacrifice on behalf of Lebanese independence. The SSNP would subsequently recognize him as a martyr, pointing to his sacrifice as evidence of the party's commitment to Lebanon and its independence. Catroux's assessment of the situation led him to conclude that only a grand gesture on the part of the French would end the crisis, an idea with which the British concurred. Thus, on 22 November, Catroux annulled Helleu's 11 November decrees, reinstated Khuri, released Lebanese leaders from detention, and reinstated the constitution in its amended form.[12] In the months that followed, SSNP detainees also

---

10 Zisser, *Lebanon*, pp. 77–78; Ziadeh, *Syria and Lebanon*, p. 77; Mujais, *SSNP*, pp. 173–174; Qubrusi, *Yatadhakkar, Vol. 2*, pp. 103–106; and Jurayj, *Haqāʾiq ʿan al-Istiqlāl.*

11 Zisser, *Lebanon*, p. 77, and Ghassan al-Khalidi, *al-Muqāwama al-Qawmiyya* (Beirut: Dār wa-Maktabat al-Turāth al-Adabī, 2000), pp. 13–14.

12 For detailed descriptions of the crisis, see Seale, *The Struggle for Arab Independence*, pp. 510–545, and Munir Taqi al-Din, *Wilādat al-Istiqlāl* (Beirut: Dar al-Nahār li-l-Nashr, 1997).

would be released from prison,[13] and the party's backing of Sulh and Khuri would be rewarded, inaugurating a new era in the SSNP's relations with the Lebanese state and political establishment.

6.1 Forging a Path Ahead as the "National Party"

At the end of February 1944, Neʿmeh Thabit visited French authorities in Beirut, providing them with a copy of the speech he planned to deliver during Saʿadeh's birthday commemoration. To his French interlocutors, he stressed his special mention of France as a "friendly country" and noted that "only sincere statements were good propaganda and that he was against making hollow and empty declarations."[14] Thabit observed that the current Lebanese government was unlike any the party had known; it was far less antagonistic than previous governments and open to dialogue with the party. In this assessment, he was undoubtedly correct, and the positive atmosphere owed much to the party's support for Lebanese independence and Sulh, Khuri, and Chamoun's political alliance. These developments were enough for Thabit to declare the era of the party's suffering had passed, its perseverance and steadfastness having preserved the movement and positioned it to reap the rewards of its struggle as it worked with the new government to eliminate the Mandate's deleterious effects.[15]

The commemoration of Saʿadeh's birth served as an appropriate point of departure for the party's renewed activity; its reconstitution and reorganization in Lebanon and Syria began in earnest. Among the top priorities was reestablishing the party's central leadership bodies, namely the Higher Council and the Council of Directors. The party's Higher Council was reconstituted in early March under Thabit's leadership and included Ashqar, Ayas, ʿAbd al-Masih, Qubrusi, and ʿAjram.[16] Focused on internal matters, the party worked to energize its local branches throughout Lebanon and Syria. In Syria, party activity had been stag-

For a more detailed description of how the decision to end the crisis was reached, see Zisser, *Lebanon*, pp. 80–82.

13 Qubrusi, *Yatadhakkar, Vol.* 2, pp. 107–108.

14 CADN 2162, Sûreté aux Armées, Beyrouth, "Compte-rendu au sujet de la visite de Nehme Tabet, Chef du P.P.S.," 29 February 1944.

15 CADN 2162, Sûreté aux Armées, Beyrouth, "Compte-rendu au sujet de la visite de Nehme Tabet, Chef du P.P.S.," 29 February 1944.

16 CADN 2162, Direction Sûreté Générale aux Armées, Beyrouth, Information, "Le Parti Populaire," 8 March 1944.

nant for much of the preceding year, but under Thabit's direction began to show signs of life in early March 1944. Propaganda tracts were distributed throughout Damascus and the provinces of Latakia and Tartus; activities in Aleppo, Homs, and Hama were also renewed.[17] In Lebanon, the SSNP received a substantial boost from the Lebanese government when Interior Minister Camille Chamoun legalized the party, declaring it a legitimate political organization. Energized by its legalization, the party increased the tempo of its public activities, but its legalization did come at a price.

The Lebanese government conditioned the party's legalization on adopting a much more palatable political platform that drastically toned down the SSNP's fierce and open commitment to Syrian nationalism. The SSNP removed the word "Syrian" from its official name and was henceforth known as the National Party (*Ḥizb al-Qawmī*). It also began to emphasize its reform principles advocating the separation of religion and state, an end to sectarianism, and an end to feudalism, minimizing or altogether avoiding any expressions related to its core Syrian nationalist tenets. Furthermore, it prohibited the party salute and chant with its declaration of 'Long live Syria' and 'Long live Saʿadeh' and redesigned its flag, removing the red tempest symbol.[18] To be sure, there were limits to the extent to which the party could accommodate itself to its Lebanese allies, and the measures taken by the party did not eliminate the marks of its Syrian nationalist beliefs. Moreover, Thabit's accommodationist approach bothered a segment within the party that believed he and his supporters were sacrificing the party's core principles and Saʿadeh to ingratiate the SSNP to a Lebanese political elite that wanted nothing of the party's Syrian nationalism or its founder.[19] While the party's steps satisfied its government allies, they were not enough for the party's traditional opponents, the Kata'ib and the Lebanese Communist Party (LCP), which considered the party's legalization a provocative and dangerous political maneuver.

17 CADN 2162, Delegation Générale de la France Libre, No. 897, Le Colonel Roget (Delegue en Syrie) a le Delegue General (Beyrouth), Damas–Beyrouth, "A/S du Parti Populaire Syrien," 5 July 1944, and CADN 2162, Delegation générale de la Combatttante au Levant, Services Politiques, Bureau de Lattaquie, No. 548/A-2, Lattaquie, "Activite actuelle du P.P.S.," 29 June 1944.

18 CADN 2162, Sûreté aux Armées, Zahle (Machgara), Information Spéciale No. 2,999, "Le P.P.S.," 26 October 1944, and CADN 2162, Sûreté aux Armées, Beyrouth, Information Spéciale No. 1,659, "Activite du P.P.S.," 17 August 1944. The party's symbol now consisted of a circle divided into four quadrants – two white and two red perpendicular to each other – each representing the party's four ideals: liberty, discipline, power, duty. This symbol was imposed on a white background.

19 Yammut, *al-Ḥaṣād al-Murr*, p. 119–129, 151–159.

Though other Lebanese political actors may have been wary, they accepted Chamoun's decision; the Kata'ib and LCP, on the other hand, vehemently opposed it. In the months that followed, the SSNP and the Communists engaged in a bitter struggle. Tensions and confrontations intensified as the SSNP reorganized while the LCP worked to prevent any such revival. Indeed, the Communists dedicated themselves to fighting the SSNP's resurgence "without mercy," and the confrontation between the two became a defining feature of the SSNP's political activities in the years to come.[20] In June, amid a fierce LCP campaign against the party, LCP leader Farajallah Helou and the editor of the LCP's *Sawt al-Sha'b* visited Chamoun to protest the SSNP's reorganization and the censorship of articles criticizing the SSNP. Helou complained that the Lebanese government was cooperating with a foreign power (i.e., Britain) to suppress the LCP and wondered how the Lebanese government could empower "agents of fascism, traitors, and Hitler's mercenaries" as the world confronted the spread of fascism. Such a decision, Helou argued, was against the principles of democracy and the patriotic spirit of Lebanese, empowering the agents of a foreign power who were the enemies of independence and liberty.[21] Helou's protests were also distributed by the Syrian Communist Party (SCP) in Damascus to counter the party's resurgence there, and anti-fascist organizations in Lebanon joined the chorus against the SSNP.[22] By early July, the activities of both the SSNP and the SCP had intensified in Homs. The SSNP's following in Homs was numerically weak and lacked broader support within the community, which tended to be more sympathetic toward the Communists. The SSNP, however, was able to establish an anti-Communist alliance with the League of National Action (LNA), enabling cooperative action to counter the SCP in the area through propaganda and other activities.[23]

LCP protests failed to hinder SSNP activities or convince the Lebanese government to intervene to prevent them. By June, the party established the publish-

---

20 See, for example, CADN 2118, Services Politique, Poste de Merdjayoun, No. 74/ME/28, Bulletin D'Informations Hebdomadaire no. 24, 19 June 1944, and CADN 2206, Service Politique, Bureau de Tyr, No. 363/TP/10, Bulletin d'informations no. 28, 29 July 1944. Communist opposition to the SSNP's legalization went beyond the borders of Lebanon and Syria. An open letter to Riad al-Sulh signed by several Iraqi intellectuals was published in the Iraqi daily *Sawt al-Ahali* and republished in the Communist party's paper in Beirut *Sawt al-Sha'b* denouncing the SSNP as "the agents of Hitlerism in Lebanon." See CADN 2162, 4 September 1944.

21 CADN 2162, Sûreté aux Armées, Beyrouth, Information Speciale No. 1,110, "Communistes contre P.P.S.," 23 June 1944, and CADN 2162, Sûreté aux Armées, Beyrouth, Information Speciale No. 1,126, "Parti Communiste et Parti Populaire," 26 June 1944.

22 CADN 2162, Sûreté aux Armées, Damas, Information, "Communistes et Parti Populaire Syrien," 27 June 1944.

23 CADN 2162, Homs, Information No. 56, "P.P.S. et le Parti Communiste," ND.

ing house Dar al-Nahda, intending to issue various publications, including novels, propaganda, and a weekly political, literary, and arts bulletin. The bulletin was to be overseen by the party's information director, Karim Azkul. The publishing house's work caused "political observers" to wonder whether it was independent or if it had been established with the help of the British. The rumor fed French concerns regarding British efforts to undermine France's standing in the Levant, but no evidence surfaced to substantiate the rumors.[24] Indeed, from the outset, the French had viewed the SSNP's legalization as the decision of a pro-British politician (i.e., Chamoun) aimed at rehabilitating a movement that the British thought could be an influential anti-communist and anti-Soviet force.[25] Though claims of British support for the SSNP were unsubstantiated, the French assessment of the party as an anti-communist force was not incorrect.

Thabit and Ayas's efforts to rebuild the party were bearing fruit after several months of actively working to draw former and current members back into the party fold. However, the French assessed that at least a third of former and current party adherents were holding out, refusing to follow Thabit and the party's current leadership whom they believed had betrayed Saʿadeh and his ideas by working with the British.[26] The nature of the party's relationship with the British remains ambiguous. The party was connected to the British through Chamoun and a shared commitment to fighting communism. Thabit seemed to suggest the British were intent on strengthening the party when he attempted to turn the Arabic daily *al-Anba*ʾ into the party's semi-official outlet and told a journalist that the party's rise aligned with Britain's broader policy of supporting groups committed to confronting the spread of communism.[27] Encouraged by the party's legalization in Lebanon, SSNP officials in Damascus appealed to the Syrian government Syrian to authorize the party's activities in the country. The Syrian

---

24 Among the first items to be published were two novels, one by Maʿmun Ayas and the other by Asad al-Ashqar, both of whom had only recently been released from Mieh Mieh and were considered among the party's ideological doctrinaires. CADN 2162, Direction Sûreté Générale aux Armées, Beyrouth, Information Speciale No. 747, "Le Parti Populaire Syrien," 17 May 1944, and CADN 2162, Direction Sûreté Générale aux Armées, Beyrouth, Information Speciale No. 851, "A/S du P.P.S.," 1 June 1944.

25 CADN 2206, Service Politique, Bureau de Tyr, No. 266/TP/10, Bulletin d'informations no. 21, 10 June 1944.

26 CADN 2162, Sûreté aux Armées, Beyrouth Information Spéciale No. 1,430, "Le Parti Populaire," 2 August 1944.

27 CADN 2162, Sûreté aux Armées, Beyrouth, Information Spéciale No. 1,458, "Le Parti Populaire et la revue al-Anba," 4 August 1944.

prime minister and interior minister promised to study the question, but no subsequent action was taken.[28]

After receiving authorization from Sulh to hold a large demonstration in Tyre in which Thabit was supposed to speak, Sulh reconsidered his decision over concerns the gathering would devolve into a violent confrontation between the SSNP and the Communists, who had threatened to raise hell should the gathering take place.[29] Despite Sulh's decision, the party made every effort to continue to court the Lebanese government and demonstrate its loyalty. On 27 August, a ceremony attended by Sulh, Majid Arslan, and other dignitaries was held in Dhour El Choueir to demonstrate the region's commitment to the government.[30] This demonstration was followed by meetings between an SSNP delegation and Sulh, Khuri, and other leading Lebanese politicians, including Salim Taqla and Majid Arslan. The purpose of the meetings was to press Lebanese leaders into permitting Saʿadeh's return to Lebanon and affirm the party remained dedicated supporters of the Lebanese government.[31]

As the party continued to regain its strength and influence, it held gatherings in support of the Lebanese government and intensified its propaganda. One such gathering was called off in Tyre due to concerns of violence between the LCP and SSNP, while another in Dhour El Choueir went ahead as planned and was attended by Sulh, Majid Arslan, and other notables.[32] Just as party gatherings were designed to attract new adherents and demonstrate the party's fielty to Lebanon, so, too, was the party's propaganda. In early September, the SSNP

28 CADN 2162, Sûreté aux Armées, Damas, Information, "Parti Populaire Syrien," 26 July 1944, and CADN 2162, Sûreté aux Armées, Damas, Information, "P.P.S.," 11 August 1944.

29 CADN 2206, Service Politique, Bureau de Tyr, No. 378/TP/10, Bulletin d'informations no. 30, 12 August 1944, and CADN 2206, Service Politique, Bureau de Tyr, No. 390/TP/10, Bulletin d'informations no. 31, 19 August 1944.

30 The ceremony and demonstrations were organized, according to the French, by the government in coordination with the SSNP: CADN 2162, Information No. 354, 30 August 1944. Images of similar SSNP events after the party's legalization in 1944 attended by leading Lebanese government officials can be found in Jurayj, *Maʿa Anṭūn Saʿādah, Vol. 3*, pp. 57–60.

31 CADN 2162, Information No. 356, 2 September 1944. In addition, the following month, Jibran Jurayj would travel to Merdjayoun for several meetings and gatherings in which the party would express praise and positive views of Sulh and Arslan, remaining consistent in its support of the Lebanese government. CADN 2118, Services Politique, Poste de Merdjayoun, No. 126/ME/28, Bulletin D'Informations Hebdomadaires no. 37, 20 October 1944.

32 CADN 2206, Service Politique, Bureau de Tyr, No. 378/TP/10, Bulletin d'informations no. 30, 12 August 1944, and CADN 2206, Service Politique, Bureau de Tyr, No. 390/TP/10, Bulletin d'informations no. 31, 19 August 1944. The ceremony and demonstrations were organized, according to the French, by the government in coordination with the SSNP. CADN 2162, Information No. 354, 30 August 1944.

released a 14-page pamphlet that declared it would lead a national renaissance that would not only lay a solid and unshakeable foundation for independence but maintain it. It asserted the party's basic and reform principles provided the foundation and political program for this national renaissance. Furthermore, the party was, in its own words, "the only movement" capable of destroying the confessional system and promoting national unity. After outlining the party's civil, social, cultural, and economic objectives, the pamphlet concluded with the observation that "independence is neither taken nor given but is built" and declared the SSNP to be the builders of independence.[33]

Distributed throughout Lebanon and Syria, the pamphlet's open declaration and commitment to safeguarding and preserving Lebanon's independence did not sit well with some members, particularly in Damascus.[34] Party officials in Damascus worried some of the ideas contradicted the party's fundamental principles and refused to accept the pamphlet's content. In search of clarification, these officials considered the possibility of dissociating themselves from their comrades in Beirut if the Beirut leadership turned its back on the party's principles.[35] Not willing to tolerate such dissent or the establishment of dissident factions, a delegation of ranking party officials led by Thabit traveled to Damascus for several meetings ostensibly to address the issue of the pamphlet. However, the discussions focused more on reorganizing the party and its activities in Syria rather than on the pamphlet's content, and it is unclear if the matter was even discussed. Following consultations, the party decided to aggressively confront the SCP through a propaganda campaign in Damascus that included the distribution of tracts, anti-communist gatherings, and appeals in local mosques.[36] It is evident that if the pamphlet's contents were discussed, no compromise or agreement was reached. Indeed, Thabit and other Beirut-based leaders made a private decision to replace several figures in the Damascene leadership. The decision was formalized in early November, on the eve of the anniversary of

33 CADN 2396, al-Ḥizb al-Qawmī, ʿUmda al-Idhāʿa, "Bayān", 1 September 1944, and CADN 2162, Sûreté aux Armées, Tripoli, Information Spéciale No. 2150 du 5.9.44, "Le Parti Populaire."

34 See, for example, CADN 2162, Sûreté aux Armées, Beyrouth, Information Spéciale No. 2,777 du 24.10.1944, "Le Parti Populaire"; CADN 2162, Sûreté aux Armées, Damas, Information du 20.10.1944, "Parti Populaire Syrien"; CADN 2162, Sûreté aux Armées, Beyrouth, Information Spéciale No. 2,889 du 28.10.1944, "Le P.P.S. a Beit-Mery"; CADN 2162, Sûreté aux Armées, Damas, Information du 15.9.44, " Parti Populaire Libanais"; and CADN 2162, Sûreté aux Armées, Saida (Tyr), Information Spéciale No. 2,781 du 16.10.1944, "Parti Populaire a Tyr."

35 CADN 2162, Sûreté aux Armées, Damas, Information du 15.9.44, " Parti Populaire Libanais."

36 CADN 2162, Sûreté aux Armées, Damas, Information du 26.9.44, "Activite du Parti Populaire Syrien," and CADN 2162, Sûreté aux Armées, Damas, Information du 5.10.44, "P.P.S."

the party's establishment, during a meeting of Beirut party leaders at Thabit's home.

Further, as part of the Thabit's efforts to consolidate control over the party and unify its message, the SSNP's Information Bureau released in October the first issue of its new monthly internal publication. Edited by Jibran Jurayj and Ibrahim Yammut, the publication was intended to keep members apprised of the party's activities, progress, and official pronouncements.[37] Content for the publication, including original articles and reproduced speeches, was primarily provided by the party's senior leadership, including Thabit (President of the Higher Council), Azkul (Director of Information), Ashqar (President of the Council of Directors), and Jurayj (Director of Finances).[38] Only four other editions would be issued before it ceased publication, the last appearing at the beginning of January.[39]

Enjoying its newfound freedom, the party intensified its activities throughout the country and kept up its pressure and attacks – verbal and physical – on the LCP.[40] For example, a group of SSNP members from Nabi Othman armed with batons, knives, and pistols ambushed a resident of El Ain who had insulted the party, dragging him from his car and beating him.[41] The party also continued to promote its reform principles and assert itself as the only movement capable of ensuring true independence. Despite enjoying the (relative) support of the Lebanese government, the party's Higher Council did urge the party's branches to reduce their political activities following Spears' departure from the country, concerned his absence would negatively impact the party's position.[42] Such caution was, perhaps, prudent. The French, who still

37 Jihad al-ʿAql, *Ṣiḥāfat al-Ḥaraka al-Qawmiyya al-Ijtimāʿiyya (1933–1949), al-Juzʾ al-Thālith (1944–1948)* (Beirut: al-Furāt, 2005), p. 22.

38 Al-'Aql, *Ṣiḥāfat, Vol. 3,* p. 25.

39 Though the party's Information Bureau ceased issuing this version of the publication in January, it would issue four editions of a similar publication between July and November 1945. Al-'Aql, *Ṣiḥāfat, Vol. 3,* pp. 95–98. In addition, the party's Bureau of Culture would begin issuing its own publication dedicated to the fine arts and culture in February 1945. Al-'Aql, *Ṣiḥāfat, Vol. 3,* pp. 133–142.

40 An informant suggested the party had more than one thousand members and countless sympathizers in the region of Koura. CADN 2162, Sûreté aux Armées, Tripoli, Information Spéciale No. 2,630 du 11.10.1944, "Parti Populaire." Also see, for example, a report on the party's activities in Merdjayoun: CADN 2118, Services Politique, Poste de Merdjayoun, No. 126/ME/28, Bulletin D'Informations Hebdomadaires no. 37, 20 October 1944.

41 CADN 2162, Sûreté aux Armées, Zahle (Ras-Baalbeck), Information Spéciale No. 3,391 du 20.11.1944, "Agression du P.P.S. a El-Ain."

42 CADN 2118, Services Politique, Poste de Merdjayoun, No. 148/ME/28, Bulletin D'Informations Hebdomadaires no. 42, 16 December 1944.

controlled the security services, remained convinced the British were providing tangible support to the SSNP in some way to help it reorganize and fight communism and were frustrated by the party's alliance with the Lebanese government.[43] Further angering the French, SSNP members had attacked a pro-French demonstration in Beit Meri, and at the beginning of February 1945, the French suspected the SSNP, in coordination with Sulh, were responsible for protests and strikes against the continuing French presence in Lebanon and Syria.[44] Yet the French did not intervene, as the activities mentioned above demonstrate, the SSNP's activities seemingly continued apace, and the party's following was notably increasing.[45]

6.2 A Special Election

At the beginning of 1945, Sulh's government was in a state of tumult. Defense Minister Majid Arslan had resigned in December, and Sulh, having failed to thwart opposition efforts to repeal the press censorship law, submitted his resignation as well. Complicating matters were President Khuri's illness and grief over the loss of his friend and Constitutional Bloc ally Salim Taqla, who had died unexpectedly on 11 January.[46] ʿAbd al-Halim Karami replaced Sulh on 9 January, and a special election was held to fill Taqla's now-vacant seat in the Chamber of Deputies. The vacancy sparked an intense and passionate campaign between the Constitutional Bloc, which put forward Taqla's son Philippe as its candidate, and the Kataʾib, which put forward Elias Rababi, the editor-in-chief of the party's newspaper *al-Amal*.

43 CADN 2162, Sûreté aux Armées, Beyrouth, Information du 18.1.1945, "Le Parti Populaire Syrien."
44 CADN 2162, Service Politique – Bureau de Beyrouth, Information No. 14, 26 January 1945, and CADN 2162, Sûreté aux Armées, Beyrouth, Information du 1.2.1945, "Activite hostile du P.P."
45 French reports noted, for example, the increasing number of youths had joined the party in the areas of Nabi Othman and El Ain in the Baalbek District, while several others reported on party gatherings in Merdjayoun and Beit–Meri and the establishment of a new SSNP directorate in Saida. See CADN 2162, Sûreté aux Armées, Zahle (Ras-Baalbeck), Information Spéciale No. 3,922 du 23.12.1944, "Activite du P.P."; CADN 2162, Sûreté au Armées, Merdjayoun, Information no. 93 du 28.12.1944, Beyrouth, du 1.1.45, "Le Parti Populare"; and CADN 2162, Sûreté aux Armées, Saida, Information du 5.1.1945, "Le P.P." On the party's activities in the Shouf, particularly Baakline, and the Druze villages of Moukhtara, Ammatour and Jbaa see CADN 48, Sûreté aux Armées, Information no. 1,129 du 23.3.1945, Beyrouth, "La Situation dans le Chouf."
46 Zisser, *Lebanon*, pp. 116–117.

Announcing Rababi's candidacy, the Kata'ib advanced its political agenda to support Lebanon's complete and absolute independence, cooperation based on equality with the Arab World, and enhancing Lebanon's prestige.[47] The SSNP, backing the government-supported candidate Taqla, dismissed the Kata'ib as nothing more than a confessional organization. At the end of February, the SSNP distributed propaganda tracts throughout Mount Lebanon, beckoning its members and other citizens to fulfill their civic duty and participate in the coming election. Kata'ib members hastened to destroy the tracts lest they sway local voters away from Rababi.[48] Arguing the Kata'ib's campaign and candidate advanced "fanatical confessionalism" that endangered Lebanese unity, the SSNP declared its full support for Taqla.[49] With the support of the government, the Constitutional Bloc, and the SSNP, Taqla won the 4 March election, a result which the Kata'ib immediately protested and deemed illegitimate.

The Kata'ib alleged a broad government conspiracy against it and its candidate. They accused Karami and Sulh of plotting armed aggression and interfering with voters. Further, they accused Lebanon's Grand Mufti Muhammad Tawfiq Khaled of issuing a *fatwa* that accused Rababi of "paganism."[50] A French inform-

47 CADN 48, Sûreté aux Armées, Beyrouth, Information No. 719 du 19.2.1945, "Les Phalanges Libanaises." For examples of the Kata'ib's election activities see: CADN 48, Sûreté aux Armées, Beyrouth, Information du 27.2.1945, "Le Meeting Phalangiste de Djounieh"; CADN 48, Sûreté aux Armées, Beyrouth, Information No. 892 du 22.2.1945, "Des Elections du Mont–Liban"; CADN 48, Sûreté aux Armées, Beyrouth, Information du 20.2.1945, "Réunion Electoral des Phalanges a Jdeide (Metn)"; CADN 48, Sûreté aux Armées, Beyrouth, Information du 22.2.1945, "4ème Tract Electoral des Phalanges Libanaises"; and CADN 48, Sûreté aux Armées, Beyrouth, Information du 27.2.1945, "Tracts Phalangistes."

48 CADN 48, Sûreté aux Armées, Beyrouth, Information du 2.2.1945, "Tract Electoral Phalangiste"; CADN 48, Sûreté aux Armées, Beyrouth, Information du 1.3.1945, "Les Phalanges Libanaises"; and CADN 2162, Sûreté aux Armées, Beyrouth, Information du 2.3.1945, "Proclamation du P.P."

49 CADN 48, "Elections au Liban 1945," E/3, Parti Populaire, 27 February 1945, and CADN 48, Sûreté aux Armées, Beyrouth, Information du 2.3.1945, "Parti Populaire." Kamal Abu Kamal, a party leader in Aley, had declared in early February that the party would support the pro-government candidate to counteract the Kata'ib. During 1 March celebrations at Thabit's home, the party reiterated its support for Taqla was for no other reason but repelling what it viewed to be a grave danger. While the party was certainly sincere in its opposition to the Kata'ib, it had other reasons for supporting Taqla, despite its assertions to the contrary, namely in generally amicable relations with Khuri and Chamoun's Constitutional Bloc, which had facilitated the SSNP legalization the previous year. CADN 48, Sûreté aux Armées, Beyrouth, Information du 5.2.1945, "Le Parti Populaire."

50 CADN 48, Sûreté aux Armées, Beyrouth, Information 8.3.1945, "Les Phalanges Libanaises," and CADN 48, Sûreté aux Armées, Beyrouth, Information du 13.3.1945, "Contre Les Phalanges Libanaises."

ant asserted that Taqla's success was owed in part to SSNP support, particularly in Dhour El Choueir, Jbeil, and Jounie, where the party allegedly mobilized many voters by audaciously buying them off for small sums of money. No evidence confirming the bribery allegations was provided. The same informant also singled out the Kata'ib for criticism, accusing them of lacking courage and the organization necessary to impact the outcome.[51]

The SSNP, in contrast, welcomed the election results as a victory over confessionalism and religious fanaticism. In a tract released on 10 March, the SSNP praised "the social and political evolution" that had taken place on 4 March and its positive meaning for Lebanon, commending Lebanese voters for their rejection of confessionalism. Unlike previous elections, the results demonstrated that in the face of a concerted campaign by the purveyors of "confessionalism" and "religious fanaticism," progressive ideas championed by the party and others had succeeded. Noting the divisive danger of confessionalism to national unity and interests, the SSNP called for all Lebanese, regardless of confession, to rally around and support the idea of a civic nation that would sustain Lebanon's existence and independence.[52] The Kata'ib brushed aside the criticism, distributing tracts dismissing the importance of the SSNP and Azkul, bluntly stating, "Hitler's agents bark, but the caravan passes."[53]

While the special election had inflamed tensions between the Kata'ib and the SSNP, the party's public activities also provoked the ire of the LCP. LCP activities and propaganda against the SSNP had intensified in February 1945 to encourage adherents to abandon the party, undermine public support for the party, and incite the public to confront the social nationalists and their aims in Lebanon.[54] In so doing, "the Communist Party aimed at eliminating the [SSNP] to consolidate [its] activities in the country."[55] On 11 March, a group of SSNP members demonstrated in Tyre where they paraded down the main thoroughfare waving

51 CADN 48, Sûreté aux Armées, Information du 6.3.1945, Zahle, "Les Elections du Mont-Liban."

52 CADN 48, Sûreté aux Armées, Beyrouth, Information no. 994 du 13.3.1945, "Ci-Apres Traducion d'un tract lance par le P.P. a la suite des elections complementaires au Mont-Liban," and CADN 48, Sûreté aux Armées, Saida (Merjayoun), Information du 16.3.1945, "Le Parti Populaire."

53 CADN 48, Sûreté aux Armées, Zahle, Information du 20.3.1945, "Activites du Parti Populaire."

54 See, for example, a report on defections from the SSNP to the Najjadeh and the Communist party in Tyre: CADN 2162, Sûreté aux Armées, Saida-Tyr, Information du 20.2.1945, "Le Parti Populaire."

55 2/1 in Youmna Asseily and Ahmad Asfahani, eds., *A Face in the Crowd: The Secret Papers of Emir Farid Chehab, 1942–1972* (London: Stacey International, 2007), p. 16.

the party's flag and chanting anti-communist and anti-French slogans. The chants derided Stalin and LCP leader Farajallah Helou, respectively, as "the ass" and "the dog" of Jouaya (a small Shiʿi village in Tyre district) and sang "down with the French." Local authorities did not intervene and let the demonstration proceed unhindered, much to the irritation of the LCP, whose entreaties proved futile.[56] The rally came only days after SSNP activists in Tyre had disrupted the screening of a pro-Soviet film, hissing and shouting insults at Stalin every time he appeared on screen and praising Hitler to provoke the LCP.[57]

Frustrated by the SSNP's resurgence, the LCP urged the Lebanese government to curtail the SSNP's increasing activity, which the LCP deemed traitorous to the nation and the cause of the Allies.[58] A little over a month later, as 1 May approached, Thabit circulated a secret directive ordering members to guard against any communist agitation or provocation. The party's approach was not merely defensive and reactionary; it also sought to actively prevent and disrupt LCP gatherings and demonstrations, creating situations where each rival provoked the other. Altercations had taken place in Jdeide after several communists publicly denounced Chamoun in front of several SSNP members, as well as in Dabbine and Tyre.[59] In Jal al-Dib, SSNP members prevented LCP partisans traveling from Antelias to Beirut to pass through the town, forcing them to turn around and abandon plans to participate in LCP demonstrations and gatherings in Beirut. The LCP did not take the act lightly and returned in the days that fol-

56 CADN 2162, Sûreté aux Armées, Saida (Tyr), Information du 13.3.1945, "Manifestation des Populaires," and CADN 2162, Service Politique, Tyr, Information au sujet d'une manifestion contra la Russie et la France," 15 March 1945.

57 CADN 2162, Sûreté aux Armées, Saida (Tyr), Information du 7.3.1945, "Entre Communiste et Populaires." Despite the SSNP's public and confrontational activities in Tyre, French reports assessed the party in the area to "be in danger" as efforts to reinvigorate the group and its activities since the beginning of 1945 there had not borne fruit and members were reportedly abandoning the party. The party's weakness owed, in no small part, to an internal rift among the local leadership that essentially divided the party locally into two factions. See CADN 2206, Service Politique, Bureau de Tyr, no. 628/TP/10, Bulletin d'informations no. 47, 9 December 1944; CADN 2206, Service Politique, Bureau de Tyr, no. 86/TP/10, Bulletin d'informations no. 6, 10 February 1945; and CADN 2206, Service Politique, Bureau de Tyr, no. 126/TP/10, Bulletin d'informations no. 9, 3 March 1945.

58 CADN 2206, Service Politique, Poste de Merdjayoun, no. 45/ME/28, Bulletin d'informations no. 7, 31 March 1945.

59 CADN 2206, Service Politique, Poste de Merdjayoun, no. 64/ME/28, Bulletin d'informations no. 10, 10 May 1945, and CADN 2206, Service Politique, Bureau de Tyr, No. 237/TP/10, Bulletin d'informations no. 17, 30 April 1945.

lowed to exact their revenge on the SSNP in the town, finding and beating several of them.[60]

60 CADN 48, Sûreté aux Armées, Beyrouth, Information no. 1813 du 12.5.1945, "Entre Communistes et Populaires."

Part Three: **The Road to a Failed Revolution and Its Aftermath**

7 Erasing the Mandate

Fayez Sayegh, the son of a Presbyterian minister, was born in 1922 in the southern Syrian village of Kharaba. He grew up in Tiberias on the Sea of Galilee's shores before moving to Beirut with his two brothers to pursue their education. In 1938, at just sixteen, Sayegh joined the SSNP, following in his two brothers' footsteps who had joined the party several years before. Saʿadeh's way of thinking and the SSNP's national doctrine provided Sayegh with a vision for a future in which the nation was strong and independent, freed from the shackles of the mandate and religious fanaticism. Sayegh made his mark leading the SSNP's student branch at AUB and eventually was appointed the party's Director of Culture and Director of Information in 1946. However, his rise in the party was cut short due to a dispute with Saʿadeh over divergent philosophical views. Their debate took place within the broader context of an ideological conflict between Saʿadeh and the party's leadership while Saʿadeh was in exile.[1] This dispute, which resulted in the expulsion of several prominent party officials, and Saʿadeh's effort to re-impose doctrinal integrity, was a defining moment in the party's history. These actions would have grave consequences, as they ultimately led the party into open confrontation with the Lebanese government.

The period preceding and immediately following Saʿadeh's return to Lebanon in March 1947 was characterized by internal party strife and renewed confrontation with Lebanese authorities. The party provocatively reiterated that Lebanon was merely part of the Syrian nation, rather than distinct from it, and was overly critical of the Lebanese government's conduct in the 1948 Arab-Israeli War. The confrontation reached its apogee in the SSNP's failed "social nationalist revolution" and Saʿadeh's subsequent execution in the summer of 1949, after which the party was outlawed in Lebanon and forced to move the center of its activities to neighboring Damascus.

7.1 The End of the Mandate

France's determination to maintain its grip over Syria and Lebanon provoked nationalists' ire and outcry in both countries. In the spring of 1945, France refused to relinquish its control over the security institutions in both countries and announced its intention to establish air and naval bases. The decision fueled the

1 Adel Beshara, *Fāyiz Ṣāyigh al-Qawmī: Tajribatuhu fī al-Ḥizb al-Sūrī al-Qawmī al-Ijtimāʿī* (Beirut: al-Furāt, 2018).

https://doi.org/10.1515/9783110729092-009

already growing sense of popular discontent and "led to widespread demonstrations and anti-French protests across Syria in May 1945."[2] The situation rapidly deteriorated, and French authorities, unable to effectively manage and police it, took a more punitive approach. French forces were ordered to quell the demonstrations using deadly force, including indiscriminate artillery and airstrikes.

Given the sensitivity of the situation in Syria, the SSNP was prohibited from holding public gatherings so as not to inflame tensions in Lebanon. In Merdjayoun, for example, a party gathering over concerns regarding the content of a planned speech. The speech was relatively innocuous, nothing more than thinly-veiled criticism of France passing as praise for the Allied victory in Europe, but was nevertheless deemed too provocative by local Lebanese authorities.[3] Several days after the canceled event, the SSNP published a tract declaring that the critical time through which Lebanon was passing would define its future. To defend Lebanon's independence, the SSNP "placed its resources at the national government's disposal" and encouraged other parties and organizations to do the same.[4] Further, Thabit issued a secret memorandum advising party adherents to remain prepared for any confrontations but not to volunteer for the Lebanese Army.[5]

The crisis devolved further as demonstrations and riots gave way to skirmishes with French forces. On 29 May, French forces laid siege to the Syrian parliament to arrest Syrian politicians before destroying the building and launching more extensive military operations in Damascus. French forces cut the city's electricity and shelled it indiscriminately while French colonial soldiers roamed the streets, looting and destroying as they saw fit. Syrian President Shukri al-Quwatli appealed to the British to intervene. British Prime Minister Winston Churchill called on the French to halt their offensive to avoid a confrontation with British forces, but British calls went unheeded, and Churchill ordered British troops to invade. Over the next several days, without bloodshed, British forces imposed their control over French forces, confining soldiers to their barracks, grounding French aircraft, and setting strict rules of engagement. By early July, France was forced to withdraw its troops from Syria to Lebanon, effectively ending its mandate over Syria. The French cursed the British for what they

---

2 Rogan, *The Arabs*, p. 244.

3 CADN 2162, Sûreté aux Armées, Saida (Merdjayoun), Information du 17.5.1945, "Le Parti Populaire."

4 CADN 2162, Sûreté aux Armées, Beyrouth, Information du 20.5.1945, "Tract du Parti Populaire."

5 CADN 2206, Service Politique, Poste de Merdjayoun, No. 70/ME/28, Bulletin d'informations no. 11, 28 May 1945.

considered a humiliating betrayal, but an all-out confrontation between the two powers had been avoided.[6]

French anger with the British manifested itself in Lebanon, where the French maintained control over the country's security apparatus and countered any challenge to its on-going presence. Given its withdrawal from Syria at the hands of the British, French intelligence was concerned by possible connections between the British and the SSNP. In July, French reports suggested a relationship between the SSNP and the British, claiming two SSNP members in Tyre had allegedly revealed party recruits were provided with British-supplied pistols and ammunition and that the party was in constant contact with the British.[7] Such allegations played to French fears of the party's cooperation with its rivals, and, given the SSNP's ties to other pro-British Lebanese political figures, it seemed to suggest deeper relations between the two.[8] However, while British and SSNP interests may have been aligned, no evidence suggests any active collaboration.

The SSNP's political activity for much of 1945 was relatively subdued, as the leadership focused on rebuilding the party. The most visible manifestations of the party's political activities typically involved confrontations with the Lebanese Communist Party. The LCP frequently accused the SSNP of working against the Lebanese cause, but given the SSNP's alliance with the government, the accusation rang hollow. In early October, for example, the SSNP held a massive, government-approved rally in Merdjayoun with an estimated 500 members in attendance and featured several prominent party officials as speakers.[9] The following month, the party joined several other Lebanese political parties to protest the Balfour Declaration, demonstrating its growing strength and expressing its solidarity in the struggle against Zionism. However, the events of that day would devolve into a violent confrontation between it and the LCP.

According to Muhammad Jamil Bayhum of the Union of Parties Opposed to Zionism, the protest's organizer, each participating political party would hold a demonstration and march that would coalesce into a single large gathering at Beirut's Cinema Roxy. The SSNP had announced its participation in the protest and, in the days preceding it, worked to stir up anti-Zionist sentiments, including

6 Rogan, *The Arabs*, pp. 245–246.
7 CADN 2162, Extrait du bulletin d'information no. 30 du 30.7.45 du poste politique de Tyr, "Les Britanniques arment le P.P.S."
8 CADN 2206, Service Politique, Bureau de Tyr, No. 379/TP/10, Bulletin d'informations no. 30, 30 July 1945.
9 CADN 2206, Service Politique, Poste de Merdjayoun, No. 415/ME/28, Bulletin d'informations no. 21, 15 October 1945.

hanging anti-Zionist posters denouncing those who sell land to Jews as "traitors."[10] The LCP "refused to join [the event] because the [SSNP] was taking part" and, instead, sought to disrupt the SSNP's protest march. Several "communists infiltrated the [SSNP's ranks] and one of them attempted to remove the [*zawbaʿa*] flag from a car, provoking a fight and causing the security forces to intervene in an attempt to separate the two groups."[11] SSNP members retreated to Assur Square and the nearby Grand Theater, but a group of LCP partisans armed with knives and sticks awaited them. In the ensuing melee, eight SSNP members were injured, and one Communist was killed. The LCP, incensed at the death of one of their own, immediately called for revenge. Encouraging attacks on the SSNP, they declared their fallen comrade, Edwar Shartuni, a martyr who had "died for Palestine in the struggle against Zionism – at the hands of the Syrian Nationalist gang."[12] The characterization of Shartuni as a casualty in the struggle against Zionism was a brazen attempt to portray the SSNP as an agent of Zionism and discredit it.

Tensions between the LCP and SSNP continued to simmer in the days and weeks following the altercation. Verbal spats and violent clashes between the two movements occurred throughout Lebanon, particularly in Merdjayoun.[13] The SSNP leadership allegedly sent funds to the party branch in Merdjayoun to obtain explosives intended for use against the local LCP branch.[14] At the end of November, two SSNP members were detained on suspicion of their involvement in bombings targeting three LCP members; no damage or injuries were caused.[15] At least one of the alleged suspects had been involved in firefights with LCP members in the village on 9 November, just one week after skir-

---

10 CADN 2206, Service Politique, Poste de Merdjayoun, No. 471/ME/28, Bulletin d'informations no. 23, 8 November 1945.

11 2/1 in Asseily and Asfahani, *A Face in the Crowd*, p. 18.

12 2/1 in Asseily and Asfahani, *A Face in the Crowd*, pp. 18–19. One SSNP member did ultimately succumb to his wounds and was declared a martyr. The commemoration of his death following forty days of morning, the party seized the opportunity to revisit the events of early November and denounce communism as "an anarchist movement delaying national renaissance." CADN 2206, Service Politique, Poste de Merdjayoun, No. 562/ME/28, Bulletin d'informations no. 26, 26 December 1945.

13 CADN 2206, Service Politique, Poste de Merdjayoun, No. 471/ME/28, Bulletin d'informations no. 23, 8 November 1945.

14 CADN 2206, Service Politique, Poste de Merdjayoun, No. 435/ME/28, Bulletin d'informations no. 22, 27 October 1945.

15 CADN 2206, Service Politique, Poste de Merdjayoun, No. 525/ME/28, Bulletin d'informations no. 25, 6 December 1945.

mishes in Beirut.[16] The party mobilized to help their detained comrades, taking up a collection and appealing to other party branches to send financial support. To get Lebanese authorities to act against the LCP, the SSNP delivered protest telegrams to the government denouncing the LCP for sowing anarchy throughout the country. Several LCP members were subsequently arrested, which resulted in LCP counter-protests and accusations that the local police chief was an SSNP member acting based on partisan motivations. Refusing to let the charge go unchallenged, the local SSNP branch in Merdjayoun responded with a telegram to the central authorities protesting the LCP's allegations.[17]

7.2 The Gathering Storm

Having gone almost four years without exchanging communication, the SSNP's leadership in Beirut reestablished contact with their exiled leader, delivering a letter through the party's branch in West Africa to Saʿadeh's brother in Brazil.[18] In response, Saʿadeh wrote Thabit and the SSNP's Higher Council requesting an update on the state of the party and the political climate in the homeland. He asked explicitly if the time was right for him to return and urged Thabit to respond with the utmost urgency.[19] The party's leadership, in turn, tasked Ghassan Tueni to correspond with Saʿadeh and update him on the party's affairs. Tueni, a Greek Orthodox Christian from Beit Meri and the son of Gibran Tueni, the founder of *al-Nahar*, had relocated to Boston for his studies. Throughout 1946, Saʿadeh corresponded not only with Tueni, but Thabit and Ashqar. Their correspondence would expose the chasm that had emerged in the preceding years between Saʿadeh and a cadre of party officials, headed by Thabit, over dissonant visions of the party's ideological and political orientation. An intense intellectual dialogue and debate ensued in private exchanges that culminated in dramatic changes within the party.

In the first exchange of letters in February, Saʿadeh directed Tueni to provide him with a comprehensive report on the party's activities since the military tribunals in August 1940 and on the state of the party in the United States.[20] Saʿa-

16 CADN 2206, Service Politique, Poste de Merdjayoun, No. 500/ME/28, Bulletin d'informations no. 24, 20 Novembre 1945.
17 CADN 2118, Service Politique, Poste de Merdjayoun, No. 32/ME/28, Bulletin d'informations no. 2, 8 January 1946.
18 Mujais, *SSNP*, p. 177.
19 "Ilā Nehmeh Thabit," in Saʿadeh, *al-Aʿmāl al-Kāmila, Vol. 11*, p. 5.
20 "Ilā Ghassan Tueni," in Saʿadeh, *al-Aʿmāl al-Kāmila, Vol. 11*, pp. 25–30.

deh acknowledged he had no details about the party's activities other than general knowledge that the "National Party" and the LCP were engaged in frequent clashes. Of primary importance to Saʿadeh was learning: (a) the extent to which the Syrian national idea had been disseminated throughout Greater Syria; (b) the reasons for the emergence of the "National Party"; (c) the state of the party's internal administration and morale; (d) the stance of the British, French, Russians, and local political parties towards the SSNP; (e) the party's current political orientation and policies; and (f) details surrounding the possibility of his return.[21]

While Saʿadeh waited for Tueni's report, the party's activities continued apace, characterized by regular confrontations with the LCP. In Machghara, the SSNP and LCP competed for the support of local *fellahin*, distributing propaganda leaflets disputing the other's claims.[22] In Merdjayoun, the SSNP protested the LCP demands for establishing a municipal council, and, in a demonstration of the often petty nature of their conflict, SSNP members in Rachaya el-Fokhar disrupted the wedding of Maronite LCP members, preventing the ceremony from taking place.[23] Further scuffles between the LCP and SSNP occurred in the same area in April, requiring the intervention of the gendarmerie and the Sûreté to disperse the fight and restore order; the altercation had caused local shops and cafes to close.[24]

The party also began publishing its new daily in Beirut, *Sada al-Nahda*. After only three editions, Lebanese Interior Minister Emile Lahud suspended its publication for three days for "disturbing public order." The party responded in protest that the order was nothing more than an effort to limit the freedom of the press and curb free speech and thought.[25] However, rather than being viewed as an assault on protected freedoms, the brief suspension is better understood as a warning to the party by Lebanese authorities to stay in line and refrain from challenging the understandings reached between the two, illuminating the boundaries of the party's political freedom.

---

21 "Ilā Ghassan Tueni," in Saʿadeh, *al-Aʿmāl al-Kāmila, Vol.* 11, pp. 30 – 31.

22 CADN 2118, Service Politique, Poste de Merdjayoun, No. 47/ME/28, Bulletin d'informations no. 2, 16 January 1946.

23 CADN 2118, Service Politique, Poste de Merdjayoun, No. 107/ME/28, Bulletin d'informations no. 4, 26 February 1946.

24 CADN 2118, Services Politique, Poste de Merdjayoun, No. 290/ME/28, Bulletin d'informations no. 9, 27 April 1946.

25 Al-'Aql, *Ṣiḥāfat, Vol. 3*, pp. 480 – 482, and "al-Taʿṭīl al-Idārī wa Ḥuriyya al-Ṣiḥāfa," *Sada al-Nahda*, 9 February 1946, reproduced in al-'Aql, *Ṣiḥāfat, Vol. 3*, p. 490.

Tueni sent his first update to Saʿadeh at the end of March.[26] Though Saʿadeh had expressed his initial satisfaction with the party's propaganda and activities during the war, a more thorough review of Tueni's report raised his concern as it revealed the party had downplayed its nationalist ideology in favor of political realism. Whereas Saʿadeh had attempted to strike a balance between the two considerations, the party under Thabit had shifted its approach toward political moderation and realism, deemphasizing the party's ideological doctrine. The shift had indeed provoked opposition within the party.

Nevertheless, Thabit, then serving as president of the Higher Council and Political Bureau and as a member of the Council of Deputies, and the cadre of his supporters in the party leadership (including Ayas, Ashqar, ʿAjram, Sayegh, Qadurra, Tueni, Qubrusi, and ʿAbdallah Saʿadeh) was able to lead the party in their desired direction. This group was determined to maintain the party's "truce" (*hudna*) with the Lebanese government. They believed the only way to advance the party's agenda and cause it to flourish was to undertake political action based on the party's reform principles, ignoring doctrinal conflicts and debates.[27] Indeed, this group had succeeded in improving the party's relations with several leading Lebanese politicians in addition to Khuri and Sulh, including Kamal Jumblatt, Gabriel Murr, Henri Pharaon, and Hamid Frangieh.[28]

Tueni defended the merits of the ideological shift in this initial report to Saʿadeh, arguing that the previous approach fiercely emphasized doctrine and ideological debate over practical political action. The former approach he characterized as "academic rigidity" (*taḥajjur akādīmī*) that had limited the party's political flexibility, while the full embrace of the party's reform principles as a political program had enabled it to spread its influence.[29] Saʿadeh argued that Tueni and others had failed to understand the party's history properly. This lack of understanding subsequently led them to erroneously conclude that this "academic rigidity" had stifled the party's creative spirit and its ability to bring about political and social reform. Even more problematic, it had led them to overemphasize the party's reform principles allowed for the introduction of individual intellectual innovations not grounded in the party's national ideology. This, he argued, could pose a danger to the party's ideological and organizational unity. To make his point, Saʿadeh singled out Fayez Sayegh, the party's young Culture and Fine Arts Director, for appealing to the authority of the Pla-

26 "Ilā Ghassan Tueni," in Saʿadeh, *al-Aʿmāl al-Kāmila, Vol. 11*, pp. 58–76.
27 Qubrusi, *Yatadhakkar, Vol. 2*, p. 137.
28 Qubrusi, *Yatadhakkar, Vol. 2*, p. 138.
29 "Ilā Ghassan Tueni," in Saʿadeh, *al-Aʿmāl al-Kāmila, Vol. 11*, pp. 96–97.

tonic values of Truth, Beauty, and Good, which suggested the authority of a value system outside of that dictated by the party's ideology.[30]

Over the preceding years, Sayegh's influence within the party had increased, his eloquence as a public speaker and writer propelling him into the ranks of the party's leadership. By 1946, he was serving as the party's Director of Culture and Director of Information.[31] Sayegh vigorously defended the party against its critics and focused a great deal of his political writing on forcefully arguing against Communism and Zionism. The content of Sayegh's speeches and articles largely conformed to the party's ideological aims and program. By 1946, however, his writings were increasingly influenced by and imbued with existentialist philosophical themes inspired by the Danish philosopher Søren Kierkegaard and the Russian philosopher Nikolai Berdyaev. Berdyaev's concept of "personalism" had served as the foundation for Sayegh's recently completed Master's thesis at AUB on "personal existence."[32] According to Berdyaev, there is a distinction between the 'individual' and the 'person'; the individual does not exist independently beyond the confines of the material world and social existence, always being part of a whole, whereas the 'person' transcends this boundary, existing independently in a spiritual category as its own unique whole. Not dependent on the material world, the 'person' is the highest and most authentic form of human existence.[33] This philosophical position directly contradicted Saʿadeh's, who argued the exact opposite: real human existence is found only within social existence. With Sayegh's views increasingly permeating party publications, a confrontation over increasingly diverging views grew ever more likely.[34]

In an April letter to Thabit, Saʿadeh expressed his happiness that the two had re-established direct contact. After a long period of disruption, they could engage once again in the national cause together. He commended Thabit for obtaining a license from the Lebanese government and welcomed the opportunities it opened for the party to operate and spread its message, though its licensing gave rise to several issues that would need to be addressed upon his return to the homeland.[35] Saʿadeh pressed Thabit to facilitate his return as soon as possible, as he desired not only to come home but to contest the upcoming Lebanese elections. The party had submitted a request to the Lebanese government to ap-

---

30 "Ilā Ghassan Tueni," in Saʿadeh, *al-Aʿmāl al-Kāmila, Vol. 11*, pp. 96–97.
31 Beshara, *Fāyiz Ṣāyigh*, pp. 41–43.
32 Beshara, *Fāyiz Ṣāyigh*, pp. 60–61.
33 Vincent J. McNamara, "Some Basic Notions of the Personalism of Nicolas Berdyaev," *Laval théologique et philosophique* 16, no. 2 (1960): pp. 279–280.
34 Beshara, *Fāyiz Ṣāyigh*, pp. 60–64.
35 "Ilā Raʾīs al-Majlis al-Aʿlā," in Saʿadeh, *al-Aʿmāl al-Kāmila, Vol. 11*, pp. 83–87.

prove his return and issue him a new passport but had yet to receive a response.[36] Complicating the party's ability to press its request was the current state of political uncertainty in Lebanon; Prime Minister Sami al-Sulh's decision to dissolve his cabinet in late May due to incessant discord had inaugurated a period of political jockeying to form a new government.[37] Saʿadeh's frustration with the delay was compounded by the fact that he had not heard from the party's central leadership in Beirut since early May. Now, in August, Saʿadeh dispatched letters to Tueni and SSNP leaders residing in Cairo and Homs imploring them to reach out to the party's leadership in Beirut to resume communication.[38] Within weeks, Thabit replied to Saʿadeh.

Despite the breakdown in communication with the party's central leadership, Saʿadeh's correspondence with Tueni and the party materials he had received, including internal reports, copies of *Sada al-Nahda*, and other party publications, was informative. These materials made him acutely aware of what he considered very problematic developments: misinterpretations of the party's history, a de-emphasis on party doctrine, and a breakdown of the party's administrative and organizational discipline. In his correspondence with Tueni, Saʿadeh stressed that his issue with Sayegh revolved around constitutional and administrative considerations and was not an issue of intellectual freedom or freedom of expression. Whereas Saʿadeh maintained Sayegh was responsible for executing his duties as the cultural director within the framework of the party's ideology and organization, Sayegh and Tueni had argued that matters of culture fell outside the party's purview. This view was incorrect according to Saʿadeh, who pointed out that cultural renaissance had been an integral part of the party's ideology and organization, and observed the dangerous implications for party unity if party leaders began to hold themselves accountable to standards other than those established by the party's constitution and ideology.[39]

Just as Tueni had attempted to do in his initial correspondence with Saʿadeh, Ashqar wrote from Cairo to explain the steps the party had taken and defended not only their necessity but their correctness. In his letter, Ashqar criticized the

---

36 "Ilā Na'aman Daw," in Saʿadeh, *al-Aʿmāl al-Kāmila, Vol. 11*, pp. 105 – 106, and "Ilā Raʾīs Maktab ʿAbr al-Ḥudūd," in Saʿadeh, *al-Aʿmāl al-Kāmila, Vol. 11*, p. 109.
37 Zisser, *Lebanon*, pp. 119 – 121.
38 See "Ilā Ghassan Tueni," in Saʿadeh, *al-Aʿmāl al-Kāmila, Vol. 11*, pp. 143 – 159; "Ilā Muhammad Shamnaq," in Saʿadeh, *al-Aʿmāl al-Kāmila, Vol. 11*, pp. 160 – 161; and "Ilā al-Ab Bulus Mas'ad," in Saʿadeh, *al-Aʿmāl al-Kāmila, Vol. 11*, pp. 141 – 142.
39 "Ilā Ghassan Tueni," in Saʿadeh, *al-Aʿmāl al-Kāmila, Vol. 11*, pp. 143 – 159, and "Ilā Ghassan Tueni," in Saʿadeh, *al-Aʿmāl al-Kāmila, Vol. 11*, pp. 203 – 210. For further discussion on their exchange, see Mujais, *Saadeh, Vol. 3*, pp. 250 – 253.

party's initial political positions and the method of its ideologues, wondering what would have happened had Saʿadeh established two parties in 1932 – the "Lebanese Reform Party" in Lebanon and the "Syrian Reform Party" in Syria – that worked together to achieve the same objectives? Ashqar, answering his question, declared Saʿadeh would have been "the undisputed leader of Lebanon" and a respected leader in the Arab League, leading the formulation of its policies.[40]

Furthermore, Ashqar related several statements he had made in a meeting of the Higher Council that were viewed as provocative and problematic by some council members. Ashqar had first asserted that the party worked "to liberate the individual from all internal and external subversive factors," before declaring that "Syrian nationalism, in the view of Nationalists, is almost a worshiped idol, and we are not idol worshipers but men of reform."[41] Most Higher Council members rejected his assertions, retorting that the party's primary purpose was to establish Syrian nationalism, to which Ashqar countered, "the party aimed to reform the social, political, and economic life of Syrians regardless of the validity of Syrian nationalism."[42] Saʿadeh dismissed Ashqar's assumptions as simplistic and contradictory, derived from a partial understanding and critical misunderstanding of the party's history and aims that stemmed from "from a serious preoccupation" with the party's political policy. In a subsequent letter to Thabit, Saʿadeh implored him to challenge Tueni, Sayegh, and Ashqar's problematic assertions. He urged them to put an end to this troublesome line of thinking.[43]

The vast majority of the party's adherents and supporters were unaware of the party leadership's intense internal exchanges and with Saʿadeh. Not only had the budding internal strife been kept quiet, the party faithful had not heard directly from Saʿadeh himself for years. This situation changed on 1 September, when the party held a large public gathering in Dhour El Choueir, marking the establishment of *Le Grand Liban*. Deemed the "Day of Reform,"[44] Saʿadeh had, at Thabit's request, prepared a short letter to be delivered to those in attendance. Its message to the party was subtle but clear: the current state of independence was not the culmination of the party's struggle. Read aloud by Sayegh,

40 "Ilā al-Ab Bulus Mas'ad," in Saʿadeh, *al-Aʿmāl al-Kāmila, Vol. 11*, pp. 141–142.
41 "Ilā Nehmeh Thabit," in Saʿadeh, *al-Aʿmāl al-Kāmila, Vol. 11*, pp. 227–228.
42 "Ilā Nehmeh Thabit," in Saʿadeh, *al-Aʿmāl al-Kāmila, Vol. 11*, p. 228.
43 "Ilā Nehmeh Thabit," in Saʿadeh, *al-Aʿmāl al-Kāmila, Vol. 11*, p. 229.
44 Several pictures from the Day of Reform and other SSNP gatherings from around the same time period, including several that were attended by Sulh, Khuri, Minister Majid Arslan, Minister Jamil Talhuk, and Gibran Tueni, are reprinted in Jurayj, *Maʿa Anṭūn Saʿādah, Vol.* 3, pp. 57–59.

Saʿadeh praised the steadfastness and determination of the SSNP's fight against French efforts and those of other foreign powers to impose their will on the nation. "The flag of the [red] tempest had spread the banner of holy national jihad against foreign colonial ambitions" and rejected the "false independence" declared by Gouraud and the French on this day in 1920. France's withdrawal from Syria and Lebanon and the countries' independence was, according to Saʿadeh, "the first tangible result of our faith in our cause and our patience in adversity." He urged his adherents to cling to their faith in "social nationalism" and continue to push for social and political reform, declaring: "This reform is not the ultimate reform we desire, and this independence is not all the independence we desire" (*fa-laisa hadhā al-iṣlāḥ ākhir iṣlāḥ nurīdahu wa laisa hadhā al-istiqlāl kull istiqlāl alladhī nabtaghīhu*).[45] Though he made no direct mention of Greater Syria or Syrian nationalism, his meaning was evident: the present situation must only be considered only as a step towards the party's ultimate goal – an undivided, fully independent Greater Syria.

The party remained focused on promoting its reform agenda, holding public gatherings in several locales in the Bekaa and Baalbek that focused on the country's *fellahin* and the party's reform agenda regarding land and agriculture.[46] The party also addressed two other issues: Palestine and the Greater Syria scheme of King ʿAbdallah. Throughout the year, the party had published articles warning of the threats posed by Zionism and Jews, condemning Zionism and opposing Jewish settlement in Mandatory Palestine.[47] In November, on the anniversary of the Balfour Declaration, the SSNP published a *bayān* lamenting America's position of establishing a Jewish home in Palestine and the Zionist movement's progress towards establishing a Jewish state. The *bayān* urged the Arab world to rise to Palestine's defense.[48] Though the party, as part of its understanding with the

45 "Ilā Muhammad Shamnaq," in Saʿadeh, *al-Aʿmāl al-Kāmila, Vol. 11*, p. 161, and "Taḥiyat al-Zaʿīm min al-Mahjar li-l-Muḥtashidīn fī Yawm al-Iṣlāḥ," in Saʿadeh, *al-Aʿmāl al-Kāmila, Vol. 7*, pp. 171–173.

46 *Sada al-Nahda*, 2, 30 September 1946, reproduced in al-ʿAql, *Ṣiḥāfat, Vol. 3*, pp. 534–536, 542–543.

47 See, for example: "Note on the Palestine Problem," in Beshara, *Fayez Sayegh*, Appendix; Beshara, *Fāyiz Ṣāyigh*, p. 49; *Sada al-Nahda*, 2 November 1946, in Beshara, *Fāyiz Ṣāyigh*, pp. 206–208; *Sada al-Nahda*, 30 July 1946, in Beshara, *Fāyiz Ṣāyigh*, pp. 204–205; *Sada al-Nahda*, 2 May 1946, reproduced in al-ʿAql, *Ṣiḥāfat, Vol. 3*, p. 582; *Sada al–Nahda*, 12 June 1946, reproduced in al-ʿAql, *Ṣiḥāfat, Vol. 3*, p. 585; *Sada al-Nahda*, 16 August 1946, reproduced in al-ʿAql, *Ṣiḥāfat, Vol. 3*, p. 590; *Sada al-Nahda*, nd, reproduced in al-ʿAql, *Ṣiḥāfat, Vol. 3*, p. 591; and *Sada al-Nahda*, nd, reproduced in al-ʿAql, *Ṣiḥāfat, Vol. 3*, p. 631.

48 *Sada al-Nahda*, 2 November 1946, reproduced in al-ʿAql, *Ṣiḥāfat, Vol. 3*, p. 592, and *Sada al-Nahda*, 2 November 1946, in Beshara, *Fāyiz Ṣāyigh*, pp. 206–208.

Lebanese government, had downplayed its Syrian nationalism and muted its call for establishing Greater Syria over the preceding years, it could not avoid addressing comments made by Jordan's King ʿAbdallah. At issue was his 11 November declaration that "'the immediate unity' of Greater Syria" was now a foreign policy objective of his kingdom.[49] Opposed by the Arab League, ʿAbdallah's Greater Syria scheme was condemned and rejected outright by the Lebanese government. Though the party was ostensibly committed to a similar objective, it, too, joined the Lebanese government in condemning ʿAbdallah's scheme and defending both Lebanon's and Syria's independence.

Two pronouncements embodied the party's public defense of Lebanese and Syrian independence. On 22 November, Lebanese Independence Day, *Sada al-Nahda* published an SSNP *bayān* and article by Sayegh, praising and defending Lebanon's sovereignty and promoting the party's reform agenda.[50] Several weeks later, on 6 December, the party published a 29-page tract written by Sayegh detailing the party's opposition to ʿAbdallah's Greater Syria scheme. Deeming it a "threat" to Lebanese and Syrian independence, Sayegh argued ʿAbdallah's plan would strengthen sectarianism in Lebanon and provide for the establishment of a Jewish home in Palestine.[51] The SSNP denounced and "categorically rejected" the scheme, calling on "the loyal citizens" of the countries targeted for unity "to resist and fight against it" (*ilā muqāwama al-mashrūʿ wa mukāfaḥatahu*).[52] The Jordanian government took exception to the criticism, issuing a statement lambasting the tract and the party's position. The party quickly responded in *Sada al-Nahda*, defending its objections and questioning why the Jordanians had singled the SSNP out of all the groups, parties, and newspapers that had voiced their opposition.[53]

Though the party's outspoken opposition to ʿAbdallah's scheme was driven in no small measure by its understanding with the Lebanese government and efforts to promote the SSNP reformist agenda rather than its Syrian nationalist doctrine,[54] its position was not necessarily at variance with Saʿadeh's. Saʿadeh had "sought from the outset to distance himself" from ʿAbdallah's scheme, eschewing comparisons between the SSNP's and ʿAbdallah's conceptions of Great-

---

49 Pipes, *Greater Syria*, p. 77.

50 *Sada al-Nahda*, 22 November 1946, in Beshara, *Fāyiz Ṣāyigh*, pp. 202–203, and *Sada al-Nahda*, 22 November 1946, reproduced in al-ʿAql, *Ṣiḥāfat, Vol. 3*, p. 594.

51 *Mashrūʿ Sūriyya al-Kubra*, pp. 19–23, 26.

52 *Mashrūʿ Sūriyya al-Kubra*, p. 27.

53 *Sada al-Nahda*, December 1946, reproduced in al-ʿAql, *Ṣiḥāfat, Vol. 3*,p. 651.

54 Beshara, *Fāyiz Ṣāyigh*, p. 50.

er Syria.[55] Specifically, Saʿadeh believed ʿAbdallah was driven by personal ambition to expand his realm. Moreover, like his father, Saʿadeh did not consider ʿAbdallah Syrian but rather Arab and, thus, an outsider who had no right to speak on behalf of the Syrian nation. Indeed, according to Saʿadeh, ʿAbdallah was an Arab nationalist "always turned to the desert, his native homeland," claiming Syrian unity was a step that must lead to Arab unity.[56] It is unlikely that the party leadership was ignorant of Saʿadeh's general views of ʿAbdallah and, while the party's unusually blunt response may not have been how Saʿadeh would have responded had he been present in Lebanon at the time, the general position is not one with which he would have disagreed.

For the sake of peace within the party, Saʿadeh sought to assure party leaders in the homeland that he did not view the policies implemented in his absence as contradictory to his directives or the party's doctrine and constitution. Further, he acknowledged that political circumstances had impacted the leadership's decisions, and they had sought to implement policies that were in the party's best interest.[57] The correspondence throughout 1946, however, demonstrated otherwise. Open confrontation loomed on the horizon in early 1947 as Saʿadeh prepared to return to Lebanon. In a second letter, Saʿadeh was more assertive and direct than he had been regarding Lebanon and the party's alliance with the government. Upon receiving the text, Sayegh presented it to members of the Higher Council and Council of Deputies, several of whom advised the party should not publish the letter's contents given the present circumstances in which they sought to maintain their good standing in the lead up to general elections. Sayegh agreed, and the letter was not publicly distributed.

The letter was a combination of praise and confrontational criticism. Once again praising the party's steadfastness, Saʿadeh understood that the party had not lost faith in him, just as he had not lost faith in them, in their struggle to build a new society. Rejecting the sectarian and feudal political order that had replaced the mandate and exchanged French influence for British, Saʿadeh declared it "was not the result of the Syrian nationalists' struggle nor did [the party] accept [it]." He stressed his rejection did not mean a rejection of "the political entities" of Lebanon and Syria, but of their political order and type of governance. Thus, though the party had struggled valiantly and effected some change, the state of the nation remained essentially the same, characterized by national discord and sectarianism.

---

55 Beshara, "Saʿadeh and the Greater Syria Scheme," p. 121.

56 "Sūriyya al-Kubra," in Saʿadeh, *al-Aʿmāl al-Kāmila, Vol. 6*, p. 444.

57 "Ilā Ghassan Tueni," in Saʿadeh, *al-Aʿmāl al-Kāmila, Vol. 11*, p. 288.

In contrast, Saʿadeh argued, authentic sovereignty, authentic independence, and authentic freedom is only realized in and through the SSNP (*fī ḥizbkum taḥaqaqat al-siyāda al-ḥaqīqiyya wa-l-istiqlāl al-ḥaqīqī wa-l-ḥuriyya al-ḥaqīqiyya*). The party's real strength, in turn, was derived from its dedication to its ideology, not the policies that enabled its political participation and attracted new supporters. The meaning was evident: Saʿadeh entirely rejected the path down which Thabit and his allies in the party leadership had led the SSNP in his absence.[58]

Determined to prevent Saʿadeh from undoing the policies and political alliances they had forged, drawing the party into open conflict with the Lebanese government and diminishing their authority over and within the party, Thabit and his allies moved to limit the potentially detrimental effects of his return. First, Thabit and Ashqar proposed amending the party's constitution to ensure their authority and limit Saʿadeh's.[59] Second, Thabit and Ashqar traveled to Cairo to intercept Saʿadeh, who had arrived there from Brazil on 18 February, to convince him to accept their approach and abandon his own, urging him to avoid provoking Lebanese authorities upon his return. Both measures failed; Thabit returned to Beirut ahead of Saʿadeh while Ashqar traveled onward to West Africa.

58 "Risāla min al-Zaʿīm li-l-Qawmiyyīn," in Saʿadeh, *al-Aʿmāl al-Kāmila, Vol. 7*, pp. 178–183.
59 Mujais, *SSNP*, pp. 185–186.

8 Return to the Field of Struggle

Khuri approved Saʿadeh's return to Lebanon in the early weeks of February, an arrangement that was concluded, according to American diplomats, in exchange for the party's support in the coming general elections.[1] Khuri hoped to secure a parliamentary majority that would support his bid to secure a second term in office, despite the constitutional provision limiting him to one term. Khuri, however, was not the only Lebanese politician interested in cooperating with the SSNP to exploit its strength and organization. So too were Henri Pharaon, Kamal Jumblatt, and Camille Chamoun.[2] Though rivals, all three had recently been appointed ministers in the new Cabinet formed by Riad al-Sulh, whom Khuri had tapped as prime minister in December 1946.[3] Arriving from Cairo on the same plane as Fawzi al-Qawuqji, the famed leader of the Arab revolt in Palestine, Saʿadeh was greeted by a mass of party members, eager to welcome him home.[4]

Saʿadeh's arrival in Beirut on 2 March and his subsequent speech shattered any illusions of cooperation between the SSNP under his leadership and Khuri. Saʿadeh's address to his supporters essentially "[declared] all previous agreements between the [SSNP] and the Lebanese government null and void,"[5] and assertively reoriented the party toward its Syrian nationalist ideology and aim of establishing Greater Syria. Echoing the contents of his January letter, Saʿadeh praised his followers for their steadfastness, stating, "today, we stand a living, free, and victorious nation over the foreign powers that sought to keep it divided between religious sects and creeds." Their struggle, he continued, had resulted in the first step toward the nation's true independence, but their work was far from over.[6] Having thus far avoided saying anything generally objectionable, Saʿadeh veered into topics more fraught with danger: Lebanon and its independence. In response to his own question, "what is the Lebanese entity?" (*mā huwa al-kiyān al-Lubnānī?*) Saʿadeh suggested that this "Lebanese entity" "[did] not represent Lebanon or the will of the Lebanese people at all" since not all its citi-

1 Telegram, 890E.00/2 – 17147, Department of State, Beirut to Secretary of State, 17 February 1947, in Walter L. Browne, *Lebanon's Struggle for Independence, 1944 – 1947 – Part II* (North Carolina: Documentary Publications, 1980), pp. 143 – 147.

2 TNA, FO 371/61724, British Legation (Beirut) to Foreign Office (London), 189/4/47, 13 March 1947.

3 Seale, *The Struggle for Arab Independence*, pp. 602 – 605, and Zisser, *Lebanon*, p. 127.

4 Qubrusi, *Yatadhakkar, Vol. 2*, pp. 141 – 144, and Saʿadeh, *Awrāq Qawmiyya*, pp. 35 – 36.

5 Beshara, *Outright Assassination*, p. 27.

6 "Khiṭāb al-Zaʿīm Yawm Wuṣūluhu ilā al-Waṭan," in Saʿadeh, *al-Aʿmāl al-Kāmila, Vol. 7*, pp. 204 – 205.

https://doi.org/10.1515/9783110729092-010

zens have a stake in it. In contrast, those assembled before him were "the Lebanese entity" and "the authentic expression of the Lebanese soul." While empowering his audience was not necessarily objectionable, his choice to refer to Lebanon as an "entity" rather than a state or nation was deliberately provocative, questioning the Lebanese state's legitimacy. His final, resounding call to the party faithful to "return to the field of struggle" (*al-ʿawda ilā sāḥat al-jihād*) only added to the unease of some in Lebanon.[7]

Figure 6: Syrian Social Nationalist Party members and supporters attended a rally in March 1947 marking Saʿadeh's return to Lebanon from his exile in South America. (Wikimedia Commons)

Saʿadeh's clear statement of the party's nationalist doctrine and the ambiguous language regarding Lebanon elicited diverse reactions. The speech immediately raised Lebanese leaders' concern that the party was a potential threat rather than an ally.[8] Further, the speech "confirmed Thabit's failure," as it effectively undid all the party's efforts under his leadership to reach "a *modus vivendi*" with Khuri and Sulh's government.[9] The Lebanese government summoned Saʿadeh to the Sûreté Générale to explain his statements. He refused, fearing ar-

7 "Khiṭāb al-Zaʿīm Yawm Wuṣūluhu ilā al-Waṭan," in Saʿadeh, *al-Aʿmāl al-Kāmila, Vol. 7,* pp. 205–207.
8 Mujais, *SSNP,* p. 188, and Yamak, *SSNP,* p. 62.
9 TNA, FO 371/61710, E13364, no. 8, "Beirut Summary," 23 April 1947.

rest, and went into hiding. In the press, the LCP and Kataʾib, for whom Saʿadeh's return was a particularly unwelcome turn of events, mercilessly attacked him and the SSNP. The LCP's *Sawt al-Shaʿb* labeled Saʿadeh a "spy" and "war criminal," and alleged the SSNP was "a band paid to serve the interests of imperialism."[10] Similarly, the Kataʾib's *al-Amal* engaged in a war of words with the SSNP's *Sada al-Nahda*, urging the government to act against the party swiftly and firmly. Pierre Gemayel, the Kataʾib's leader, wrote "one must choose" between Lebanese nationalism and Syrian nationalism, the two being distinct and entirely incompatible nationalist worldviews. Foreign Minister Hamid Frangieh echoed Gemayel's criticism, stating, "[Saʿadeh had] learned nothing," and had ignored the new political reality created by the National Pact. Together with Sulh, Gemayel and Frangieh declared they would forcibly confront anyone who undermined the Pact and Lebanon's independence.[11]

Having gone into hiding rather than be arrested, the Sûreté issued a warrant for Saʿadeh's arrest, "and the minister of interior declared that [Saʿadeh] was wanted dead or alive."[12] Saʿadeh remained in hiding for months in the mountains outside of Beirut, protected by armed party members (*ḥaras al-zaʿīm*). By 18 March, Lebanese authorities had suspended *Sada al-Nahda*, in whose pages the party had vociferously defended Saʿadeh. However, the government remained undecided on what measures to take against the party beyond refusing to tolerate its challenge to the idea of Lebanon's independence.[13] Despite its confrontational rhetoric, "the government's efforts to capture [Saʿadeh] were halfhearted." Even the officer tasked with arresting him, Farid Chehab, avoided doing so because he assessed it to not be in the country's best interest.[14] Moreover, the government rescinded *Sada al-Nahda*'s suspension at the beginning of April before banning it once again several weeks later, further reflecting its ambiguous, confused policy vis-à-vis the SSNP.[15]

Still in hiding, Saʿadeh, as he was wont to do after making provocative declarations, tried to strike a conciliatory tone to bring the affair to an end, declaring he and his movement posed no threat to Lebanon.[16] In a letter to the Sûreté's

---

10 Airgram, American Legation (Beirut) to Secretary of State, A-107, 4 March 1947, in Browne, *Lebanon*, pp. 157–158.

11 Seale, *The Struggle for Arab Independence*, pp. 667–668.

12 Mujais, *SSNP*, p. 189.

13 Airgram, American Legation (Beirut) to Secretary of State, A-130, 18 March 1947, in Browne, *Lebanon*, pp. 166–167.

14 Yamak, *SSNP*, p. 62, and Beshara, *Outright Assassination*, p. 29.

15 Al-ʿAql, *Ṣiḥāfat, Vol. 3*, pp. 482, 484.

16 Zisser, *Lebanon*, p. 182.

director, Saʿadeh argued that he had not attacked the Lebanese entity in his speech, but had instead declared the SSNP support for it, clarifying the party was not Lebanon's enemy. Further, Saʿadeh stated he considered Lebanon to be a bastion of free thought, and he had no desire to eliminate it.[17] Subsequently, in a *bayān* issued on 6 March, Saʿadeh beseeched the Lebanese people to ignore the rumors and disinformation being spread about the content of his speech, reiterating that he and the party "recognize and respect Lebanon's existence." Declaring himself a "son of Lebanon," he reiterated that it was not his intention "to be at war with this entity [Lebanon] but to be a force within and for it."[18] His statement did not go far enough in Lebanese authorities' eyes, and they refused to rescind the order for his arrest.

Undeterred, Saʿadeh continued to appeal to the broader public for support. On 28 March, he issued a second *bayān* urging the Lebanese people not to be "fooled by noise," contending that it is the people who are sovereign, the real owners of Lebanon who possess the power and freedom to decide its future. The Lebanese government was, Saʿadeh argued, preventing the people from exercising their power and freedom. Portraying himself as their defender, he attacked the government's campaign against him as nothing more than an effort to distract the people from its corruption and failures as it took the country to new elections.[19] Saʿadeh also made his case in the press, giving interviews to Lebanese and Syrian journalists who visited him in hiding.[20] However, Saʿadeh's confrontational approach and refusal to report to the Sûreté were not entirely supported by some party members.

8.1 Saʿadeh Versus Thabit: The Struggle for the Party

With their frustration mounting, Thabit and his supporters in the party leadership strongly urged Saʿadeh to reconsider his approach, which had done little more than drag the party into open conflict with the government. Saʿadeh, in contrast, believed his approach had invigorated the party's base. To Saʿadeh,

---

17 "Ilā al-Mudīr al-Āmn al-ʿĀmm al-Lubnānī," in Saʿadeh, *al-Aʿmāl al-Kāmila, Vol. 11*, p. 304.
18 "Bayān Awal min al-Zaʿīm ilā al-Shaʿb al-Lubnānī," in Saʿadeh, *al-Aʿmāl al-Kāmila, Vol. 7*, pp. 208–209.
19 "Bayān Thāni min al-Zaʿīm ilā al-Shaʿb al-Lubnānī," in Saʿadeh, *al-Aʿmāl al-Kāmila, Vol. 7*, pp. 217–219.
20 "Ḥadīth al-Zaʿīm ilā Jarīda al-Qabas," in Saʿadeh, *al-Aʿmāl al-Kāmila, Vol. 7*, pp., 213–216; "Ḥadīth al-Zaʿīm ilā Majalla al-Jumhūr," in Saʿadeh, *al-Aʿmāl al-Kāmila, Vol. 7*, pp. 235–236; and "Ḥadīth al-Zaʿīm ilā Jarīda al-Naṣr," in Saʿadeh, *al-Aʿmāl al-Kāmila, Vol. 7*, pp. 220–223.

the best path forward was to seize on the momentum generated by his return to press the party's claims on the Lebanese government. Their entreaties having failed, and determined to maintain their quickly eroding power within the party, Thabit's faction worked to obstruct Saʿadeh's ability to conduct the party's administrative affairs and undermine and limit his authority. Absent from meetings and adopting a generally combative and contrarian stance, they paralyzed the party's leadership bodies. To impair and limit Saʿadeh's power, they made a concerted effort to convince their peers on the Higher Council and Council of Deputies that Saʿadeh's approach reflected his ignorance and misunderstanding of the existing social and political reality in Lebanon. This lack of understanding rendered him incapable of devising an appropriate strategy for the party and made him unsuitable to do so. To further democratize the party and preserve their influence, Thabit's faction formally urged the Council of Deputies to amend the party constitution to check Saʿadeh's power by stipulating that he, as the party leader, was accountable to the Higher Council.[21]

Discord within the party came to a head the first week of April at an emergency meeting of the Higher Council. With Ashqar still abroad and Ayas having excused himself from attending, Thabit and Karim Azkul were left to make their case for amending the party constitution. Saʿadeh defended himself before the Council, arguing that his approach and a return to the party's nationalist principles better reflected "the desires of the broader [party] constituency."[22] The Council agreed, tabling the proposal to amend the constitution and, in the process, delivering a significant blow to Thabit and his faction. Taking advantage of this endorsement of his authority, Saʿadeh immediately ordered the dissolution of the Higher Council and the party's political bureau, removing Thabit, Ayas, Ashqar, Azkul, and others from their positions. Now lacking any official authority, their efforts to lead the party down a more moderate and pragmatic path were severely hampered.[23]

The struggle between Saʿadeh and Thabit's faction was far from over. Though support for Thabit and Asqhar was eroding, the dispute now spilled into the party's preparations for the upcoming general elections scheduled for 25 May.[24] Saʿadeh dismissed Lebanon's traditional political class, with whom Thabit chose to align, as a group only concerned with promoting personal, religious, and feudal interests, which led to mismanagement, corruption, and the

21 "Ilā Rafīq al-Ḥalabī," in Saʿadeh, *al-Aʿmāl al-Kāmila, Vol. 11*, pp. 308–311.

22 Mujais, *SSNP*, p. 191.

23 "Ilā Rafīq al-Ḥalabī," in Saʿadeh, *al-Aʿmāl al-Kāmila, Vol. 11*, pp. 310–311.

24 For a comprehensive analysis of the 1947 election, see Zisser, *Lebanon*, Chapter 7.

failure to serve the people. In contrast, Saʿadeh argued the SSNP strove to advance socio-economic and political reforms in Lebanon's interest.[25] Though there was broad agreement within the party regarding its reform agenda, the dividing line was drawn at Saʿadeh's confrontational and more overtly ideological approach. His approach largely rendered the party an unpalatable partner among both the government's supporters and opponents, which reduced the party's chances for electoral success. There remained, however, the possibility of forming a coalition with opposition politicians provided its would-be partners accept the party's reform principles as the foundation for cooperation.[26] No such alliance would be built, and the SSNP would run independent candidates in each of Lebanon's five electoral districts.

The party's electoral platform was grounded upon four guiding principles: (1) securing Lebanon and ensuring it remained an open society in which the party could spread its doctrine; (2) make independence a real fact, not a new form of colonialism; (3) promote closer political ties, and cultural and economic unity between Lebanon and the other entities of Greater Syria; and (4) participate in the common defense of Greater Syria's constituent entities – Syria, Jordan, Palestine, and Iraq. Furthermore, the party promoted comprehensive reform in five areas: social, economic, political, judicial, and administrative. The foundation for its agenda's success lay, first and foremost, in promoting several electoral reform measures, including increasing the number of representatives in parliament and reorganizing Lebanon's voting districts.[27] In 1947, with only a 55-seat parliamentary chamber and the country divided into only five electoral districts, the party believed structural changes were necessary to enhance the chances for its electoral success. Increasing the number of electoral districts in the country was particularly important as the situation, as it stood in 1947, significantly enhanced the power and influence of local, traditional elites throughout the country, rendering a candidate's success mostly dependent on their degree of loyalty to local notables. Increasing the number of districts, it was argued, would aid in decreasing the power of local notables and the electoral corruption such power often carried with it. Among the SSNP candidates to contest the elections were: Dr. ʿAbdallah Saʿadeh and Dr. Afif ʿAbd al-Wahhab (North Lebanon); Adib Qadurra and Dr. Adib Maʿaluf (Beirut); ʿAbdallah Muhsin

---

25 "Maʿraka al-Intikhābāt al-Muqabila," in Saʿadeh, *al-Aʿmāl al-Kāmila, Vol. 7*, pp. 227–230.
26 "Bayān Rābiʿ min al-Zaʿīm ilā al-Shaʿb al-Lubnānī," in Saʿadeh, *al-Aʿmāl al-Kāmila, Vol. 7*, p. 258.
27 "Bayān Murashiḥī al-Ḥizb al-Qawmi fī Jabal Lubnān," in Saʿadeh, *al-Aʿmāl al-Kāmila, Vol. 7*, pp. 256–257, and "Bayān al-Ḥizb al-Qawmī wa Minhājahu al-Niyābī ʿan Irāda al-Shaʿb al-Lubnānī," in Saʿadeh, *al-Aʿmāl al-Kāmila, Vol. 7*, pp. 245–253.

and Dr. Karim Azkul (Bekaa); Hafiz Munadhir (Mount Lebanon); and Nazmi Azkul and Beshara Trabulsi (South Lebanon).[28] Saʿadeh viewed most of the party's candidates warily, as they were closely aligned with Thabit and Ashqar, but resigned himself to their candidacies. Indeed, Saʿadeh accused every candidate except Qadurra, Muhsin, and ʿAbdallah Saʿadeh of not faithfully representing the party's ideology and pursuing individual interests and opportunism instead. Thabit had tried to secure a spot on Chamoun's pro-government electoral list in Mount Lebanon but could not convince Chamoun that he could still dictate the SSNP's agenda. Saʿadeh also vetoed Thabit and Ashqar's participation on any pro-government list in Mount Lebanon because any such list must include at least four, not two, SSNP candidates given the party's electoral strength in the region.[29]

On the eve of the election, the SSNP issued a *bayān* calling on the Lebanese people to support the party's candidates. The *bayān* declared that, if elected, the party's representatives would advance the people's interests and initiate real reforms, urging the Lebanese: "March with the Nationalists, march to glory!" (*sir maʿa al-Qawmiyyūn, tasir ilā al-majd!*).[30] Glory was elusive, however, as no SSNP candidates were elected. Instead, government-aligned candidates secured an overwhelming forty-nine of the fifty-five seats "in the first elections to be held in independent Lebanon."[31] The "sweeping victory for Khuri's government" was immediately mired in controversy, as the government was accused of egregious acts of meddling, voter intimidation, and electoral fraud. Even several of the victors, including Chamoun and Jumblatt, protested the election results, demanding their nullification and new elections. Ultimately, Jumblatt would resign his seat, while Chamoun would accept the election results.[32]

Along with other electoral losers, the SSNP also questioned the legitimacy of the election results. Saʿadeh, who remained in hiding from authorities, issued a *bayān* published five days after the election. In it, he decried the government's continued campaign against him and stated he had expected nothing less

---

28 "Qawāʿid al-Tarshīḥ li-l-Niyāba fī al-Ḥizb al-Qawmī al-Ijtimāʿī," in Saʿadeh, *al-Aʿmāl al-Kāmila, Vol. 8*, pp. 247–249; Saʿadeh, *Awrāq Qawmiyya*, pp. 40–41; and Qubrusi, *Yatadhakkar, Vol. 2*, pp. 160–165.

29 "Qawāʿid al-Tarshīḥ li-l-Niyāba," in Saʿadeh, *al-Aʿmāl al-Kāmila, Vol. 8*, pp. 246–251.

30 "Bayān Thālith min al-Zaʿīm ilā al-Shaʿb al-Lubnānī," in Saʿadeh, *al-Aʿmāl al-Kāmila, Vol. 7*, pp. 254–255.

31 Zisser, *Lebanon*, p. 128.

32 Zisser, *Lebanon*, pp. 136–138; TNA, FO 371/61710, E5207/909/88, "Lebanon: Summary No. 10," 18 June 1947; TNA, FO 371/61710, E6621/909/88, "Lebanon: Summary No. 11," 24 July 1947; and *The Black Book of the Lebanese Elections of May 25, 1947* (New York: Phoenicia Press, 1947).

from the government than their interference in the election to ensure the maintenance of their power and prestige. Criticizing the corrupt political bargaining designed to advance individual interests, Saʿadeh also reproached the Lebanese people for tolerating and acquiescing to the nonsense that undermined the foundations of national sovereignty and independence. The rigged election may have been a "terrible shock and hilarious calamity," an act of tyranny, but the primary issue was one of national values. So long as the Lebanese clung to the backward principles of feudalism and sectarianism, they would not experience true freedom and real sovereignty, merely exchanging existing "reactionary" and "opportunistic" leaders for new ones cut from the same cloth. Only the values of the SSNP offered a path to the nation's glory.[33]

Privately Saʿadeh expressed satisfaction that the elections had been marred by corruption and that none of the party's candidates had been elected, arguing their success would have reinvigorated the internal rebellion against him. Instead, Saʿadeh was pleased that the party's internal situation had greatly improved and stabilized, as Thabit, Ayas, and Ashqar's influence and support continued to erode.[34] The party's failure in the elections had further weakened the triumvirate, who increasingly found themselves lacking the means and mechanisms to counter Saʿadeh effectively. The election failure did not so much reflect the merit or lack thereof of Thabit's political strategy as it did the realization of Saʿadeh's efforts to undermine that strategy. In early July, just a little over a month after the elections, Saʿadeh decided the time was right to end the ongoing dispute. To that end, he issued an order suspending Thabit, Ayas, and Ashqar from all party activities. Portraying the order as "the natural outcome of conditions created by [the three] comrades themselves," Saʿadeh's note of justification lambasted their commitment to "isolationist tendencies," their hostile attitude towards him, their cooperation with the party's opponents in a campaign against him, and their general pursuit of individual interests to the detriment of the party's nationalist creed.[35]

Thabit and Ayas responded by establishing a new political party, *al-Ḥizb al-Jumhūrī al-Lubnānī al-Dimūqrāṭī*, inviting their supporters to abandon Saʿadeh and the SSNP.[36] They published a highly critical and biting statement against

---

33 "Bayān Rābiʿ," in Saʿadeh, *al-Aʿmāl al-Kāmila, Vol. 7*, pp. 258 – 262. Also see "al-Ḥukm bi-l-Irhāb wa Muṣādarat al-Silāḥ min al-Shaʿb," in Saʿadeh, *al-Aʿmāl al-Kāmila, Vol. 7*, pp. 268 – 271.
34 "Ilā Rafīq al-Ḥalabī," in Saʿadeh, *al-Aʿmāl al-Kāmila, Vol. 11*, pp. 310 – 311.
35 "al-Amīnān Thābit wa Ayās wa Asad al-Ashqar – Balāgh," in Saʿadeh, *al-Aʿmāl al-Kāmila, Vol. 7*, pp. 272 – 273.
36 Qubrusi, *Yatadhakkar, Vol. 2*, pp. 180 – 189, and TNA, FO 371/61710, E7657/909/88, "Lebanon: Summary No. 12," 20 August 1947.

Saʿadeh, arguing he was an ineffective leader who led the party toward disaster by stubbornly clinging to his ideas. In their minds, they were no less committed to the party's ideology than Saʿadeh but continued to maintain that remaining a committed ideologue need not preclude taking a pragmatic and flexible political approach, adapting itself to existing realities. Not letting the accusations go unanswered, Saʿadeh penned a lengthy rebuttal in which he defended his leadership, steadfastness, and sacrifice while refuting Thabit's claims and denouncing his arrogance and betrayal. Saʿadeh dismissed Thabit's talk of "the exhausting struggle and precious sacrifices" waged in his absence, retorting Thabit had forgotten "the blissful four years of [legalization], ideological retreat, and tea and cocktail parties that demonstrate the advantage of sacrifice and relentlessness." Thabit and Ayas' "treasonous" efforts, according to Saʿadeh, had resulted only in their demise, not a schism in the party.[37] The long-winded response was in keeping with Saʿadeh's character, but it was perhaps unnecessary. Thabit and Ayas' supporters, including Qubrusi, ʿAbdallah Saʿadeh, Qadurra, and Sayegh, had abandoned them en masse and refused to follow them out of the party.[38] Even Ashqar, who had been expelled with them, refused to join their new political party and refrained from publicly criticizing Saʿadeh. Ashqar's decision would prove fortuitous, as months later he would offer a public apology for his actions and be reinstated to the party.

Having quashed internal dissent, Saʿadeh turned the party's attention to countering the government's ongoing campaign against them. Though he was far from the only figure to denounce the rigged elections, the government had taken particular offense to Saʿadeh's criticism and reiterated its desire to capture him "dead or alive."[39] Rumors spread in the press that the SSNP, together with members of the Lebanese gendarmerie, was plotting to overthrow the government. Fueled by reports that Saʿadeh had recently visited Amman, the press also reported the SSNP had reached an understanding with King ʿAbdallah to advance the cause of Greater Syria together.[40] Furthering their efforts to harass the

---

37 "Niʿmah Thābit Baṭal al-Khiyāna," in Saʿadeh, *al-Aʿmāl al-Kāmila, Vol. 7,* pp. 298–304.

38 Qubrusi, *Yatadhakkar, Vol. 2*, pp. 166–172, 185–189; Saʿadeh, *Awrāq Qawmiyya*, pp. 35–38; and Yamak, *SSNP*, p. 63. Reflecting on their expulsion several years later, a British diplomat would lament that "[one] cannot find men like them in the party nowadays." TNA, FO 1018/62, No. 250, P.P.S. in Lebanon, "Parti Populaire Syrien," 2 April 1949.

39 Beshara, *Outright Assassination*, p. 29.

40 *The Palestine Post*, 6 July 1947; "Ḥadith al-Zaʿīm ilā Jarīda al-Ḥayāt," in Saʿadeh, *al-Aʿmāl al-Kāmila, Vol. 7,* pp. 281–287; and "Ḥadith al-Zaʿīm ilā Jarīda Bayrūt al-Masāʾ," Saʿadeh, *al-Aʿmāl al-Kāmila, Vol. 7,* pp. 288–290. In his interviews, Saʿadeh demurs and states that he is currently not present in Amman, sidestepping the question of whether he visited, which he had, in fact, done. In August, in an official announcement, Saʿadeh denied any formal agreement had been

party, government security forces launched periodic raids on party strongholds and locations where Saʿadeh was reported to be hiding.

The SSNP, under Saʿadeh's orders, avoided violent engagements with government forces and refrained from responding to the government's campaign, maintaining a state of calm. Meanwhile, Saʿadeh carried out his attack in interviews with various periodicals. In these interviews, Saʿadeh emphasized the government's guilt in the fraudulent elections, its violations of fundamental freedoms such as the freedom of expression and the press, and its unjustified persecution of the party. At the same time, he stressed the party's right to freely express its political views and emphasized that it posed no threat to Lebanon.[41] After months of conflict, the Lebanese government and the SSNP had reached an impasse as "neither side had enough political or military power to win the standoff."[42] By September, the government had stopped conducting raids against party offices and personnel, and the SSNP had made it clear it was open to reaching a mediated solution to end the whole affair. The struggle between the two entities ended on 9 October after Saʿadeh met with Lebanese Justice Minister Ahmad al-Husyani, declared his "respect" for Lebanon, and the arrest warrant was withdrawn.[43] While he may have struck a conciliatory tone with the minister, Saʿadeh, unsurprisingly, struck a defiant tone in a message to his followers. He spun the reconciliation agreement as a great victory for the party and its ideology over the "forces of reaction, sectarianism, and utilitarianism."[44]

8.2 Rebuilding the Party and The Palestine Question

No longer pursued by Lebanese authorities, Saʿadeh emerged from hiding and dedicated himself to rebuilding the party he had struggled lead since his return, and "returning its doctrine to its pristine state."[45] Among his first steps was pub-

---

concluded with the Jordanians. Mujais, *SSNP*, p. 194, and "Balāgh min Maktab al-Zaʿīm," in Saʿadeh, *al-Aʿmāl al-Kāmila, Vol. 7*, p. 306.

41 "Ḥadith al-Zaʿīm ilā Jarīda Kull Shay'," in Saʿadeh, *al-Aʿmāl al-Kāmila, Vol. 7*, pp. 294–297, and "Ḥadith al-Zaʿīm ilā Majalla al-Kawkab," in Saʿadeh, *al-Aʿmāl al-Kāmila, Vol. 7*, pp. 307–308.

42 Mujais, *SSNP*, p. 196.

43 Yamak, *SSNP*, p. 63.

44 "Risāla al-Zaʿīm ilā al-Qawmiyyīn al-Ijtimāʿiyyīn," in Saʿadeh, *al-Aʿmāl al-Kāmila, Vol. 7*, pp. 335–336.

45 Zisser, *Lebanon*, p. 182.

lishing a revised version of the party's principles and aims.[46] The revised doctrinal statement included three significant additions: (1) expansion of the geographic boundaries of the Syrian homeland to include Cyprus and Iraq; (2) elucidation of his comprehensive social philosophy, social nationalism (*al-qawmiyya al-ijtimāʿiyya*); and (3) officially changing the party's name, adding the word "social" to make it the Syrian Social Nationalist Party. Saʿadeh had made the revisions without consulting the SSNP's executive and legislative councils, believing it was his prerogative as the party's leader to make any decision he deemed appropriate independent from these bodies.[47] The additions, which were accepted with little protest, exacerbated Saʿadeh's ongoing dispute with Fayez Sayegh.

Though Sayegh had been part of Thabit's faction, he had been wary of the Thabit's efforts to move the party away from its national doctrine. Given his hesitancy on the matter, he had remained in the background as Thabit and Saʿadeh struggled over who would lead the party and had even supported Saʿadeh's decision to purge Thabit, Ayas, and Ashqar.[48] Since August, the two had engaged in intense private philosophical debate over Sayegh's existentialist leanings and his insertion of these ideas into party publications.[49] Sayegh maintained that his philosophical convictions fell outside of the party's purview, as the party had no philosophy of its own that Sayegh's ideas could adhere to or contravene. Saʿadeh argued to the contrary that the party did indeed have a philosophy that permeated its principles and aims. Despite numerous conversations and the pleas of several party leaders for Sayegh to drop the matter for the party's good, their philosophical conflict remained unresolved and, following Saʿadeh's doctrinal revisions of the party's principles and aims, took on a whole new meaning.[50]

Sayegh resisted the new additions to the party's doctrine, arguing that Saʿadeh's actions amounted to blatant abuse of power and contravened the party's constitution, which, according to Sayegh, did not grant Saʿadeh carte blanche. Sayegh's protests shifted their disagreement away from philosophy to matters of constitutionality and authority. Saʿadeh, however, remained primarily concerned with their philosophical dispute, resulting in an increasingly divergent

46 "Balāgh min Maktab al-Zaʿīm," in Saʿadeh, *al-Aʿmāl al-Kāmila, Vol. 7,* p. 342, and "Kitāb al-Taʿālīm al-Sūriyya al-Qawmiyya al-Ijtimāʿiyya," in Saʿadeh, *al-Aʿmāl al-Kāmila, Vol. 7,* pp. 309–330.
47 Beshara, *Fāyiz Ṣāyigh*, p. 74.
48 Beshara, *Fāyiz Ṣāyigh*, p. 70.
49 Qubrusi, *Yatadhakkar, Vol. 2*, p. 196.
50 Beshara, *Fāyiz Ṣāyigh*, pp. 73–74.

and more antagonistic discourse.[51] Indeed, after Sayegh published two letters in the party's cultural bulletin that were understood as being directed toward Saʿadeh, Saʿadeh acted swiftly, abolishing its publication and establishing in its place the "Official Bulletin of the Social Nationalist Movement." Also, Saʿadeh removed Sayegh from his position as director of information and replaced him with Wadih al-Ashqar.[52] Notably, Ashqar was given the title of "deputy director" (*wakīl ʿamīd*), a designation reflecting the fact that Saʿadeh had "assumed full control of the departments of culture and information."[53]

By December, Saʿadeh had had enough and gave Sayegh an ultimatum: cease making references to existentialist philosophy and conduct himself in a manner consummate with the party's principles, or he would be expelled from the party.[54] Though initially receptive, Sayegh instead became quite resistant to Saʿadeh's demand and made another bid to challenge him. He failed and was subsequently expelled from the party on 7 December. On 10 December, not prepared to go silently, Sayegh published a front-page editorial in *al-Nahar*, the newspaper of his friend and party ally Ghassan Tueni, harshly criticizing Saʿadeh and airing the party's dirty laundry in public. In addition, Tueni, Yusuf al-Khal, and Yusuf Nuheid published a joint statement on 11 December announcing their withdrawal from the SSNP in protest of Saʿadeh's unilateral additions and changes to the party's doctrine and the lack of freedom of thought within the party. In response to these critical articles, other party members closed ranks around Saʿadeh. They accused Sayegh, their former friend and comrade, of going too far in making the dispute public. His reckless act of defiance, to them, amounted to nothing less than betrayal.[55]

Amid the doctrinal dispute, the party's attention focused on developments in Palestine. In May 1947, the United Nations Special Committee on Palestine (UNSCOP) was established to study the conflict and recommend solutions for

51 Beshara, *Fāyiz Ṣāyigh*, p. 74.
52 Beshara, *Fāyiz Ṣāyigh*, pp. 75–76, and al-ʿAql, *Ṣiḥāfat, Vol. 2*, pp. 818, 820.
53 Yamak, *SSNP*, p. 64.
54 "Kitāb al-Zaʿīm ilā ʿAmīd al-Idhāʿa," in Saʿadeh, *al-Aʿmāl al-Kāmila, Vol. 7*, pp. 378–381, and "Qaḍiyya al-Rafīq Fāyiz Ṣāyigh," in Saʿadeh, *al-Aʿmāl al-Kāmila, Vol. 7*, pp. 388–390.
55 Beshara, *Fāyiz Ṣāyigh*, pp. 78–82, and *al-Nahar*, 11 December 1947. On the Sayegh affair, also see: Qubrusi, *Yatadhakkar, Vol. 2*, pp. 192–209. Among those who abandoned and vociferously criticized Sayegh was Labib Yamak, his friend and protégé of sorts, who accused Sayegh of deceit, pretentiousness, and being filled with nonsense. (Beshara, *Fāyiz Ṣāyigh*, p. 80) Yamak, however, would ultimately offer a mea culpa of sorts in his monograph on the party, lamenting the fact that Sayegh's expulsion "had been met with equanimity even by Sayegh's closest associates" and criticizing the prevailing sense among party members that Saʿadeh "could do no wrong," admitting more issues should have been openly debated. Yamak, *SSNP*, p. 63.

its resolution. The Committee submitted its report at the beginning of September, recommending the end of Britain's mandate and proposing a partition plan. At the end of the month, Britain "announced its intention to withdraw unilaterally from Palestine and entrust its mandatory responsibilities to the United Nations," declaring 14 May 1948 the official date of its withdrawal.[56] Demonstrations against UNSCOP's recommendations brought Beirut to a standstill on 3 October, just days before the Arab League was to meet in the city to discuss the Palestine issue.[57] At the Arab League meeting, the participants made three decisions: (1) implement the agreements made at Bludan the previous year[58]; (2) make preliminary military preparations to facilitate intervention; and (3) extend financial and other assistance to Arabs in Palestine.[59] "The gap between the resolution and Arab realities, however, was well understood by all sides."[60]

The SSNP supported the Arab League's actions in principle; they were in line with the party's aim of establishing an Arab Front to resist foreign ambitions in the region and advance progress in the Arab World. As it had in the past, the party sought to use the Balfour Declaration's anniversary to mobilize support for Palestine. The SSNP planned to hold a mass demonstration in Beirut and called on party members to participate throughout Lebanon and Syria, including Damascus, Homs, and Aleppo. The Lebanese government, wary of the idea of allowing such a large gathering of SSNP members in the capital and its potential to foster dissent, issued a general ban on public demonstrations and gatherings. They informed the party the night of 1 November to cancel its plans or be confronted by force. The party acceded to the request to avoid an unnecessary clash, turning back the buses and convoys that had made their way to Beirut from Syria and other locales in Lebanon. Incensed, the party issued a *bayān* reiterating it was not at war with the Lebanese government and only sought to express its support for Palestine, which it called Southern Syria. The Lebanese government

56 Rogan, *The Arabs*, p. 252.
57 TNA, FO 371/68489, E11425, No. 15, "Beirut Political Summary for the month of October 1947," 4 December 1947.
58 At Bludan, the participants agreed on three matters: "(1) the reconstitution of an expanded, Mufti-dominated Arab Higher Committee, (2) the pledging of measures to tighten the Arab boycott of Zionist goods and to forestall the selling of land to Jews, and most importantly, (3) the adoption of "secret" resolutions that no new economic concessions were to be granted to Great Britain and the United States, and that the withdrawal of existing concessions would be considered." Bruce Maddy–Weitzman, *The Crystallization of the Arab State System, 1945–1954* (Syracuse, New York: Syracuse University Press, 1993), p. 36.
59 TNA, FO 371/68489, E11425, No. 15, "Beirut Political Summary for the month of October 1947," 4 December 1947.
60 Maddy-Weitzman, *Arab State System*, p. 50.

justified its decision by claiming it was following the requests of the Arab Higher Committee (AHC) in Palestine and the Arab League, which had asked for financial support rather than demonstrations. The SSNP dismissed the claim, arguing the AHC did not have a monopoly on deciding courses of action in Palestine and accused the Lebanese government of hindering national unity and of "reviving Jewish aspirations... and revealing the paralysis of Lebanese and Syrian society."[61] The party's protests fell on deaf ears, as the Lebanese government would pursue a policy of financial support for Palestine and limit its military involvement.

While the Lebanese public grew increasingly riled over developments in Palestine, Sulh and Khuri initially hoped to reach an acceptable solution before an "all-out war" requiring Lebanon's military involvement broke out.[62] The UN's decision to partition Palestine at the end of November 1947, which was met with massive protests in Beirut and Damascus, undercut their approach and forced them to reassess their policies. The initial response involved the Lebanese Chamber resolving to raise money for Palestine's defense by leveling a tax on luxury goods, among other financial measures, and "registering volunteers for fighting in Palestine."[63] In contrast, the SSNP stated that the partition of Palestine was a tragic disaster that was the inevitable consequence of the arbitrary political policies of religious and tribalistic parties (*siyāsa al-ḥizbiyyāt al-dīniyya wa-l-ʿashāʾiriyya*). Declaring the social nationalists now to be at war for Palestine, the statement called for volunteers to join the "Social National Army to fight under the banner of the Tempest."[64] However, the party was weak and unable to raise, mobilize, and arm such a militia. Moreover, its efforts to do so, as well as to participate in the military campaign, would be severely hampered.[65] Instead, it would concentrate its efforts over the coming year to maintain its fierce rhetoric, demanding forceful and organized intervention in Palestine to prevent its partition and establish a Jewish state.

---

61 "Bayān al-Zaʿīm al-Ḥaraka al-Qawmiyya al-Ijtimāʿiyya ilā al-Qawmiyyīn," in Saʿadeh, *al-Aʿmāl al-Kāmila, Vol. 7,* pp. 352–353, and "Risāla al-Zaʿīm ilā al-Qawmiyyīn al-Ijtimāʿiyyīn wa-l-Umma al-Sūriyya," in Saʿadeh, *al-Aʿmāl al-Kāmila, Vol. 7,* pp. 356–368.

62 Zisser, *Lebanon*, p. 152, and Seale, *The Struggle for Arab Independence*, pp. 632–638.

63 TNA, FO371/68489, E11744, No. 16, "Beirut Political Summary for the month of December 1947," 6 February 1948, and Zisser, *Lebanon*, p. 152.

64 "Balāgh al-Zaʿīm fī Ṣadad Qarār Taqsīm Filasṭīn," in Saʿadeh, *al-Aʿmāl al-Kāmila, Vol. 7,* pp. 382–383.

65 Hisham Sharabi, *Embers and Ashes: Memoirs of an Arab Intellectual* (Northampton: Olive Branch Press, 2008), pp. 63–64.

While the party remained mindful of developments in Palestine and pressed for more aggressive intervention, Saʿadeh dedicated much effort toward strengthening the party's ideological foundations and revitalizing his movement. Beginning in early January 1948 and continuing through the first week of April, Saʿadeh delivered ten lectures to the party's cultural forum. The talks, attended by hundreds, provided Saʿadeh an opportunity to expound upon the party's basic and reform principles at length and in detail. Recorded by George ʿAbd al-Masih, the lectures were ultimately transformed into a widely disseminated ideological text known as *al-Muḥāḍarāt al-ʿAshr* (The Ten Lectures).[66] Complementing his talks, the party began issuing a new publication called *al-Niẓām al-Jadīd* (The New Order) that declared "the establishment of a new order for a new life" to revive the nation.[67] A total of six editions would be published, all of which addressed important intellectual topics related to the party's social nationalist philosophy, Syrian history, poetry, and literature.[68]

Seeking to spread the party's message of national revival beyond the confines of the SSNP, it began publishing a new political daily called *al-Jil al-Jadid* (The New Generation). In an open letter to the paper's readers, Saʿadeh explained the logic behind its name, stating, "it had been created to serve the new generation and its great mission… proclaiming the new truth" of a new, rising young generation. This "new generation," whose values of sincerity and courage inspired it to renew and advance the nation, stood opposed to the "old generation," whose values of fear and hypocrisy inspired it to embrace the past and delay the nation's progress.[69] Only five editions were published before the Lebanese government banned the periodical, claiming it "threatened public security." The ban was likely in response to an article penned by Saʿadeh entitled "The Lebanese Entity between Two Leaders," in which he argued that the foundations of the Lebanese state were "weak" and criticized leadership that had a greater interest in perpetuating personal conflicts and competition than working for the good of the people.[70] The periodical would reappear a year later in April 1949 for only two months before its printing press was shuttered once more.[71]

In the spring of 1948, Saʿadeh visited party branches throughout Lebanon and Syria to increase support and inspire its adherents. The speeches he delivered were filled with the familiar rousing rhetoric. He declared the party's deter-

66 The text of *The Ten Lectures* can be found in Saʿadeh, *al-Aʿmāl al-Kāmila, Vol. 8*, pp. 1–141.
67 "al-Niẓām al-Jadīd," in Saʿadeh, *al-Aʿmāl al-Kāmila, Vol. 8*, pp. 159–162.
68 See Mujais, *SSNP*, p. 200, and al-ʿAql, *Ṣiḥāfat, Vol. 2*, pp. 833–863.
69 *Al-Jil al-Jadid*, 4 April 1948.
70 *Al-Jil al-Jadid*, 8 April 1948.
71 Al-ʿAql, *Ṣiḥāfat, Vol. 2*, p. 637.

mination to resist foreign domination and the forces of reaction at home, that it was on the march to achieving the final victory in its struggle to revive and liberate the nation and that its influence was the key to establishing a strong and independent nation.[72] Saʿadeh's trip to Damascus was of particular importance, as he met with Syrian Minister of Defense Ahmad Sharabati and visited with party officials. Saʿadeh and Sharabati discussed a range of issues, and Saʿadeh was keen to stress the SSNP was not hostile to the Syrian government headed by President Shukri al-Quwatli and had no intention to agitate against it. Both were sentiments that Sharabati reciprocated.[73] In Sharabati, Saʿadeh found a largely sympathetic ear, and the two men were able to reach a personal understanding on the national issue and work to be accomplished in the Arab world.[74]

Until 15 May, the day after David Ben Gurion had declared the establishment of the State of Israel, the Arab military struggle for Palestine had been conducted by irregular volunteer forces, the *Jaysh al-Inqādh* (Army of Deliverance, commonly referred to as the Arab Liberation Army, ALA), organized by the Arab League. Though the Arab League had established the ALA, Syria took the lead in backing its efforts. Fawzi al-Qawuqji commanded the ALA, and several Syrian officers with ties to the SSNP served under him, specifically, Adib al-Shishakli and Ghassan Jadid. It led the Arab military effort against the Zionist Yishuv in Palestine until May when Arab states ordered their regular forces to invade.[75] However, the Lebanese army did not participate in the invasion even though it had been tasked to do so. The ALA, instead, took its place. Lebanon's inaction was notable given Sulh's efforts with Syrian prime minister Jamil Mardam over the preceding months "to bring about full Arab cooperation on Palestine." It was also understandable, to a certain degree, as the Lebanese army was unprepared to engage in battle.[76] Its inaction, however, resulted in much criticism, particularly from the SSNP and the government's opponents.

---

72 See "Khitāb al-Zaʿīm fī al-Qalamūn," in Saʿadeh, *al-Aʿmāl al-Kāmila, Vol. 8*, pp. 145–146; "Khitāb al-Zaʿīm fī Jal al-Dīb," in Saʿadeh, *al-Aʿmāl al-Kāmila, Vol. 8*, pp. 149–155; "Khitāb al-Zaʿīm fī Riyāq," in Saʿadeh, *al-Aʿmāl al-Kāmila, Vol. 8*, p. 201; and "Khitāb al-Zaʿīm fī al-Biqāʿ al-Awsaṭ," in Saʿadeh, *al-Aʿmāl al-Kāmila, Vol. 8*, pp. 202–206.

73 For more on Sharabati, see Sami Moubayed, *The Makers of Modern Syria: The Rise and Fall of Syrian Democracy, 1918–1958* (London: I.B. Tauris, 2018).

74 "Riḥla al-Zaʿīm ilā Dimashq," in Saʿadeh, *al-Aʿmāl al-Kāmila, Vol. 8*, pp. 165–167. Part of the reason for Sharabati's receptivity was likely due to his grave concerns over developments in Palestine and his growing frustration with the "negligence and ignorance" of Syrian politicians that undermined the effectiveness of the Syrian Army in battle. Moubayed, *The Makers of Modern Syria*, p. 177.

75 Rogan, *The Arabs*, p. 255.

76 Zisser, *Lebanon*, pp. 153–154, and Seale, *The Struggle for Arab Independence*, pp. 648–649.

Though the SSNP had endeavored to arm its military force, it required outside support to do so. Such assistance was not forthcoming; the Lebanese government blocked the transfer of arms to the party due to its reluctance to arm a movement it feared could, in the end, turn against and attempt to overthrow it.[77] Unable to mobilize its militia, SSNP members made their way to fight in Palestine either as volunteers or enlisted members of the Syrian army. Individual and small brigades of SSNP fighters participated in battles around Haifa, Acre, Ramle, Lod, Safed, and Jerusalem. One SSNP unit was known as "The Red Tempest" and fought around Safed.[78] In battles in Lubya west of Tiberias, near Malikiyya, and Mishmar HaYarden in May-June 1948, several SSNP volunteers fighting with the ALA were killed. Almost a dozen other SSNP members serving in the Syrian army perished in battles in Palestine.[79]

After ten days of renewed fighting, the second UN-brokered truce took effect on 18 July. Saʿadeh declared this turn of events in Palestine to be a disaster. In his statement to the party, Saʿadeh lamented the fact that the entry of regular Arab armies into Palestine had done little to change the situation. The Arab intervention, he argued, had been doomed from the beginning. The reactionary and divisive policies of Arab leaders had failed to heed the SSNP's warnings of impending disaster and had been unable to utilize the party to advance the Arab cause in the political and military spheres. He concluded with a plea to enable the party to do whatever was necessary to save Palestine and preserve Syria. He absolved the party of any responsibility for events transpiring there, placing the blame entirely on the government's decisionmakers.[80] He was not alone in criticizing the government's policies.[81]

Throughout the fall of 1948 and into the early spring of 1949, as military operations continued in Palestine, the SSNP maintained its strident criticism of the Lebanese government. Saʿadeh broadened the party's attacks on Lebanese nationalism and Arab nationalism, describing them as religiously based ideas whose adherents only helped perpetuate division, disunity, and sectarianism. In visits to Ain Zhalta, Bshamoun, Jezzine, and Koura, Saʿadeh passionately ela-

---

77 Beshara, *Outright Assassination*, p. 31.

78 *Al-Khālidūn: Sīrat Shuhadā' al-Ḥaraka al-Sūriyya al-Qawmiyya al-Ijtimāʿiyya* (Syria: ND), p. 69.

79 Al-Khalidi, *al-Muqāwama al-Qawmiyya*, pp. 19–21, and *al-Khālidūn*, pp. 70–75, 78–79.

80 "Balāgh min Maktab al-Zaʿīm fī Ṣadad Filasṭīn," in Saʿadeh, *al-Aʿmāl al-Kāmila, Vol. 8*, pp. 235–236.

81 TNA, FO 371/68489, E10497, No. 7, "Beirut Political Summary for July 1948," 19 August 1948; TNA, FO 371/68489, E12619, No. 8, "Beirut Political Summary for August 1948," ND; and, TNA, FO 371/68489, E13454, No. 9, "Beirut Political Summary for September 1948," ND.

borated on these themes, lambasting how the war in Palestine was being conducted, defending the party against criticisms of corruption and misguidance, and decrying the reactionary policies of Arab states. In a pointed reproach, he accused the Syrian, Egyptian, and Arab armies of fighting not only the Jews in Palestine but the Palestinians themselves, driven by self-interest and hope for personal aggrandizement rather than advancing the Palestinian cause. In another speech, he essentially stated Lebanese independence was a sham as the country remained controlled by foreign interests, acerbically observing the foreign powers had not left but "had merely moved away just as a cat does from a mouse when it wants to play with it."[82] Saʿadeh did not limit his ever more provocative and aggressive rhetoric to a Lebanese audience, embarking on a journey through Syria in November and December 1948 to rouse the party faithful and strengthen its organization in Damascus, Homs, Latakia, Aleppo, and elsewhere.[83] His campaign did not escape the notice of Sulh and other Lebanese authorities who were growing disturbed by his confrontational rhetoric challenging the ideals of Lebanese and Arab nationalism. However, of more practical concern to authorities was the SSNP's emerging alliance with Chamoun and Jumblatt in opposition to Sulh and Khuri's Palestine policy.

82 See "ʿAyn Zaḥaltā," in Saʿadeh, *al-Aʿmāl al-Kāmila, Vol. 8*, pp. 394–399; "Bashāmūn," in Saʿadeh, *al-Aʿmāl al-Kāmila, Vol. 8*, pp. 400–406; "Jazīn," in Saʿadeh, *al-Aʿmāl al-Kāmila, Vol. 8*, pp. 407–409; and "al-Kūra," in Saʿadeh, *al-Aʿmāl al-Kāmila, Vol. 8*, pp. 410–414.

83 Saʿadeh would visit Damascus, Homs, Hama, Aleppo, Latakia, Tarsus, Banias, and Safita. See, for example "Dimashq," in Saʿadeh, *al-Aʿmāl al-Kāmila, Vol. 8*, pp. 417–423; "Ḥalab," in Saʿadeh, *al-Aʿmāl al-Kāmila, Vol. 8*, pp. 427–432; and "al-Lādhaqiyya," in Saʿadeh, *al-Aʿmāl al-Kāmila, Vol. 8*, pp. 433–440. For more on Saʿadeh's visit to Syria, particularly his time in Lattakia and the ʿAlawi region along the Syrian coast where he interacted with local dignitaries, leaders, and party members, including those from the well-established and prominent Makhluf family, see Jamil Makhluf, *Maḥaṭṭāt Qawmiyya* (Beirut: al-Rukn li-l-Ṭibāʿa wa-l-Nashr, 2006), pp. 44–67.

9 An Inglorious Revolution

The tide of the battle in Palestine had decisively turned against the Arabs as Israel continued to make significant military advances and secure further territory. "By the end of 1948, the Arab front, both militarily and politically speaking, was on the point of collapse," and Khuri and Sulh were determined to pursue an end to the hostilities. They reached an armistice agreement with Israel at the end of March 1949, a month after Egypt signed a similar agreement.[1] The Arab defeat in Palestine had revealed Arab governments' weakness and their conflicting political and territorial objectives, the reality of which provided plentiful fodder for critics like Saʿadeh and the SSNP.

The events in Palestine presented the party with opportunities to forge new political alliances and broaden its appeal in communities where it had previously held little appeal, particularly among Sunnis. In addition to deepening the party's ties to Chamoun and Jumblatt, Saʿadeh found common cause with disenchanted Arab nationalists in Lebanon, foremost among whom were Muhammad Baʿalbaki and Saʿid Taqi al-Din. Baʿalbaki, a Sunni, was the editor of the political weekly *Kull Shay'*, a paper known for its Arab nationalist leanings and support for Sulh, while Taqi al-Din, a Druze, was a prominent writer and playwright who also worked at the newspaper. Both would later join the SSNP and serve in influential positions in the party's leadership. At the time, Baʿalbaki had grown increasingly frustrated with Sulh and increasingly disillusioned with Arab nationalism and found himself more sympathetic to Saʿadeh and his ideas. Their budding relationship's immediate outcome was Baʿalbaki's decision to publish a series of Saʿadeh's articles critical of Arab nationalism and the Lebanese government in *Kull Shay'*. The publication provided the SSNP with a valuable platform and exposure to a new audience.

Appearing on the paper's front page, Saʿadeh's articles constituted a clear departure from the periodical's previous editorial line, a fact not lost on Arab nationalists and Sulh. Not mincing his words, Saʿadeh declared Arab nationalism and Lebanese nationalism to be bankrupt, reactionary doctrines. The defeat in Palestine was merely the latest and most humiliating manifestation of the damage caused by "false Arabism." Rather than acknowledging the reality of division in the Arab world and establishing cooperative agreements to further common interests, Arab nationalists deluded themselves into believing they could form

1 Zisser, *Lebanon*, pp. 156–158, and TNA, FO 371/75318, E5443, No. 3, "Beirut Summary for the Month of March 1949," 29 April 1949.

https://doi.org/10.1515/9783110729092-011

Figure 7: A Syrian Social Nationalist Party gathering in Lebanon on 1 March 1949, commemorating Saʿadeh's birthday. (Courtesy of The Palmach Archive)

a unified Arab nation and society. This fantastical mentality was the source of the Arab defeat.[2]

Similarly, Saʿadeh railed against the reactionary mindset of Lebanese nationalism that sought to isolate the Lebanese from the Syrian nation and was, in fact, hostile toward them. Deeming it "an idea contrary to social reality and truth," Saʿadeh lambasted the religious underpinnings of the Lebanese national idea (as he did with Arabism), the internal fragmentation, and the calamity the

2 "Al-ʿUrūba Afalsat," in Saʿadeh, *al-Āʿmāl al-Kāmila, Vol. 8*, pp. 256–258, and "Ḥārabnā al-ʿUrūba al-Wahmiyya," in Saʿadeh, *al-Āʿmāl al-Kāmila, Vol. 8*, pp. 267–271.

Figure 8: Syrian Social Nationalist Party members and others listen to speeches in honor of Saʿadeh and the party's struggle in March 1949. (Courtesy of The Palmach Archive)

enshrinement of sectarianism had wrought.[3] The confrontational rhetoric did not fail to generate a response, appealing to some while others defended both doctrines' merits and attacked the SSNP. However, the attacks did not diminish the validity of Saʿadeh's criticisms, which were considered legitimate "in many well-informed Arab circles."[4]

The resonance of Saʿadeh's message in Lebanon "among those segments of the population whom [Sulh and other traditional political leaders] regarded as

3 "Al-Inʿizāliyya al-Lubnāniyya Afalsat," in Saʿadeh, *al-Āʿmāl al-Kāmila*, *Vol. 8*, pp. 259–262.
4 Yamak, *SSNP*, p. 65.

their natural supporters" was increasingly viewed as a threat.[5] Indeed, "[Sa'adeh's] attacks on the war issue and his cooperation with the opposition leaders had now stamped him as an enemy of both Sulh and Khuri."[6] The strength and influence of the SSNP's propaganda aside, the extent to which the party posed a serious political or military threat to the Lebanese government is debatable. At the time, the SSNP was estimated to have no more than 4,000 members in Lebanon, predominately from the Druze and Greek Orthodox communities. The center of the party's activities was Beirut, its branch mostly filled by AUB students and professors who were assessed to be unlikely to engage in armed conflict. The SSNP was most active in Mount Lebanon, while in North Lebanon, the party attracted educated members from the Sunni and Greek Orthodox communities of Tripoli and Koura. In the Bekaa, the party had grown among the largely uneducated Shi'i and Greek Orthodox communities opposed to feudalism. In South Lebanon, the party largely failed to appeal to the Shi'i and Sunni communities there, only gaining a foothold among the Druze and Greek Orthodox communities in Merdjayoun and Hasbaya.[7] Regarding military affairs, the Lebanese government had successfully prevented the transfer of arms to the party over the preceding year, and the party's militia was poorly trained and had little fighting experience. Furthermore, the party lacked allies or a patron to provide it with finances and arms for an uprising.

At the end of March, the dramatic and unexpected coup of Husni al-Za'im in Syria changed the Lebanese government's calculus, significantly adding to its sense of unease vis-à-vis the SSNP. Za'im's coup "was badly received in official Lebanese circles," particularly by Sulh, whose personal friend Shukri al-Quwatli had been removed from power.[8] The Lebanese government's immediate response was non-committal as it hesitated to recognize the new government for three weeks, a decision that enraged the ill-tempered and unpredictable Za'im, who responded by banning the export of meat and other foodstuffs from Syria to Lebanon, driving up prices and deepening tensions between Beirut and Damascus.[9] Further complicating matters was the extreme level of distrust between Za'im and Sulh; Za'im believed Sulh was "encouraging elements hostile to him to operate from Lebanon," while Sulh thought Za'im was encouraging the Lebanese

5 Yamak, *SSNP*, p. 65.
6 Zisser, *Lebanon*, p. 182.
7 TNA, FO 1018/62, No. 250, P.P.S. in Lebanon, "Parti Populaire Syrien," 2 April 1949.
8 TNA, FO 371/75318, E6549, No. 4, "Beirut Summary for the Month of April 1949," 26 May 1949, and Seale, *The Struggle for Arab Independence*, p. 672.
9 For details, see Zisser, *Lebanon*, Chapter 9, and Seale, *The Struggle for Arab Independence*, p. 676.

opposition – holding meetings with Chamoun and Jumblatt – and developing strong ties with the SSNP.[10]

The SSNP, meanwhile, reacted to the coup with cautious optimism. An editorial published in *al-Jil al-Jadid* several weeks later was optimistic, welcoming Zaʿim's proposed reforms and expressing hope the party would be granted freedom to expand its activities.[11] In private, Saʿadeh had instructed party officials in Damascus to contact Zaʿim and offer him the party's support. A letter was drafted, and a small delegation delivered it to Zaʿim's representatives.[12] At the same time, Lebanese officials began receiving reports suggesting the SSNP intended to instigate a popular revolt to overthrow the government with the support of the opposition and an unnamed foreign country.[13] While Lebanese officials viewed these reports as credible, no concrete plans for such an uprising existed, nor were they being made. However, a new diplomatic crisis between Lebanon and Syria in May and the party's response to that crisis would only confirm mounting suspicions among Sulh, Khuri, and others that the SSNP posed a credible threat to Lebanon.

In early May, a Syrian military patrol crossed the border into Lebanon and attempted to arrest a Lebanese smuggler accused of being a spy for Israel, but instead shot and killed him. The Lebanese gendarmerie arrested the Syrians before they could slip back across the border and took them to Beirut to stand trial. Syria demanded their immediate extradition, but the Lebanese government refused, claiming the Syrian request had no legal basis. In response, Syria closed the border as tensions soared.[14] The party reviewed the episode and concluded the Syrians were mainly in the right on the matter, publishing its conclusions in *al-Jil al-Jadid*.[15] The party's stance on the case caught one of Zaʿim's advisors' attention, who suggested Zaʿim meet with Saʿadeh. A meeting was arranged, and Saʿadeh traveled to Damascus on 27 May, where the two agreed, in principle, out of their shared sense of grievance, to work together to oppose the Lebanese government.[16]

---

10 124/1, 7 June 1949, No. 21, "al-Za'eem," in Asseily and Asfahani, *A Face in the Crowd*, pp. 23–25; Seale, *The Struggle for Arab Independence*, pp. 676–677; and Zisser, *Lebanon*, pp. 166–169.

11 *Al-Jil al-Jadid*, 13 April 1949.

12 *Al-Jil al-Jadid*, 25 May 1949.

13 "Taqrīr bi-Tārīkh 19/4/1949, Taqrīr bi-Tārīkh 21/4/1949, and Taqrīr bi-Tārīkh 27/4/1949," in Asfahani, *Anṭūn Saʿādah*, pp. 40–42.

14 TNA, FO 371/75318, E7778, No. 5, "Beirut Summary for the Month of May 1949," 24 June 1949.

15 *Al-Jil al-Jadid*, 25 May 1949.

16 Beshara, *Outright Assassination*, pp. 33–35.

News of their meeting quickly made it to Beirut, where Khuri and Sulh's suspicions and fears were now confirmed. Further adding to their irritation were the results of local elections in which the SSNP made significant gains. Suggesting a rising level of popular support for the party, this only strengthened their conviction that the SSNP posed a threat to Lebanon that must be confronted.[17] Sulh and Khuri failed to grasp, however, just how fragile and unproven the ties between the SSNP and Zaʿim were; Zaʿim had his suspicions of the party, particularly its several thousand adherents in the Syrian army.[18] However, the confrontation between the Lebanese government and the SSNP erupted into open conflict and violence, as a clash between the SSNP and the Kataʾib in Beirut's Jummayzh district provided it with the pretext it needed to suppress the party.

Jummayzh, a predominately Maronite district, was known to be the Kataʾib's domain, but the SSNP had recently moved its printing press into a building there owned by a relative of Asad al-Ashqar.[19] The building sat opposite a café often frequented by Kataʾib members and used for their meetings. On 9 June, Saʿadeh visited the printing works, his arrival coinciding with a large Kataʾib gathering at the café.[20] Trouble began soon after the Kataʾib's gathering ended and happened to coincide with Saʿadeh's departure from the printing press to the loud shouts of "Long live Syria, long live Saʿadeh" by the SSNP members accompanying him. Taking exception to the slogans and following a brief exchange of fire, a clash broke out between hundreds of Kataʾib and SSNP members.[21] During the brawl, the building housing the printing was set on fire and destroyed. Lebanese police eventually arrived and dispersed the brawl, arresting over 20 SSNP mem-

---

17 Beshara al-Khuri, *Ḥaqāʾiq Lubnāniyya, al-Juzaʾ al-Thālith* (Beirut: Manshūrāt Awrāq Lubnāniyya, nd), pp. 228–229, and Beshara, *Outright Assassination*, p. 36. On the local elections, see *al-Jil al-Jadid*, 20 May–7 June 1949.

18 Zaʿim was wary of Shishakli, Hawrani, and several other officers who he believed could move against him. He also had arrested 21 SSNP-affiliated soldiers "in whose possession he [had] found copies of secret military orders they intended to send to [Saʿadeh]." 124/1, 7 June 1949, No. 21, "al-Za'eem," in Asseily and Asfahani, *A Face in the Crowd*, p. 26.

19 Sharabi, *Embers and Ashes*, p. 157.

20 Dylan Baun, "The Gemmayzeh Incident of 1949: Conflict Over Physical and Symbolic Space in Beirut," *Arab Studies Journal* 25, no. 1 (2017): p. 107.

21 Baun, "The Gemmayzeh Incident," p. 108. As Baun describes in detail and with great clarity, the Kataʾib and SSNP promoted divergent accounts of how the events of 9 June transpired (Ibid., pp. 108–114). Furthermore, scholars are divided over whether the Lebanese government ordered the Kataʾib to instigate a confrontation with the SSNP so that it could then suppress it. Given the lack of evidence proving the Lebanese government did, in fact, conspire to goad the SSNP, the reasons why the incident took place remain unclear. Baun, "The Gemmayzeh Incident," p. 95, and Zisser, *Lebanon*, pp. 183–184

bers but not a single Kata'ib member.[22] The government's crackdown on the SSNP began immediately. The party was declared illegal, SSNP members were arrested en masse, party offices were raided, and weapons and documents were seized.[23] Saʿadeh fled Beirut and made his way to Damascus, where he was welcomed by Zaʿim, who promised to provide Saʿadeh and the party with weapons, money, and Syrian soldiers to assist in an SSNP-led uprising in Lebanon. Other party officials also fled Lebanon to avoid arrest.[24]

The immediate reaction to the government's crackdown on the SSNP was mostly positive.[25] However, some questioned the vigor of the Lebanese government's pursuit of the SSNP and the validity of its claims regarding the SSNP, finding the evidence regarding the party's intentions and capabilities to be unconvincing.[26] Meanwhile, in Damascus, Saʿadeh and party officials grappled with responding to the Lebanese government's offensive. Buoyed by Zaʿim's offer of support, Saʿadeh intensified his rhetoric against the Lebanese government, speaking of a "decisive conflict" and "day of reckoning," openly challenging it to fight.[27] Unsurprisingly, the Lebanese government viewed the statement as confirmation its campaign against the party was wholly warranted. Expanding its security operations, the Lebanese government charged Saʿadeh *in absentia* with collaborating with Israel to overthrow it, essentially accusing both him and the party of committing treason. Amid the SSNP and Lebanese government's escalating battle, Zaʿim's commitment to the SSNP appeared to waver. He began to pursue reconciliation with Sulh and, internally, dissolved all political parties in Syria, including the SSNP.[28] Though wary of Zaʿim's commitment, the party nevertheless continued to plan for an armed popular rebellion. According to the agreed-upon strategy, the SSNP would prioritize seizing territory in areas where the Lebanese government's control and presence were weak, while at the same time launch attacks against government forces and rally local populaces to the party's cause in areas in and around Beirut.[29] However, the plan would

---

22 TNA, FO 1018/62, No. 250, "Parti Populaire Syrien," Telegram no. 358, Beirut to Foreign Office, 10 June 1949.
23 *The Palestine Post*, 12 June 1947.
24 "Taqrīr bi-Tārīkh 18/6/1949," in Asfahani, *Anṭūn Saʿādah*, p. 44, and Zisser, *Lebanon*, p. 185.
25 *The Palestine Post*, 22 June 1949, and TNA, FO 371/75318, E9483, No. 6, "Beirut Summary for the Month of June 1949," 4 August 1949.
26 Beshara, *Outright Assassination*, pp. 41–43.
27 "Bayān al-Zaʿīm ilā al-Qawmiyyīn al-Ijtimāʿiyyīn wa-l-Umma al-Sūriyya," in Saʿadeh, *al-Āʿmāl al-Kāmila, Vol. 8*, pp. 383–387.
28 Beshara, *Outright Assassination*, pp. 45–47; Zisser, *Lebanon*, pp. 185–186; and Rathmell, *Secret War*, pp. 47–48.
29 Mujais, *SSNP*, p. 209.

prove woefully fanciful and ill-conceived, "well beyond the party's capabilities," and fail even to achieve the limited goal of forcing the Lebanese government to relent in its suppressive campaign.[30]

Armed clashes between Lebanese security forces and the SSNP broke out on the night of 2 July. SSNP fighters attacked several Gendarmerie posts, resulting in the death of one gendarme and two wounded, and cut telephone lines in North Lebanon.[31] In a communiqué issued the same day, Saʿadeh urged SSNP members in the security forces to join the party's uprising and renounce their responsibilities to the Lebanese government.[32] On 4 July, Lebanese security forces besieged Bshamoun, a village in Mount Lebanon known as an SSNP stronghold, to prevent SSNP fighters from joining their comrades. The commanding officer of the Lebanese gendarmerie was killed, while several SSNP members were wounded, and dozens were arrested. In response, Saʿadeh proclaimed a revolution whose aim was to overthrow the Lebanese government and establish a new social and political order based on the party's doctrine. The proclamation confirmed the Lebanese government's worst fears of a Syrian-backed SSNP uprising.[33]

The uprising was on the verge of collapse within hours. Lacking proper training, weapons, leadership, and numbers, the SSNP's revolution stumbled along. A group of an estimated 100 SSNP fighters crossed the Syrian border and attacked gendarmerie posts in Rachaya and Machghara. Having been warned of the impending attacks, the gendarmerie was ready and able to repel the attackers, who fled back to Syria to evade arrest. The government responded by blowing up the houses of known SSNP sympathizers.[34] In the northern Bekaa, the party's offensive faltered as its would-be allies, the Dandash clan, refused to join the uprising, depriving the SSNP of a capable fighting force in the area.[35] On 6 July, Zaʿim would deal the most significant blow to the rebellion.

The Syrian regime had transferred weapons into Lebanon on 3 July for the SSNP, but Zaʿim's assessment of the situation soon changed. He no longer felt

---

30 Beshara, *Outright Assassination*, p. 48; ʿAbdallah Qubrusi, *ʿAbd Allah Qubruṣī Yatadhakkar, Vol. 4* (Beirut: al-Furāt, 2004), p. 51; and Sharabi, *Embers and Ashes*, p. 175.

31 TNA, FO 371/75318, E10339, No. 7, "Political Summary for the month of July 1949," 25 August 1949.

32 "Amr ilā al-Qawmiyyīn al-Ijtimāʿiyyīn fī al-Silk al-ʿAskarī," in Saʿadeh, *al-Āʿmāl al-Kāmila, Vol. 8*, p. 454.

33 "Balāgh al-Thawra al-Qawmiyya al-Ijtimāʿiyya al-ʿUlyā al-Awwalī," in Saʿadeh, *al-Āʿmāl al-Kāmila, Vol. 8*, pp. 455–460. On Sulh and Khuri's response, see Khuri, *Ḥaqāʾiq Lubnāniyya, Vol. 3*, pp. 236–240.

34 TNA, FO 371/75318, E10339, No. 7, "Political Summary for the month of July 1949," 25 August 1949.

35 Sharabi, *Embers and Ashes*, p. 174, and Mujais, *SSNP*, p. 210.

it advisable to pursue a policy supporting the party and antagonistic toward the Lebanese government. Consequently, Zaʿim sought to repair bilateral relations with Sulh and Khuri by turning on Saʿadeh and agreeing to extradite him. Zaʿim invited an unknowing Saʿadeh to the presidential palace in Damascus on the evening of 6 July. Saʿadeh was detained and handed over to Farid Chehab, the police chief and head of the Lebanese gendarmerie, who then transferred Saʿadeh to Beirut.[36] Simultaneously, the Syrian army began detaining SSNP members throughout the country.

In the early hours of 7 July, Saʿadeh was arraigned before a military court on charges of conspiracy, treason, attempting to overthrow the government, collaborating with Israel, attacking the army, and being responsible for the deaths of several people.[37] By evening, after only several hours of deliberation, Saʿadeh was convicted and sentenced to death. Khuri refused to commute the death sentence. Saʿadeh was executed by firing squad in the dawn hours of 8 July. The arrest, extradition, deliberation, and sentencing took less than twenty-four hours. The haste with which the process had been conducted provoked an outcry among Saʿadeh's supporters and opponents alike.[38]

9.1 The Aftermath: Revenge and Reorganization

In the weeks following his death, Lebanese-Syrian rapprochement would occur rapidly. The countries signed a bilateral trade agreement, and Sulh made an official state visit to Syria. Legal proceedings against several hundred detained SSNP members would continue until early September. Of the first 68 SSNP members tried before the Military Tribunal in Beirut, twelve would be sentenced to death, three to life imprisonment, eleven to 10–15 years, thirty-nine to 3–7 years, and three acquitted. Only six of the twelve condemned to death would be executed; the others' sentences were commuted to life imprisonment. The remainder of those SSNP members put on trial would receive sentences of only several months, the most notable exception being George ʿAbd al-Masih, who was sentenced to death in absentia.

The government's crackdown on the SSNP met with little protest among most Lebanese, though some argued that party members should not be held re-

36 Rathmell, *Secret War*, pp. 48–50.

37 *The Palestine Post*, 10 July 1949.

38 For a detailed analysis of the trial, see Beshara, *Outright Assassination*, Chapters 3 and 4, and al-Khalidi, *Saʿādah wa-l-Thawra al-Awwalī*. For the Lebanese government's case against the party, see Wizārat al-Iʿlā al-Lubnāniyya, *Qaḍīyat al-Ḥizb al-Qawmī* (Beirut, 1949).

sponsible for Saʿadeh's decisions. Predictably, the Kataʾib urged the government to respond with even more severity, going so far as to demand the government shutter the American University of Beirut because it had been an SSNP stronghold. No such step was taken, and the Kataʾib was forced to retract its statement; Pierre Gemayel, its leader, formally apologized to the AUB's president.[39] Ironically, despite its outspoken support for the government, the Kataʾib would not escape the repercussions of the failed uprising, as the Lebanese government ordered the dissolution of all armed movements, including it and the Najjadeh.[40]

Public opinion was less forgiving and far more critical on the matter of Saʿadeh's execution. Several demonstrations protesting actions against the party were held in Lebanon, while more than 200 Lebanese residing in Brazil signed a telegram protesting Saʿadeh's trial and execution. The Lebanese government was aware of and tried to dampen these sentiments by issuing a short public statement defending its actions. However, the statement failed to satisfy some government supporters as even *al-Hayat*, a newspaper known for its sympathies for Sulh, dismissed it as insufficient, demanding the government provide a detailed account justifying its months-long campaign against the SSNP.[41] Ghassan Tueni, who had been expelled from the party, penned a scathing editorial in *al-Nahar* denouncing Saʿadeh's hasty execution. In it, he contended the government's actions defied understanding: was it an execution or an assassination, a trial or a plot? Tueni argued the government's deed had only transformed Saʿadeh into a martyr, not only to his followers but also to those who disagreed with him and did not believe he should be executed.[42]

In parliament, Chamoun and Jumblatt denounced the government's actions. In August, Jumblatt, a more vocal critic than Chamoun, published a manifesto in which he accused the government of having conducted an unfair trial in which false evidence was used to convict an innocent man and execute him. Jumblatt charged the government's actions were not only shameful but illegal. He submitted his manifesto for debate in the parliament, but his colleagues refused to discuss it the three times they were in session that month.[43]

The initial Syrian reaction to Saʿadeh's execution was relatively subdued, owing to the Syrian regime's censorship of the press. The Damascene *al-*

39 Beshara, *Outright Assassination*, p. 147.
40 TNA, FO 371/75318, E10339, No. 7, "Political Summary for the month of July 1949," 25 August 1949.
41 Beshara, *Outright Assassination*, p. 144.
42 Seale, *The Struggle for Arab Independence*, pp. 686–687.
43 TNA, FO 371/75318, E12106, No. 8, "Political Summary for the month of August 1949," 7 October 1949. For the manifesto's text, see al-Khalidi, *Saʿādah wa-l-Thawra al-Awwalī*, pp. 322–336.

Qabas, for which Saʿadeh had worked as a journalist in the early 1930s, lauded him as a patriot and criticized Lebanese citizens for not opposing their government's actions toward the SSNP.[44] An editorial in the same paper by the Archbishop of Hama went even further, comparing the Lebanese government's betrayal to that of Herod, who had offered John the Baptist's head on a platter to his daughter.[45]

Zaʿim's betrayal of Saʿadeh also contributed to growing discontent with his rule among Syrian Army officers and some Syrian politicians. Zaʿim's dismissal of several officers, including Adib al-Shishakli, angered their allies in the military, while his appointment of Muhsin al-Barazi as prime minister angered and inflamed Zaʿim's intense political rivalry with Akram al-Hawrani.[46] In the early hours of 14 August, Zaʿim was overthrown in a coup led by Colonel Sami al-Hinnawi and Lt. Colonel Bahij Kallas. Zaʿim was declared a tyrant and, without being brought to trial, was executed by Fadlallah Abu Mansur, a Syrian Army officer and member of the SSNP who proclaimed it an act of revenge on Saʿadeh's behalf.[47] Hinnawi reinstated Shishakli and other dismissed army officers to their former positions. He also appointed Hashim al-Atasi to form a government and withdrew the military from politics.

Zaʿim's overthrow greatly benefited the party. As a gesture to the Lebanese government, Zaʿim had dissolved the SSNP in Syria, suppressed its activities, and detained some party members. Under the new Syrian government, the party was reinstated, and its property and funds seized by Zaʿim were returned in their entirety.[48] Further improving the party's standing in Syria was the renewed and strengthened prominence of army officers with direct ties to, or sympathies for, the SSNP, including Shishakli, Abu Mansur, and the Jadid brothers, Salah and Ghassan. While the party continued to operate clandestinely in Lebanon, the Lebanese government's crackdown forced the SSNP to move its headquarters to Damascus. There, the party's newly elected president George ʿAbd al-Masih rallied the party around the death of their martyred leader and consoli-

---

44 *The Palestine Post*, 19 August 1949.

45 Beshara, *Outright Assassination*, pp. 138 – 139, and al-Khalidi, *Saʿādah wa-l-Thawra al-Awwalī*, pp. 371 – 374.

46 Seale, *The Struggle for Syria*, pp. 73 – 74, and *The Palestine Post*, 15 August 1949.

47 TNA, FO 371, E10944, No. 13, Man to Attlee "Background of the Zaim Regime in Syria: Factors Leading up to the "Coup d'Etat,"" 3 September 1949, and Fadlallah Abu Mansur, *Aʿāṣīr Dimashq* (ND), pp. 70 – 75.

48 *The Palestine Post*, 31 August 1949.

dated its organization in Syria, building on the existing strength of party branches in the country.[49]

The party's first taste of success in Syria came in November when the SSNP secured nine seats in Syria's parliament during general elections. The most significant victory of all was that of ʿIsam Mahayri, the party's general secretary in Damascus.[50] Mahayri, unmarried and under thirty years of age, hailed from a prominent land-owning family in Damascus and had distinguished himself in the party's Damascus branch. The party's small presence in parliament enabled it to advance legislation in line with its reform principles.[51] The more amicable atmosphere in Syria also allowed the party to be openly active, the most visible manifestation of which would be the establishment of a network of primary and secondary schools throughout Syria to promulgate the party's principles and "raise a new generation."[52] One of the secondary schools the party established was the New Order School (*Madrasa al-Nidhām al-Jadīd*) in the predominately Greek Orthodox village of al-Sawda in the Tartus Governorate. One of the school's anthems (*anāshīd*) captured its mission of educating and preparing the youth to serve their nation and contribute to its advancement, declaring they were "building a virtuous life for our new generation" and that "knowledge and jihad are the pillars of the country."[53] The school was also a practical way to advance the SSNP's political agenda as its establishment was an effective way of countering the Communist Party's influence in al-Sawda.[54]

Adib al-Shishakli's rise to power in a bloodless coup in December 1949 did little to assuage Lebanese concerns of deepening ties between Syrian rulers and the SSNP, particularly given Shishakli's former links to the party and his relationship with Mahayri. These connections worried the Lebanese government, which was convinced "that Syria had hostile intentions toward it."[55] More concerning, at least for Sulh, was the party's determination to avenge Saʿadeh's death by assassinating him, an outcome he sought to avoid by reaching an arrangement

49 Inʿam Raʿad, *al-Kalimāt al-Akhīra: Mudhakkirāt wa Wathāʾiq* (Beirut: Muʾassasat Inʿām Raʿad al-Fikriyya, 2002), p. 66.
50 Raʿad, *al-Kalimāt al-Akhīra*, p. 65, and Yamak, *SSNP*, p. 68.
51 Yamak, *SSNP*, p. 69.
52 Qubrusi, *Yatadhakkar, Vol. 4*, p. 107, and Raʿad, *al-Kalimāt al-Akhīra*, p. 66.
53 "The New Order School in al-Sawda (Tartus)," accessed 10 October 2020: https://www.ssnp.info/?article=86053.
54 The SSNP and Communist Party were the two main political organizations in the village. The Communists also established a secondary school in al-Sawda, but it was not as popular or successful. See "The New Order School in al-Sawda (2)," accessed 10 October 2020: https://www.ssnp.info/?article=118301.
55 Zisser, "The Downfall of the Khuri Administration," p. 496.

with the SSNP. By early 1950, party members were operating more openly in Lebanon, though unofficially and not to the degree they had previously.[56] In early February 1950, Mahayri traveled from Damascus to Beirut, where he met with party members. A rumor spread that he had met with Sulh to discuss the possible amnesty of detained SSNP members, likely in return for the party abandoning its efforts to exact revenge. In truth, a Lebanese government minister had arranged a meeting without his knowledge, but when Mahayri learned of the minister's intentions, he refused to meet Sulh or negotiate on the party's behalf.[57]

The first attempt on Sulh's life occurred several weeks after Mahayri's trip. In Beirut on 9 March 1950, a Druze SSNP member named Tawfiq Hamdan opened fire on Sulh as he stepped out of his vehicle. Sulh was not wounded, but the incident resulted in two bystanders' deaths and the wounding of three others. It is unclear whether the party ordered the attempted assassination or if Hamdan carried out the act on his own accord to exact revenge for his cousin, a fellow SSNP member who had been executed in July 1949 for his participation in the failed uprising. Regardless, the party made no apologies for the attempt on Sulh's life and, except for Kamal Jumblatt, was widely condemned by Lebanese politicians for the assassination attempt. Hamdan was sentenced to death; however, Sulh commuted his sentence as a gesture of goodwill toward the party. The SSNP, unimpressed, remained committed to exacting its revenge.[58]

Perturbed by the recent attempt on his life, Sulh expressed his displeasure with Syria's legalization and open support of the SSNP and bristled at reports of party members being "smuggled into Lebanon to stir up trouble" with Syrian assistance.[59] While there is no evidence this was occurring, the SSNP, which had put great hopes in Shishakli, was reaping the benefits of being on amicable terms with the Syrian regime. In the summer of 1950, the party was particularly active in Aleppo and Damascus. Public opinion in Aleppo had shifted in the party's favor thanks to the influence of Syrian Army officers, who gave the party credibility. Actively recruiting from among the *fellahin* and peasants, the party held a large, well-attended public gathering in Aleppo's Balleramoun district. They opened new branches in Idlib, al-Bab, Haram, and Jabal Sama'an. By the end of the summer, the party had an estimated 3,000 members in northern

---

56 Raʿad, *al-Kalimāt al-Akhīra*, p. 67.
57 Seale, *The Struggle for Arab Independence*, p. 690, and "Taqrīr bi-Tārīkh 4/2/1950," in Asfahani, *Anṭūn Saʿādah*, p. 71.
58 *The Palestine Post*, 10 March 1950; Seale, *The Struggle for Arab Independence*, p. 691; and Qubrusi, *Yatadhakkar, Vol. 4*, p. 122.
59 *The Palestine Post*, 15, 21 March 1950.

Syria, Aleppo, and Latakia.[60] In September 1950, the party began publishing a new periodical in Damascus, *al-Jil al-Jadid*. As with all its publications, *al-Jil al-Jadid* would serve as a platform for the party to propagate its doctrine and views on domestic and foreign affairs. The periodical would run until June 1952.[61]

As general elections approached in the spring of 1951, Lebanese officials were concerned the party may try to disrupt them. With broad support for the Khuri-Sulh administration eroding and public discontent rising, Sulh and his allies felt particularly vulnerable to the SSNP.[62] Their concern would prove partially correct. Though the party's standing in Lebanon remained diminished, it had worked to build opposition to the government and planned to offer its support for several candidates in the coming elections. Sulh's resignation from the premiership in February, amid mounting criticism and growing tensions in his relationship with Khuri, rendered the party's opposition to him null.[63] In the April elections, the party actively supported Ghassan Tueni, Kamal Jumblatt, and Camille Chamoun in the Shouf, while supporting Pierre Eddé's National Bloc against pro-government Pierre Gemayel in Metn. All four were victorious,[64] though overall, the opposition failed to make any substantial gains. There was, however, a silver lining: under Chamoun and Jumblatt's leadership, "[the opposition] emerged more cohesive and united around a single and explicit aim: the downfall of [Khuri]."[65]

Despite Sulh's resignation from the government, he remained a target for revenge. In July, at the Jordanian monarch's request, Sulh traveled to Amman to discuss inter-Arab affairs. Following his meeting with King ʿAbdallah, Sulh departed the Philadelphia Hotel for the Amman airport, where he was to board a flight to return to Beirut. On the way, his car was overtaken by another vehicle in which three assassins were traveling. The three – Wadiʿ Nikola Spiro, Michel Gabriel al-Dik, and Muhammad ʿAbd al-Latif al-Salahi – were members of the SSNP who had decided to exact their revenge on the man responsible for Saʿa-

---

60 "Taqrīr min Ḥalab bi-Tārīkh 25/6/1950 and Taqrīr min Ḥalab bi-Tārīkh 7/1950," in Asfahani, *Anṭūn Saʿādah*, pp. 71–73.

61 Jihad al-ʿAql, *Ṣiḥāfat al-Ḥaraka al-Qawmiyya al-Ijtimāʿiyya, 1950–1955, Vol. 4* (Beirut: Dār al-Rukn, 2005), pp. 39–47.

62 "Taqrīr ghayr Muʾarikh 1950," in Asfahani, *Anṭūn Saʿādah*, p. 75.

63 Mustafa ʿAbd al-Satir, *Ayyām wa Qaḍiyya: Min Muʿānayāt Muthaqaf ʿArabī* (Beirut: Muʾassasat Fikr li-l-Abḥāth wa-l-Nashr, 1982), p. 153, and Seale, *The Struggle for Arab Independence*, p. 713.

64 *L'Orient*, 17 April 1951; Raʿad, *al-Kalimāt al-Akhīra*, 86, and TNA, FO 371/91434, EL1016/11, No. 50, British Legation (Beirut) to FO, "Lebanese General Elections," 24 April 1951.

65 Zisser, *Lebanon*, p. 223.

deh's execution.[66] Firing several shots into the vehicle, the assailants succeeded in wounding Sulh, who later died from his wounds. News of the assassination provoked anger and grief among Sulh's sympathizers, many of whom took to Beirut's streets to protest his death. SSNP leaders in Beirut were summoned to provide an account for the party's alleged involvement in the assassination, but initial investigations into the party's liability produced no evidence of its involvement.[67] In Damascus, the SSNP was denounced by the Baʿth party's Michel ʿAflaq and by the National Party. Condemning the assassination, the National Party also accused the party of working against Syria's Arabism and spreading its Syrian nationalist propaganda among ʿAlawis and Kurds. The National Party's denouncement came on the same day that Mahayri and Hawrani walked out of Syria's parliament when it paid tribute to Sulh by observing a minute of silence.[68]

9.2 Emerging from the Shadows

At the end of November 1951, Shishakli swiftly consolidated his rule after disposing of Dawalibi's government, firmly establishing his authority over Syrian security forces.[69] Lacking the support of Syria's largest political blocs, the People's Party and the National Party, Shishakli was forced to rely on "the numerically weak" SSNP, the Baʿth, and Hawrani's Arab Socialist Party (ASP).[70] Shishakli believed the SSNP and ASP would be reliable sources of support given his previous membership with the SSNP and his relationships with Mahayri and Hawrani. Moreover, he wanted to exploit the SSNP's broad appeal among Syria's minority communities "from whom many army officers [were] drawn," and the SSNP's firm opposition to communism.[71] The SSNP did not disappoint. It fully supported

---

66 *Le Jour*, 17–18 July 1951; TNA, FO 371/91434, EL1016/24, No. 384, Beirut to FO, "Assassination of former Prime Minister," 16 July 1951; TNA, FO 371/91434, EL1016/25, No. 385, Beirut to FO, "Assassination of former Prime Minister," 16 July 1951; and TNA, FO 371/91434, EL1016/26, No. 388, Beirut to FO, "Assassination of Riad Solh," 17 July 1951.

67 *Le Jour*, 20 July 1951; "Taqrīr bi-Tārīkh 21/7/1951," in Asfahani, *Anṭūn Saʿādah*, p. 77; and *al-Qabas*, 23 July 1951.

68 "Taqrīr bi-Tārīkh 17/7/1951 and 12/8/1951," in Asfahani, *Anṭūn Saʿādah*, pp. 76–77.

69 TNA, FO 371/6/EY1016/1, "General Correspondence No. 4: Political Situation in Syria," Montagu-Pollock to Eden, Damascus, 8 January 1952.

70 TNA, FO 371/6/EY1016/1, "General Correspondence No. 4: Political Situation in Syria," Montagu-Pollock to Eden, Damascus, 8 January 1952.

71 TNA, FO 371/6/EY1016/1, "General Correspondence No. 4: Political Situation in Syria," Montagu-Pollock to Eden, Damascus, 8 January 1952.

Shishakli, providing him favorable press in *al-Jil al-Jadid*. Further evidence of the party's close ties to Shishakli was found in the content of his first official pronouncement, which, according to Hawrani, "bore the [party's] fingerprints."[72]

Hawrani was bothered by the close relationship between the party and Shishakli. He believed the SSNP exploited its relations with Shishakli to attack the ASP and Baʿth, incite against other political parties, and portray itself as Shishakli's party.[73] Hawrani's perception of the SSNP-Shishakli relationship was not mistaken. In a meeting with SSNP leaders before seizing power, Shishakli had promised party officials positions in his government and had expressed his desire for the SSNP to play a prominent role in governing Syria. Shishakli hoped to forge an official alliance between the SSNP, Hawrani's ASP, the Baʿth, and the National Party after eliminating the Communists and People's Party from the political scene. However, the party turned him down, feeling it was not yet able to fulfill such a role.[74] By the summer of 1952, however, relations between the SSNP and Shishakli would sour after Shishakli banned *al-Jil al-Jadid* after publishing a negative article about him.[75]

Further straining ties was Shishakli's establishment of the Arab Liberation Movement (ALM, *Ḥarakat al-Taḥrir al-ʿArabī*) in Damascus in late August 1952. Shishakli hoped the newly formed ALM "would give his regime the broad, popular base" of support it needed, unifying Syria's diverse groups and political parties into one, strong movement that would carry the banner of Arabism and help Syria assert its leadership in the Arab World.[76] The ALM's establishment frustrated the SSNP, as it had hoped to play the role of "Shishakli's party" and was angered by his efforts to recruit SSNP members to join the ALM. Another consequence of the ALM's establishment was the banning and dissolution of all political parties, though the measure was not enforced on the SSNP, which continued to be active and free from harassment.

---

72 Akram al-Hawrani, *Mudhakkirāt Akram al-Hawrānī, Vol. 2* (Cairo: Maktabat Madbūlī, 2000), p. 1513.

73 Hawrani, *Mudhakkirāt, Vol. 2*, p. 1513.

74 Raʿad is critical of the party's shortcomings regarding its relations with Shishakli. He argues that though Shishakli offered to have the party be his partner in ruling Syria, the party leadership hesitated, believing it was not up to the task of governing. Raʿad wonders how it is that a party filled with highly educated and cultured members with an organized presence throughout the country could deem itself insignificant and unfit for such a role. Raʿad, *al-Kalimāt al-Akhīra*, p. 72.

75 TNA, FO 371/6/EY1015/9, "Work of the New Government," Samuel to Eastern Department, Damascus, 11 July 1952. The ban would prove short-lived as the paper would reappear as *al-Binaʾ* in August.

76 Seale, *The Struggle for Syria*, pp. 124–125.

Meanwhile, in Lebanon, opposition to Khuri had intensified. His accumulation of power, concurrent with the decline in Lebanon's regional and international standing, engendered resentment and discontent.[77] The growing opposition coalesced around Chamoun and Jumblatt's National Socialist Front (NSF, *al-Jabha al-Ishtirākiyya al-Waṭaniyya*), a parliamentary bloc that had first taken shape in 1951. The SSNP was tied to the NSF from the beginning through Ghassan Tueni,[78] who had been elected the previous spring as part of Jumblatt and Chamoun's electoral list in Mount Lebanon. The party had participated in NSF activities throughout the preceding year, including the NSF's general strike in the summer of 1952. Khuri had done his best to fragment the opposition in early 1952, even going so far as making overtures to the SSNP, but the party rebuffed his advances and maintained its commitment to the NSF.[79] Though the party had mobilized its supporters in the previous election and had played a minor role in the NSF's activities, it had not yet fully re-emerged on the Lebanese political scene. This would happen in August 1952 at a mass rally in Deir al-Qamar organized by the NSF.

The rally in Deir al-Qamar, a predominately Maronite village in Mount Lebanon and the home of Chamoun, was a powerful demonstration of the opposition's resolve and determination, featuring fiery speeches denouncing Khuri and the government. Hassan Tawil, the party's leader in Lebanon, had acceded to the SSNP's symbolic participation in the event, concerned with the possible repercussions of the party's overt involvement in the rally. His deputies did not share his misgivings and, without his knowledge, mobilized the party to participate fully in the event. No SSNP officials spoke at the rally, but the party's presence was significant and was a strong signal that it had returned.[80]

The opposition would ultimately emerge victorious, as Khuri resigned his office the following month. A week after, Chamoun was elected president. His supporters, including the SSNP, hoped the new government would implement the NSF's reform program. Their hopes would be quickly dashed, as Chamoun and Jumblatt had a falling out over the former's reluctance to implement the NSF's radical reform program, a rift that would continue until Chamoun left office in the summer of 1958. To be sure, Chamoun would attempt to implement several significant reforms, including in the judicial and civil service systems, increasing press freedoms, giving women the right to vote, and amending electoral

77 Zisser, *Lebanon*, pp. 221–222.
78 On Tueni's return to the party see Qubrusi, *Yatadhakkar, Vol. 4*, pp. 116–119.
79 Zisser, *Lebanon*, p. 231.
80 ʿAbd al-Satir, *Ayyām wa Qadiyya*, p. 112, and Raʿad, *al-Kalimāt al-Akhīra*, pp. 68–70.

laws, but several of these reforms were ultimately unsuccessful.[81] However, for the SSNP, Chamoun's rise to the presidency would inaugurate a new era of its activity in Lebanon.

81 Attié, *Struggle in the Levant*, pp. 51–54.

Part Four: **Advance and Retreat**

10 Out of the Shadows: Contesting Elections in Syria and Lebanon

ʿAbdallah Qubrusi and ʿIsam Mahayri were lawyers by training who joined the SSNP in their mid-twenties. Though they shared a common profession and a commitment to the party's creed, their socio-economic and religious backgrounds differed significantly. Qubrusi, the elder of the two, hailed from a Greek Orthodox family of modest means – his father was a cobbler – from a small village in Lebanon's Koura district; Mahayri, in contrast, hailed from a prominent Sunni Damascene land-owning family. Qubrusi had been one of the first to join the party in the early 1930s and had quickly emerged as a leader, pushing for the creation of a party constitution and serving in key leadership positions. Similarly, Mahayri, who had joined the party in the mid-1940s, had also quickly risen the ranks of party leadership and, by the early 1950s, had served in various ranking positions in the party leadership. Given their positions of influence within the party, each would leave their indelible marks on the SSNP in the 1950s as the party worked to reestablish itself in Lebanon and consolidate its position in Syria.

Qubrusi and Mahayri were confronted with a challenging task. In the 1950s, Lebanon and Syria found themselves caught in a regional geopolitical struggle between Egypt and Iraq that was magnified by the intrusion of the Cold War rivalry between the West and the Soviet Union. As the region experienced change because of this struggle, both Lebanon and Syria underwent domestic transformations as well. This chapter and those that follow address how the SSNP acted to shape the emerging regional and domestic orders in accordance with its ideological vision. Having reemerged on the Lebanese political scene following Khuri's downfall, the SSNP would build a cooperative relationship with Camille Chamoun. This relationship enabled the party to organize and advance its agenda in a way it had been unable previously. While the party would voice its frustration over the direction of Chamoun's domestic policies during his six-year administration, their shared assessment of regional developments and their likely negative impact on Lebanon and its independence superseded the former. In Syria, where the party had been headquartered since 1949, the SSNP worked to further consolidate its influence in government and the armed forces under Shishakli's regime. Shishakli's resignation led the party to conclude it had an opportunity to expand its power, but its popular appeal was lacking, and poor decision-making led it into open conflict with its increasingly powerful rivals the Baʿth and the Communists. In the end, the bitter, often violent struggle between the party and its rivals in Syria resulted in its demise and retreat from the Syrian public sphere.

https://doi.org/10.1515/9783110729092-012

10.1 The Electoral Struggle

In October 1952, the SSNP was navigating the new political realities in Syria and Lebanon. In Syria, the SSNP remained in the regime's good graces despite the ban on political parties and Shishakli's efforts to build the ALM.[1] The party continued to publish *al-Bina'*, its leadership resided in the country without harassment, its activities continued though were not overtly public, and Mahayri remained close with Shishakli. Further, the number and influence of SSNP affiliated officers in the Syrian army continued to increase, mainly thanks to Ghassan Jadid, an SSNP member and personal friend of Shishakli who served as the director of the Homs Military Academy where he recruited and spread party doctrine. The party also benefited from Shishakli's curtailment of Ba'thist influence and the activities of regime opponents.[2] Despite this, a considerable amount of tension existed between the party and Shishakli's regime. The SSNP considered the ALM's establishment a betrayal of its arrangement with Shishakli that purportedly guaranteed the party would play a leading role in building popular support for the regime. Moreover, the divide between the SSNP and Shishakli had deepened over the latter's embrace of Arab nationalist positions and ideas, declaring Syria to be the birthplace of Arabism and an Arab nation. The SSNP derided Arab nationalism but was careful to temper its views and restrained its criticism, fearful of provoking Shishakli's harsh response.[3]

Meanwhile, in Lebanon, the party had recently emerged from the shadows to offer its public support for Beshara al-Khuri's resignation and Camille Chamoun's election as his replacement at the end of September 1952.[4] Relations between the party and the Lebanese state during the Khuri years had been fraught with contention and violence. However, Chamoun's election upended this state of affairs and inaugurated "a new era" in the party's relations with the Lebanese government as Chamoun was far more tolerant of the party's political activities than his predecessor.[5] The SSNP understood that a meaningful change had taken place, but what this meant practically remained uncertain. For example, in the middle of December 1952, SSNP leaders met at Ghassan Tueni's Beirut office,

1 TNA, FO 371/6/EY1016/17, No. 156, Samuel to Eden, Damascus, "The Arab Liberation Movement: Activities of Colonel Shishakli," 10 October 1952.

2 Moubayed, *Steel and Silk*, pp. 58–59.

3 Seale, *The Struggle for Syria*, pp. 123–125.

4 *Sada Lubnan*, 3, 16 November 1952.

5 Beshara, *Lebanon*, pp. 36–37. Chamoun also toleratd the party because he sought to strengthen and broaden his base of support and his aim to use the party to gain an advantage over his rivals. Beshara, *Lebanon*, pp. 37–38.

where a heated discussion ensued over moving the party's headquarters back to Beirut from Damascus.[6] Most of the participants favored the move, but others argued it should only occur after the Lebanese government granted amnesty to all social nationalists, a measure that would enable party exiles to return to the country. No decision on the matter was taken.[7] The party tentatively, but prudently, waded back into the thick of Lebanese politics in the spring of 1953, aware of the prevailing political instability resulting from disagreements over Chamoun's reform program.[8]

By early May 1953, however, the party had officially declared its return to public activity, embracing and hoping to bolster the "new spirit" and "new era" that now existed in the country.[9] At an afternoon press conference, Tueni proclaimed that the SSNP had been determined to make its activities official though the wider public may not have been aware of its intent. To this end, party officials had informed the Lebanese interior minister of the SSNP's intention to officially reorganize the party according to the Lebanese Constitution's requirements. In their official letter, SSNP officials declared the party was a movement working in the Lebanese political arena to preserve the Lebanese entity, its status as the domain of protected free thought, and the promoter of civic nationalism. Therefore, the party advanced a six-point platform grounded in its reform principles, calling for, among other things, the separation of religion and state, removing the barriers separating Lebanon's sects and communities, national economic reform, and strengthening the army. Tueni also defended the party's agenda and addressed the controversies surrounding its political activity in Lebanon, given its contentious past, arguing that the party's objective in the summer of 1949 had been to "strengthen Lebanon's independence based on the people's

6 Qubrusi, *Yatadhakkar, Vol. 4*, pp. 116–119.

7 "Taqrīr bi-Tārīkh 17/12/1952," in Asfahani, *Anṭūn Saʿādah*, p. 89.

8 In the spring of 1953, disagreements between Jumblatt and Chamoun intensified over the latter's failure to adhere to the terms of the pact they had forged prior to overthrowing Khuri, which Chamoun refused to fulfil until the security situation in the country stabilized. Jumblatt approached the Najjadeh movement in the hope of forming an alliance and sparking a mass movement to unseat Chamoun and sought to cooperate with leftists and communists in his efforts, while Jumblatt's Progressive Socialist Party (PSP) attacked Chamoun and accused him of "working to bring foreign domination back and implement the colonialists' plans." See 74/13, n.d., "The dispute between Chamoun and Jumblatt" and "Onset of the serious rift between Jumblatt and Chamoun," in Asseily and Asfahani, *A Face in the Crowd*, pp. 152–153. See also Attié, *Struggle in the Levant*, pp. 48, 51–53.

9 The headline in *al-Bina'* stated it plainly: "The Syrian National Party announces its return to official public activity." *Al-Bina'*, 10 May 1953. Also *Sada Lubnan*, 11 May 1953.

free will" (*tawṭīd al-istiqlāl al-Lubnānī ʿalā irādat al-shaʿb al-hurra*), not to destroy the country.[10]

The timing of their announcement was no coincidence. Lebanese parliamentary elections were slated to be held later that summer in July 1953 and August 1953.[11] The SSNP, which had not officially participated in any election since its rebellion in 1949, considered the time ripe to take advantage of the "new spirit" in Lebanon. Preparations thus began in earnest to organize an electoral campaign in several districts. The party's candidates were selected at a joint meeting of the Higher Council and Council of Deputies presided over by ʿAbd al-Masih and included Adib Qadurra (Beirut – fourth district), Asad al-Ashqar (Metn), ʿAbdallah Saʿadeh (Koura), Ali Halawa (Tyre), and Nadhmi Azkul (Bekaa el-Gharbi).[12] Campaigning began in earnest in late June 1953, but the party, from the outset, tempered expectations for electoral success, fully aware of its contentious recent past and its ambiguous standing in the emerging Lebanese political order. In a campaign speech, Ashqar stated plainly, "Electoral victory is not our objective as we feel that the great victory is people understanding their rights and obligations," and declared it was the party's mission to give voice to these rights and obligations and awaken the people.[13] The approach to temper expectations proved prudent as not a single official party candidate secured a seat.[14] The results notwithstanding, the party found solace in its very participation, declaring it a victory in and of itself given it occurred just years after the party's failed attempt to overthrow the Lebanese government and its assassination of Riad al-Sulh. Moreover, though he had not been an official party candidate, Tueni was reelected, giving the SSNP a parliamentary voice, and, in time, he

---

10 *Al-Binaʾ*, 10 May 1953, and *Sada Lubnan*, 11 May 1953.

11 This was the first–time elections were held in this manner in the country. As Hudson observes, "...President Chamoun in 1953 instituted the practice of holding elections on successive Sundays in the various districts in order to give the government more time to mobilize its security forces in case of violence." Hudson, *Precarious Republic*, p. 220.

12 *Sada Lubnan*, 13, 17–18 June 1953; *al-Binaʾ*, 7 July 1953; and Qubrusi, *Yatadhakkar, Vol. 4*, pp. 158–160. Ghassan Tueni ran in Beirut's second district but was not an official SSNP candidate in the elections despite the fact he was a member of the party. Tueni went on to serve in a prominent role in the body as speaker of the Chamber, champion the party's agenda, and was, in general, identified as an SSNP's MP.

13 *Al-Binaʾ*, 19, 27 June 1953.

14 On election results, see *al-Binaʾ*, 13, 21, and 27 July 1953, and *Sada Lubnan*, 13 and 22 July 1953.

would play a leading role in the Chamber.[15] The party's return to the Lebanese political field did not escape the notice of its rivals.[16]

In Syria, meanwhile, the SSNP maintained its tacit support for Shishakli, doing its best not to run afoul of Syria's ruler. Seeking to legitimize his regime, Shishakli drafted a new constitution, published 21 June 1953, and called for a constitutional referendum and presidential election on 10 July.[17] Several days later, on 24 June, *al-Bina'* published the first of eleven articles analyzing Shishakli's proposed constitution under its column "Toward the Light" ("*Naḥwa al-Nūr*"); the last article was published on the eve of the constitutional referendum and presidential election.[18] While the party had "comments and objections" (*mulāḥaẓāt wa iʿtirāḍāt*) to the new constitution, it nevertheless welcomed it "as a fundamental step in the transition from individual rule to the rule of the people."

Moreover, the SSNP supported Shishakli's presidential candidacy and reportedly forged an agreement with him to cooperate in the parliamentary elections he planned on calling that fall. According to the alleged agreement, Shishakli guaranteed the SSNP would be the second-largest parliamentary bloc behind his ALM, securing 15 seats to the ALM's 50.[19] At the beginning of August 1953, several weeks after Shishakli's election and the new constitution's passage, the Syrian government passed a new election law. The following month, the parliamentary election date was set for October, and the government passed another law enabling Syrians to establish and join political groups and parties.[20] Accordingly, the SSNP registered itself as a legal political entity.

---

15 On Tueni's parliamentary activity see, for example, *al-Bina'*, 4 September 1953; *Sada Lubnan*, 2 December 1953; and *al-Bina'*, 7, 23 December 1953.

16 The new political climate and the SSNP's return is best exemplified in the efforts of Khuri to reach an understanding with the party that would put all outstanding issues between the two sides, particularly the SSNP's desire to kill him, to bed. In late September, an intermediary worked to reach an understanding between the two rivals. According to the proposed understanding, the SSNP would rescind the death sentence it had pronounced on Khuri and, if this were done, Khuri would pay the party 25,000 Lebanese Lira. The proposal was discussed by the party leadership in both Lebanon and Syria. The efforts to reach an understanding, however, failed as the SSNP's leadership did not agree to the proposal and no rapprochement between the party Khuri ever took place. See "Taqrīr bi-Tārīkh 29/9/1953" and "Taqrīr bi-Tārīkh 14/10/1953," in Asfahani, *Anṭūn Saʿādah*, p. 92; and Zisser, "The Downfall of the Khuri Administration," p. 504.

17 *Al-Bina'*, 21 June 1953.

18 See *al-Bina'*, 24 June 1953, and *al-Bina'*, 9 July 1953.

19 "Maʿlūmāt min Faysal al-ʿAsali bi-Tārīkh 25/7/1953," in Asfahani, *Anṭūn Saʿādah*, p. 92.

20 *Al-Bina'*, 3 August 1953, and *al-Bina'*, 2, 14 September 1953. For more on the Constitution of 1953 and subsequent election and party laws passed by Shishakli's government, see Karim Atassi, *Syria – The Strength of an Idea: The Constitutional Architectures of Its Political Regimes* (Cambridge: Cambridge University Press, 2018), pp. 230 – 248.

By the beginning of October 1953, election campaigning in Syria was in full swing. On 3 October, Mahayri gave a rousing stump speech in the Damascus neighborhood of al-Jura, while party members canvased throughout several of the city's neighborhoods promoting the party's message of a nation full of potential waiting to be realized.[21] Mahayri asserted the SSNP worked for the betterment of the entire nation and not on behalf of individuals, i.e., special interests or particular elites. In Aleppo, the party's candidate Nuri al-Khalidi spoke of the legacy of colonialism and the present threats confronting the country and urged the people to vote for those who would champion the national cause.[22] Elsewhere in Syria, party activists busied themselves campaigning on behalf of the party's other 19 candidates in locales such as Homs, Tel Kalkh, Mayadin, Safita, Dayr al-Zur, Qamishli, Suwayda, and Latakia, calling on the public to embrace the party's principles and program.[23] On the eve of the 9 October elections, expectations for success were building within the party though SSNP officials acknowledged party candidates' faced some challenges.

The election results, however, shocked the party. Shishakli's ALM secured at least 60 of the 82 seats in the new Chamber of Deputies and, of the 20 SSNP candidates, only Mahayri was elected, well short of the 15 seats allegedly promised to the party.[24] The electoral defeat was humiliating and painful, leaving the party embittered and alienated; Shishakli had not honored the arrangement and, adding insult to injury, ensured a resounding victory for his ALM and allegedly spread damaging rumors that the United States was financing the SSNP.[25] However, the SSNP's defeat also pointed to a deeper, more problematic issue: the party's message had failed to resonate widely with Syrian voters.[26] To be sure, the general sense of apathy among Syrian voters and the low voter turnout in the election contributed to the SSNP's poor showing and were beyond its control, but the party had nevertheless failed to mobilize Syrians and get them to the polls. Despite Shishakli's apparent betrayal, the party leadership in Lebanon was hesitant to criticize him, arguing it was not in the party's interest to do so as it would likely result in a crackdown on its activities. The party leadership in Syria, believing the election to have been rigged, ceased cooperating with Shishakli though it stopped short of joining the opposition and actively working

---

21 *Al-Bina'*, 4 October 1953.
22 *Al-Bina'*, 4 October 1953.
23 *Al-Bina'*, 5–7 October 1953.
24 TNA, FO 371/7/EY1018/21, No. 170, Gardener to Eden, "Recent Syrian Elections: The Formation of a Chamber of Deputies," 14 October 1953, and *Sada Lubnan*, 12 October 1953.
25 Yamak, *SSNP*, pp. 69–70.
26 "Taqrīr bi-Tārīkh 14/10/1953," in Asfahani, *Anṭūn Saʿādah*, pp. 92–93.

to bring about Shishakli's downfall. By January 1954, however, the party would cease supporting Shishakli as his campaign against the Syrian opposition intensified.

10.2 Consequences: Navigating the Post-Shishakli Political Order

In late 1953, opposition to Shishakli's regime was intensifying and was centered in Jabal Druze, Homs, and Aleppo.[27] In December, student protests devolved into clashes with police and more extensive demonstrations and strikes supporting them. Syrian security forces detained several students and even arrested their lawyers. These developments sparked further protests, demonstrations, and strikes in Homs, Damascus, and Jabal Druze.[28] Most disconcerting for Shishakli were the demonstrations in Jabal Druze. Shishakli's relations with the Druze were fraught with distrust, and he feared the idea of a Druze-led revolt against his regime. Thus, when leaflets attacking the Syrian regime were circulated in Jabal Druze – likely by the Baʿth – Shishakli's reaction was swift and harsh. Government forces, commanded by Shishakli's brother Salah, were sent to the Jabal to quell any revolt, and several leading Druze leaders, including Hassan al-Atrash, were arrested. By the end of January, the Druze and Syrian armed forces had been engaged in intense fighting while demonstrations and protests raged in Aleppo and Damascus. The Druze bore the brunt of the Syrian regime's violence, the heavy fighting and pursuit of Druze leaders causing some to flee to Jordan and raising the loud protest of Druze in Lebanon who protested the treatment of their brethren. The SSNP's leadership held an emergency meeting to discuss developments in the country, but it is unclear if the party leadership took any decisions.[29] Publicly, *al-Bina'* was silent regarding the unrest but also did not express support for Shishakli.

At the end of February 1954, in a final desperate attempt to squelch the opposition, Shishakli ordered the military police to arrest leading opposition figures, including Mahayri.[30] Within days of issuing the order, however, Shishakli

---

27 According to Seale, Shishakli uttered the following saying regarding opposition to his regime: "My enemies are like a serpent: the head is the Jabal Druze, the stomach Homs, and the tail Aleppo. If I crush the head, the serpent will die." Seale, *The Struggle for Syria*, p. 132.
28 Seale, *The Struggle for Syria*, pp. 135–136.
29 Ahmad, *SSNP*, p. 146.
30 "Juzaʾ min Taqrīr ʿan al-Ijrāʾāt allatī Ittakhadhhā Adīb al-Shīshaklī ḍidda Muʿāraḍiyya, Muʾarrakh fī 28/2/1954," in Asfahani, *Anṭūn Saʿādah*, p. 99. Among the others ordered arrested

resigned and fled the country. His resignation led to a brief period of uncertainty as SSNP officials in Lebanon waited to receive an assessment from their comrades in Damascus of the party's standing vis-à-vis the new Syrian government. The party leadership in Syria responded to their inquiries, declaring the party's goals remained unaffected despite the change in government. Indeed, "whether the government was hostile to it or supportive of it, [the party] would work to realize whatever it viewed to be in line with its interests and objectives."[31] Notwithstanding these declarations and the poor state of relations between the party and Shishakli at the time, Shishakli's departure was a setback for the SSNP and did not provide the party with an opportunity to expand its influence and activity effectively.[32]

Cooperation between the SSNP and Shishakli was limited throughout his rule, but Shishakli's friendship with Mahayri, and Mahayri's role as one of his political advisors, at least gave the party access and a voice in policymaking.[33] This was now gone. Moreover, the true nature and extent of the ties between Shishakli and the party mattered little in the public and Syrian opposition's eyes, who did not hesitate to directly link the SSNP to the former regime, diminishing its standing in the emerging political order. Overcoming this negative popular perception proved difficult as the party failed to broaden its public appeal, and its leaders, specifically Mahayri and ʿAbdallah Muhsin, were excluded from forming a new government.[34] Further, Shishakli's resignation also resulted in the reinstatement and promotion of military officers dismissed due to their "leftist sympathies" at the time. Many of these officers were now members or sympathizers of the Baʿth Party. The Baʿth's resurgence within the officer corps challenged SSNP officers' dominance within the military's ranks and contributed to the increasing political factionalism within the army, increasing tensions between the two rival movements.

While the party navigated the new domestic political reality in Syria, it also turned its attention to other pressing regional and internal issues. In early 1954, Iraqi Prime Minister Fadhil al-Jamali had once again promulgated a plan to es-

---

were the Baʿth leaders Akram Hawrani, Michel ʿAflaq, and Salah al-Din al-Bitar. For Hawrani and Mahayri, who had previously enjoyed close relations with Shishakli, the arrest order was far more personal.

31 "Taqrīr bi-Tārīkh 10/3/1954,"in Asfahani, *Anṭūn Saʿādah*, p. 101.

32 Yamak, *SSNP*, p. 70.

33 Moubayed, *Steel and Silk*, p. 288.

34 Raʿad, *al-Kalimāt al-Akhīra*, p. 73. To be sure, the Baʿth and Hawrani were also left out of Sabri al-ʿAsali's new government, which he had formed based on a coalition comprised of the National Party, People's Party, and Independent politicians. Seale, *The Struggle for Syria*, p. 166.

tablish a Hashemite-led federation, including Iraq, Syria, and Jordan. The SSNP, which had opposed the same Fertile Crescent scheme promoted by the Iraqis since the 1940s, remained skeptical of the Hashemite proposal, a position shared by several regional powers, including Saudi Arabia.[35] According to a report filed by an informant with the Lebanese Sûreté, Mahayri had met with Saudi Ambassador Prince ʿAbd al-Aziz bin Zayd in Damascus to express the party's commitment to thwarting the Fertile Crescent project and explore "the role that the Nationalists [i. e., the SSNP] in Syria and Lebanon could play towards this end." Simultaneously, similar discussions were also held between ʿAbdallah Qubrusi and Saudi Arabia's Chargé d'Affaires at the Saudi Embassy in Beirut.[36] Internally, the party formalized and regularized communications between the party headquarters in Lebanon and Syria as communication between the two had been infrequent and often only took place as needed.[37]

Within Lebanon, meanwhile, Druze leader Kamal Jumblatt sought to mend relations between his Progressive Socialist Party and the SSNP in Lebanon, perhaps hoping he could shake the party's commitment to Chamoun.[38] While visiting Damascus in March 1954, Jumblatt reached out to Mahayri and arranged a meeting with Saʿadeh's widow, in which he expressed his desire for reconciliation between the two movements and hoped Ms. Saʿadeh would use her influence and "prevail upon [the SSNP in Lebanon] to reciprocate [his] gesture."[39] Within weeks, however, any chance of reconciliation between the two sides at that time was scuttled by a new dispute between the two sides that arose after the pro-PSP newspaper *al-Anbaʾ* published documents purporting to demonstrate the SSNP's support and complicity in Shishakli's violent suppression of the revolt in Jabal Druze. The documents were ultimately deemed to be forgeries by a Lebanese court and, in the SSNP's view, a cheap attempt to weaken support for the party among Lebanon's Druze.[40] Despite their quarrel's public nature, the

---

35 Seale, *The Struggle for Syria*, p. 168.

36 20/2F, 19 March 1954, in Asseily and Asfahani, *A Face in the Crowd*, p. 44.

37 "Taqrīr bi-Tārīkh 25/3/1954," in Asfahani, *Anṭūn Saʿādah*, p. 102.

38 Since cooperating in 1952 to help bring about Beshara al-Khuri's downfall and Camille Chamoun's election as president of Lebanon, tensions had grown between the erstwhile allies. Jumblatt and the PSP had grown frustrated with Chamoun's failure to implement the domestic reforms it advocated and, as a result, had become increasingly vocal in its opposition to Chamoun's nascent presidency. In contrast, the SSNP's support for Chamoun remained steadfast despite any misgivings the party may have shared with the PSP regarding Chamoun's administration.

39 20/2F, 19 March 1954, in Asseily and Asfahani, *A Face in the Crowd*, p. 44.

40 Jumblatt's affiliated newspaper *al-Anbaʾ* published telegrams in the name of "the Syrian Nationalists in Baakline" that it claimed had been sent to Shishakli and his aides offering the par-

party continued to maintain a relatively low profile in Lebanon, taking care not to rouse opposition to its public activity.

In early June, Syria's transition from Shishakli's rule under the auspices of a coalition government led by Sabri al-ʿAsali sputtered; ʿAsali's government collapsed, and Saʿid al-Ghazzi replaced him. Under Ghazzi, the "[Syrian government's] first and only task [was] to conduct free and fair elections [under] a new electoral law."[41] This turn of events prompted Syrian political parties, including the SSNP, to prepare for 20 August's coming elections. At the time, Mahayri was the party's sole elected representative in the Syrian parliament, representing one of Damascus' districts. The party had followers throughout the country, however, including its traditional areas of influence along the coast (Tartus and Latakia) and other predominately ʿAlawi areas (Tel Kalkh, Safita, and Masyaf), urban centers (Damascus, Aleppo, and Homs), and predominately Druze regions of the south (Dera'a and Sweida). The party, now focused on the coming election, intensified its efforts to promote itself and its ideology to the Syrian public to win supporters to its cause. Throughout June, the party published several articles in its on-going series on its ideology, specifically regarding its views on Arabism and economics.[42] At the beginning of July, a delegation of party officials in Lebanon traveled to Damascus for discussions – ostensibly on the upcoming elections and formulating an electoral strategy – with the party leadership there.[43]

The beginning of the election campaign coincided nicely with an important date on the party's calendar: the 8 July commemoration of its failed 1949 revolution and Saʿadeh's execution. The occasion provided the party an opportunity to propagate its ideological message and imbue the events of 1949 with meaning for the party at present, which it did through an "interview" with Fuʾad Abu ʿAjram, the president of the party's Higher Council, that was published in *al-Bina*ʾ. ʿAjram provided readers a concise and detailed overview of the SSNP's ideology and political views, which served as a helpful introduction to the par-

ty's support for the Syrian army's efforts putting down the revolt in Jabal Druze. The SSNP claimed the telegrams were forgeries and ranking party member Hassan Tawil, in whose name at least one of the telegrams was signed, filed a lawsuit against Jumblatt for defamation. The courts lifted Jumblatt's immunity from prosecution as a parliamentarian so the case could proceed. In the end, the court found Jumblatt's newspaper guilty of forging and inventing the documents with the intent of damaging the party's name and cause. See *al-Bina*ʾ, 4, 8–9, 23 April 1954; *Sada Lubnan*, 26 March 1954; and *Sada Lubnan*, 1–4 April 1954.

41 Seale, *The Struggle for Syria*, p. 172.

42 *Al-Bina*ʾ, 1, 21, 28 June 1954.

43 "Taqrīr bi-Tārīkh 2/7/1954," in Asfahani, *Anṭūn Saʿādah*, p. 103.

ty's electoral platform's core principles before turning to the events of 1949. ʿAjram argued that the reforms the party attempted to achieve through its armed insurrection, implementing its five reform principles and combatting communism, were the same as those the people sought to realize by forcing Khuri to resign in 1952. Further, the party's aim had not been to destroy Lebanon or fight against its existence; instead, it had been to rid Lebanon of the ruling tyrants and liberate the people from this "new slavery," ensuring their freedom.[44] Linking it to the present, ʿAjram stated these reforms and aims were the same the party emphasized today and would champion throughout its electoral campaign in the hope of ushering in a new era in Syria's political order and leave the days of Shishakli behind.

In mid-July, SSNP regional executive directors recommended the party run candidates in 16 electoral districts at a party conference.[45] At the meeting, SSNP president George ʿAbd al-Masih urged his comrades to seize the opportunity before them and dedicate themselves to political activities that advanced the party's cause and the betterment of the people. ʿAbd al-Masih stressed the party's populist agenda rooted in its foundational principles to eliminate the people's woes and promote national unity, though he did not mention Greater Syria.[46] A week later, the Higher Council and Council of Deputies convened for deliberations on the party's list of candidates, and ʿAbd al-Masih traveled to Homs and Tel Kalkh to give the first of many stump speeches to sway voters to the party's cause.[47] The Higher Council announced 15 of the party's candidates running in 14 districts; the Council of Deputies selected the remaining candidates. Among the candidates were ʿIsam Mahayri and ʿAbdallah Muhsin (Damascus); Hanna Kaswani (Ghouta); Issa Salameh (Tel Kalkh); Nuri al-Din al-Khalidi (Aleppo); and Dr. Sami Sahlul (Homs).[48]

Campaigning began in earnest in early August and continued through the month as the party and its candidates actively mobilized voters and party supporters to generate additional support. At public and private gatherings, party candidates, local leaders, and, at times, ʿAbd al-Masih, delivered speeches and appealed for votes. Campaigning was particularly intense in locales where the party had an established presence dating to the 1930s and traditionally enjoyed strong support, particularly in the towns and villages around Tel Kalkh, Masyaf,

---

44 *Al-Bina'*, 11 July 1954.
45 *Al-Bina'*, 18 July 1954.
46 *Al-Bina'*, 18 July 1954.
47 *Al-Bina'*, 22–25 July 1954.
48 *Al-Bina'*, 26 July 1954, and "Taqrīr Akhīr bi-Tārīkh 27/7/1954 ʿan al-Intikhābāt al-Sūriyya," in Asfahani, *Anṭūn Saʿādah*, pp. 103–104.

Tartus, Latakia, and Deraa.[49] SSNP candidates propagated a populist discourse rooted in the party's reform principles and ideology, which they argued would lead to national revival and lead the Syrian people from victory to victory. In their telling, the social nationalist message was one for the people, seeking not the glory of the party, but the betterment and glory of the Syrian nation, desiring what was in the national interest (*maṣlaḥa al-umma*). Issa Salameh from Tel Kalkh declared the SSNP was "entering the elections to extricate [the Syrian] people from this deviation leading to the abyss," and that only the party's principles could transform the Syrian nation into a living nation.[50] For Salameh and the party, this, then, is what the party struggled for, determined to eliminate the injustices and conditions that prevented the Syrian nation's rise. ʿAbd al-Masih stated plainly: "Those who fight against us because we fight against their injustice, will be overcome by their injustice. And those who are tormented by tyranny, we give [our] blood to save them from their condition."[51] That the party had somewhat enabled the very tyranny it now claimed to oppose through its limited and tacit support of the Shishakli regime was irrelevant.

In early September 1954, just several weeks before the election, the SSNP published a *bayān* in which it presented its electoral platform in detail and at great length.[52] Published on two full pages in *al-Bina'*, the party's platform covered a broad range of relevant topics grounded in its precepts of reform in the areas of virtue, economics, society, law, administration, military, and politics. In line with its ideology, this push for change was all-encompassing, touching on all aspects of life from politics to culture and the family. Campaigning continued apace as party candidates in Damascus and Homs held rallies and meetings in a push to further win votes by convincing the public that the party sought only their betterment and empowerment.[53] In addition to addressing domestic matters, the *bayān* discussed foreign affairs, particularly its views on the Arab world and Syrian-Iraqi unity schemes.

In keeping with Saʿadeh's ideas, the party maintained that Syria was an Arab nation and was not an entity separate from "the Arab world" or existing outside of it. Moreover, the party's message of revival and Syrian unity only strengthened the Arab world, and a strong, unified Syria would neither undermine nor weaken its strength. Regarding Syrian-Iraqi unity schemes, the party refrained from ex-

---

49 See, for example *al-Bina'*, 2, 4–6, 15–17, 22, 29 August 1954.
50 *Al-Bina'*, 4 August 1954.
51 *Al-Bina'*, 6 August 1954.
52 *Al-Bina'*, 7 September 1954.
53 See, for example, the party's campaign activities in Damascus, Jableh, Latakia, Homs, and Eastern Syria: *al-Bina'*, 8–9, 13–15 September 1954.

plicitly calling for such a unity and instead acknowledged that "since Iraq and Syria, as we have stated, are two parts of one homeland, the interest in a united destiny exists" (*al-ʿirāq wa-l-shām juzān, ka-mā akadnā, min waṭan wāḥid mawjūd al-maṣlaḥa muwaḥḥad al-maṣīr*). They further acknowledged that the party embraced the idea of unity in principle and that it welcomed efforts to advance its realization. Indeed, while eschewing any mention of "Greater Syria," the statement embraced whatever helped generate a unified national will, whether it be in the area of politics, economics, culture, or society, as unity in these areas would help advance the larger goal of one united nation.[54]

The party's electoral push, particularly in Damascus, garnered the attention of more established politicians. Indeed, though the SSNP had been left out of the government formed after Shishakli's departure, National Party leader Sabri al-ʿAsali spoke positively about the party at a public gathering in Damascus, even voicing an appeal for cooperation to advance the interests of the nation. While important, ʿAsali's bid was more likely an attempt to sway voters away from the SSNP's candidates in Damascus rather than a genuine call for cooperation.[55] Despite the SSNP's concerted campaign efforts, the election ended in overwhelming defeat as it had before. Only one of the party's candidates, Hanna Kaswani of Ghouta, was elected; perhaps the greatest disappointment and the most painful loss was ʿIsam Mahayri's failure to win re-election.[56]

Mahayri, who had served in the Syrian parliament since 1950, lost his seat to Salah al-Din al-Bitar, the Baʿth party co-founder.[57] The frustration of Mahayri's loss to Bitar was further compounded by the impressive gains the Baʿth made in the election, as it secured a total of 22 seats, and the fact that the Communist Party, another SSNP rival, succeeded in getting its leader, Khalid Bakdash, elected as well.[58] However, more disconcerting to the SSNP was what the Baʿth's gains represented: its triumphant reemergence on the Syrian political scene after Shishakli's resignation now complemented its rising influence among the Syrian officer corps. Grappling with yet another resounding electoral defeat and in light of its rivals' gains, simmering internal tensions boiled over as a crisis developed between the Higher Council and the party president.

54 *Al-Binaʾ*, 7 September 1954.
55 *Al-Binaʾ*, 15 September 1954.
56 Raʿad, *al-Kalimāt al-Akhīra*, p. 74.
57 Raʿad, *al-Kalimāt al-Akhīra*, p. 73.
58 Yamak, *SSNP*,p. 69.

10.3 New Challenges from Within and Without

Higher Council members had grown increasingly frustrated by what they believed to be ʿAbd al-Masih's authoritarian and tyrannical leadership of the party in contravention of the party constitution. Indeed, the Higher Council felt marginalized by ʿAbd al-Masih, claiming he never submitted comprehensive reports on the party's activities and finances to the Council and did not appropriately consult it on decisions. The mounting frustration culminated in the Higher Council's demand that ʿAbd al-Masih resign his presidency, a request which he obliged. However, having submitted his resignation and the Higher Council accepting it, ʿAbd al-Masih objected and questioned the constitutional legitimacy of its action in a letter to the Higher Council.[59] On 24 October, the Higher Council convened, dissolved itself, and declared elections for a new council. The following week, a special session was held in which a new Higher Council was elected, most of whom had been members of the previous Higher Council. In the Council's first meeting later that day, it elected Hassan Tawil as its head, ʿAbd al-Masih party president, and Mahayri Deputy of Information. In a second meeting, ʿAbd al-Masih and Mahayri resigned their seats on the council to maintain the separation between the executive and legislative authority within the party; Qubrusi and Inʿam Raʿad replaced them.[60] The new council and the cooperative relations between Mahayri and ʿAbd al-Masih enabled the party to emerge from the internal crisis and move forward. The resolution, however, would only be temporary.

Amid the infighting, Qubrusi published a book detailing the party's position on Lebanon entitled *Nahna wa Lubnān (Us and Lebanon).* Since reengaging in public political activity under Chamoun's administration, the party had been keen to avoid embroiling itself in any significant controversy. This pragmatic approach did not prevent the party from voicing criticism when deemed necessary, nor constitute an abandonment of its principles. In late August 1954, for example, the SSNP criticized the shortcomings of the government's reformist agenda, criticizing the continuing the roles of sectarianism and communalism in Lebanese society and their malign influence on politics and society. The party also called for transforming Lebanon into a proper national entity inclusive of all its people and amending the constitution to reflect this nationalist outlook. The party singled out the Kataʾib for condemnation, accusing them of betraying

59 Raʿad, *al-Kalimāt al-Akhīra*, p. 74.

60 "al-Nashra al-Rasmiyya li-l-Ḥarakat al-Qawmiyya al-Ijtimāʿiyya 1955," in Asfahani, *Anṭūn Saʿādah*, pp. 133–134; Raʿad, *al-Kalimāt al-Akhīra*, p. 78; Yammut, *al-Ḥaṣād al-Murr*, p. 277; and Qubrusi, *Yatadhakkar, Vol. 4*, pp. 165–186.

Figure 9: Syrian Social Nationalist Party official ʿIsam Mahayri gives a speech on Saʿadeh's birthday at a large party celebration in Damascus in the mid-1950s. (*Sada Lubnan*, 26 August 1955 – Courtesy of The Arabic Press Archive, The Moshe Dayan Center, Tel Aviv University)

the nation by perpetuating sectarianism and collaborating with foreigners (i.e., the French).[61] Qubrusi's book, published several months later, addressed similar themes as the party worked to portray itself as a defender of Lebanon and its independence rather than a movement that sought its destruction.

Dedicated to "all those who love Lebanon," Qubrusi's study argued that "social nationalism, principally, is a Lebanese discovery and a Lebanese achievement," and that Lebanon is a valued part of the Syrian homeland. Qubrusi explained, "the phrase 'long live Syria' is one that emerges from the depths of Lebanese who love Lebanon because it has the same meaning as 'long live Lebanon'"; thus, how could the phrase possibly mean 'death to Lebanon' since Lebanon is the head and heart of Syria?[62] Moreover, "every social nationalist shouts from the depths of his being 'long live Lebanon' because the life of Lebanon is necessary for the life of the rest of the Syrian homeland."[63] He emphasized that the party "works positively within the Lebanese entity for the success of the Lebanese people" in contrast to the enemies and traitors of Lebanon "who want it to remain in its present state of confusion and deterioration," the social nationalists were devoted, faithful Lebanese citizens dedicated to advancing Lebanon out of its present state.[64] In this manner, the party redefined and justified its past activities and political positions, doing away with their subversive nature vis-à-vis Lebanon and casting them in an entirely different light. Though the party's "reorientation" may have been unconvincing to many, it helped facilitate cooperation with Chamoun and the Lebanese government as it enabled them to allow the SSNP to operate openly and made the party's support more palatable. This reorientation would prove even more valuable in the coming months amid significant regional developments that further strengthened the bonds of cooperation between the party and the Lebanese government under Chamoun.

In February 1955, Britain, Iraq, and Turkey signed a regional defense agreement known as the Baghdad Pact, which sought to contain the spread of Soviet influence in the Middle East by creating a security organization that would work in close cooperation with the North Atlantic Treaty Organization (NATO). The Pact provided Britain an opportunity to preserve its weakened position of influence in the Middle East. Egypt strongly opposed the Pact, as Nasser believed it perpetuated foreign domination, i.e., imperialism, in the region, and instead sought to orient Egyptian foreign policy to allow the country to navigate between the American and Soviet Blocs. Moreover, Nasser was particularly enraged that

61 *Al-Bina'*, 22 August 1954.
62 ʿAbdallah Qubrusi, *Nahna wa Lubnān* (Beirut: 1954), p. 8.
63 Qubrusi, *Nahna wa Lubnān*, p. 9.
64 Qubrusi, *Nahna wa Lubnān*, pp. 90–91, 186–187.

Iraq, Egypt's regional rival, had acceded to the Pact, a step that had "adverse implications...for Egypt's regional position" as it threatened to curtail Egyptian regional influence, particularly in Syria where it fiercely competed with Iraq for dominance. Thus, Nasser sought to do to Iraq what he feared the Pact would do to Egypt and moved to isolate Iraq regionally and launched a vicious propaganda campaign against the country on Egypt's "Voice of the Arabs" (*Sawt al-'Arab*). To prevent Syria from falling into Iraq's sphere of influence, it mounted a rigorous diplomatic effort led by the newly appointed Ambassador and Nasser confidant, Mahmud Riyad. He used clandestine means to help sway Syrian opinion, including providing "subsidies to Arab nationalist and anti-Baghdad Pact newspapers" and, possibly, bribes to Syrian officials.[65]

Lebanon, too, found itself caught between Nasser and the West, as the former urged Chamoun to oppose the Pact while the latter urged him to make Lebanon part of the new regional alliance. Together with Saudi Arabia, Egypt used similar clandestine means in Lebanon to sway Lebanese public opinion and those in government to oppose the pact. Egypt and Saudi Arabia also urged Chamoun to be part of their counter-alliance, but Chamoun declined and refused to oppose the Baghdad Pact.[66] While Egypt and Saudi Arabia viewed Chamoun's decision as a slight and an "act of hostility," Chamoun also declined to join Lebanon to the Baghdad Pact and maintained Lebanon's neutrality between the two emerging camps.[67] As for the SSNP, it, too, took a cautious and non-committal approach to the evolving situation. In 1954, members of the party's political bureau – Ashqar, Jurayj, Taqi al-Din, Tueni, Azkul, and Baʿalbeki – had held meetings with Iraqi Foreign Minister Fadil al-Jamali, a friend of Taqi al-Din, about the Iraqi-SSNP relations. In particular, Jamali hoped to persuade the party to take a more aggressive anti-communist line and move closer to the Iraqi camp. Thus, when the Baghdad Pact was announced, some within the party leadership found supporting the alliance attractive. Yet, most party officials urged taking a more prudent and cautious approach, a position that won the day.[68] At a press conference in March, Qubrusi stated that the party, in principle, did not object to cooperating with Western powers so long as such cooperation was based on mutual understanding and agreement that cooperation must ensure and advance Lebanese and Syrian freedom and independence. He also accepted the Lebanese government's approach to the Baghdad Pact and Egypt's counter alli-

65 James Jankowski, *Nasser's Egypt, Arab Nationalism, and the United Arab Republic* (Boulder: Lynne Rienner Publishers Inc, 2002), p. 74.

66 Attié, *Struggle in the Levant*, pp. 82–83, and Hudson, *Precarious Republic*, pp. 282–283.

67 Hudson, *Precarious Republic*, p. 283.

68 Yammut, *al-Ḥaṣād al-Murr*, pp. 279–281.

ance, stating that the party supported any decision the government took so long as it aligned with the will of people, which, in this case, the party argued it was.[69]

In contrast to Lebanon, Syria's situation was far more acute as the Syrian government was in crisis following the resignation of Prime Minister Faris al-Khuri and Sabri al-ʿAsali's appointment as his replacement. Khuri's government had attempted to keep Syria neutral as pressure mounted for it to accept the Baghdad Pact advocated by Britain and the United States and effectively choose sides in the Western-Soviet struggle over the Near East. Indeed, as one British diplomat assessed, the internal divisions and personal rivalries of Syrian leaders "[were] becoming increasingly connected with the question of where Syria stands in relation to the West."[70] However, 'Asali's new government was expected to be "less well inclined towards the West" and to "gravitate" towards Egypt rather than Iraq.[71] This shift toward Egypt was reinforced by the increasing support within the Syrian army for the Baʿth's positions, which were more sympathetic to Egypt than Iraq, advocated neutralism, and criticized the West.[72] While the new government did move towards Egypt, by April, it had yet to make a formal decision stating its support or rejection of either pact, effectively maintaining the previous government's policy of indifference and doing little to ease the pervasive political tensions within the country.

Further adding to the tense atmosphere in Syria was the return of Adib Shishakli's brother Salah, who had fled the country together with his brother in 1954. Salah's presence was viewed with suspicion by the Baʿth, and an armed confrontation between Baʿthists and Shishakli supporters in Shishakli's hometown on Evacuation Day – which commemorates the end of the French mandate and Syria's full independence – resulted in the death of one of Shishakli's relatives and the wounding of Akram Hawrani's brother. Clashes were not limited to Hama, as armed disputes between the SSNP and Communists in Tartus resulted in several wounded and at least one death, while a scuffle between the SSNP, Baʿthists, and Communists in the village of Saidnaya prompted the inter-

69 *Al-Bina'*, 22 March 1955.

70 TNA, FO 371/115945/VY1015/14, Confidential Despatch No.21, Gardner to Eden, 17 February 1955.

71 TNA, FO 371/115945/VY1015/14, Confidential Despatch No.21, Gardner to Eden, 17 February 1955.

72 TNA, FO 371/115945/VY1015/32, 10104/36/55, Gardner to Rose, "Political Unrest in Syria," 22 April 1955, and Malik Mufti, *Sovereign Creations: Pan-Arabism and Political Order in Syria and Iraq* (Ithaca: Cornell University Press, 1996), p. 72.

vention of government authorities to restore public order.[73] These incidents reflected street-level efforts by the parties involved to demonstrate and assert their power locally.

73 TNA, FO 371/115945/VY1015/30, 10104/35/55, Chancery Damascus to Levant Department, "Return of Captain Salah Shishakli," 23 April 1955, and TNA, FO 371/115945/VY1015/32, 10104/36/55, Gardner to Rose, "Political Unrest in Syria," 22 April 1955. Humorously, when the gendarmerie arrived in Saidnaya to restore order, the assailants joined to disarm and detain the gendarmes.

11 The Malki Affair: The Uprooting of the SSNP in Syria

In the afternoon of 22 April 1955, Yunis Kamal ʿAbd al-Rahim, an ʿAlawi military police sergeant and member of the SSNP from Safita, approached Colonel Adnan Malki, a respected Sunni military officer. Shortly after a football match between the Egyptian and Syrian army teams began, Rahim fired two shots from his pistol, wounding Malki, before turning the weapon on himself, taking his life to avoid arrest. Malki, who was considered a Baʿthist sympathizer and proponent of the Syrian-Egyptian-Saudi tripartite military pact, subsequently succumbed to his wounds and died.[1] While Rahim had committed suicide, two other SSNP members serving as his back up, sergeants Badiʿ Makhluf[2] and ʿAbd al-Munʿim Dubusi, were quickly arrested. The Syrian government deemed the SSNP responsible for the murder and its retaliation, driven by the Baʿth and the Communists and spearheaded by the Syrian army under Chief of Staff Shawqat Shuqayr and the Deuxième Bureau (military intelligence) under the recently appointed ʿAbd al-Halim Sarraj, was swift and harsh.[3]

---

1 *Sada Lubnan*, 23 April 1955; TNA, FO 371/115945/VY1015/25, No. 195, Gardner to FO, "Assassination of Adnan Malki," 22 April 1955; and TNA, FO 371/115945/VY1015/26, No. 196, Gardner to FO, "Disturbances in Syria," 23 April 1955. The reasons why Adnan Malki was assassinated are the source of controversy and dispute. The Syrian government and Arab nationalists would paint the assassination as part of a wider US–backed conspiracy against Syria and the work of the SSNP. The SSNP, on the contrary, denied the existence of such a conspiracy and an official internal party investigation placed full responsibility for the affair on ʿAbd al-Masih who, motivated by personal grievances, had ordered Malki's killing without consulting the party leadership. (The party also found then-party defense commissioner Iskander Shawi guilty of complicity in ʿAbd al-Masih's decision.) Rahim, the assassin, was also accused of harboring a personal grudge against Malki. One theory suggests Rahim believed Malki, a Sunni, was responsible for preventing him from attending the Syrian military academy because he was ʿAlawi. Malki's crime, thus, was discriminating against ʿAlawis like himself, a grievance exploited by ʿAbd al-Masih in selecting him for the mission. Another theory, which remains unsubstantiated, was suggested by American diplomats. According to a State Department report, Rahim killed Malki to restore his family's honor since Malki had impregnated Rahim's younger sister while she was a worker in his house. See Seale, *The Struggle for Syria*, p. 240; Rathmell, *Secret War*, pp. 98–102; and Martin, *Syria's Democratic Years*, p. 78.

2 Badiʿ was the first cousin of Anisa Makhluf, the future wife of Syrian president Hafiz al-Asad and the mother of current Syrian president Bashar al-Asad. The Makhlufs were an influential ʿAlawi landowning family in Syria's northern coastal region in Latakia Governorate who were known supporters of the SSNP and would largely remain so.

3 *Sada Lubnan*, 24–26 April 1955; *L'Orient*, 26–27 April 1955; and *Lisan al-Shaʿb*, 27 April 1955. The convergence of interests between the Baʿth and Communists on the matter of confronting

https://doi.org/10.1515/9783110729092-013

Tensions within the Syrian army between Baʿthist and SSNP military officers and between Malki and SSNP president George ʿAbd al-Masih had intensified in the months preceding the assassination. Malki's Arab nationalist views, particularly his affinity for Gamal ʻAbd al-Nasser, and his desire to propagate these views within the Syrian armed forces met with the strong resistance of the SSNP and officers aligned with it, such as SSNP's Director of Defense Ghassan Jadid, the former head of the Homs Military Academy. The dispute between Malki and the two prominent SSNP leaders was quite personal. Malki was suspected of having a hand in Jadid's dismissal from the Syrian army on account of Jadid's SSNP-related political activity, while he had also personally threatened to extradite ʿAbd al-Masih to Lebanon where he had been sentenced to death for his role in the failed 1949 uprising.

By 26 April, an estimated 150 SSNP members and more than two dozen military officers suspected of supporting the party had been detained. Party offices in Damascus and throughout the country were shuttered. Several prominent party leaders, including ʿAbd al-Masih, Ghassan Jadid, Iskander Shawi, ʿAbd al-Karim al-Shaykh, and Dr. Sami Khuri, managed to evade arrest and flee Syria, finding refuge in neighboring Lebanon.[4] In Damascus, the party's printing press was destroyed in an arson attack, effectively silencing its voice in the Syrian public sphere as *al-Bina'* ceased publication. The Syrian government and the SSNP traded accusations of responsibility for the arson, the government alleging the party set aflame its printing press to destroy incriminating evidence of its suspect activities. At the same time, the SSNP denied the charge and held the government responsible for its destruction.

News of Malki's assassination took the SSNP's leadership in Lebanon somewhat by surprise as it had not been consulted or sanctioned such an operation.

---

the SSNP, their ideological rivals, should not be misconstrued as a natural or straightforward alliance. In an interview with Patrick Seale, Michel ʿAflaq succinctly captured the Baʿth's reservations, stating, "No positive aims brought us together." Seale, *The Struggle for Syria*, p. 256.

4 *Sada Lubnan*, 24 April 1955. It was rumored, and an unproven allegation, that ʿAbd al-Masih and Jadid had fled Damascus several hours prior the assassination, an accusation suggesting their culpability in the affair. See TNA, FO 371/115945/VY1015/31, No. 61, 10106/40/55, Gardner to Macmillan, "Assassination of Colonel Malki," 27 April 1955. Other rumors emerged in early May that the two were hiding in the ʻAlawi mountains along the coast and were being protected by locals. See TNA, FO 371/115945/VY1015/36, 10104/57/55, Chancery Damascus to Levant Department, "Repercussions of Col. Malki Assassination," 7 May 1955, and *L'Orient*, 7 May 1955. Dr. Sami Khuri is an interesting figure. A 34-year-old physician at a hospital in Damascus, Khuri was the nephew of former Syrian President Faris al-Khuri, highlighting the party's potential to appeal to not only the young, highly educated but to individuals hailing from the elite classes. A similar observation can be made about Mahayri.

On 24 April, the party's Higher Council issued an official statement decrying the arrest of their comrades in Syria and the destruction of the *al-Bina'* printing press. The *bayān* condemned the Syrian regime's distortion of events and the increasing influence of the communists, urging the authorities in Damascus to respect the rule of law and conduct a legitimate investigation; the *bayān* reminded the regime and fellow SSNP members that the party had experienced difficulties in the past and, in fact, had thrived on them.[5] Several days later, the party issued another *bayān* in response to reports that 18 SSNP detainees in Damascus' al-Qalʿa Prison had confessed their guilt in the Malki Affair under torture and duress and, consequently, had been hastily sentenced to death without trial. The party claimed the cries of their tortured comrades could be heard outside of the prison's walls and demanded the Syrian government allow Arab ambassadors to investigate and oversee medical exams of the detainees to verify whether any "barbaric Soviet torture" (*al-taʿdhīb al-muskūvī al-hamajī*) had occurred. In another official statement issued the same day, the party asserted that Shuqayr had deemed the entire party responsible for the assassination before any evidence was produced or investigation concluded. Further, it accused the government in Damascus of other abuses and crimes against the party, including harassing SSNP students at schools and universities, burning unguarded party offices to the ground, and arresting hundreds, all under the guise of enforcing the law.[6]

The Syrian army expanded its crackdown beyond the SSNP, arresting pro-Iraqi Syrian leaders and threatening them with court-martial. To solidify support for a Syrian pact with Egypt, the Baʿth and Communist parties worked to foment anti-Western sentiments by spreading disinformation accusing Western powers – specifically, the Americans and the British – of being behind Malki's assassination; they also fomented anti-Iraq sentiments and portrayed the SSNP as the servant of imperialism.[7] The crackdown prompted some in the Iraqi government to consider military intervention, a prospect that concerned the Turkish officials with whom the idea had been broached. Iraqi authorities, however, assured British diplomats they had no intention of intervening militarily in the country.[8] A segment of the Syrian also urged the Syrian parliament to remove Hanna Kaswa-

5 *Sada Lubnan*, 24 April 1955.

6 *Sada Lubnan*, 28 April 1955.

7 TNA, FO 371/115945/VY1015/28, No. 201, Gardner to Foreign Office, "Political Disturbances," 26 April 1955; 113/12, n.d., "Regarding al-Malki's assassination," in Asseily and Asfahani, *A Face in the Crowd*, p. 140.

8 TNA, FO 371/115945/VY1015/29, No. 202, Gardner to Foreign Office, "Situation in Syria," 26 April 1955.

ni, the SSNP deputy representing Ghouta, from its Chamber, a demand to which the parliament ultimately acceded, waiving Kaswani's immunity and arresting him.[9] The Syrian government and army, supported by the Syrian Communist Party and other leftists, worked in tandem to construct the narrative surrounding the events, portraying Malki as a martyred national hero who was killed for trying to preserve the country's freedom from foreign interference. In contrast, his assassin and the SSNP were depicted as the agents of colonialism "who [were] trying to drag a reluctant Syria into the [Baghdad Pact]."[10] Further charges, allegedly based on seized party documents, claimed the SSNP's conspiracy against Syria extended well beyond killing Malki and was supported by the United States, including further political assassinations and a coup d'état that would establish a government more inclined to "imperialist" interests, an accusation the United States adamantly protested.[11]

The keen longing to eliminate the SSNP from Syria's political landscape and armed forces led the Syrian army to seek to impose martial law in areas like Damascus and Latakia to legalize widespread arrests and quick military trials that would circumvent the civilian judicial system. The president and several other government officials balked at this and other proposals suggesting amending the penal code and, failing that, the constitution itself. Indeed, they considered these proposed amendments unconstitutional and feared the precedent their passage would establish.[12] The Syrian army also thwarted Lebanese law-

---

9 *L'Orient*, 26 April 1955. Kaswani penned a strongly-worded letter at the end of May 1955 to his former colleagues in the Syrian parliament decrying the government's persecution of the SSNP, warning that while the SSNP was the movement being suppressed today tomorrow it could be another nationalist party that found itself suppressed by the communists and their helpers. See al-Khalidi, *al-Ḥizb al-Qawmī wa Qaḍīyat al-Mālikī, Vol. 2*, pp. 16–19.

10 TNA, FO 371/115945/VY1015/31, No. 61, 10106/40/55, Gardner to Macmillan, "Assassination of Colonel Malki," 27 April 1955. For a thorough study on how the Syrian government and the press in Damascus – from official military publications to daily periodicals – constructed this narrative, see Kevin W. Martin, *Syria's Democratic Years: Citizens, Experts, and Media in the 1950s* (Bloomington: Indiana University Press, 2015), pp. 61–81.

11 *L'Orient*, 4 May 1955; TNA, FO 371/115945/VY1015/33, 10104/46/55, Chancery Damascus to Levant Department, "Assassination of Malki," 30 April 1955; TNA, FO 371/115945/VY1015/32, 10104/49/55, Gardner to Rose, "Assassination of Malki," 3 May 1955; *Foreign Relations of the United States (FRUS)*, 1955–1957, Volume XIII, Near East: Jordan – Yemen, Editorial Note 295; and *FRUS*, 1955–1957, Volume XIII, Near East: Jordan – Yemen, Document 297.

12 TNA, FO 371/115945/VY1015/33, 10104/46/55, Chancery Damascus to Levant Department, "Assassination of Malki," 30 April 1955; TNA, FO 371/115945/VY1015/36, 10104/57/55, Chancery Damascus to Levant Department, "Repercussions of Col. Malki Assassination," 7 May 1955. Indeed, ʿAbd al-Masih, Jadid, Shawi, al-Shaykh, and Khuri remained at large. *L'Orient*, 6 May 1955.

yers' efforts to provide legal aid to detained SSNP members, preventing a delegation from seeing detainees.[13]

The military's failure to produce evidence of a wider SSNP conspiracy, or arrest members of the SSNP's leadership accused of organizing the assassination, raised doubts and caused many to believe the allegations were "unfounded and that the murder may have a private act of revenge by [ʿAlawi] members of the [SSNP] against the head of a party which had persecuted fellow [ʿAlawis]."[14] Also shaking confidence in the army's account were persistent allegations in the Syrian and Lebanese press that detained SSNP members had been subjected to torture and abuse and had, therefore, confessed under duress.[15] The party itself propagated these claims in *Sada Lubnan* as it established a counter-narrative that absolved it of wrongdoing and protested the Syrian government's campaign against it. Even former SSNP member Salah Labaki publicly called for an to the mistreatment of SSNP prisoners.[16] Worried allegations of torture would further erode support for its campaign against the party, the Syrian government banned the import of Lebanese newspapers and threatened to prosecute local journalists who published stories on the matter.[17]

In strongly-worded proclamations, the SSNP advanced four central demands: an end to political persecution and torture; the establishment of an independent investigative committee comprised of important individuals from various Arab states; no amendments to the Syrian constitution be allowed throughout the course of the investigation and trial; and banning all political parties, including the SSNP, Baʿth, and Communists, from the Syrian armed forces.[18] Another SSNP statement condemned the Syrian authorities' distortion of the content of five letters sent to the party by Hisham Sharabi, an SSNP member teaching at Georgetown University, portraying them as incontrovertible evi-

---

13 *Sada Lubnan*, 28 April 1955.

14 TNA, FO 371/115945/VY1015/32, 10104/49/55, Gardner to Rose, "Assassination of Malki," 3 May 1955.

15 TNA, FO 371/115945/VY1015/32, 10104/49/55, Gardner to Rose, "Assassination of Malki," 3 May 1955, and *L'Orient*, 4 May 1955.

16 *Sada Lubnan*, 6 May 1955.

17 TNA, FO 371/115945/VY1015/36, 10104/57/55, Chancery Damascus to Levant Department, "Repercussions of Col. Malki Assassination," 7 May 1955. It should be noted that not all Lebanese papers, particularly those affiliated with the party's traditional opponents in Lebanon, voiced hostility to the Syrian government's policy against the SSNP. The Kata'ib's newspaper *al-Amal* attacked the party, accusing it of committing treason and cruel acts of terrorism. *L'Orient*, 1 May 1955.

18 *Sada Lubnan*, 1, 4–7 May 1955.

dence the party was collaborating and conspiring with the United States.[19] Qubrusi called on Syrian authorities to respect the rule of law and condemned the torture and abuse of SSNP detainees in Syrian prisons.[20] Moreover, in an interview with *al-Nahar*, Qubrusi declared that the party, despite the charges leveled against it, was – and would never – deny that it was a revolutionary party in both spirit and thought that sought to implement its vision for the good and advancement of the Syrian nation.[21]

The party also worked to distance itself from the United States. In an article in *Sada Lubnan*, for example, the SSNP argued it had attempted to foil the efforts of US Ambassador Eric Johnson to resolve the water dispute in the Jordan Valley, arguing that the American proposal would harm Syrian interests. Further demonstrating the party's anti-American bona fides, the party's aggressive campaign against illicit profiteering by oil companies in Syria allegedly had prompted the Syrian government to request the party tone down its rhetoric to not to infuriate the United States. Though the examples provided may have been true, and despite any reservations or protests to the contrary, the SSNP was more favorably disposed to the United States and its aims in the region due to their shared interests in countering communism and Arab nationalism. The article concluded with a challenge to the rulers in Damascus to harshly punish the actual perpetrators of the assassination but do so through a transparent legal process by publicly releasing evidence against the accused and refraining from spreading disinformation concealing the truth.[22]

Despite Syrian protests, Lebanese authorities did little to stem the party's aggressive criticism of the Syrian regime, particularly in the pages of *Sada Lubnan*. Several Lebanese leaders did ask the party to temper the intensity of its criticism. The Information minister asked *Sada Lubnan*'s managing editor Ali Hashim to "moderate the campaign against Syria" in the paper, but Hashim refused after consulting with the party's information director, Saʿid Taqi al-Din.[23] Regardless, Syrian authorities continued their vigorous campaign against the now-dissolved

19 *Sada Lubnan*, 10 May 1955.
20 113/12, n.d., "Regarding al-Malki's assassination," in Asseily and Asfahani, *A Face in the Crowd*, p. 140, and *Sada Lubnan*, 4 May 1955.
21 *Sada Lubnan*, 5 May 1955.
22 *L'Orient*, 1 May 1955.
23 "Ittiṣāl bitārīkh 13 Ayār 1955," in Ahmad Asfahani, *al-Tanaṣṣut ʿala al-Hātif fī Lubnān: Anṭūn Saʿādah wa-l-Ḥizb al-Sūrī al-Qawmī al-Ijtimāʿī Namūdhajan, 1947–1958* (Beirut: Dār Kutub li-l-Nashr, 2014), p. 53. It is interesting that the Information minister approached Hashim about changing the tone of the paper, not *Sada Lubnan*'s owner and editor-in-chief Muhammad Baʿalbaki. See also the effort of ʿAbdallah Yafi and Saeb Salam to intercede with Qubrusi the following week. "Ittiṣāl bi-Tārīkh 22/5/1955," in Asfahani, *al-Tanaṣṣut ʿala al-Hātif*, pp. 54–55.

party, leveling new accusations against it and arresting additional party members and suspected party sympathizers. The party was pursued even in Saudi Arabia, which expelled over 70 Palestinian Saudi Aramco employees on charges that they belonged to the SSNP.[24]

By the end of May, however, British diplomats in Syria suggested public opinion was "becoming increasingly skeptical" of the zealous campaign against the party and the official narrative of events. They noted Syrian authorities had failed to produce any evidence of either foreign involvement in Malki's assassination, a foreign-backed broader conspiracy against Syria, or sufficient information to bring any of the detained to trial.[25] While such skepticism may have existed, it was not widely or openly proclaimed. The SSNP, too, continued to scornfully reproach Syrian authorities and the logic of their case, declaring that "after 35 days of investigation, torture and promises to release documents," they will only release a document written in 1938 stating Saʿadeh hoped to become Syria's emperor. The statement, written by Taqi al-Din, continued, "Let us supposes this absurd statement is correct that Saʿadeh wanted to be emperor over Syria, so this then means that his party would (1) kill Malki, (2) conspire with a foreign power to execute a coup, and (3) burn its printing press?"

11.1 Military Tribunals and Syria's Pursuit of the SSNP in Lebanon

Moreover, the party condemned the falsification of confession statements, particularly that obtained from Mahayri.[26] Ostensibly acknowledging its failure to prove the party had ordered Malki's assassination, Syrian authorities released some party members on bail and began legal proceedings against those remaining in custody charged with either belonging to an illegal organization or with Malki's murder.[27] Of the first twenty-five SSNP members facing the military tribunal, twenty were civilians, and five were members of the armed forces; the five soldiers received light sentences up to one-year's imprisonment.[28]

---

24 *Al-Anba'*, 27 May 1955.

25 TNA, FO 371/115945/VY1015/37, 11901/725/55, Gardner to Rose, "Situation between right- and left-wing parties," 25 May 1955.

26 *Sada Lubnan*, 7 June 1955.

27 *Al-Anba'*, 5 June 1955, and TNA, FO 371/115946/VY1015/44, 11901/703/55, Gardner to Rose, "Reduction of Tension in Syria," 15 June 1955.

28 TNA, FO 371/115946/VY1015/44, 11901/703/55, Gardner to Rose, "Reduction of Tension in Syria," 15 June 1955.

The ongoing persecution of the SSNP strained relations between Syria and Lebanon as Lebanese authorities refused to pursue, apprehend, or extradite SSNP members residing in Lebanon despite multiple Syrian requests. When pressed by the Syrian government, Lebanese authorities consistently denied they possessed any information on the whereabouts of wanted SSNP members or stated they could not verify Syrian claims.[29] Further straining bilateral relations was that the Lebanese government allowed the party to publish its official statements and allowed the Lebanese press to express their disapproval of Syria's policies regarding the party freely.[30] These actions reflected the amicable state of relations between the party and Chamoun's government, though Lebanese authorities would, at times, disrupt party meetings, prevent the distribution of party propaganda, and arrest party members.[31]

The official indictment against 68 SSNP members was published at the end of June, the day before the memorial service for Malki was to be held, to stir public anger toward the party and make it more inclined to support harshly punishing the accused.[32] Almost half of the indicted party members were charged in connection with Malki's assassination, "while the others were charged for activities relating to their membership [in] the party."[33] The Syrian government also sought the arrest and extradition of at least 15 SSNP members in Lebanon – all of whom were leading party officials, and many were Lebanese citizens – for their alleged complicity in the plots. Lebanon refused the request.[34] According to the indictment, the SSNP, supported by the United States and Iraq, treasonously aspired to overthrow the Syrian regime and unite Syria with Iraq as an initial step towards fulfilling the Fertile Crescent plan. The prosecution sought the death penalty for those conspirators, including Ghassan and Fu'ad Jadid, ʿAbd al-Masih, Shawi, and Khuri, accusing them of organizing the plot against the state, murdering Malki, and collaborating with a foreign power.[35] Makhluf and Dabussi, the fellow ʿAlawi SSNP members and non-commissioned officers acting as Rahim's back up, were also sentenced to death and executed. Once

---

29 *Lisan al-Shaʿb*, 28 April 1955; *L'Orient*, 26–28 April 1955; and *L'Orient*, 7 May 1955.

30 *Al-Anba'*, 27 May 1955.

31 *L'Orient*, 26 April 1955.

32 According to Islamic tradition, a memorial ceremony is held forty days following an individual's death, marking the end of the mourning period. Malki's memorial should have taken place in early June but was delayed several weeks. *L'Orient*, 26 June 1955, and TNA, FO 371/115946/VY1015/46, 10104/83/55, Chancery Damascus to Levant Department, "Assassination of Malki," 2 July 1955.

33 Rathmell, *Secret War*, p. 99.

34 *L'Orient*, 28, 29 June 1955, and *Sada Lubnan*, 2, 5 July 1955.

35 Rathmell, *Secret War*, p. 99.

again, the party categorically denied the charges, arguing the SSNP had nothing to do with Malki's assassination, Rahim having acted independently.[36]

The public military tribunal proceedings were covered extensively by the local press, which took a mostly hostile position towards the party that echoed the official line to incite the Syrian public against the SSNP and the West.[37] To this end, military prosecutors renewed their accusations regarding foreign involvement in Malki's assassination and a broader Western-backed plot by the United States to overthrow the Syrian government, charging the party with committing multiple acts of treason.[38] The prosecution accused the United States Military Attaché in Damascus of having contacts with SSNP members and attempting to bribe Malki to end his opposition to the Baghdad Pact.[39] The prosecution also focused once again on Sharabi's correspondence with the party leadership in Syria that discussed possible US-SSNP cooperation, producing reports on discussions between Sharabi and Lebanese Ambassador to the United States Charles Malik, and Sharabi's proposal that Mahayri travel to America to lead talks regarding cooperation with the United States. No actions had been taken regarding the letters' contents beyond general discussions, indicating the only thing that bound the SSNP and US government was their shared commitment to combatting communism and desire to move Syria into the West's sphere of influence.[40]

Though under intense pressure, the party marked the sixth anniversary of Saʿadeh's execution on 8 July, using the occasion as an opportunity to inspire and lift the spirits of the party faithful. The party leadership reminded adherents that the party's path was not an opportunistic one but one of suffering and martyrdom; the social nationalists, who have chosen their way and their leader, understand that changing the nation's state and its affairs requires effort and sacrifice.[41] By August, both the Syrian public and press had lost interest in the whole Malki Affair and focused their attention on news regarding the coming Sy-

36 *Sada Lubnan*, 30 June 1955.

37 Martin, *Syria's Democratic Years*, pp. 62–63.

38 *FRUS*, 1955–1957, Volume XIII, Near East: Jordan – Yemen, Document 300.

39 TNA, FO 371/115946/VY10345/1, 10104/165/55, Chancery Damascus to Levant Department, "Assassination of Colonel Malki," 28 September 1955.

40 Rathmell, *Secret War*, pp. 99–100; Seale, *The Struggle for Syria*, pp. 241–242; al-Khalidi, *al-Ḥizb al-Qawmī wa Qaḍīyat al-Mālikī, Vol. 1*, pp. 311–332. The section from al-Khalidi's book is a reproduction of Mahayri's testimony addressing Sharabi's letters and the party's relations with the United States.

41 *Sada Lubnan*, 8 July 1955.

rian presidential election.[42] By this time, the SSNP had managed to reorganize enough in Syria to begin to resist and counter the ongoing campaign against it. SSNP members attempted to assassinate several military judges overseeing the trial, targeting a military prosecutor and a military judge at their homes, shooting one outside of his house, and detonating an improvised explosive device in front of the other's home.[43]

The Lebanese government's continuing refusal to cooperate with the Syrian government's prosecution and pursuit of the SSNP remained a point of contention between the two countries, though tensions had eased by the end of summer as Syria temporarily ceased pressing the Lebanese on the matter. Further adding to the atmosphere of détente was the fact that neither had become a party to the joint defense pacts the other viewed as suspect – Lebanon had not joined the Baghdad Pact, and Syria had not entered the tripartite agreement with Saudi Arabia and Egypt. Despite the détente, Syria remained determined in its efforts to capture and repatriate fugitive SSNP members condemned by the military tribunal. By October, Lebanon's firm refusal to cooperate in the pursuit and extradition of wanted SSNP members and curtail accusations in the press of torture by the "communist-infiltrated" Syrian army against SSNP detainees inflamed tensions once again.

Syrian authorities did not let Lebanese intransigence hinder their efforts, and when Syrian intelligence received information that Ghassan Jadid and Iskander Shawi were reportedly hiding in north Lebanon, they launched an operation to capture them. The operation, which was dependent on the success of bribing locals to hand the wanted men over, was an embarrassing failure. Two Syrian intelligence officers clandestinely entered the country and traveled to northern Lebanon, where they paid off a local SSNP member who belonged to an influential local clan and Shawi's whereabouts. The informant, Mashhur Dandashi, was given 50,000 Lebanese pounds to bring Jadid and Shawi to an agreed-upon location where the Syrian intelligence officers would arrest them and whisk them back to Syria. Dandashi accepted the money but had other ideas, notifying Jadid and Shawi of the Syrian plan. Jadid and Shawi decided to turn the tables on their would-be captors and, together with a small contingent of armed SSNP members, went to the meeting location and waited for the Syrians. When the intelligence officers arrived, they were caught off guard by the SSNP members lying in wait and were detained. After an unknown period, the Syrian government,

42 TNA, FO 371/115946/VY1015/54, No. 91, 10104/03/53, Gallagher to Macmillan, "Presidential Elections," 2 August 1955.

43 TNA, FO 371/115946/VY10345/1, 10104/165/55, Chancery Damascus to Levant Department, "Assassination of Colonel Malki," 28 September 1955.

which had been unable to contact the officers or determine their whereabouts, was forced to inform Lebanese authorities about the two missing intelligence agents and request their return, thus revealing the bungled operation. Lebanese authorities contacted the SSNP to ask them to release the two men, and the party, not wanting to anger the Lebanese government, subsequently handed them over to Lebanese security forces, who returned the men to Syria, ending the fiasco.[44] In response, Syria demanded the Lebanese government arrest Jadid and other SSNP leaders and extradite them to stand trial in Syria; the Lebanese government refused.

Much to the Western Powers' dismay, Egyptian and Soviet influence were ascendant in Syria in the Malki Affair's aftermath. Shukri al-Quwatli was elected president of Syria in August 1955, which frustrated Iraq but was generally welcomed by Lebanese, who hoped relations between the two countries would improve.[45] SSNP-affiliated newspapers responded cautiously and argued that Quwatli's victory was a reflection of his predecessors' failures, "[warned] against over optimism," and encouraged him to pursue alliances with "the Fertile Crescent countries."[46] Yet, under new Prime Minister Saʿid al-Ghazzi, Syria moved further into Egypt's sphere of influence rather than Iraq's, signing a bilateral defense pact establishing the foundation for military cooperation with the Egyptian government. Moreover, Syrian relations with the Soviet Union deepened diplomatically and militarily. A Soviet military attaché was appointed, its diplomatic mission upgraded to an embassy, and the Syrian military began receiving Soviet weapons.[47] However, it was not until the following summer that the Baʿth would increase its power within the Syrian government, securing the vital ministerial posts of foreign and economic affairs in the Syrian Cabinet.[48]

44 TNA, FO 371/115731/VL10389/2, 10323/5/55, Chancery Beirut to Levant Department, 20 October 1955, and TNA, FO 371/115731/VL10389/3, 10302/1/55, Chancery Damascus to Levant Department, 19 October 1955.

45 TNA, FO 371/115946/VY1015/67, 1025/61/55, British Embassy Baghdad to Levant Department, "Iraqi Attitude to Syrian Presidential Elections," 17 August 1955, and TNA, FO 371/115947/VY10345/71, 1028/4/69/55, Chancery Beirut to Levant Department, "Lebanese reactions to Quwatly's election," 23 August 1955.

46 TNA, FO 371/115947/VY10345/71, 1028/4/69/55, Chancery Beirut to Levant Department, "Lebanese reactions to Quwatly's election," 23 August 1955.

47 Seale, *The Struggle for Syria*, pp. 253–254.

48 Seale, *The Struggle for Syria*, p. 258.

11.2 A Bitter Struggle: The Clandestine Battle Against the Syrian Regime

The SSNP was determined to reverse the course of affairs in Syria, exacting its revenge on the regime and seizing power. As early as August 1955, rumors swirled regarding Adib al-Shishakli's return to Syria with thoughts of launching a military coup to bring a change to the country's direction and, in part, to the persecution of the SSNP.[49] Shishakli had, in fact, secretly come to Lebanon with such intentions, his arrival facilitated by the party and several of its members in the Lebanese army. His efforts to cultivate support in Beirut and among his associates in Damascus bore no fruit, and he eventually left Lebanon, abandoning his plans.[50] Months later, in early December 1955, Quwatli raised his concerns with British diplomats in Damascus about a possible British- and American-backed SSNP coup plot to restore Shishakli to power and establish a Fertile Crescent union.[51] According to Quwatli, the British, together with the Americans, were working with the party in Lebanon and had devised a plan to use Iraq as the base of operations for his overthrow. The British diplomat sought to calm Quwatli's nerves, dismissing the rumors as false and observing that Shishakli was not an SSNP member, but the ALM's leader, and would have to overcome his hostility to Iraqi prime minister Nuri al-Saʿid if any plot were to develop.[52] Quwatli's suspicions would prove correct in part, however, as a British-American plan to overthrow the Syrian regime with the help of Iraq and the SSNP began to take shape in the spring and summer of 1956.

Both Great Britain and the United States were growing ever more concerned by Syria's drift into the Soviet orbit and were determined to stop and reverse it. Initially, the Eisenhower administration was hesitant about undertaking a major covert military operation to install a more Western-friendly government in Damascus. Prime Minister Eden's government did not share these reservations, and

49 *The Times*, 19, 23, and 26 August 1955; TNA, FO 371/115946/VY1015/66, Telegram No. 617, Beirut to FO, 22 August 1955; and TNA, FO 371/115947/VY1015/76, 10104/135/55, Chancery Damascus to Levant Department, 31 August 1955.

50 82/16, n.d., "Adeeb Shishakli. Attempts to stage military coups in Syria," in Asseily and Asfahani, *A Face in the Crowd*, pp. 183–185, and "Taqrīr bi-Tārīkh 18/8/1955," in Asfahani, *Anṭūn Saʿādah*, p. 122.

51 TNA, FO 371/115947/VY1015/95, 10104/180/55, Gardner to Rose, "Plot to restore Shishakli to power," 5 December 1955.

52 TNA, FO 371/115947/VY1015/95, 10104/180/55, Gardner to Rose, "Plot to restore Shishakli to power," 5 December 1955. Rumors of a possible coup involving Shishakli and the SSNP continued to appear in the Syrian press well into early January; such rumors were not without merit. *FRUS*, 1955–1957, Volume XIII, Near East: Jordan – Yemen, Document 318.

Eden ordered the Foreign Office and the British Secret Intelligence Service (SIS) to be more aggressive and formulate plans for regime change.[53] Sharing London's view and pushing for military action in Syria were Baghdad Pact members Turkey and Iraq, both of whom had grown more convinced only direct intervention could bring about the desired change in Syria's regional and international posture. By the end of March, American reservations regarding a more aggressive approach to Syria had softened following the Eisenhower administration's failure to persuade Egypt's Nasser to support American efforts to counter the Soviet Union in the region. Instead, the United States would work to weaken Nasser by denying military and economic assistance to Egypt, dividing the Egyptian-Saudi alliance, giving more significant support to the Baghdad Pact, expanding support for "pro-Western elements in the region," and beginning to work more closely with the British to advance their complementary strategic agenda in the region.[54] Nevertheless, the United States remained skeptical of Britain and Iraq's approach to Syria.

The SSNP's view of regional developments complemented that of the United States and Britain, given its strong opposition to communism and desire to stem the spread of Arab nationalism. In October 1955, according to one Lebanese Sûreté report, SSNP members employed in Saudi Arabia's oil company were suspected of working against King Saʿud and the Saudi government on behalf of Anglo-American interests to draw Saudi Arabia into the Baghdad Pact.[55] In late December 1955 and early January 1956, the SSNP leadership began discussing the possibility of overthrowing the Syrian regime with Western support, motivated by both a desire for revenge and concern over increasing communist influence. It also explored ways to unify the Syrian opposition behind the party's initiative. Party representatives broached the subject with American officials in Beirut, but American officials, skeptical of more aggressive plans to confront and repel Soviet expansion in Syria, quickly rebuffed the "SSNP request for help in carrying out a coup in Syria."

Furthermore, the US made its refusal clear, so there would be no misunderstanding of any real or perceived support for such a plan.[56] Rebuffed by the Americans, the SSNP approached Iraq to discuss Iraqi cooperation and support for an SSNP-led military action in Syria. A delegation led by Adib Qadurra trav-

---

53 Rathmell, *Secret War*, pp. 112–113.

54 Rathmell, *Secret War*, pp. 115–116.

55 "Taqrīr bi-Tārīkh 7 Tishrīn al-Awwal 1955 ʿan al-Suʿūdiyya," in Asfahani, *Anṭūn Saʿādah*, p. 123.

56 *FRUS*, 1955–1957, Volume XIII, Near East: Jordan – Yemen, Document 318, and *FRUS*, 1955–1957, Volume XIII, Near East: Jordan – Yemen, Document 319.

eled to Baghdad in December 1955, but talks between the two sides failed to achieve any mutual understanding.[57] However, the delegation's failure did not signal the end of either side's efforts to court the other. In January 1956, further discussions on military cooperation between the SSNP and Iraq occurred in Beirut, where Taqi al-Din and Jadid met with Colonel Mehdi al-Samarra'i, the Iraqi Military Attaché, and the head of Iraqi Military Intelligence.[58] However, the meetings did not result in any concrete plans for cooperation or action, though both sides remained open to the idea.

By June, American and British fears regarding Syria's deepening ties to Egypt and the Soviet Union intensified with the formation of a new unity government in Damascus led by Sabri al-ʿAsali and recent Soviet economic and military overtures to Syria. The fall of Ghazzi's government provided an opportunity for the Baʿth to flex its enhanced strength, securing the foreign affairs and economics portfolios in ʿAsali's new government and conditioning its membership in the ruling coalition on its demand that Syria enter unity talks with Egypt.[59] Egypt's standing had been considerably enhanced thanks to Nasser's nationalization of the Suez Canal Company in July 1956 – a decision that the Syrian government enthusiastically supported – and his subsequent appeals for Syria to work together to advance the cause of Arab unity.[60] Nasser's growing regional influence and Soviet activity in Syria were viewed with alarm by Beirut and Baghdad.

Under the leadership of Nuri Saʿid, the Iraqi government was particularly perturbed by the rise of its regional rival and its increasing sway in Syria, developments that further encouraged Iraqi desires for military intervention. With its British allies, Iraq, as previously mentioned, had worked to establish a different regional order under the auspices of the Baghdad Pact but had failed over the preceding year to bring Damascus under its sphere of influence. Now, the two found themselves intensively plotting an intervention to change their fortunes in Syria and nullify Nasser's gains. Despite these developments, the American government remained committed to its cautious approach, which it believed was bearing fruit. However, as summer ended and turned to fall, American misgivings subsided, and the CIA became involved in the ongoing British and Iraqi operational planning for military intervention.[61]

Joining the British-Iraqi supported plot to overthrow the Syrian regime, officially known as 'Operation Straggle,' was an assortment of Syrian exiles, includ-

57 Rathmell, *Secret War*, p. 120.
58 Rathmell, *Secret War*, p. 120.
59 Seale, *The Struggle for Syria*, p. 259, and Rathmell, *Secret War*, p. 117.
60 Seale, *The Struggle for Syria*, pp. 260–261.
61 Rathmell, *Secret War*, p. 118.

ing former politicians, former military officers, and SSNP members, brought together by their shared sense of grievance against the Syrian regime and little else. The conspirators' rivalries threatened at several points to undermine the plot in its planning stages and required the mediation of intermediaries to soothe egos and smooth over differences. Among the exiled Syrian officers involved in the developing plot was Jadid, the SSNP's director of defense, Captain Salah al-Shishakli, Colonel Muhammad Maʿruf, Colonel Muhammad Safa, and Adib al-Shishakli, Syria's former president and Salah's brother. Apart from Adib, the other four officers resided in Lebanon, where they each maintained a relationship with the Iraqi Military Attaché in Beirut, Colonel Mehdi al-Samarra'i. To this military committee, a separate political committee was formed that ultimately comprised Sami Kabbara, a former Syrian Justice Minister, ʿAdnan al-Atasi, the son of the former Syrian president, Hassan al-Atrash, a Druze leader, Subhi al-Amari, Munir ʿAjlani, a former member of parliament, Adil ʿAjlani, and Saʿid Taqi al-Din, the SSNP's director of information. All were involved in deliberations regarding the post-coup order and establishment of a new government.[62]

The Iraqi government, particularly Nuri al-Saʿid, believed that Adib al-Shishakli would be the best suited to lead the coup and seize the reins of power in Damascus. In July, Adib traveled to Beirut where he held several meetings with the conspirators planning the military operation and received updates on the current political climate in Syria from two trusted associates, one of whom, Burhan Adham, turned out to be an informant for Syrian military intelligence (the Deuxième Bureau). It is unclear whether the coup plan presented to Adib by Jadid and the others was the same one the conspirators later agreed upon, but whatever the scenario, Adib was unimpressed and unconvinced it would be successful. Frustrated, Adib returned to France with the money the Iraqis had paid for his participation "[claiming] he disapproved of the plans" and refused to participate in the plot in its current form.[63] His brother Salah and Colonel Maʿruf implored Adib to reconsider, and a meeting in Geneva was set for Adib to meet with Iraqi Deputy Chief of Staff Ghazi Daghestani and Iraqi Foreign Minister Burhan al-Din Bashayan. This meeting, however, failed to persuade Adib, and he withdrew from any further plotting. Despite the setback, the conspirators continued preparing for the coup they scheduled to take place in late October.

62 Rathmell, *Secret War*, p. 119, and Seale, *The Struggle for Syria*, pp. 269–270.
63 Rathmell, *Secret War*, p. 119; TNA, FO 371/128220/VL1015/6, 1023/9/57, Beirut Chancery to Levant Department, "Conspiracy trial in Damascus," 18 January 1957, and "Taqrīr bi-Tārīkh 9 Kānūn al-Thānī 1957," in Asfahani, *Anṭūn Saʿādah*, p. 140.

In need of a future head of state, the conspirators decided to enlist former Syrian president Hashim al-Atasi. The idea was raised with Hashim's son Adnan, but it is unclear what, if anything, Adnan told his father about the planned coup, their hopes to install him as president, or even whether Hashim agreed to the proposal. The conspirators' political committee also began to explore ways to mobilize popular support for their planned revolt among the Druze, ʿAlawi, and Bedouin tribesmen throughout Syria and discussed technical matters regarding forming a new government and policies.[64] While the SSNP was determined to translate its participation in the coup into significant influence in any newly formed government, the party's fellow conspirators were hesitant, believing the new government's legitimacy would be put at risk if the SSNP held any ministerial posts. Instead, the party accepted the pledge that it would be legalized and allowed to operate freely in the country once again.[65] Meanwhile, the military committee finalized an operational plan for the coup.

According to the plan, several hundred SSNP fighters, divided into different units, would spearhead the attack. One, disguised as military police, would seize critical locations in Damascus and assassinate key political and military figures, while another, disguised as a Syrian army unit under Jadid's command, would seize Homs, where he had formerly served as the head of the military academy, and join forces with SSNP officers and the units under their command in the city. At the same time, Salah al-Shishakli and his followers would take Hama, the city from which he hailed, while other rebels would move on Aleppo, effectively targeting the country's four most significant urban centers. As the rebels moved, it was hoped that sympathetic SSNP officers would command their forces to join in support of the rebellion in each city. Meanwhile, to spread Syrian forces thin, the conspirators hoped with local allies' help to foment rebellion in three regions: the ʻAlawi mountains, southern Syria, and the eastern Syrian desert. In the ʿAlawi area, Maʿruf would lead the revolt; in Jabal Druze, Druze fighters under tribal leaders Hassan al-Atrash and Shakib Wahhab and backed by the SSNP would lead the rebellion; and in the east, the uprising would be led by Bedouin tribesmen armed and trained by Iraq.[66] With Iraqi and CIA arms and funding, Jadid focused his attention on preparing the party's militiamen at camps in

---

64 TNA, FO 371/128221/VY1015/17, 1028/20/57, Chancery Beirut to Levant Department, "Damascus Trials," 7 February 1957.

65 Seale, *The Struggle for Syria*, pp. 275–276.

66 Seale, *The Struggle for Syria*, pp. 271, 276; Rathmell, *Secret War*, p. 121; TNA, FO 371/128220/VL1015/9, 1028/14/57, Beirut Chancery to Levant Department, "Trials in Damascus," 25 January 1957; "Taqrīr bi-Tārīkh 9 Kānūn al-Thānī 1957," in Asfahani, *Anṭūn Saʿādah*, p. 140; and *Daily Star*, 24 January 1957.

the Bekaa and Metn. Iraq secured Turkish diplomatic support for the coup, as the Turks also feared communist expansion in Syria like the Americans and British.[67] The coup was scheduled to take place in late October, but the date was changed several times. Ultimately plans for the coup were overtaken by dramatic regional events as Israel, backed by the British and the French, invaded the Sinai sparking the Suez Crisis.[68]

Israel's invasion of Egypt and the subsequent British-French air and ground campaign, including the seizure of the Suez Canal, was a watershed moment that, in the end, shifted the regional balance of power toward Nasser and his anti-Western camp. The SSNP, wary of Nasser and not on good terms, gave its reluctant, but full, support to Egypt, condemning the "tripartite aggression" of Israel, Britain, and France, and put itself at Egypt's disposal. Jadid, one of Operation Straggle's key conspirators, argued the coup should be postponed as it was inconceivable that an internal revolution takes place while Syria was exposed to foreign invasion, a position with which the party's Higher Council agreed.[69] Indeed, while the British continued to push the conspirators to carry out their coup in Syria amid the crisis in Egypt, the SSNP refused. The delays, however, did the conspirators no favors as Syria's Deuxième Bureau successfully uncovered the plot and arrested dozens of suspects, putting an end to yet another attempt to overthrow the government in Damascus and doing further damage to the SSNP's reputation and its efforts to regain its footing in the country, though it managed to continue to operate underground [70]

The failure of the coup plot, Egypt's diplomatic victory in the Suez Crisis, and Nasser's greater prestige further enabled the Arab nationalist Baʿth to enhance its power and influence in Syria. Throughout 1956, the Baʿth party had consolidated its political position in power. It supported ʿAsali's government, encouraged opposition to the West and the Baghdad Pact, established a sizeable presence in the National Assembly, and secured two ministerial positions in the Cabinet. Within the army, the Baʿth had almost 3,000 members among enlisted soldiers and commissioned officers, its influence further augmented by other members of the Syrian armed forces who sympathized with the party's anti-colonialist aims and anti-Iraq views. The Baʿth also expanded its power due to cooperation with the Syrian Communist Party, promoting stronger relations with

67 Rathmell, *Secret War*, pp. 121–122.

68 For more on the SSNP's internal deliberations in light of the Suez Crisis and its coup plot see Yammut, *al-Ḥaṣād al-Murr*, p. 314–316.

69 ʿAbd al-Satir, *Ayyām wa Qaḍiyya*, p. 132.

70 TNA, FO 371/128220/VL1015/4, Foreign Office Minute, "New Syrian Government," 1 January 1957.

the Soviet Union and working with the communists to promote socialist policies in rural Syria to combat feudalism.[71] In early 1957, with the swearing-in of the new Syrian Cabinet in which Baʿth Party member Salah al-Din al-Bitar was appointed foreign minister, it was evident that the Syrian government was firmly in the grip of leftists. Allying with Communists opposed to the West and desiring closer relations with Nasser's Egypt, the continuing ascendance of the Baʿth party was a source of concern among Western diplomats.[72]

Court proceedings against the Iraqi plot's alleged conspirators began the second week of January 1957 in Damascus. Charged with treason and threatening the state's security, proceedings against the 29 defendants, both those in custody and those who remained at large, were overseen by Colonel Afif Bizri, one of the Malki trial judges.[73] Proceedings against a reserve lieutenant and ʿAdnan al-Atasi revealed the establishment of paramilitary training camps for the SSNP. They confirmed a meeting involving Atasi, Taqi al-Din, Jadid, and Safa regarding coup preparations that Salah al-Shishakli hoped would be executed without delay. Atasi also described that Taqi al-Din had told him the SSNP had received funds and weapons from Iraq for the coup.[74] Former minister of justice Munir ʿAjlani, who had been deemed one of the plots principal conspirators, pleaded not guilty, arguing that he had merely met with Jadid, Safa, and Taqi al-Din and had paid no attention to their "puerile" musings.[75] As the proceedings continued throughout January, the SSNP repudiated accusations made in court, and arguments that confessions had been obtained as a result of torture were reported in several papers, including the pro-SSNP periodicals *al-Nahar* and *Sada Lubnan*; other newspapers suggested Syria's Deuxième Bureau had exaggerated the extent of the plot to prevent further challenges to the Syrian government.[76]

In late January, the public prosecutor issued a histrionic statement of committal, portraying the accused as the children of "treachery and...enmity" who conspired to undermine the foundations of the state in the service of imperial-

---

71 139/12 (26/11/1956), in Asseily and Asfahani, *A Face in the Crowd*, pp. 141–142.

72 TNA, FO 371/128220/VL1015/7, War Office, "Form at a Glance, Syria, 1957," 17 January 1957, and TNA, FO 371/128220/VL1015/8, Foreign Office Minute, "Discussion with a Syrian business-man," 20 January 1957.

73 *Sada Lubnan*, 9 January 1957; *L'Orient*, 9 January 1957; and *Le Jour*, 9 January 1957.

74 *Sada Lubnan*, 10 January 1957, and *L'Orient*, 10 January 1957.

75 *Sada Lubnan*, 11 January 1957; *L'Orient*, 11 January 1957; *Daily Star*, 24 January 1957; and TNA, FO 371/128220/VL1015/11, 1028/17/57, Beirut Chancery to Levant Department, "Damascus Trials," 29 January 1957.

76 TNA, FO 371/128220/VL1015/6, 1023/9/57, Beirut Chancery to Levant Department, "Conspiracy trial in Damascus," 18 January 1957, and TNA, FO 371/128220/VL1015/8, Foreign Office Minute, "Discussion with a Syrian business-man," 20 January 1957.

ism, colonialism, and Israel. The "root of all crimes" was the Baghdad Pact and the effort of "imperialists" to undermine the Egyptian and Syrian led "Arab awakening" in any way possible, finally resorting to using the SSNP to do so. The SSNP, the statement continued, had sought to "dominate politics through the army," making every effort to infiltrate its ranks but, having failed, changed course and attempted to mobilize the masses to revolt. Further, the SSNP, which since early 1955 had "[stood] side by side with imperialism in its hostile attitude against the Arab Nation," was complicit in Iraqi attempts to sow chaos in Syria.[77] The trials raised the tension between Lebanon and Syria as Lebanon, as it had before, rebuffed Syrian demands to extradite Syrian exiles deemed traitors and criminals by Syrian authorities.[78]

As the Damascus trials proceeded, the party and the Syrian government's struggle extended beyond the courtroom's confines as the SSNP and Syria's Deuxième Bureau waged a violent covert campaign against each other. Though the party had been significantly weakened in Syria in the period following Malki's assassination, it had remained a formidable opponent capable of frustrating the Syrian government due to its organizational strength, dedication to its cause, and access to armaments.[79] In early February, pamphlets denouncing the Syrian government and "its left-wing tendencies" that included warnings for parents to keep their children home from school on 5 February were distributed throughout Aleppo.[80] That day, several attacks took place involving SSNP members who threw several improvised explosive devices at the local officers' club, Baʿth and Communist party offices, and the residences of Baʿth and Communist Party leaders in the city of Aleppo. The explosives caused little damage, and no individuals were wounded in the attacks. Following 26 SSNP members' arrest on charges related to conducting these attacks, the party conducted a new wave of bombings in protest.[81]

The threat posed by the Syrian Deuxième Bureau to SSNP members in Lebanon was "a very real one," which reportedly led the SSNP to order several members to carry arms for personal protection and kidnap some of the party's oppo-

---

77 TNA, FO 371/128220/VL1015/11, 1028/17/57, Beirut Chancery to Levant Department, "Damascus Trials," 29 January 1957.
78 TNA, FO 371/128014/VL10389/1, 10611/4/57, No. 27, Middleton to Lloyd, "Lebanon-Syria," 31 January 1957.
79 Rathmell, *Secret War*, p. 126.
80 TNA, FO 371/128221/VY1015/20, 10217/9/57 (S), Scott to Watson, "Conditions in Syria (and Egypt)," 15 February 1957.
81 TNA, FO 371/128221/VY1015/18, 10212/9(S), Bowker to Watson, "Political Situation in Syria," 8 February 1957, and Rathmell, *Secret War*, p. 126.

nents. The Lebanese authorities "turned a blind eye" to the SSNP's security measures and precautions, which ultimately failed to prevent the assassination of Ghassan Jadid on 19 February in Ras Beirut.[82] In the days preceding the killing, a Syrian Deuxième Bureau officer had surveilled Jadid's comings and goings from the party's Information Office in Ras Beirut, posing undercover as a street vendor selling brooms to blend in with the crowd. Early in the afternoon on 19 July, the Syrian intelligence officer opened fire on Jadid as he drove his car towards the party's offices, hitting him at least 12 times and killing him instantly.[83] The assassin briefly evaded capture, hiding in a nearby building, but was eventually wounded and detained by a Lebanese gendarmerie unit after a brief firefight. Yet, just as the injured assassin exited the building in custody, an SSNP member charged through the police barricade and shot and killed him.[84]

In the days that followed, the SSNP defiantly rallied around their slain comrade, publishing images of Jadid's mourning family and his children giving the party salute in honor of their deceased father. Many odes praising Jadid were published, and a large funeral honoring him was scheduled to take place in Beirut on 22 February.[85] According to one estimate, 50,000 party members and regular Lebanese citizens lined the streets and participated in Jadid's funeral procession through Beirut. During the ceremony, SSNP president Asad al-Ashqar addressed the crowd, praising Jadid as a great martyr who died honorably on behalf of the struggle to revive the Syrian nation, vowing the SSNP would continue the battle to reform and renew the nation.[86]

Just days after Jadid's assassination, the military tribunal in Damascus pronounced its verdicts on the conspiracy trial's defendants, including Jadid, who was among the conspirators condemned to death despite having already been assassinated; others were sentenced to hard labor.[87] Undeterred by the verdicts and with passions enflamed by Jadid's killing, the party turned its attention to combatting the newly formalized Arab Solidarity Pact signed by Egypt, Syria, Jordan, and Saudi Arabia. Indeed, the party's new defense commissioner, the

---

82 TNA, FO 371/128014/VL10389/4, 1011/33/57, Middleton to Rose, "Lebanese/Syrian Relations," 21 February 1957.

83 Rathmell, *Secret War*, p. 127.

84 *Sada Lubnan*, 20 February 1957.

85 *Sada Lubnan*, 21–22 February 1957.

86 *Sada Lubnan*, 23–24 February 1957. Images from the funeral procession can be seen in *Sada Lubnan*, and Ahmad Asfahani and Nasif Rizkallah, eds., *Jūzif Rizq Allāh: Sīrat Munāḍil Qawmī, 1926–1970* (Beirut: al-Furāt, 2020), p. 412.

87 TNA, FO 371/128221/VY1015/27, 1025/24/57, Chancery Beirut to Levant Department, "Damascus Trials," 28 February 1957, and TNA, FO 371/128221/VY1015/27 (A), 1025/24/57, No. 274, Beirut to FO, "Damascus Trials," 7 March 1957.

former Syrian officer Fadlallah Abu Mansur, reportedly approached the Iraqis once again to win their support for another American-backed coup attempt in Syria that April.[88]

88 Rathmell, *Secret War*, p. 127.

12 The Struggle for Lebanon

In late February 1957, a little over a month after the Arab Solidarity Pact was signed, representatives of the four countries met again in Cairo to further formalize their position on the Eisenhower Doctrine. Articulated in early January 1957, the Eisenhower Doctrine enabled countries in the Middle East to request American military and economic assistance if they believed they were threatened by communist expansion, particularly "overt armed aggression," threatening their "territorial integrity and political independence."[1] At the February meeting, the four countries issued a joint communiqué proposing the region's countries embrace a policy of "positive neutralism" in the American-Soviet conflict. The doctrine of "positive neutralism" provoked a strong response in the region, particularly in Lebanon.

In a series of editorials reflecting the SSNP's position published in early March, *Sada Lubnan* proprietor and editor Muhammad Baʿalbaki firmly rejected the doctrine of "positive neutrality." He derided "positive neutrality" as bereft of any meaning and found the idea the four participants had agreed on a common course of action laughable, characterizing it as an attempt to "blackmail" other countries in the region.[2] In his first editorial, Baʿalbaki rhetorically asked whom they [i.e., the signatories] were trying to deceive and what political victory they thought their announcement had achieved.[3] In his two subsequent pieces, he demanded to know what Egypt and Syria wanted from Lebanon and Iraq, their calls for neutralism merely a euphemism for adopting policies that were more favorable to the Soviets than the Americans.[4] While criticizing the doctrine, Baʿalbaki praised Chamoun's anti-communist stand and argued America's fight against communism and an offer of aid could only benefit Arab countries.[5]

Chamoun's government believed securing American economic and military aid was vital for strengthening the country and helping Lebanon resist Syrian and Egyptian political pressure and, accordingly, announced its formal accept-

---

1 "The Eisenhower Doctrine, 1957," accessed 7 January 2019: https://history.state.gov/milestones/1953–1960/eisenhower–doctrine. Attié observes that "In view of the limited Soviet presence in the Middle East in 1957 and the remote possibility of aggression by a communist-controlled country, the political significance of the new American policy statement, the Eisenhower Doctrine, was in the restraint that it tried to impose on Egypt and Syria in allowing the Soviets further entry into the area." Attié, *Struggle in the Levant*, p. 113.

2 *Sada Lubnan*, 3–8 March 1957, and *L'Orient*, 5–9 March 1957.

3 *Sada Lubnan*, 3 March 1957.

4 *Sada Lubnan*, 6–8 March 1957.

5 *L'Orient*, 7, 12 March 1957.

https://doi.org/10.1515/9783110729092-014

ance of the doctrine on 16 March.[6] The Lebanese government's official endorsement of America's policy, which went further than any other pro-American Arab government, was a divisive decision that "further polarized the divided loyalties of the [Lebanese] population and worsened already strained relations with [Egypt's] Nasser."[7] Indeed, Chamoun's overt declaration in support of American regional policy and newly enacted domestic policies that limited the freedom of expression and expanded the scope of the government's censorship of the press only served to galvanize opposition to his government further and resulted in the dissolution of the Lebanese parliament. Among the opposition, support for Nasser, predominately among Sunnis who viewed Chamoun's acceptance of the Eisenhower Doctrine as a slight towards their community and a violation of the National Pact of 1943, was particularly strong. However, the Lebanese opposition was divided between those opposed to Chamoun's foreign and domestic policy and those solely opposed to his domestic policy. The former formed a Sunni-led, pro-Nasser opposition coalition known as the National Front under the leadership of ʿAbdallah al-Yafi and Saeb Salam. At the same time, the latter coalesced around Kamal Jumblatt's Progressive Socialist Party and Beshara al-Khuri's Constitutional Union Party (CUP).[8] Meanwhile, as internal opposition to Chamoun organized, an infuriated Nasser ordered the intensification of Egypt's propaganda attacks and subversive activities to destabilize Chamoun and his government.[9]

Tensions and hostility between Beirut and the Cairo-Damascus alliance only intensified over the following months as summer parliamentary elections approached. The SSNP continued to denounce growing communist infiltration and influence in Syria through its mouthpiece *Sada Lubnan* and remained concerned about the Syrian Deuxième Bureau's activities in Lebanon designed to counter its activities and undermine Chamoun.[10] While the party had enjoyed the Lebanese government's protection, it grew concerned that Lt. Colonel Antun Saʿad, the head of Lebanon's Deuxième Bureau, was working closely with his Syrian counterparts, providing them with important information on the party's activities in Lebanon.[11] To be sure, Saʿad and Sarraj did not have

---

6 Attié, *Struggle in the Levant*, p. 112.

7 Attié, *Struggle in the Levant*, p. 117.

8 Attié, *Struggle in the Levant*, pp. 119–120.

9 Attié, *Struggle in the Levant*, pp. 117–119; Samir Khalaf, *Civil and Uncivil Violence in Lebanon: A History of the Internationalization of Communal Conflict* (New York: Columbia University Press, 2002), p. 112.

10 *L'Orient*, 30 March 1957.

11 "Taqrīr bi-Tārīkh 16 Nīsān 1957," in Asfahani, *Anṭūn Saʿādah*, p. 142.

the best of relations, but whatever tensions may have existed between them and their respective intelligence bureaus would not necessarily preclude cooperation on matters in which both had a vested interest. The party also worked to thwart Syrian and Egyptian efforts to subvert Jordan, whose policy orientation had shifted towards the West and its anti-communist views became more pronounced. The Syrian military's limited participation in an attempted putsch to overthrow King Hussein in early April heightened already strained tensions between Amman and Damascus and hardened Jordan's anti-Nasserist and anti-communist stance. It also led Jordan to intensify its subversive campaign against Syria, which included making overtures to the Syrian opposition. In this context, King Hussein invited Asad al-Ashqar and Salah al-Shishakli to his palace to discuss Syria and forge a cooperative relationship of some sort. According to British reports, the SSNP offered to assist Jordanian security services during the Saudi monarch's planned visit to thwart any Syrian effort to cause trouble or harm to King Saʿud.[12]

At the end of May, as parliamentary elections neared, the opposition accused the Lebanese government of interfering in the elections and demanded a "neutral" government oversee the elections were free and fair, calling for a general strike should its demands not be met. The Lebanese government denied the accusations and prohibited public demonstrations of any sort. Ignoring the order, opposition leaders Salam and Yafi "called for a general strike and peaceful demonstration to mobilize popular support on behalf of [the opposition's] demands," but "the peaceful demonstration degenerated into a violent scuffle between the opposition and security forces."[13] Adib Qadurra, the head of the SSNP's Higher Council and a candidate in the coming elections, called on all involved to avoid sowing discord, denouncing the influence of sectarianism and communism, and the SSNP issued a statement supporting free elections and the preservation of Lebanon as a bastion of thought and freedom.[14] While Lebanese elections were generally free, the opposition's claims of interference were not entirely unfounded as foreign meddling had already manifested itself in the parliamentary contest. The United States, through the CIA, was providing funds to Chamoun that were used to support pro-Western candidates, particularly those supportive of the Eisenhower Doctrine,[15] while the British, determined to maintain Leba-

---

12 Rathmell, *Secret War*, pp. 131–136.

13 Khalaf, *Civil and Uncivil Violence*, p. 108, and *Sada Lubnan*, 1 June 1957. For a thorough assessment of the 1957 Lebanese parliamentary elections, see Attié, *Struggle in the Levant*, pp. 128–153.

14 *Sada Lubnan*, 1–2 June 1957.

15 Attié, *Struggle in the Levant*, pp. 136–137.

non's pro-Western orientation, were supportive of efforts to strengthen Chamoun and his allies. On the other hand, Egypt and Syria, possibly with Soviet backing, financially supported opposition candidates, and Syrian intelligence smuggled weapons to opposition forces in-country.[16] Notably, however, "while Syrian and Egyptian assistance was blatant, that of the Western powers was far subtler and was a well-kept secret at the time."[17]

The fiercely contested elections in June centered on presidential succession; Chamoun's term in office was set to end the following year in October, and with it, Chamoun's unabashedly pro-Western foreign policy orientation. Voting for the Chamber of Deputies, whose number of seats Chamoun had increased from 44 to 66 to the opposition's chagrin, took place over four consecutive Sundays beginning on 9 June in Beirut and South Lebanon and ending on 30 June in North Lebanon. Voting was staggered to ensure public order. While public order was maintained, voting was marred by acts of voter intimidation, bribery, and outside interference. With parliamentary seats divided based on religious confession, voters in various constituencies did not vote for political parties per se but candidates of different religious confessions in the same constituency.[18] Despite its steadfast opposition to confessionalism and traditionalism, the very organization of the electoral system compelled the SSNP to mostly play by its rules, forcing the party to consider the confessional backgrounds of its candidates and to build electoral alliances that inherently stood little chance of winning as they were often not forged with leading individuals, families or clans. Despite the SSNP's pro-government stance, the summer 1957 election was no exception as only one of the party's candidates secured a seat in the new Chamber.

In Beirut, on 9 June, Tueni and Qadurra lost their election bids in the city's first and second districts, respectively, even though the pro-government list won almost all the seats.[19] The following week in Mount Lebanon, a region where the SSNP was strongest, government-supported candidates – though none affiliated

---

16 *The Times*, 3 June 1957; TNA, FO 371/127999/VL1015/32, No. 1022, Amman to FO, 7 June 1957; and Rathmell, *Secret War*, pp. 128–130.

17 Attié, *Struggle in the Levant*, p. 142.

18 "For example, a voter in [Beirut's second constituency] can vote for two [Sunnis], one [Shi'a], one Armenian Catholic, one Armenian Catholic, and [one] for religious minorities." TNA, FO 371/127999/VL1015/17, 10110/35/57, No. 81, Middleton to Lloyd, "General Election," 9 May 1957. Furthermore, "regions and districts are allocated enough seats to represent them "fairly" in the Chamber and to reflect the sectarian balance within the constituency of each district. The device for accomplishing this double basis of representation is the list system." Hudson, *Precarious Republic*, p. 213.

19 TNA, FO 371/127999/VL1015/33, No. 623, Beirut Chancery to FO, 10 June 1957, and *Sada Lubnan*, 11 June 1957.

with the SSNP – won all twenty parliamentary seats, and one opposition leader, Kamal Jumblatt, suffered a stunning defeat. On 23 June in the Bekaa region, the party supported Higher Council member Mustafa ʿAbd al-Satir and Faysal Nasr al-Din, a young party member from one of the larger clans in the Hermel, in the region's northern in Baalbek-Hermel district. However, Nasr al-Din withdrew his candidacy mistakenly believing it would benefit Satir, who could not overcome Sabri Hamadeh's influence with local clans. Meanwhile, Satir resisted calls from the party leadership, first and foremost Qubrusi, to join a list with other local politicians, but ultimately relented, allying with local figures Nasri Maʿaluf and Salim Haydar.[20] In any case, the political maneuvering did not matter as Satir failed to secure a seat. However, this result did not stop a victorious Sabri Hamadeh from accusing Satir of being a "government candidate," a charge Satir refuted.[21] Having failed to secure an electoral victory, the party's last remaining hopes came down to the election's final week with voting in North Lebanon and Metn. The SSNP had focused its campaign efforts on the vote in Metn, a district historically intensely contested between the SSNP and Kataʾib, and in which SSNP president Asad al-Ashqar was a candidate. In the first weeks of June, Ashqar allied with Salim Lahud and Albert Munir, a list that ultimately turned out to be quite formidable as it was victorious.[22] Ashqar's election was a significant political victory in its own right, but it also represented the party's defeat of its fierce rival, the Kataʾib.

At the election's conclusion, government-backed candidates had secured 53 of the 66 seats in the Chamber, a result that only further enraged the opposition. The opposition denounced the election results, deeming them illegitimate and the product of illegal manipulation, and called for the annulment of the results and for new elections to be held.[23] Opposition leaders Salam and Yafi were defeated, as was Jumblatt, whose defeat left him greatly embittered and prompted him to commit himself to oppose Chamoun and demand "the dissolution of the new parliament."[24] The SSNP and its supporters, however, remained firmly be-

---

20 *Sada Lubnan*, 30 May 1957; ʿAbd al-Satir, *Ayyām wa Qaḍiyya*, pp. 158, 161; and *Sada Lubnan*, 11, 13, 15, 23 June 1957.

21 TNA, FO 371/127999/VL1015/37, No. 675, Beirut Chancery to FO, "Elections in Bekaa area," 24 June 1957, and *Sada Lubnan*, 29 June 1957. Notably, Satir laments the fact that Chamoun did not openly support his candidacy or those of other SSNP members beyond that of Ashqar, observing Chamoun's "nationalist" quota was no more than one. ʿAbd al-Satir, *Ayyām wa Qaḍiyya*, p. 163.

22 *Sada Lubnan*, 5, 11–12 June 1957; Raʿad, *al-Kalimāt al-Akhīra*, p. 86; ʿAbd al-Satir, *Ayyām wa Qaḍiyya*, p. 163; and Yamak, *SSNP*, p. 71.

23 *L'Orient*, 3 July 1957, and *Sada Lubnan*, 4 July 1957.

24 Attié, *Struggle in the Levant*, pp. 121, 144, and *L'Orient*, 4 July 1957.

hind Chamoun and the election results. In an editorial in *Sada Lubnan*, Muhammad Baʿalbaki responded to the opposition's accusations stating, "if any crime was committed, then you were an accessory to it!"[25] The SSNP, inspired by Ashqar's victory, sought to further energize its partisans with large celebrations commemorating Saʿadeh's execution in which declarations of the party's commitment to protecting the nation "from the forces of confusion and conflict" were pronounced.[26]

12.1 The Road to Civil War

Tensions continued to rise in the late summer and fall between the government and opposition despite internal divisions in the opposition between those opposed to Chamoun's foreign and domestic policy and those only opposed to the latter. The Lebanese government continued to deepen its pro-Western orientation and curb opposition activities.[27] Egypt and Syria, meanwhile, courted Lebanese opposition leaders such as former ministers Salam and Yafi and funneled money to opposition politicians in critical areas while also supporting infiltration and subversive activities in Lebanon and continuing to pursue exiled SSNP members residing in Lebanon.[28] Indeed, Salam and Yafi "became the leading Nasserist spokesmen of the opposition that formed against Chamoun in 1957."[29] In mid-August, Jumblatt's PSP bombed the Beirut-Damascus railway. In September, Lebanese security forces prevented several attempts to smuggle weapons into the country from Syria. In early October, unknown perpetrators threw several bombs at the offices of *Sada Lubnan* and pro-Saudi *al-Hayat.*[30] The general ineffectiveness of the bombs, the newspaper office bombings the only exception, led one British diplomat to wryly remark that "it is a fortunate characteristic of bombs as used in this part of the world that they very seldom

25 *Sada Lubnan*, 4 July 1957.
26 *Sada Lubnan*, 10 July 1957.
27 The Lebanese government, for example, requested the United States provide the Lebanese Gendarmerie with light weapons, vehicles, and communications equipment, which the United States granted. *FRUS*, 1955–1957, Volume XIII, Near East: Jordan–Yemen, Documents 141 and 142.
28 Rathmell, *Secret War*, p. 129, and *Sada Lubnan*, 14 July 1957.
29 Attié, *Struggle in the Levant*, pp. 104–105.
30 *L'Orient*, 18 August 1957; *L'Orient*, 4, 13 September 1957; TNA, FO 371/128014/VL10389/11, No. 978, Middleton to FO, "Lebanese–Syrian clash near frontier," 13 September 1957; TNA, FO371/128000/VL1015/51, 1011/103/57, Chancery Beirut to Levant Department, "Incidents in Lebanon during the last month," 12 September 1957; and *L'Orient*, 9 October 1957.

do any damage."[31] Both *Sada Lubnan* and the Kata'ib's *al-Amal* accused Syria's Deuxième Bureau of complicity in the bombings, denouncing Syria's ever more aggressive anti-Lebanese activities and urging the Lebanese government to take all necessary measures to end Syrian subversive activities in the country.[32]

The SSNP added to the growing tensions through its vocal opposition to Egypt and Syria's interference in Lebanon's domestic affairs and its bitter struggle against the Syrian regime, particularly its Deuxième Bureau. The party viewed favorably Saudi-led efforts to organize an inter-Arab conference, hoping that the meeting of Arab heads of state would result in tangible steps to curb Egyptian militancy and interference in the internal affairs of Arab countries, particularly the subversive activities of Egyptian and Syrian intelligence services in Lebanon.[33] In September, the SSNP allegedly conducted several attacks in Damascus, bombing the Egyptian and Soviet embassies and then-defense minister Khalid al-ʿAzm's home.[34] In October, Syrian authorities announced they had uncovered another alleged SSNP plot against the Syrian regime supported by the United States and accused exiled Syrian army officer Muhammad Maʿaruf of training SSNP militiamen in Lebanon for Syria operations. As evidence, Syrian authorities cited the discovery of an arms cache in the ʿAlawi mountains allegedly belonging to the party.[35]

While the SSNP continued to struggle against the Syrian regime and the rising tide of Arab nationalism, within the party, personal and policy differences among the leadership were becoming ever more fraught, threatening a party split. In early October, conflicting reports emerged that Ghassan Tueni had been either suspended or expelled from the party, perhaps owing to his issuing a joint statement with Kata'ib leader Pierre Gemayel and former parliamentarians Yusuf Salem and Gabriel Murr criticizing Chamoun's domestic policies.[36] The most divisive issue, however, centered around former SSNP president George ʿAbd al-Masih. A growing bloc within the party's leadership, frustrated by ʿAbd al-Masih's past decisions as party president and seeking to limit his influence within the party, searched for a way to oust him. ʿAbd al-Masih's supporters,

---

31 TNA. FO371/128000/VL1015/51, 1011/103/57, Chancery Beirut to Levant Department, "Incidents in Lebanon during the last month," 12 September 1957

32 *L'Orient*, 10 October 1957.

33 *L'Orient*, 12, 19 October 1957.

34 Rathmell, *Secret War*, p. 127.

35 *L'Orient*, 19 October 1957, and Rathmell, *Secret War*, p. 127. Rathmell suggests the weapons cache was likely left over from Operation Straggle and not a new one for newly smuggled weapons.

36 *L'Orient*, 12 October 1957, and Attié, *Struggle in the Levant*, pp. 104, 146–147.

the so-called "conservatives," were determined to prevent ʿAbd al-Masih's diminished role within the party and any attempt to expel him. Under pressure from the Higher Council, ʿAbd al-Masih resigned the party presidency in the Fall of 1956, stating he had done so "... for the benefit of the [national] cause as there can be no schism in our party," and was replaced by Mustafa Arshid.[37] A subsequent internal party investigation chaired by Qubrusi absolved the deceased Jadid of responsibility in the Malki Affair, laying the blame for the entire debacle on the shoulders of ʿAbd al-Masih who was uncooperative and evasive, refusing to answer questions or acknowledge responsibility for his role in the affair.[38] In late October 1957, the Higher Council met and declared their judgment, expelling ʿAbd al-Masih for unilaterally ordering Malki's assassination without the party leadership's consent, a decision that had brought nothing but calamity, woe, imprisonment, and persecution and damaged the party's constitution and institutions.[39]

The decision to expel ʿAbd al-Masih, one of the party's first members, was momentous and resulted immediately in a schism that divided the party into two distinct factions. The first faction, led by Ashqar and Qubrusi, was referred to as *al-Markaziyyun* (the Center), while the second, led by ʿAbd al-Masih and Iskander Shawi, was referred to as *al-Intifāḍa* (the Uprising), though each continued to refer to itself as the SSNP and Saʿadeh's authentic successors. While the vast majority of the party leadership and party faithful remained firmly in Ashqar's camp, many leaders and members maintained their commitment to ʿAbd al-Masih, including Ibrahim Yammut, Hassan al-Tawil, Joseph Rizkallah, and Hana Kaswani.[40] Over the following months, besides establishing a parallel political organization, ʿAbd al-Masih's faction would compete with Ashqar's faction to lay claim to Saʿadeh's legacy, focusing first and foremost on establishing the *Intifāḍa*'s ideological purity and correctness through the publication of an internal periodical called *al-Nashra al-Rasmiyya li-l-Ḥarakat al-Sūriyya al-Qawmiyya al-ʿIjtimāʿiyya.*[41] ʿAbd al-Masih's efforts failed to shift the balance of power between the two factions in any significant manner. Indeed, Ashqar's faction continued with business as usual, using the 25th anniversary of the party's founding

---

37 *Sada Lubnan*, 7 October 1956, and Saʿadeh, *Awrāq Qawmiyya*, p. 60.
38 Qubrusi, *Yatadhakkar, Vol. 4*, pp. 212–215.
39 TNA, FO 371/128235/VY1017/1, BBC Monitoring Report, "Expulsion of Members of Syrian Nationalist Party," 23 October 1957, and *Sada Lubnan*, 23 October 1957.
40 Suleiman, *Political Parties in Lebanon*, p. 99.
41 Jihad al-ʿAql, *Mawsūʿat Ṣiḥāfat al-Ḥaraka al-Qawmiyya al-ʿIjtimāʿiyya fī 75 ʿĀman, 1933–2008, Vol. 5* (Beirut: al-Furāt, 2011), pp. 98–114.

to hold public gatherings and celebrations throughout Lebanon, demonstrating its growing strength.[42]

The October 1957 purge was a victory for Ashqar and those in the "Lebanese school" within the party leadership that enabled Ashqar to deepen the party's alliance with Chamoun and pursue a more accommodationist policy vis-à-vis the Lebanese political establishment.[43] Though Chamoun had yet to officially legalize the party and thereby legitimize the SSNP's political activity, he made several conciliatory gestures that further deepened the alliance between the two sides. These included releasing several SSNP members serving life sentences for their participation in the failed July 1949 uprising and protecting the party from Syrian efforts to pursue SSNP members in Lebanon.[44]

By January 1958, Egyptian and Syrian support for, and direction of, subversive operations inside Lebanon, from bombing campaigns to cross-border raids, had continued to increase and raised the Lebanese government's concern and its Western supporters.[45] The declaration of Egyptian-Syrian unity and the establishment of the United Arab Republic (UAR, *al-Jumhūriyya al-ʿArabiyya al-Muttaḥida*) on 1 February 1958 only further destabilized Lebanon's domestic affairs, intensifying the dispute between Lebanon's opposition and the government. Indeed, Nasser's supporters, who hailed predominately from Lebanon's Sunni community, publicly celebrated in Beirut, Tyre, and Tripoli's streets and called for Lebanon to join the UAR.[46] The enthusiastic support for Nasser within Lebanon and the rising tide of Arab nationalist fervor within the country and in the broader region was not, however, a welcome development among the supporters of Lebanon's government, many of whom hailed from Lebanon's Christian communities who rejected Nasserism and Arab nationalism and wanted to preserve Lebanon's independence and pro-Western orientation.

---

42 *Sada Lubnan*, 16, 20 November 1957.

43 Beshara, *Lebanon*, p. 41.

44 *Sada Lubnan*, 1 October 1957; Yamak, *SSNP*, p. 71; Beshara, *Lebanon*, p. 41; and Suleiman, *Political Parties in Lebanon*, p. 99. The government decision to release SSNP members was denounced by the opposition deputy Sabri Hamadeh during a parliamentary session. Seeking to blunt Hamadeh's criticism, Prime Minister Sami al–Sulh said the government's decision was based on humanitarian considerations as the prisoners were in bad health, but Ashqar, not willing to let exchange end, contradicted Sulh and stated the prisoners were released because the government recognized their convictions were unjust. *Sada Lubnan*, 13 December 1957. In early January 1958, the Deuxième Bureau succeeded in assassinating two Syrian SSNP members in Beirut in a bombing. *Sada Lubnan*, 8 January 1958.

45 *FRUS*, 1958–1960, Volume XI, Lebanon and Jordan, Document 1.

46 Attié, *Struggle in the Levant*, pp. 154–158.

Days after the UAR's establishment, Inʿam Raʿad, the party's director of information, penned an editorial in *Sada Lubnan* in which he distinguished "artificial unity" (*al-itiḥād al-iṣṭināʿī*) and "natural unity" (*al-waḥda al-ṭabīʿiyya*), characterizing the unity of Egypt and Syria as an example of the former, and Jordanian-Iraqi union as an example of the latter.[47] In line with this view, the party criticized the establishment of the UAR while it welcomed the Arab Federation (AF, *al-Ittiḥād al-ʿArabī*) as a step toward realizing complete national unity, a cause on behalf of which the SSNP had been struggling for twenty-five years.[48] Indeed, while praising the new Arab Federation, the SSNP called upon the AF to spread the message of unity, promote internal national, social, and economic reforms that would unify the people and diminish the influence of sectarianism and tribalism, and adopt economic and foreign policies in line with the SSNP's views.[49] The party vocally pushed its message that the social nationalist renaissance was the only solution to the societal problems in Greater Syria through editorials and the public demonstrations it held in honor of Saʿadeh's birthday at the beginning of March.[50]

The formation of the UAR was such a profound development that it brought about a détente between the SSNP and the Kata'ib, as both movements now found themselves on the same side defending Lebanon's independence from outside attack. The Kata'ib and SSNP made strange bedfellows given the contentious history between the two groups and their conflicting visions for Lebanon. However, considering the external threat facing Lebanon, the two found common cause, the SSNP being committed to stopping the spread of communism and supporting the Lebanese government "primarily because an independent and pro-Western Lebanon was its only refuge." In contrast, the Kata'ib remained devoted to its *raison d'être:* preserving Lebanon's territorial sovereignty and national independence.[51] From the UAR's establishment into the summer months of the crisis, the SSNP and the Kata'ib would provide their consistent, outspoken support for Chamoun's government, uncompromisingly criticizing and attacking the UAR and the Lebanese opposition in their respective periodicals, *Sada Lubnan* and *al-Amal.* In early March, both condemned the UAR for alleging Saudi Arabia had concocted a plot to prevent Syrian-Egyptian unity and assassinate Nasser. They also decried the Lebanese opposition for attempting to incite artificial

47 *Sada Lubnan*, 2 February 1958.
48 *Sada Lubnan*, 16, 21 February 1958.
49 *Sada Lubnan*, 21 February 1958.
50 *Sada Lubnan*, 19, 22–23 February 1958, and *Sada Lubnan*, 1, 4March 1958.
51 Yamak, *SSNP*, p. 71.

crises and drag Lebanon into conflicts that threatened its independence[52] In April, when battles in the Shouf erupted between Kamal Jumblatt's militiamen and Lebanese security forces and subsequently spread to the Hermel, both decried and condemned the opposition's resort to violence.[53]

The SSNP's support for the Lebanese government was not, however, without limits. In March, after government supporters held a massive public demonstration against Nasser's supporters in Lebanon and called for Chamoun to serve another term as president, the SSNP distanced itself from the rally and declared its indifference. In April, while condemning the opposition for the armed revolt in the Shouf and Hermel, the party criticized the government for not being proactive and allowing the situation to deteriorate to a point where people considered taking up arms.[54] Later that month, though firmly on the government's side, the party's willingness to criticize it and their hesitancy to support Chamoun's second term perhaps influenced the decision of Kamal Jumblatt and Sabri Hamadeh to approach Ashqar to persuade him to end the SSNP's support for the government and adopt a position of neutrality. Should the party do so, Jumblatt and Hamadeh asserted the SSNP would receive funding and weapons from Nasser as a token of gratitude. Ashqar rejected the proposal, arguing that if the conflict engulfing Lebanon were only an issue of national renewal and advancement, he would not hesitate to be their allies, but the conflict was not about this. Instead, it was about Nasser's ambition to subsume Lebanon into Egypt's sphere of influence and exert his control over the country, an outcome the SSNP could not abide.[55]

12.2 The Civil War

The crisis in Lebanon intensified quickly in the early weeks of May. On 9 May, following the murder of an opposition newspaper editor, Jumblatt and other opposition leaders called for a general strike in protest. Over the following days, strikes in Tripoli and Beirut devolved into rioting and violent clashes between security forces and rebels. Jumblatt's militiamen fought government forces in the Shouf, quickly gaining the advantage and establishing control over the area. While fighting also raged in Tripoli, south Lebanon remained relatively

52 *L'Orient*, 11–14 March 1958.
53 *L'Orient*, 15 April 1958.
54 *Sada Lubnan*, 18 March 1958; *L'Orient*, 19 March 1958; and *L'Orient*, 15 April 1958.
55 Fu'ad Awad, *al-Ṭarīq ilā al-Sulṭa* (Beirut: Kadmus Publications, 1973), Chapter 2.

free of conflict.[56] Chamoun scathingly rebuked the opposition for the destructive strikes and attacks even as sporadic clashes, bombings and strikes between the two sides continued, the most intense fighting taking place in Tripoli, Beirut, the Shouf, and the Bekaa near the Syrian border.

The UAR's push to intervene in the crisis it had helped foster through support for the opposition, propaganda attacks, and subterfuge was of great concern to Britain, France, the United States, and Iraq, all of whom were determined to prevent Nasser's influence from expanding into Lebanon. Indeed, US State Department officials were increasingly troubled by reports the UAR provided military assistance to the opposition from Syria and emphasized to the Egyptian leader that the United States would help Lebanon defend its sovereignty and independence. Predictably, Nasser denied the charges and distanced himself and the UAR from Lebanon's situation, claiming he had always respected Lebanon's sovereignty.[57] The UAR's interference in Lebanon was not, however, the only concern of Western powers. While France, Britain, and the United States sought to ensure Lebanon's sovereignty and independence were overseen by "a strong and pro-Western President," they began to question the wisdom of backing Chamoun for a second term. A growing sense among the three powers that Chamoun was perhaps more of an obstacle to solving the Lebanese crisis than a help led them to explore possible alternatives, ultimately focusing their attention on General Fuad Chehab.[58] The British, French, and American Ambassadors separately broached the subject with Chamoun, who, after considering the "Chehab formula," accepted the idea in principle.[59]

---

56 TNA, FO 371/134118/VL1015/97, No. 548, Beirut to FO, 19 May 1958; TNA, FO 371/134118/VL1015/107, No. 554, Beirut to FO, 19 May 1958; and TNA, FO 371/134118/VL1015/107, No. 555, Beirut to FO, 20 May 1958.

57 *FRUS*, 1958–1960, Volume XI, Lebanon and Jordan, Document 39; *FRUS*, 1958–1960, Volume XI, Lebanon and Jordan, Document 44; TNA, FO 371/134118/VL1015/103, No. 539, Beirut to FO, 19 May 1958; TNA, FO 371/134118/VL1015/100, No. 1175, Washington to FO, 17 May 1958; TNA, FO 371/134118/VL1015/119, No. 1244, Washington to FO, 21 May 1958; and TNA, FO 371/134118/VL1015/119, No. 579, Beirut to FO, 22 May 1958. Notably, Egyptian propaganda on its Voice of the Arabs radio station and its leading dailies would continue to attack Chamoun, urging his removal, even by assassination if necessary. Attié, *Struggle in the Levant*, p. 103.

58 TNA, FO 371/134118/VL1015/102, No. 1191, Washington to FO, 17 May 1958; TNA, FO 371/134118/VL1015/98, No. 829, Baghdad to FO, 18 May 1958; TNA, FO 371/134118/VL1015/98, No. 1200, Washington to FO, 19 May 1958; *FRUS*, 1958–1960, Volume XI, Lebanon and Jordan, Document 41; *FRUS*, 1958–1960, Volume XI, Lebanon and Jordan, Document 42; and *FRUS*, 1958–1960, Volume XI, Lebanon and Jordan, Document 43.

59 TNA, FO 371/134118/VL1015/119, No. 565, Beirut to FO, 21 May 1958, and *FRUS*, 1958–1960, Volume XI, Lebanon and Jordan, Document 43.

SSNP leaders who had initially supported the idea of Chamoun seeking a second term now expressed their concern and reservations. In response, Ashqar established a special committee to discuss and formulate policy recommendations regarding the party's approach. The committee submitted a memorandum to Ashqar in which it stated that, in its struggle, the party must remain faithful to its basic principles to ensure Lebanon is not divided along sectarian lines. Furthermore, it encouraged the party: (1) not to play a divisive role; (2) to ask Chamoun to state that he did not seek to renew his term, was dissolving the parliament and planned to amend the constitution; (3) elect a new caretaker parliament comprised of cultured and learned men; and (4) state that disputes between Muslims and Christians be resolved through dialogue and understanding, not through foreign interference. A joint meeting of the party's Higher Council and Council of Deputies was scheduled to discuss the memorandum, but Ashqar rejected its recommendations out of hand because the party could not make such demands to Chamoun. No meeting was held.[60]

In late May, two SSNP members were killed in clashes with rebels in the village of Adbil in North Lebanon's Akkar district.[61] SSNP fighters had succeeded in repelling the rebels' attack without Lebanese security forces' assistance, which merely watched the confrontation unfold.[62] As party members fought in North Lebanon, Ashqar issued a statement denouncing foreign – communist and UAR – interference in Lebanon and reiterated the SSNP's support for the government. In an interview with the *New York Times*, he also noted that the party had 2,000 men-at-arms who helped the government defend Lebanon's sovereignty.[63] The party also augmented its voice in the public sphere. It began publishing its official periodical *al-Bina'* beginning on 16 May, providing it with an additional media outlet to the hitherto unofficial *Sada Lubnan* to disperse its propaganda, news, and official statements to the public at large. The editors of the new publication were the poet Adonis and Muhammad Ba'albaki.[64] Unlike *Sada Lubnan*, *al-Bina'* included much more party-driven content concerning political and cul-

---

60 Ahmad, *SSNP*, pp. 173–174.

61 *Al-Bina'*, 25 May 1958, as cited in Ahmad, *SSNP*, p. 172.

62 Beshara, *Lebanon*, p. 43.

63 *The New York Times*, 30 May 1958.

64 Al-'Aql, *Mawsū'at, Vol. 5*, pp. 363–365. Adonis is the pen name of Ali Ahmad Said Esber, an 'Alawi poet and writer from Al Qassabin in Syria's Latakia Governorate. A philosophy graduate of the Syrian University, he joined the SSNP in the early 1950s, contributing articles to the party's periodicals that were published in Damascus, and arrested with other party members in the aftermath of the Malki assassination in 1955. In 1956, Adonis moved with his wife to Beirut and the following magazine, he co-founded the poetry magazine *Shi'r* with former SSNP member Yusuf al-Khal. He, too, would distance himself from the party ultimately.

tural thought. Indeed, a significant section of the paper promoted culture and the nation's cultural revival, including publishing the poems of leading poets of the emerging Arabic Modernist movement, such as party members Kamal Kheir Bek, Adonis, and Muhammad Maghut.[65]

The revolt against Chamoun's government continued into June, and Chamoun increasingly sought the intervention of the United States and Great Britain. In the press, the SSNP and the Kata'ib continued to support Chamoun's government outspokenly, condemning the UAR's actions in Lebanon and its propaganda campaign against the country in the pages of *al-Bina'*, *Sada Lubnan*, and *al-Amal.*[66] At the beginning of June, Lebanon filed official complaints with the Arab League and the UN Security Council against the UAR for interfering in its internal affairs. However, the appeals failed to alter the status quo as the UAR continued to wage an intense propaganda campaign against Lebanon's government and maintained its support for rebel factions. The SSNP strongly condemned the inaction of the UN and Arab League in the face of the UAR's aggression. In *al-Bina'*, the SSNP criticized the Arab League, characterizing it as a bankrupt and laughable institution that had essentially accepted the legitimacy of Nasser's subversive activities in Lebanon. At the same time, editorials in *Sada Lubnan* and *al-Bina'* suggested Lebanon conclude a defense pact with the Arab Federation.[67] Throughout June, both periodicals would continue to attack the UAR and hold it responsible for the ills gripping Lebanon.[68] Meanwhile, on the domestic front, *Sada Lubnan* attacked the opposition, accusing it of having transformed into an insurrectionist movement and lacking sincerity in its intentions as it had not ended the strikes that, contrary to what it claimed, had not been peaceful.[69] The paper also criticized Sunni leaders for fomenting confessionalism and several Sunni 'ulema for interfering in Lebanon's political affairs, urging them to limit their activity to their religious duties.[70]

On the military front, Lebanese security forces and rebels remained engaged in sporadic combat with intense fighting predominately around Tripoli, the Shouf, Beirut, and Baalbek. Local SSNP directors urged the party's defense com-

---

65 Al-ʿAql, *Mawsūʿat, Vol. 5*, pp. 365–366. On Arabic Modernism in Beirut and the relationship of some of movement's leading poets to the SSNP, see Robyn Creswell, *City of Beginnings: Poetic Modernism in Beirut* (Princeton: Princeton University Press, 2019), pp. 52–93.

66 *L'Orient*, 1 June 1958.

67 *L'Orient*, 8–12 June 1958.

68 For the SSNP press campaign against the UAR, which occurred in tandem with that of the Kata'ib's, see *L'Orient*, 20–26 June 1958.

69 *L'Orient*, 4 June 1958.

70 *L'Orient*, 14–15 June 1958.

missioner Fadlallah Abu Mansur to arrange training exercises in light weaponry, indirect fire, explosives, and urban combat tactics at one of the party's training camps in Dhour El Choueir. At the time, the party also had at least three other training camps in Lebanon in Dik El Mehdi, Shemlan, and Koura. An estimated 300 SSNP fighters were based in Dik El Mehdi, supported by another 150 fighters from the northern Bekaa and Nabi Osman. Another 300 SSNP fighters were evenly divided between Shemlan and Koura.[71] At the end of June, SSNP forces entrenched in Suq al-Gharb and Shemlan, where they, together with Lebanese gendarmerie, fought and skirmished with Druze forces loyal to Jumblatt, beating back an assault on Shemlan after three days of fighting.[72] Shemlan was of great strategic significance to both the government and opposition, owing to its geographic location overlooking Beirut's international airport, whose seizure was the likely intent of Jumblatt's offensive. Fighting in the Shouf continued for several more days before the government established its complete control over the areas south of Aley, its forces inflicting severe casualties on Jumblatt's forces.[73] The fierce fighting between the SSNP and PSP would remain an open, festering wound affecting relations between the two movements for several years despite reconciliation efforts.[74]

As fighting in the Shouf wound down, the United Nations Observer Group in Lebanon (UNOGIL) published a report on its investigation into the UAR's interference in Lebanon. Much to the SSNP's discontent, the report concluded it could not substantiate claims or produce conclusive evidence of any significant infiltration or arms smuggling to the opposition by the UAR. The observers admitted that they lacked access to opposition-held areas to investigate and verify claims, but this did not prevent the SSNP and Lebanese government from fiercely attacking the report. In late June, the SSNP submitted a memorandum to the UN detailing the UAR's interference in the country, stating its firm opposition to any foreign intervention in Lebanon, which it claimed had been ignored, as evidenced by the report's flaws and failure to censure the UAR for its crimes.[75] Sev-

---

71 "Taqrīr Raqm (1)," in Asfahani, *Anṭūn Saʿādah*, pp. 145–147.

72 "Juzʾ min Taqrīr bi-Tārīkh 30/6/1958," in Asfahani, *Anṭūn Saʿādah*, p. 145; TNA, FO 371/134127/VL1015/415(a), No. 879, Beirut to FO, 30 June 1958; TNA, FO 371/134127/VL1015/415(b), No. 885, Beirut to FO, 1 July 1958; TNA, FO 371/134127/VL1015/415(c), No. 893, Beirut to FO, 2 July 1958; *L'Orient*, 1–3 July 1958; and *Sada Lubnan*, 1 July 1958.

73 TNA, FO 371/134127/VL1015/415(e), No. 913, Beirut to FO, 4 July 1958; TNA, FO 371/134127/VL1015/415(f), No. 926, Beirut to FO, 5 July 1958; and TNA, FO 371/134127/VL1015/415(h), No. 938, Beirut to FO, 7 July 1958.

74 Raʿad, *al-Kalimāt al-Akhīra*, p. 87.

75 *Sada Lubnan*, 27 June 1958, and *L'Orient*, 10 July 1958.

eral weeks later, the SSNP strongly condemned the arrival of US forces in Lebanon. In an official statement published in *Sada Lubnan* and *al-Bina'*, the SSNP denounced the presence of "foreign forces" in Lebanon, explaining that its opposition to the presence of American forces was "the same position" it had taken to stop communist interference in Lebanese affairs and the position it had advocated in its memorandums to the UN. The *bayān* further held both the government and opposition responsible for the foreign military presence and the crisis.[76]

While the Ashqar-led SSNP remained fully engaged in Lebanon's ongoing political and military happenings, ʿAbd al-Masih's group maintained its position of neutrality, refusing to engage.[77] Discussions between the opposition and government were making headway on an agreement to replace Chamoun and nominate Chehab to the presidency. The SSNP, while remaining loyal to the government, also supported the effort to nominate Chehab, the party's Higher Council adopting a resolution to that effect before the 31 July elections in which Chehab was elected president.[78] Indeed, the party welcomed Chehab's election as a positive step towards lifting Lebanon out of the current state of confrontation and division and viewed him as a leader capable of reconciling and rebuilding the country.[79] However, the SSNP's opinion of Chehab quickly changed as Chehab courted former opposition leaders for positions in his new cabinet, something the party vehemently opposed.

12.3 An Unwelcome Change

Though the SSNP and Chehab shared a vision of a modernized Lebanon in which the traditional elite's power was broken, and socio-economic reforms were implemented to alleviate existing inequalities, Chehab's courting of former rebels and opposition figures to his new government set the two sides at odds. In early September, Chehab was absorbed in discussions with both the former supporters and opponents of Chamoun's government to form a new cabinet but struggled to make progress. Chehab sought to make Karameh, who had led the opposition to Chamoun in Tripoli, his prime minister, a decision that was the source of dismay among loyalists like the SSNP and Christians who strongly protested the appointment of a person who had led the fight against the government

76 *Sada Lubnan*, 17 July 1958, and *L'Orient*, 18 July 1958.
77 "Taqrīr Raqm 3," in Asfahani, *Anṭūn Saʿādah*, 151.
78 Beshara, *Lebanon*, p. 49.
79 Beshara, *Lebanon*, pp. 45, 48–49.

to the position of prime minister.[80] Chamoun, hoping to organize loyalists – his former allies – into a robust and united opposition front to the new Chehab-Karameh government, had established a new political party under his leadership called the Liberal Patriotic Party (*Parti des Patriotes Libres*). Ashqar was among the twenty-two deputies who supported Chamoun's new party, all of whom "demanded that those responsible for the crisis – i.e., opposition leaders – be brought to trial on charges of subversion."[81] Further, the party "declared that it would refuse to cooperate with any future government [that] included any opposition leader."[82] In return for Ashqar's support, the Lebanese interior ministry, acting on Chamoun's directive on the eve of Chehab's ascent to power, legalized the SSNP on the grounds that the party and its reform principles aimed to preserve the country's independence.[83]

Amid the last-minute political maneuvering, conflicts between loyalists and oppositionists continued. In Beirut, unknown assailants thought to be intelligence officers with Syria's Deuxième Bureau kidnapped a prominent Christian journalist, which prompted retaliatory kidnappings and attacks on Muslims and others accused of having a hand in the journalist's disappearance by the Kata'ib.[84] The kidnappings further strained communal tensions between Christians and Muslims. Outside Beirut, armed confrontations between the SSNP and Jumblatt's PSP were still taking place, particularly near Shemlan. A sizeable contingent of SSNP fighters maintained the party's control over the strategic village, ostensibly defending the town and local SSNP members from Jumblatt's militiamen in the surrounding Druze villages.[85] In Beirut, a group of SSNP and Kata'ib fighters skirmished with Armenian militiamen, resulting in one SSNP fighter's death.[86]

---

80 TNA, FO 371/134134/VL1015/613, No. 1358, Beirut to FO, 18 September 1958, and TNA, FO 371/134134/VL1015/622, 1011/241/58, Beirut Chancery to Levant Department, 18 September 1958.

81 TNA, FO371/134135/VL1016/2, Beirut Chancery to Levant Department, 11 September 1958; *L'Orient*, 5 September 1958; and Beshara, *Lebanon*, p. 52.

82 Beshara, *Lebanon*, p. 52.

83 TNA, FO371/134135/VL1016/3, BBC Monitor, "Approval of the foundation of the Socialist Nationalist Party," 17 September 1958, and TNA, FO371/134135/VL1016/4, 1677/3/58, Chancery Beirut to Levant Department, "Parti Populaire Syrien," 10 October 1958.

84 TNA, FO 371/134134/VL1015/615, No. 1370, Beirut to FO, 20 September 1958; TNA, FO371/134134/VL1015/616, No. 1372, Beirut to FO, 21 September 1958; and TNA, FO371/134134/VL1015/618, No. 1375, Beirut to FO, 22 September 1958.

85 TNA, FO 371/134134/VL1015/619, No. 1367, Beirut to FO, 20 September 1958, and TNA, FO371/134134/VL1015/625, No. 1384, Beirut to FO, 24 September 1958

86 TNA, FO 371/134134/VL1015/624, No. 1383, Beirut to FO, 24 September 1958.

Chehab declared a new Cabinet on 25 September, two days after he was sworn in as Lebanon's new president; the SSNP was left on the outside looking in. The SSNP, frustrated by its failure to thwart Karameh's establishment of a new government and the emerging role of former opposition figures in the evolving post-crisis order, voiced its discontent in a pamphlet it disturbed throughout the country. In a nine-point declaration, the party reiterated its opposition to communism and rejection of sectarianism and religious interference in political affairs while also dedicating itself to promoting social unity, economic advancement, and independence from local and international intervention.[87] The restatement of the party's basic reform principles met with little objection among its allies in Chamoun's camp and was even advanced in the pro-Chamoun newspaper *Le Soir.*[88]

However, without its partner Chamoun in power, and lacking meaningful representation in the army and the emerging post-crisis political order under Chehab, the SSNP's political position had been weakened, despite its contributions to preserving the Lebanese state and reported following of 25,000.[89] By the beginning of 1959, the Chehab's government had already begun pressuring the party, threatening to prosecute SSNP members for any role they played in armed skirmishes that erupted in Irsal in December 1958 and expelling twenty-eight SSNP members from Lebanon in February 1959.[90] Despite its best efforts, the party's political influence would continue to diminish as the party could not regain what it had lost with Chehab's election and the former opposition's empowerment. This decline fueled a sense of frustration and discontent within the party that would contribute to imprudent decision-making and lead the party into another disastrous fiasco in the early 1960s when it would attempt to overthrow Chehab's government by force.

---

87 TNA, FO 371/134134/VL1015/653, 1011/309/58, Chancery Beirut to Levant Department, 24 October 1958.
88 TNA, FO 371/134134/VL1015/653, 1011/309/58, Chancery Beirut to Levant Department, 24 October 1958.
89 Toufic Mokdessi and Lucien George, *Les Partis Libanais en 1959* (Beirut: Editions l'Orient al-Jarida, 1959), p. 69.
90 Beshara, *Lebanon*, p. 52.

Figure 10: Portrait of Antun Saʿadeh (*Sada Lubnan*, 9 July 1959 – Courtesy of The Arabic Press Archive, Moshe Dayan Center, Tel Aviv University)

13 Epilogue: The Rise of Factionalism

The publication of Shehadeh al-Ghawi's 2019 book *Tārīkh Istishhād Saʿādah wa-mā Baʿdah* provoked a hostile reaction. The hostility was expected given the book's controversial content, which copiously documented and aired the party's dirty laundry in public, leveling accusations against former party figures for aiding in Saʿadeh's downfall and leading the party away from his teachings. Indeed, there was even talk in the party about suppressing its publication. However, the controversy that it stirred was even more dramatic given its appearance at a moment when the party found itself – and continues to find itself – mired in a deep internal crisis, factionalized and divided into three separate organizations bearing the same name and internal opposition movements.

More than six decades have passed since the 1957 schism divided the SSNP into two organizations – the larger Beirut-based *Markaz* faction and the smaller Damascus-based *Intifada* faction. The two have remained at odds ever since despite unification efforts, divided over questions of ideology and how the party should engage in politics in the countries in which it operates. Indeed, while the *Markaz* faction has adopted a more pragmatic and accommodationist approach to political engagement and ideology, the *Intifada* faction has taken a more rigid approach, eschewing political arrangements that would compromise its firm commitment to ideological purity. Moreover, while the *Markaz* faction has been beset by internal divisions, infighting, and rebellion, the *Intifada* faction has remained a cohesive organization. The most significant recent division in the *Markaz* occurred in 2012 when the party's Damascus-based leadership established a separate organization, known as *al-Amāna* (the Trusteeship or the SSNP in the Syrian Arab Republic) without consulting with the Beirut-based leadership. Three years later, the *Markaz* faction was embroiled in another crisis over a constitutional dispute provoked by the party president's effort to extend his term in office by forcing through a constitutional amendment that would enable him to do so. In response, a new reform trend announced itself within the *Markaz* known as the July 8th Movement (*Ḥarakat al-Thāmin min Tammūz*).[1] Several years later, some July 8th movement members would formally organize an opposition faction with its own institutions known as the Syrian Nationalist Renaissance Movement (*Ḥarakat al-Nahḍa al-Sūriyya al-Qawmiyya*).[2]

Divided among competing organizations and internal opposition movements, one party intellectual, ʿAli Himaya, issued a stark warning in May

---

1 *Al-Nahar*, 9 July 2016 and 5 August 2018, and *al-Akhbar*, 11 July 2016.
2 *Al-Akhbar*, 19 February 2019.

https://doi.org/10.1515/9783110729092-015

2020, declaring that the party stood "on the brink of the abyss." For him, the situation is dire, with members abandoning the party, the party failing to attract new members, particularly among the youth, and its aging membership, with most party members over the age of forty, and pleaded for unity to reverse the party's direction and reinvigorate its ranks.[3] However, at the time of this writing, Himaya's warning has been ignored and gone unheeded as the SSNP finds itself mired in internal conflict and crisis. How did the party arrive here?

13.1 From Failed Coup to Civil War in Lebanon

The party's frustration[4] with its diminished position following the 1958 conflict would only grow throughout the years of Fuad Chehab's rule. Despite the declaration that there would be "no victor and no vanquished" (*la ghalib wa la maghlūb*), the SSNP found itself outside looking in as its Arab and Lebanese nationalist opponents, as well as the Lebanese Army, extended their influence over Lebanon's political scene. The SSNP's opposition to Chehab's government grew only more hostile and belligerent following the party's failure in the 1960 parliamentarian elections and ʿAbdallah Saʿadeh's election as the party's new president.[5] By the end of 1961, the SSNP, succumbing to its dissatisfaction with the status quo and its more militant tendencies, decided to overthrow the Chehab government with a cadre of army officers.[6] The failure to garner more support from the army, tactical ineptitude, the lack of strategic planning, and the ineffectiveness of the party's militia and participating army units doomed the coup from its earliest hours, and Lebanese security forces quickly defeated it. By 3 January, nearly two thousand party members and rebel soldiers had been arrested, and the SSNP was officially dissolved by the executive order of the Lebanese government.[7]

Despite the government's successful decimation of the party and its political prospects in Lebanon, the SSNP was not eliminated. For two years, the party

3 *Al-Akhbar*, 14, 28 May 2020.

4 The idea of the SSNP as a "frustrated" movement is inspired by Beshara's *Lebanon: The Politics of Frustration.*

5 Saʿadeh, *Awrāq Qawmiyya*, p. 71, and Raʿad, *al-Kalimāt al-Akhīra*, pp. 101–105.

6 For works, including memoirs, on the failed 1961 coup, see Awad, *al-Ṭarīq ila al-Sulṭa*; Saʿadah, *Awrāq Qawmiyya*, pp. 93–152; Beshara, *Lebanon*; Raʿad, *al-Kalimāt al-Akhīra*, pp. 103–125; ʿAbdallah Qubrusi, *ʿAbd Allah Qubruṣī Yatadhakkar, Vol. 5* (Beirut: Dār wa Maktabat al-Turāth al-Adabī, 2019); and, Ghassan al-Khalidi, *al-Ḥizb al-Qawmī wa-l-Thawra al-Thāniyya, Vol. 1.*

7 *Al-Ayaam*, 2–3 January 1962.

waged a dedicated and public legal battle with the Lebanese government during the military tribunals that followed the failed coup. As in the times of the French mandate, party members who had avoided imprisonment began operating in secret, guided by former party president ʿAbdullah Muhsin, focused on attempting to reconstitute the party, campaigning for the release of their imprisoned comrades, and protesting the Lebanese justice system's corruption.[8] By 1969, the party had resumed its activities after its leaders were released from prison, and the following year, the SSNP was legalized by then-interior minister Kamal Jumblatt. The party's reemergence on the Lebanese political scene less than a decade after launching a failed coup was a significant achievement for the SSNP.

The reconstituted party differed significantly from the one that had existed at the start of the decade as it allied itself with the leftist Lebanese Nationalist Movement (LNM), Arab nationalists, and the Palestinian Liberation Organization (PLO), an orientation it formalized at a party conference at Beirut's Melkart Hotel.[9] However, the proceedings of the Melkart conference also brought festering internal disagreements to light over assigning blame for the coup debacle, the party's ideological orientation, amendments to the party's constitution, which would prove to be an ongoing source of contention, and disagreement over the party's alliances with Syria and the PLO.

The outbreak of the Lebanese civil war in 1975 led to further divisions within the party over accepting the patronage of Syria or Libya and whether the party should remain supportive of the PLO, particularly following Syria's direct military intervention in Lebanon in 1976. ʿAbd al-Masih's *Intifada* faction turned a cold shoulder to overtures from Damascus, as did the *Markaz* faction led by Raʿad and ʿAbdallah Saʿadeh, which remained committed to the LNM and PLO, condemned Syria's intervention, and was courted by Libya. However, another *Markaz* faction, known derisively as the *khawarij*, led by ʿIsam al-Mahayri aligned itself with the Syrian regime.[10] By 1978, though, this internal rift within the *Markaz* over the party's alliance with Syria had been resolved. Aligned with Syria, the party's militia received financial and military support from the Asad regime and advanced Syria's objectives in Lebanon.

---

8 Beshara, *Lebanon*, p. 157, and Asfahani and Rizkallah, *Jūzif Rizq Allāh*, p. 414.
9 Zisser, "The Syrian Phoenix," p. 199; Raʿad, *al-Kalimāt al-Akhīra*, pp. 162–163; and Saʿadeh, *Awrāq Qawmiyya*, pp. 219–229.
10 Rabinovich, *The War for Lebanon*, p. 82. On the SSNP-*Markaz*'s relationship with Syria and Libya at the time see Raʿad, *al-Kalimāt al-Akhīra*, pp. 196–198, 203–206, and Saʿadeh, *Awrāq Qawmiyya*, pp. 301–310.

From the outset, the SSNP's militia had been a small, but involved, fighting force in the conflict. With Israel's invasion in 1982, the party's prominence was significantly enhanced with its participation in the Lebanese National Resistance Front (LNRF, *Jabhat al-Muqāwama al-Waṭaniyya al-Lubnāniyya*, or Jammoul) as it played an essential role in targeting the Israel Defense Forces and Israel's Lebanese allies, including the Lebanese Forces (LF) and South Lebanon Army (SLA).[11] Until 1987, the SSNP, together with its armed partners in Jammoul, participated in battles – including the famous War of the Mountain (*Ḥarb al-Jabal*) – and conducted dozens of guerilla operations, including suicide attacks, several by female bombers. Perhaps even more infamous than the party's use of suicide attacks was its assassination of Kataʾib leader Bachir Gemayel in September 1982 just weeks after being elected Lebanon's president.[12] The consequences and impact of the assassination, allegedly carried out at the behest of Syrian intelligence, still profoundly resonate to this day.

Israel's withdrawal to southern Lebanon in late 1985 opened the door for Syria's return to Lebanon in force and enabled Damascus to reassert its influence that had eroded over time. For the party, Syria's renewed presence in the country would exacerbate internal tensions as the SSNP-*Markaz* found itself divided once again over constitutional matters over the separation of powers within the party and questions over how the party should balance its support for the PLO with its relations with Damascus. Ultimately, the two factions split at the end of 1987: Mahayri led the more pro-Syrian "Emergency Faction" (*Lajnat al-Tawāriʾ*) while Raʿad led the "Higher Council Faction" (*Majlis al-Aʿlā*).[13] The tensions between the two factions were far from benign: two pro-Syrian SSNP leaders, Mohammed Salim and Habib Kayrouz, were assassinated in 1985 and 1987, respectively, for their pro-Syrian views, while later on, the division would occasionally manifest itself in violent brawls.[14] This split would last until 1998 when the factions united.[15]

---

11 Pipes, *Greater Syria*, pp. 125–126.

12 *New York Times*, 15 September 1982. Habib Shartouni was the SSNP member who conducted the attack. He was sentenced to death in Lebanon in 2017. *Al-Nahar*, 20 October 2017. See also Ghassan al-Khalidi, *Baṭal min Umatī Ḥabīb al-Shartūnī* (Beirut: Dār wa Maktabat al-Turāth al-Adabī Lubnān, 2020).

13 Saʿadeh, *Awrāq Qawmiyya*, pp. 337–345; Shawqi Khayrallah, *Mudhakkirāt Shawqī Khayr Allah, Vol. 2, 1971–1997* (Beirut: al-Markaz al-ʿIlmī li-l-Nashr wa-l-Tawziʿ, 1998), pp. 174–189; and Walid Zaytuni, *al-Thābit wa-l-Mutaghayyir fī Masār al-Ḥizb al-Qawmi* (Beirut: Dār wa Maktabat al-Turāth al-Adabī, 1988), pp. 42–43.

14 *Daily Star*, 13 July 1998.

15 *Daily Star*, 23 October 1998, and 5 November 1998.

Following the end of the war, Syria, together with its allies – including the SSNP – worked to assert and expand its influence, mainly through the Taif Accord's implementation. The SSNP did not hesitate to join the fray and vie for influence in Lebanon's emerging political order. The party participated in municipal and parliamentary elections and openly engaged with other parties, asserting its "belonging" as a legitimate part of a political establishment that had often tried to ostracize it. The party's success in this area essentially transformed it, over time, into an establishment party. The SSNP also navigated the new post-war reality, charting a path to deepen relations with Syria, support resistance to Israel's ongoing presence in south Lebanon, which entailed close cooperation with the Shiʿi Amal and Hezbollah movements and advance its secular reform agenda.

The SSNP's most significant electoral success in Lebanon would come in the 1992 parliamentary elections when Mahayri's faction secured six seats in the Lebanese parliament. Over the next two decades, its parliamentary presence would diminish, as it proved unable to sustain and build upon its initial success, securing only between two and three seats in general elections held since 2005. However, the SSNP's parliamentary delegations would play a pivotal role in promoting the party's secular and anti-sectarian legislative agenda that would define its political platform until now. This agenda pushed for the implementation of civil laws, including legalizing civil marriages and electoral reforms.[16] The first time the party proposed legalizing civil unions, it was supported by Lebanese president Elias Hrawi and several other parties. However, the proposed legislation provoked a backlash among Lebanon's religious establishments, which argued such legislation advanced "atheism," and the tensions were so severe that Syria was required to step in and mediate a solution.[17] The party also promoted electoral reform, proposing, as it had in the past, that Lebanon become a single electoral district with no seats set aside based on sect to break the influence of geography and sectarianism on the electoral process.[18]

Beyond articulating and emphasizing its anti-sectarian positions, the SSNP also promoted its role as a defender of Lebanon and its independence, pushing several interconnected narratives to bolster its identity as part of the "resistance." The party worked to publicly commemorate the sacrifices its members had made on behalf of the country, including commemorating Saʿid Fakhr al-Din's bravery in confronting the French mandate.[19] In addition to highlighting

16 *Daily Star*, 23 March 2000.
17 *Daily Star* 29 December 1997, 13 February 1998, and 27 March 1998.
18 *Daily Star*, 19 March 1999.
19 *Daily Star*, 22 November 1997.

"the martyr of independence," the SSNP also drew attention to its "martyrs" of the civil war to emphasize its contributions to resisting Israel's presence in the country in the 1980s and its continued dedication to removing Israel from south Lebanon [20] With Israel's withdrawal from Lebanon in 2000, the party joined Hezbollah and Amal in taking credit for defeating Israel and forcing it to retreat.

13.2 Divided They Stand: The SSNP's March to Irrelevance in Lebanon

Hezbollah, its allies, and Syria emerged as the dominant political forces in Lebanon following Israel's withdrawal from the south of the country in May 2000. In parliamentary elections held at the end of August, Hezbollah and Amal each secured ten seats, while the SSNP secured four. Seeking to build upon broader political developments and concluded its transitionary reunification period, the SSNP-*Markaz* selected Gibran Araiji to succeed Ali Qanso as party president, capitalizing on Araiji's broad-based internal and external support and hopes that he could facilitate the party's legalization in Syria.[21] Over the next several years, the SSNP worked to secure support for Syria in Lebanon, promoting Syrian-Lebanese economic cooperation and justifying Syria's continued de-facto control of the country through its pervasive military and intelligence presence.

The assassination of Lebanese president Rafiq al-Hariri in 2005 shook Lebanon to its core and divided the country as many Lebanese, with the support of the international community, demanded an end to Syria's presence in the country and that Hezbollah relinquish its weapons, which it had retained in the wake of Israel's withdrawal under the justification that they were "the weapons of the resistance."[22] The country was divided into two political camps, March 8 and March 14, named after the Hezbollah-led pro-Syrian demonstration and the Christian and Sunni-led anti-Syrian counterdemonstration on those respective dates. Though Syria was formally forced to evacuate Lebanon and anti-Syrian forces appeared on the rise, Hezbollah, supported by the SSNP, Amal, and others, remained a powerful and formidable force.

20 On the party's anti-sectarianism and its promotion of "resistance" in the 1990s, see, for example, Tawfiq Muhanna, *La-Yabqā al-Hilāl al-Sūrī... Khasīban* (Beirut: al-Furāt, 2017), pp. 65 – 100.

21 *The Daily Star*, 6 January 2000.

22 Mordechai Nisan, *Politics and War in Lebanon: Unraveling the Enigma* (London: Transaction Publishers, 2015), pp. 180 – 187.

Post-Hariri Lebanon entered a period of sustained instability, witnessing several political assassinations and violent clashes, several in which the SSNP was involved.[23] Closely aligned with the Hezbollah-led March 8 coalition and with Syria, the SSNP was derided by opponents as a puppet and "tool" of Syrian intelligence, particularly SSNP minister of parliament Assad Hardan. In late 2006, Hardan was accused of ordering an SSNP member to bomb a Kata'ib party gathering in Koura, a charge the party denied and attempted to deflect by shifting the conversation to sectarianism and the nature of Lebanon's national identity, indirectly attacking the Kata'ib as "sectarian force."[24] Two years later, the SSNP would be involved in at least two violent clashes with Lebanese Forces and Future Movement forces. The SSNP-LF clashes took place in the village of Dedde in Koura, and six individuals were wounded in the violent brawl, five of which were SSNP supporters who had been shot; the LF blamed the SSNP for trying to provoke an incident, while the SSNP stated the LF had started it by insulting a party member.[25] A far more lethal clash occurred just months later in May in Halba following clashes in Beirut in which the SSNP joined Hezbollah and Amal fighters in attacking March 14 forces. In Halba, 11 SSNP members were killed and their bodies mutilated by Future Movement forces in what was considered retribution for the party's participation in the Hezbollah offensive in Beirut.[26]

Internally, the party's leadership was coming under increasing scrutiny for the party's poor political performance and declining influence as a member of the Hezbollah-led opposition with only two parliament members. The pressure the party faced was a byproduct of the pressure being placed on Hezbollah to give up its weapons and the party's alliance with Hezbollah and Syria. Nevertheless, the party praised itself for remaining steadfast in the face of the challenges confronting it and vowed to keep pressing its agenda; however, little changed after parliamentary elections in 2009 as the party failed once again to increase its parliamentary presence.[27] Further complicating matters were rising tensions

---

23 Among others, for example: June 2008 clashes between the SSNP and PSP in Aley (*Daily Star*, 10 June 2008); SSNP members assaulted a reporter affiliated with the March 14 coalition in December 2008 (*Daily Star*, 4 December 2008); and a July 2009 gun battle between SSNP and Future Movement supporters in the Bekaa (*Daily Star*, 17 July 2009).

24 *Al-Akhbar*, 25 December 2006.

25 *Daily Star*, 25 February 2008.

26 *Daily Star*, 10 – 11 May 2008; Nisan, *Politics and War in Lebanon*, pp. 194 – 197; and Nir Rosen, *Aftermath: Following the Bloodshed of America's Wars in the Muslim World* (New York: Nation Books, 2010), pp. 406 – 412.

27 *Al-Akhbar*, 6 May 2008.

within the party's leadership bodies between supporters of party president Asaad Hardan and his opponents. These tensions would come to define the next decade of the party's existence, reaching its nadir at the time of this writing.

The outbreak of civil war in Syria presented yet another formidable challenge to the SSNP-*Markaz*. The *Markaz* and *Intifada* leaderships backed the Asad regime, deeming the uprisings to be nothing more than Zionist and Western imperialist plots to destroy Syria.[28] Viewed in such terms, the new struggle for Syria was nothing less than an existential battle for the SSNP on behalf of the nation. The *Markaz* faction offered its vocal support to the regime in the early months of the crisis. However, Asad managed to deliver – intentionally or unintentionally – a crushing blow to the *Markaz*'s unity, instituting a constitutional reform that prompted the party to split into the *Markaz* and *Amana* factions.

While the *Markaz* and *Amana* remained at odds over the coming years, the *Markaz* and *Intifada* factions examined reunification. Periodically, rumors would surface that the two factions were considering taking steps toward unification or looking for ways to bridge the gap that had grown between them since 1957. Seemingly the most serious discussion of unity occurred in June 2016. At that time, Hardan and Haidar jointly announced "their readiness for unity" and declared their intention to form committees to work out the practicalities of uniting the two organizations that had been divided for almost sixty years.[29] But the reconciliation efforts, mediated by Syria's ambassador to Lebanon, faltered and became virtually impossible as the *Markaz* faction occupied itself with internal squabbling.[30]

The *Markaz*'s infighting took place against a backdrop of political gridlock. Lebanon had been without a president since 2014, parliamentary elections had been postponed, and the country's economy faltered, weakened by the state of political affairs and the effects of the Syrian Civil War, including absorbing over 1.5 million Syrian refugees. The dismal situation in Lebanon did little to encourage the party to right its ship. Once again, the party found itself embroiled in a constitutional and leadership crisis owing to deep divisions between Hardan's supporters and his opponents that has yet to end. The event that precipitated it was Hardan's reelection as the party's president for a third term despite, and in

---

28 As will be discussed later, younger members in the party, particularly those in Syria, were less enthusiastic about supporting the regime and some openly supported the opposition. *Al-Akhbar*, 27 July 2011.

29 *Al-Akhbar*, 8 June 2016. Similar discussions about unifying the *Markaz* and *Intifada* factions were broached in 2010. See *al-Akhbar*, 16 November 2010.

30 *Al-Akhbar*, 11 June 2016 and 2 June 2017.

contravention of, party regulations limiting him to two terms. After his reelection, Hardan attempted to force through a constitutional amendment to legalize his new term, which was accepted by the party's Higher Council. However, the party's legal tribunal overturned the amendment, a decision Hardan accepted, but the damage had already been done and would only worsen over the next four years.[31]

Hardan succeeded in getting his ally and previous party president, Ali Qanso, elected to replace him, perpetuating the crisis. That ballot was just as contentious with several members of the Higher Council boycotting the election and the July 8th Movement deriding Qanso as nothing more than "Hardan's puppet."[32] Qanso's term ended in late 2017, and he was replaced by Hanna al-Nashif, a long-time party official who had served in numerous leadership positions within the party and was sympathetic to the reformist agenda of the July 8th movement. Nashif, however, struggled to advance his agenda for the party, due in no small part to Hardan and his obstructionist efforts as head of the party's Higher Council. By the summer of 2019, Hardan had secured enough support among Higher Council members to force Nashif out of the presidency. Hardan and his supporters blamed the party's crisis and internal division on Nashif and demanded he resign or be dismissed by the Council. Nashif refused to be held responsible for the internal issues that had divided the party for more than a decade and, to retain his dignity, submitted his resignation more than a year before his term was to finish, which the Higher Council accepted.[33]

Nashif was replaced by Faris Saʿad on 7 July 2019, making him the fourth party president in just three years. His selection, too, did not pass without controversy, as six of the seventeen members of the Higher Council boycotted the vote, and Saʿad only received nine votes, barely a majority. Saʿad would resign his office at the end of February 2020 in protest over unaddressed and unresolved constitutional violations but was essentially pushed out by Hardan and his allies.[34] Waʾil Hasaniyya, a close associate of Hardan, was appointed as Saʿad's temporary replacement, tasked with overseeing the party until elections for the Higher Council and presidency were held in the fall. Under Hasaniyya's stewardship, little progress was made in resolving outstanding internal issues, nor was there any reconciliation between Hardan and his opponents. These sim-

31 *Daily Star*, 23 July 2016. For a detailed examination of the party's internal tribunal and the crisis, see Jihad al-ʿAql, *Azmat al-Maḥkama al-Markaziyya fī al-Ḥizb al-Sūrī al-Qawmī al-Ijtimāʿī* (Beirut, 2019).

32 *Al-Nahar*, 5 August 2016.

33 *Al-Akhbar*, 20 June 2019 and 6 July 2019.

34 *Al-Akhbar*, 26–27 February 2020.

mering tensions and divisions boiled over in September as the elections laid bare the bitter struggle over the party's future direction and the internal power struggle. A new generation of younger leaders supported by prominent party members succeeded in replacing an older generation of leaders aligned with Hardan. These new leaders seek to chart a new course for the party by implementing internal reforms, promoting internal reconciliation, and returning to its principles.[35]

Unsurprisingly, Hardan refused to accept the election results, which significantly diminished his power, and took the unprecedented step of filing two lawsuits with the Lebanese courts to prevent the party from swearing in a new Higher Council and electing a new president.[36] The move sent shockwaves through the party, but, undeterred and having rejected the efforts of the Syrian ambassador in Lebanon to mediate a compromise, the newly-elected Higher Council selected Rabiʿ al-Banat as president.[37] While Banat and the Higher Council struck a conciliatory tone that appealed for party unity, mending internal divisions, and strengthening the party's institutions, the crisis would only deepen as Hardan refused to back down and abandon his fight, insisting that the party's elections, which he had called for, were illegal and their results nullified.[38] The deteriorating situation raised fears that the party was returning "to the era of internal fighting in the eighties," or, even worse, experiencing a calamity like never before.[39] Though the internal struggle between Hardan and his opponents remains unresolved at the time of this writing, it does appear that the SSNP-*Markaz* under Banat's leadership has succeeded in bringing an internal opposition faction, the Syrian Nationalist Renaissance Movement, back into the fold.[40]

13.3 Political Defeat, Ideological Victory: The SSNP in Syria under Hafiz al-Asad

Its activities and political influence decimated by the Baʿth in Syria in the mid-1950s, decades would pass before the SSNP would engage in public political activity in the country. Yet, as Zisser notes, its absence from Syria's political arena "did not end support for its ideology, namely Syrian unity, the Syrian nation as a

35 *Al-Liwaa*, 19 October 2020.
36 *Al-Akhbar*, 10 October 2020.
37 *Al-Nahar*, 15 October 2020.
38 *Al-Akhbar*, 16 October 2020.
39 *Al-Akhbar*, 16 October 2020, and *Nidaʾ al-Watan*, 31 October 2020.
40 *LBCI News*, 1 November 2020, accessed 1 November 2020: https://bit.ly/2TNNcPF.

distinctive historical entity, and the establishment of Greater Syria."[41] Asad's seizure of power in the 'Corrective Revolution' (*al-thawra al-taṣḥīḥiyya*) was a seminal event in Syria's history, as Asad transformed the country from a weak, unstable state into a more politically stable and economically prosperous state capable of effectively projecting regional power under the leadership of a pragmatic, strong, and centralized regime. As part of this transformation, Asad gradually strengthened local nationalism and identity and emphasized Syrian national interests (*waṭaniyya*) over broader pan-Arab identity and interest (*qawmiyya*).

Asad occasionally alluded to Syrian nationalist ideas in public speeches in the early 1970s, for example, referring to Syria and Lebanon's historical and eternal "special relationship" and to Palestine constituting part of southern Syria.[42] It also manifested itself in the cautious rapprochement between the Baʿth and the SSNP, particularly following Syria's direct military intervention in the Lebanese civil war in 1976. At this time, the Syrian regime allowed Lebanese writer and SSNP member Shawqi Khayrallah to publish articles on notions related to Greater Syria in the Baʿth's official daily *al-Thawra*, including promoting the establishment of a federation including Syria, Lebanon, Jordan, and Palestine.[43]

Another, more personal, facet to Asad's Syrian nationalist utterances was his wife, Anisa Makhluf. Anisa hailed from a prominent, established land-owning ʿAlawi family from the village of Bustan al-Basha in Latakia Governorate; the town and the Makhluf family were known for their allegiances to the SSNP and its cause. Several of the Makhlufs were prominent party activists, including Jamil Makhluf and Badiʿ Makhluf, who took part in the assassination of Adnan al-Malki in April 1955.[44] The family's staunch support for the SSNP nearly jeopardized Anisa's betrothal to Hafiz in the 1950s. Her father strongly opposed the marriage of his daughter to a Baʿth party member due to the fierce ideological and political rivalry between the two nationalist movements (the fact that Hafiz hailed from a different, historically rural, ʿAlawi tribe, the al-Kalbiyah, rather than the Makhluf's more affluent al-Haddadin tribe also did not help matters). More than sixty years later, the Makhluf family's ties to the SSNP would become the focus of renewed intrigue. After almost a decade of war, Anisa's nephew, Rami, who had helped revive the SSNP in Syria beginning in the

41 Zisser, "The Syrian Phoenix," p. 202.

42 Moshe Maoz, *Asad: The Sphinx of Damascus* (New York: Weidenfeld & Nicolson, 1988), pp. 114, 124.

43 *Al-Thawra*, 29 August 1976 and 18 January 1977.

44 See Jamil Makhluf, *Maḥaṭṭāt Qawmiyya* (Beirut: al-Rukn li-l-Ṭibāʿa wa-l-Nashr, 2006).

mid-2000s and worked to expand its influence through his financial patronage, openly clashed with his cousin, Anisa's son, Bashar, Syria's ruler.

However, further Baʿthist ideological shifts toward Syrianism would evolve only slowly. Despite any credence Asad gave Greater Syria and the Syrian national idea, it did not translate into the party's rehabilitation and resumption of activity in Syria during his rule. Instead, Asad cultivated the party in Lebanon, considering it a useful ally to advance Syria's aims in Lebanon. Beyond the appearance of Khayrallah's articles in *al-Thawra*, a faction within the SSNP-*Markaz* also took steps to align itself with the Asad regime and soften its ideological views on Arab nationalism, suggesting Syrian unity could serve as the cornerstone of broader Arab unity. Only after the rift within the *Markaz* had been resolved in 1978 did it fully align itself with Damascus and, in a signal of the new era of SSNP relations with the Syrian regime, a party delegation was officially invited to meet with Asad and other Syrian leaders in December 1979 to discuss the situation in Lebanon.[45]

Only towards the end of the 1990s would the SSNP's political activity be slowly revived in Syria, having accepted its political defeat at the hands of the Baʿth while emerging ideologically triumphant as the Baʿth "[adopted] many of the SSNP's ideological precepts" as they related to conceptualizing Syria and the Syrian nation.[46] Indeed, in 2001, prominent regime figure Mustafa Tlass, then serving as defense minister, published a book *Sūriyya al-Tabīʿiyya* (Natural Syria) in which he discussed ideas related to the "concept of the uniqueness and unity of the 'Syrian Nation,'" and its historical existence.[47] The book caused waves owing to its clear echoes of the SSNP's Syrian nationalist ideas, yet it should not have come as a surprise considering that the Asad regime had been soft-peddling these ideas as it worked to construct a Syrian identity and a type of Syrian "Arabism."[48] The Asad regime also worked to rehabilitate the party's image, in part by promoting a revisionist narrative about the party's involvement in the assassination of Adnan al-Malki that downplayed or absolved

45 Saʿadeh, *Awrāq Qawmiyya*, pp. 306–308, 315–317. Inʿam Raʿad and Bashir Obeid had traveled to Damascus four years earlier in 1975 for meetings to support the PLO. It was the first time Raʿad had visited Syria since the 1955, when he had been sentenced to 15 years in prison for his alleged role in the Malki assassination. There, they met with Syrian foreign minister ʿAbd al-Khalim Khaddam, and upon their return to Lebanon, where they published an article praising Damascus and "the party's return to Damascus after a twenty-year absence." Raʿad, *al-Kalimāt al-Akhīra*, p. 196.

46 Zisser, "The Syrian Phoenix," p. 188.

47 Zisser, "The Syrian Phoenix," p. 189.

48 Eyal Zisser, "Who's Afraid of Syrian Nationalism? National and State Identity in Syria," *Middle Eastern Studies* 42, no. 2 (March 2006): pp. 179–198.

the SSNP of any guilt. For example, Tlass, in his memoirs, suggested it was the CIA, together with Egyptian Ambassador Mahmud Riad and Syrian military intelligence head ʿAbd al-Hamid al-Sarraj, that had been pushing the SSNP's leader at the time, ʿAbd al-Masih, to assassinate Malki. In promoting this conspiracy theory, which has been rejected by scholars such as Rathmell, Tlass removed some of the blame from the SSNP.[49]

13.4 From Damascus Spring to Civil War: The SSNP in Syria after 2000

The return of the SSNP to Syria's public sphere came in the early years of Bashar al-Asad's rule and the aftermath of the Damascus Spring, the brief period following the death of Hafiz al-Asad marked by open political debate and hopes for reform. The party's first public gathering in almost fifty years took place in July 2002, when the party commemorated Saʿadeh's execution. The following year, the SSNP was legalized, and the *Markaz* faction joined the National Progressive Front (NPF, *al-Jabhat al-Waṭaniyya al-Taqdumiyya*), the Baʿth-led political coalition of nationalist and anti-imperialist Syrian political parties. Both developments enabled the party to participate in the parliamentary elections held in March of that year. Twenty SSNP candidates ran for office, but only four were elected, including the head of the party's political bureau, Joseph Suweid, and Basil Dahduh; most participated as independents, while only a few were included on NPF lists, specifically in Qamishli and Homs.[50]

Over the next several years, the SSNP would slowly begin to carve out space in both the political and social-cultural spheres, openly spreading its ideas online and in print and holding public gatherings to commemorate key dates in the party's history. Notably, in 2004, the party could celebrate Saʿadeh's 100th birthday; in locales where the party had deep roots, such as Safita and Masyaf, SSNP commemorations were attended by Syrian regime figures and Baʿth party dignitaries. By 2006, Suweid would be appointed minister without portfolio, a further sign of the party's acceptance in Syria's political sphere. However, Suweid's role and that of the party were to build support for the regime, not develop into a formidable political party that could challenge the Baʿth or Asad's grip on power. Indeed, the party's position in Syria would not change dramatically until the outbreak of the civil war in 2011, when its ranks began to expand, and the regime

49 Mustafa Tlass, *Mirāt Hayātī, Vol. 1* (Damascus: Dār Ṭlāss, n.d.), pp. 434–438.
50 *Daily Star*, 1 March 2003, and Zisser, "The Syrian Phoenix," p. 203.

made use of its factions for different purposes, all designed to help the regime stave off defeat.

The response of the SSNP's *Markaz* and *Intifada* factions to the Syrian uprisings that broke out in Deraa revealed new fissures within the *Markaz* over supporting or opposing the Baʿthist regime or the rebels. These fissures reflected divergences of opinion between the party leadership and its members and between the party faithful in Lebanon and Syria. This convoluted response reflected each faction's deep-seated desire to see real reforms implemented in Syria and the creation of space for each to grow and exert their influence more openly. The party faithful in Beirut loyal to the *Markaz* and long-time Syrian ally Asaad Hardan took to the streets of Hamra to chant defiantly "*Allāh Sūriyya Bashār wa bas!*" (God, Syria, Bashar, and Nothing else!), while those in locales like Hama, Deraa, and Suweida, both members of the *Markaz* and *Intifada*, chanted in unison with the opposition "*al-shaʿb yurīd isqāṭ al-nidhām!*" (The people want the regime's downfall).

In contrast, the leadership of the party's factions lined up behind the regime with little hesitation, viewing the preservation of Syria's security and stability, as well as confronting Israel (which it blamed for sowing the seeds of rebellion and internal strife), to be paramount and existential. Indeed, one party leader remarked that Syria's destabilization would result in the national scene's complete dismantling.[51] The *Markaz* faction leadership began immediately speaking of Western-inspired treachery, and its representative met with then-Syrian vice president Farouk al-Shara and *Intifada* faction leader Ali Haider to discuss the SSNP's support for the regime.[52] Aligned with the regime against those seeking to overthrow it, the SSNP deemed the opposition and rebels either "internal Jews" (*yahūd al-dākhil*) or "terrorists" (*irhabiyyin*), mimicking and amplifying the regime's narratives and talking points.

In the first year of the conflict, SSNP factions predominately limited their support to vocal political backing to the regime, and those party members who did take up arms against the rebels did so not as members of a party militia or armed unit, but as members of the state security apparatus. ʿAli Haidar, the leader of the SSNP's *Intifada* faction and a friend of Bashar al-Asad, with whom he had studied ophthalmology, was appointed Reconciliation Minister in June 2011. Haider was responsible for making overtures to moderate opposition members to reach a political solution to the conflict's end and advance reconciliation. However, his role was essentially to offer the Syrian opposition a

51 *Al-Akhbar*, 27 July 2011.
52 *Al-Akhbar*, 27 July 2011.

poisoned chalice: the opposition would give up their demands and possibly be granted limited concessions on reforms, and Bashar al-Asad would remain in power. Perhaps he did believe he was doing some good in bridging the gap between the sides; he suffered a loss due to the conflict – his son was killed in May 2012 by armed opposition members. Notably, he refused regime offers to arm his faction's members. He held the position until 2018, at which point Haider, though remaining the *Intifada*'s president, withdrew from public life.

The early years of the crisis also produced a new split within the *Markaz* faction. In 2012, the Syrian government revised the constitution, adding a clause that political parties participating in the elections could not be led or based outside of the country. The *Markaz*'s Syrian branch, led by ʿIsam Mahayri and heavily supported by Rami Makhluf, Asad's cousin, decided, without consulting the party leadership in Beirut, to form an independent party in Damascus. Mahayri's decision to create the *Amana* faction and an entirely separate organization, officially known as the Syrian Social Nationalist Party in the Syrian Arab Republic, infuriated the party leadership in Beirut. However, besides raising their ire and outrage, no action was taken to censure the new faction or its members. Of concern to the *Markaz* leadership in Beirut, particularly Hardan, was Makhluf's expanding influence over the party in Syria and the potential ramifications of Makhluf's rise on the party in Lebanon.[53] This concern only worsened in the years that followed as Makhluf became more open about his affiliation with the party and arranged for former Lebanese MP Nasser Qandil to become the editor-in-chief of the SSNP-*Markaz*'s official newspaper, *al-Bina'*.[54] By 2013, the SSNP-*Markaz*'s militia, *Nusūr al-Zawbaʿa* (Eagles of the Whirlwind), fought in Syria alongside the Syrian army. The SSNP-*Markaz*'s engagement on the battlefield marked a definitive step in the party's efforts to openly reassert itself in Syria's public in a way that would have been previously unheard.[55]

In May 2012, six SSNP members were elected in parliamentary elections, many of whom belonged to the newly established *Amana* faction. Four years later, the *Markaz* faction would manage to re-establish its footing in the country

---

53 *Al-Nahar*, 20 May 2020.

54 *Al-Arabi al-Jadid*, 5 March 2014.

55 *ElNashra*, 27 December 2013. The exact date the party's militia became engaged in the fighting in Syria is unclear. However, the first martyrdom announcements appeared in late 2013 together with statements that the deceased had died while performing their national duty in confronting terrorism and "internal Jews." *Nusūr al-Zawbaʿa* has an estimated 6,000 – 8,000 members. On the party's role in Syria, see Chris Solomon, Jesse McDonald, and Nick Grinstead, "Eagles riding the storm of war: The role of the Syrian Social Nationalist Party," *CRU Policy Brief* (January 2019).

and get seven of its members elected in parliamentary elections that year. The leading figure to emerge as part of the *Markaz*'s parliamentary delegation was Ahmed Marʿi, a young, ambitious party member from Jarabulus. A lawyer, Marʿi would transform into a vocal defender and proponent of the Asad regime, becoming a visible presence in Syrian media and the parliament.[56] His most audacious contribution to defending the regime was his 2018 book *Sūriya wa-l-Kīmiyāʾī bi-l-Waqāʾiʿ wa-l-Wathāʾiq*, in which he denied Syria's use of chemical weapons and declared Syria would never use chemical weapons.[57] More importantly, the 2016 election results underscored the SSNP-*Markaz*'s growing political influence in the country.

As the party's parliamentarians and leaders engaged on the political front, other SSNP members were actively participating on the military front. The *Markaz*'s Eagles of the Whirlwind, comprised of both Lebanese and Syrian party members, fought alongside the Syrian Arab Army (SAA), Hezbollah, and the National Defense Forces (NDF)throughout the country. Militia members also provided security in several Christian towns and villages outside of Damascus. Though the Amana and Intifada factions did not establish or operate their own armed groups, members of those factions took part in the fighting as members of the SAA, NDF, or other local defense forces established by the regime.

However, despite the appearance of progress and expanding influence, the SSNP's factions have been given a rude reminder of the limits of their political power. The *Intifada* faction, always small and politically reclusive, has faded into the background as has its president ʿAli Haider. In the fall of 2019, the regime moved against the Makhluf-backed *Amana* faction, dissolving it and withdrawing its license. The exact reasons why the *Amana* faction was disbanded remain unclear, but it is likely related to the personal dispute between Rami Makhluf and Bashar al-Asad. Over the course of the war, Makhluf had amassed further wealth through his ownership of Syriatel, laundered money for the regime, funded regime-backed militias, established his charity and militia, and funded the SSNP, enhancing his power and base of support, though not his popularity overall.[58] Asad, perhaps influenced by his wife who does not care for

56 Other prominent members of the delegation included Talal Khouri and Samir Hajar. Examples of Marʿi's relatively prominent media status can be seen on the Facebook Page of the SSNP's parliamentary block in Syria. See, for example, Facebook Page, "The Syrian Social Nationalist Party Bloc in the Syrian Parliament," accessed 8 June 2020: https://www.facebook.com/permalink.php?story_fbid=1282346538822719&id=742626412794737.

57 Ahmed Marʿi, *Sūriyya wa-l-Kīmiyāʾī bi-l-Waqāʾiʿ wa-l-Wathāʾiq* (Beirut: Dār al-Abʿād, 2018).

58 *Al-Arabiya*, 4 June 2020, accessed 25 August 2020: https://english.alarabiya.net/en/features/2020/06/04/Makhlouf-and-Assad-A-feud-at-the-heart-of-the-Syrian-regime.

Rami or the Russians, decided to seize Makhluf's assets, igniting an internal dispute between the two families that have ruled Syria hand-in-hand since 1970.[59] In the meantime, the *Markaz* has escaped a similar fate. However, the regime sent a clear message to it in the recent parliamentary elections: only three, as opposed to seven, *Markaz* candidates were elected.[60] The loss of four seats was a heavy blow to the party as it had entered the elections believing it would increase its share of seats, in part as a reward for its loyalty and contributions to the regime. Such was not the case.

13.5 To Where? A Movement Frustrated

The history of the SSNP is the story of frustrated and unfulfilled ambition. Judging the party against its aims, its failure to become a mass movement, attain significant, lasting political power, and effect the transformative social and political change it pursues is evident to any scholar or observer of the modern Middle East. As this study has demonstrated, several reasons explain this glaring disparity between the SSNP's aims and its accomplishments, mainly due to its inability to overcome the Levant's enduring socio-political realities.

Foremost among the reasons for its failure was in the realm of ideas: the party's rigid, puritanical Syrian nationalism did not resonate broadly, nor did its aim of wholly replacing the existing socio-political structures of the societies in which operated, which antagonized the traditional social and political elites of Lebanon and Syria. In Lebanon, Lebanese nationalist and Arab nationalist ideas found more fertile soil among the numerically more significant Maronite and Sunni communities than did Syrian nationalism, which held greater appeal among minority communities like the Greek Orthodox, Druze, and Shiʿi. Further, the establishment parties and the ideological political movements that embraced and propagated Lebanese and Arab nationalist ideas wielded more political and social influence. They were able to obtain a more significant share of political

---

59 On the Makhluf-Asad feud, see Faysal Itani and Bassam Barabandi, "The Makhlouf Incident and the Infighting Within the Syrian Regime," *Center for Global Policy,* 4 May 2020, accessed 25 August 2020: https://cgpolicy.org/articles/the-makhlouf-incident-and-the-infighting-within-the-syrian-regime/ and Anonymous, "The Intractable Roots of Assad-Makhlouf Drama in Syria," *Center for Global Policy,* 15 May 2020, accessed 25 August 2020: https://cgpolicy.org/articles/the-intractable-roots-of-assad-makhlouf-drama-in-syria/.

60 Facebook Page, "The Syrian Social Nationalist Bloc in the Syrian Parliament," accessed 22 July 2020: https://www.facebook.com/permalink.php?story_fbid=1388402004883838&id=742626412794737.

power while at the same time endeavoring to thwart the SSNP's growth and impact. In Syria, Arab nationalist ideas held more appeal among its majority Sunni community (~60 % of the population), while the SSNP's Syrian nationalism tended to attract followers from Syria's much smaller minority communities, the ʿAlawis, Druze, and Greek Orthodox. This reality, which continues to exist today, severely impeded the SSNP's ideological appeal, ensuring it largely remained on the margins. Moreover, its arguable ideological victory over its Baʿthist rivals in Syria was mostly a hollow one that resulted primarily in its further political marginalization in the country, its ideas successfully coopted and reshaped into a new type of Baʿthist Syrianism.[61]

The party's aim of comprehensive social and political reform also engendered firm opposition in both countries. The existing socio-political structures were not only an obstacle to overcome but played an active role in constraining and resisting the party's efforts to attain power and implement far-reaching reforms. The French Mandate posed one of the primary obstacles to the party's success as France, determined to perpetuate its rule in the Levant, implemented security policies to suppress and thwart nationalist activities that would endanger its authority. While Lebanese and Syrian politicians were often more forgiving of the party, the SSNP did not escape their censure, nor was the party able to enter political alliances as the stronger actor, enabling it to press its demands and enact its agenda.

In Lebanon, another hindrance was the country's social cleavages based on kinship, religious, and communal ties. Lebanon's political system reflected and sustained these cleavages, and the pervasive influence of confessionalism and familism only undermined nationalism, whatever its variety.[62] These cleavages not only weakened the party's appeal but damaged its political strength, particularly in elections. Even among those communities and political circles in which the SSNP's ideology and political stances would ostensibly appeal to or form the basis for political alliances, it failed to secure cooperation or a foothold for its movement. These structural challenges remain today, and the party faces a new challenge, particularly post-Ta'if – it has become an establishment party. Despite its fiery rhetoric promoting resistance and secularism, it behaves like all other Lebanese political actors, cutting deals and sacrificing principles to maintain its modest influence and standing.

---

61 As early as 1988, Inʿam Raʿad declared the party's ideological victory over the Baʿth during the SSNP's Third General Conference, stating, "the Syrian truth won." Raʿad, *al-Kalimāt al-Akhīra*, pp. 318.

62 Halim Barakat, *Lebanon in Strife: Student Preludes to the Civil War* (Austin: University of Texas Press, 1977), p. 187.

The party's failure can also be attributed to poor decision-making and poor reading of the political climate. The most egregious of these are arguably Saʿadeh's antagonistic posture towards the Lebanese government upon his return in 1947, his decision two years later to launch an ill-thought-out and ill-prepared uprising, the party's assassination of Adnan al-Malki in 1955, and the party's failed coup on the eve of 1962. At no point in its history has the party been strong enough to implement the change it desires, a fact that the party has acknowledged at certain times.

In addition to the above, in Saʿadeh's absence, the party has divided itself over issues ranging from personal, political, and ideological disputes to disagreements over constitutional matters of the separation of powers between the party's executive and legislative bodies. At the core of these issues lies the familiar accusation or claim that one side or the other is acting in accordance or in contravention of Saʿadeh's teachings, or that the party's leadership has proven unable take responsibility for its poor guidance and questionable decisions.

Does this mean, however, that the SSNP should be classified as a "failed" movement? As this study has demonstrated, such a conclusion would not only be misleading but would overlook the party's historical achievements in Lebanon and Syria. Among the party's most notable achievements was establishing a social and political movement that cut through social and political cleavages. Though the party would count Greek Orthodox and Druze as most of its adherents, it succeeded in recruiting members from among the religious communities of Lebanon and Syria. Further, though the party would hold great appeal among the young, educated, urban middle class comprised of students, teachers, merchants, and white-collar professionals, it would also make inroads in Lebanon and Syria's rural and peripheral areas. Significantly, a veritable who is who of prominent Palestinian, Lebanese, and Syrian intellectuals, artists, and politicians would embrace, at least in the party's early years, Saʿadeh's Syrian nationalist creed. In the political realm, the party benefited from the relationships and alliances it built. To be sure, these alliances had their share of problems and never enabled the SSNP to implement its program. However, they were arguably successful partnerships: the party's allies got the political and organizational support they sought, and the SSNP was able to pursue and expand its activities relatively unhindered. The SSNP also enjoyed limited electoral success in both countries, but "had a considerable influence on the development of other political parties and the formulation of other political ideologies,"[63] including the Kata'ib, Najjadeh, and the Baʿth. In the realm of ideas, the party served as a con-

63 Salem, *Bitter Legacy*, p. 256.

sistent voice promoting the notion of "secularism in politics," a banner that other movements, particularly Arab nationalist movements, would be inspired to carry.[64]

Despite its many shortcomings, its legacy of frustrated ambition, and the pervasiveness of internal divisions, the SSNP has managed to survive as an organized political movement. Saʿadeh's legacy and ideas have retained their appeal and resonate with a relatively small, but significant, number of Lebanese and Syrians. How is it that Saʿadeh's legacy and the movement he founded have proven so resilient despite confronting acute internal and external challenges and multiple divisions and infighting? Indeed, how is it that despite its legacy of frustration and factionalism, the SSNP remains undeterred, marching onward in its struggle for Greater Syria behind the banners of the red tempest.

64 Salem, *Bitter Legacy*, p. 256–257. Salem suggests the promotion of secularism in politics is, perhaps, "the SSNP's greatest legacy," a suggestion with which this author largely agrees.

Bibliography

Archives

Centre des Archives Diplomatiques de Nantes (CADN).
MDC Arabic Press Archives, Tel Aviv University (MDC).
The National Archives of the United Kingdom, Kew (TNA).
United Nations Archive, Geneva (UNA).

Periodicals

Correspondence d'Orient
Filastin (Jaffa)
L'Orient (Beirut)
Le Jour (Beirut)
al-Akhbar (Beirut)
Mirat al-Sharq (Jaffa)
Lisan al-Shaʿb (Damascus)
Sada Lubnan (Beirut)
al-Anbaʾ (Damascus)
al-Difaʿ (Jaffa)
al-Ma'rad (Beirut)
Sawt al-Shaʿb (Beirut)
al-Zawba'a (Buenos Aires)
al-Jil al-Jadid (Beirut)
al-Binaʾ (Damascus)
Daily Star (Beirut)
al-Thawra (Damascus)
The New York Times (New York)
The Palestine Post (Jerusalem)
The Times (London)
Oriente Moderno (Rome)
al-Arabi al-Jadid (London)
LBCI News (Beirut)
Nidaʿ al-Watan (Beirut)
al-Liwaa (Beirut)
al-Arabiya (Dubai)
ElNashra (Beirut)

https://doi.org/10.1515/9783110729092-016

Published Books, Articles and Other Material in Arabic, French, and German

ʿAbd al-Masih, George. *Ayyām Qawmiyya: Min ʿAmāṭūr ilā al-Iskandarūn* [Nationalist Days: From Ammatour to Alexandria]. Beirut: al-Rukn li-l-Ṭibāʿa wa-l-Nashr, 2004.

ʿAbd al-Satir, Mustafa. *Ayyām wa Qaḍiyya: Min Muʿānayāt Muthaqaf ʿArabī* [Days and a Cause: On the Sufferings of an Arab Intellectual]. Beirut: Muʾassasat Fikr li-l-Abḥāth wa-l-Nashr, 1982.

Abu Mansur, Fadlallah. *Aʿāṣīr Dimashq* [Whirlwinds of Damascus]. ND.

al-ʿAql, Jihad. *al-Iltizām fī Jarīdatay 'al-Nahḍa' wa 'Sūriyyā al-Jadīda'* [Ideological Commitment in the Newspapers 'al-Nahda' and Suriyya al-Jadida']. Beirut: al-Furāt, 2002.

al-ʿAql, Jihad. *Ṣiḥāfat al-Ḥaraka al-Qawmiyya al-Ijtimāʿiyya fī-l-Waṭan wa-l-Mahjar, 1933–1949, Vol. 1 and 2* [The Social Nationalist Movement's Press in the Homeland and the Diaspora, 1933–1949, Vol. 1 and 2]. Beirut: al-Furāt, 2004.

al-ʿAql, Jihad. *Ṣiḥāfat al-Ḥaraka al-Qawmiyya al-Ijtimāʿiyya, 1933–1949, Vol. 3* [The Social Nationalist Movement's Press, 1933–1949, Vol. 3]. Beirut: al-Furāt, 2005.

al-ʿAql, Jihad. *Ṣiḥāfat al-Ḥaraka al-Qawmiyya al-Ijtimāʿiyya, 1950–1955, Vol. 4* [The Social Nationalist Movement's Press, 1950–1955, Vol. 4]. Beirut: Dār al-Rukn, 2005.

al-ʿAql, Jihad. *Mawsūʿat Ṣiḥāfat al-Ḥaraka al-Qawmiyya al-Ijtimāʿiyya fī 75 ʿĀman, 1933–2008, Vol. 5* [Encyclopedia of the Social Nationalist Movement's Press at 75 Years, 1933–2008, Vol. 5]. Beirut: al-Furāt, 2011.

al-ʿAql, Jihad. *Azmat al-Maḥkama al-Markaziyya fī al-Ḥizb al-Sūrī al-Qawmī al-Ijtimāʿī* [The Crisis of the Central Court in the Syrian Social Nationalist Party]. Beirut: 2019.

al-Hawrani, Akram. *Mudhakkirāt Akram al-Hawrānī, Vol. 2* [Memoirs of Akram al-Hawrani, Vol. 2]. Cairo: Maktabat Madbūlī, 2000.

al-Husri, Satiʿ. *al-ʿUrūba bayna Duʿātihā wa Muʿāriḍīha* [Arabism between its Supporters and Opponents]. Beirut: 1951.

al-Husri, Satiʿ. *Difāʿ ʿan al-ʿUrūba* [A Defense of Arabism]. Beirut: 1956.

al-Khalidi, Ghassan. *Saʿādah wa-l-Thawra al-Awwalī* [Saʿadeh and the First Revolution]. Beirut: Dār wa Maktabat al-Turāth al-Adabī, 1997.

al-Khalidi, Ghassan. *al-Ḥizb al-Qawmī wa-Qaḍīyat al-Mālikī: Haqīqa am Ittihām, al-Juzaʾ al-Awwal* [The National Party and the Malki Affair: Facts or Doubts, Vol. 1]. Beirut: Dār wa Maktabat al-Turāth al-Adabī, 1999.

al-Khalidi, Ghassan. *al-Ḥizb al-Qawmī wa-Qaḍīyat al-Mālikī: Haqīqa am Ittihām, al-Juzaʾ al-Thānī* [The National Party and the Malki Affair: Facts or Doubts, Vol. 2]. Beirut: Dār wa Maktabat al-Turāth al-Adabī, 2000.

al-Khalidi, Ghassan. *al-Muqāwama al-Qawmiyya* [The Nationalist Resistance]. Beirut: Dār wa-Maktabat al-Turāth al-Adabī, 2000.

al-Khalidi, Ghassan. *al-Ḥizb al-Qawmī wa-l-Thawra al-Thāniyya 1961–1962, al-Inqilāb wa-l-Muhākamāt, Vol. 1* [The National Party and the Second Revolution 1961–1962, The Coup and the Trials, Vol. 1]. Beirut: Dār wa Maktabat al-Turāth al-Adabī, 2003.

al-Khalidi, Ghassan. *Baṭal min Umatī Ḥabīb al-Shartūnī* [A Hero from My Nation: Habib al-Shartuni]. Beirut: Dār wa Maktabat al-Turāth al-Adabī Lubnān, 2020.

al-Khālidūn: Sīrat Shuhadāʾ al-Ḥaraka al-Sūriyya al-Qawmiyya al-Ijtimāʿiyya [The Immortals: The Lives of the Martyrs of the Syrian Social Nationalist Movement]. Syria: ND.

al-Khuri, Beshara. *Ḥaqāʾiq Lubnāniyya, al-Juzaʾ al-Thālith* [Lebanese Realities, Vol. 3]. Beirut: Manshūrāt Awrāq Lubnāniyya, ND.

al-Sulh, Adil. *Ḥizb al-Istiqlāl al-Jumhūrī: Min al-Muqāwama li-Waṭaniyya Ayām al-Intidāb al-Faransī* [The Republican Independence Party: From Resistance to Patriotism – The French Mandate Era]. Beirut: Dār al-Ṭalīʿa li-l-Tibāʿa wa-l-Nashr, 1970.

al-Qays, Fayez ʿIlm al-Din. *Ḥizb al-Baʿth al-ʿArabī al-Ishtirākī, Vol. 1* [The Arab Socialist Baʿth Party, Vol. 1]. Beirut: Dār al-Fārābī, 2017.

Ahmad, Ahmad Salim. *Ḥizb al-Sūrī al-Qawmī al-Ijtimāʿī, 1932–1962: Dirāsa Tārīkhīya* [The Syrian Social Nationalist Party, 1932–1962: A Historical Study]. Beirut: Dār wa Maktabat al-Turāth al-Adabī, 2014.

Asfahani, Ahmad. *Anṭūn Saʿādah wa-l-Ḥizb al-Sūrī al-Qawmī al-Ijtimāʿī fī Awrāq al-Amīr Farīd Shihāb al-Mudīr al-ʿĀmm li-l-Amn al-ʿĀmm al-Lubnānī* [Antun Saʿadeh and the Syrian Social Nationalist Party in the Papers of Emir Farid Chehab, the General Director of Lebanese General Security]. Beirut: Kutub, 2006.

Asfahani, Ahmad. *al-Tanaṣṣut ʿala al-Hātif fī Lubnān: Anṭūn Saʿādah wa-l-Ḥizb al-Sūrī al-Qawmī al-Ijtimāʿī Namūdhajan, 1947–1958* [Wiretapping in Lebanon: Antun Saʿadeh and the Syrian Social Nationalist Party as an Archetype]. Beirut: Dār Kutub li-l-Nashr, 2014.

Asfahani, Ahmad. *Mafhum al-Ḥizb ʿinda Saʿādah* [Understanding the Party with Saʿadeh]. Beirut: al-Furāt, 2016.

Asfahani, Ahmad and Yumna ʿAsaili (eds.). *Fī Khidmat al-Waṭan: Mukhtārāt min al-Wathāʾiq al-Khaṣṣa li-l- Amīr Farīd Shihāb* [On Behalf of the Nation: Selections from the Private Papers of Emir Farid Chehab]. Beirut: Kutub, 2005.

Asfahani, Ahmad and Nasif Rizkallah (eds.). *Jūzif Rizq Allāh: Sīrat Munāḍil Qawmī, 1926–1970* [Joseph Rizkallah: The Life of a Nationalist Fighter, 1926–1970]. Beirut: al-Furāt, 2020.

Awad, Fuʾad. *al-Ṭarīq ilā al-Sulṭa* [The Path to Power]. Beirut: Kadmus Publications, 1973.

Beshara, Adel. *Fāyiz Ṣāyigh al-Qawmī: Tajribatuhu fī al-Ḥizb al-Sūrī al-Qawmī al-Ijtimāʿī* [Fayez Sayegh the Nationalist: His Experience in the Syrian Social Nationalist Party]. Beirut: al-Furāt, 2018.

Dayah, Jan. *Saʿādah wa-l-Nāziyya* [Saʿadeh and Nazism]. Beirut: Fajr al-Nahḍa, 1994.

Dayah, Jan. *Muḥākamat Anṭūn Saʿādah: Wathāʾiq al-Taḥqīq al-Rasmī* [The Trial of Antun Saʿadeh: Official Investigation Documents]. Beirut: Fajr al-Nahḍa, 2002.

Facebook Page, "The Syrian Social Nationalist Bloc in the Syrian Parliament," accessed 22 July 2020: https://www.facebook.com/permalink.php?story_fbid=1388402004883838&id=742626412794737.

Facebook Page, "The Syrian Social Nationalist Party Bloc in the Syrian Parliament," accessed 8 June 2020: https://www.facebook.com/permalink.php?story_fbid=1282346538822719&id=742626412794737.

Faris, George. *Fuʾād Sulaymān bayn al-Waṭaniyya wa-l-Qawmiyya* [Fu'ad Suleiman between Patriotism and Nationalism]. Beirut: Khāṣ Lubnān, 2011.

Haddad, Maʿin. *Jadaliyya al-Jughrāfiyā wa-l-Siyāsa* [The Dialectic of Geography and Politics]. Beirut: al-Furāt, 2019.

Hajal, Masʿad. *Lam Ubaddil... wa Lan: al-Mujallad al-Awwal* [I Have Not Changed...And I Will Not, Vol. 1]. Beirut: 2018.

Hallaq, Hassan. *Muʾatamar al-Sāḥil wa-l-Aqḍiya al-Arbaʿa 1936* [The Conference of the Coast and the Four Districts 1936]. Beirut: 1983.

Hardan, Nawaf. *Saʿādah fī al-Mahjar, Vol.1* [Saʿadeh in Exile, Vol. 1]. Beirut: Dār Fikr li-l-Abḥāth wa-l-Nashr, 1989.

Hokayem, Antoine, Daad Bou Malhab ʿAtallah, and Jean Charaf, eds. *Documents Diplomatiques Français Relatifs à l'Histoire du Liban et de la Syrie à l'Époque du Mandat: 1914–1946, Tome* 1 [French Diplomatic Documents Relating to the History of Lebanon and Syria during the Mandate Era: 1914–1946, Vol. 1]. Paris: L'Harmattan, 2003.

Ibrahim, Mutaniyus Yusuf. *Anṭūn Saʿādah wa-l-Niẓām al-Lubnānī* [Antun Saʿadeh and the Lebanese Government]. Beirut: al-Jāmiʿa al-Lubnāniyya, 2016.

Jurayj, Jibran. *Maʿa Anṭūn Saʿādah, Vol. 3* [With Antun Saʿadeh, Vol. 3]. Beirut: Ḥuqūq al-Ṭabʿa wa-l-Nashr Maḥfūẓa li-l-Muʾallif, 1979.

Jurayj, Jibran. *Min al-Juʿbat: Marwiyyāt, Mustanadāt wa Adabiyyāt ʿan al-Ḥizb al-Sūrī al-Qawmī al-Ijtimāʿī, Vol. 1* [From the Files: Stories, Documents, and Literature on the Syrian Social Nationalist Party, Vol. 1]. Beirut: 1985.

Jurayj, Jibran. *Min al-Juʿbat: Marwiyyāt, Mustanadāt wa Adabiyyāt ʿan al-Ḥizb al-Sūrī al-Qawmī al-Ijtimāʿī, Vol.2* [From the Files: Stories, Documents, and Literature on the Syrian Social Nationalist Party, Vol. 2]. Beirut: 1986.

Jurayj, Jibran. *Min al-Juʿbat: Marwiyyāt, Mustanadāt wa Adabiyyāt ʿan al-Ḥizb al-Sūrī al-Qawmī al-Ijtimāʿī, Vol. 3* [From the Files: Stories, Documents, and Literature on the Syrian Social Nationalist Party, Vol. 3]. Beirut: 1988.

Jurayj, Jibran. *Min al-Juʿbat: Marwiyyāt, Mustanadāt wa Adabiyyāt ʿan al-Ḥizb al-Sūrī al-Qawmī al-Ijtimāʿī, Vol. 4* [From the Files: Stories, Documents, and Literature on the Syrian Social Nationalist Party, Vol. 4]. Beirut: 1993.

Jurayj, Jibran. *Haqāʾiq ʿan al-Istiqlāl: Ayyām Rāshayā* [Facts about Independence: Days of Rashaya]. Beirut: Dār Amwāj Lubnān, 2000.

Khayrallah, Shawqi. *Mudhakkirāt Shawqī Khayr Allah, Vol. 2, 1971–1997* [Memoirs of Shawqi Khayrallah, Vol. 2, 1971–1997]. Beirut: al-Markaz al-ʿIlmī li-l-Nashr wa-l-Tawziʿ, 1998.

Lammens, Henri. *La Syrie et Son Importance Géographique* [Syria and its Geographic Importance]. Lourain, 1904.

Lammens, Henri. *La Syrie: Précis Historique* [Syria: A Precise History]. Beirut, 1921.

Lyautey, Pierre. *Gouraud* [Gouraud]. Paris: 1949.

Makhluf, Jamil. *Maḥaṭṭāt Qawmiyya* [Nationalist Stations]. Beirut: al-Rukn li-l-Ṭibāʿa wa-l-Nashr, 2006.

Marʿi, Ahmed. *Sūriyya wa-l-Kīmiyāʾī bi-l-Waqāʾiʿ wa-l-Wathāʾiq* [Syria and Chemical Weapons: Facts and Documents]. Beirut: Dār al-Abʿād, 2018.

Mokdessi, Toufic & Lucien George. *Les Partis Libanais en 1959 [*Lebanese Parties in 1959*]*. Beirut: Editions l'Orient al-Jarida, 1959.

Muhanna, Tawfiq. *La-Yabqā al-Hilāl al-Sūrī... Khasīban* [To Keep the Syrian Crescent... Fertile]. Beirut: al-Furāt, 2017.

Mujais, Salim. *Anṭūn Saʿādah wa-l-Iklīrūs al-Mārūnī* [Antun Saʿadeh and the Maronite Clergy]. Beirut: 1993.

Mujais, Salim and Badr el-Hage. *al-Duktūr Khalīl Saʿādah: Sūriyya min al-Ḥarb wa-l-Majāʿa ila Muʾtamar al-Ṣulḥ, al-Mujallad al-Awwal* [Dr. Khalil Saʿadeh: Syria from the War and Famine to the Peace Conference, Vol. 1]. Beirut: Muʾassasat Saʿādah li-l-Thaqāfa, 2014.

Mujais, Salim and Badr el-Hage. *al-Duktūr Khalīl Saʿādah: Sūriyya wa-l-Intidāb al-Faransiyya, al-Mujallad al-Thānī* [Dr. Khalil Saʿadeh: Syria and the French Mandate, Vol. 2]. Beirut: Muʾassasat Saʿādah li-l-Thaqāfa, 2014.

Mujais, Salim and Badr el-Hage. *al-Duktūr Khalīl Saʿādah: Mabāḥith ʿUmrāniyya wa Falsafiyya, al-Mujallad al-Rābiʿ* [Dr. Khalil Saʿadeh: Civilizational and Philosophical Discussions]. Beirut: Kutub, 2016.
Qubrusi, ʿAbdallah. *Nahna wa Lubnān* [Us and Lebanon]. Beirut: 1954.
Qubrusi, ʿAbdallah. *ʿAbd Allah Qubruṣī Yatadhakkar, Vol. 1* [ʿAbdallah Qubrusi Remembers, Vol. 1]. Beirut: Muʾassasat Fikr li-l-Abḥāth wa-l-Nashr, 1982.
Qubrusi, ʿAbdallah. *ʿAbd Allah Qubruṣī Yatadhakkar, Vol. 2* [ʿAbdallah Qubrusi Remembers, Vol. 2]. Beirut: Muʾassasat Fikr li-l-Abḥāth wa-l-Nashr, 1982.
Qubrusi, ʿAbdallah. *ʿAbd Allah Qubruṣī Yatadhakkar, Vol. 4* [ʿAbdallah Qubrusi Remembers, Vol. 4]. Beirut: al-Furāt, 2004.
Qubrusi, ʿAbdallah. *ʿAbd Allah Qubruṣī Yatadhakkar, Vol. 5* [ʿAbdallah Qubrusi Remembers, Vol. 5]. Beirut: Dār wa Maktabat al-Turāth al-Adabī, 2019.
Raʿad, Inʿam. *al-Kalimāt al-Akhīra: Mudhakkirāt wa Wathāʾiq* [Final Words: Memoirs and Documents]. Beirut: Muʾassasat Inʿām Raʿad al-Fikriyya, 2002.
Saʿadeh, ʿAbdallah. *Awrāq Qawmiyya: Mudhakkirāt ʿAbdallah Saʿādah* [Nationalist Papers: The Memoirs of ʿAbdallah Saʿadeh]. Beirut: 1987.
Saʿadeh, Antun. *al-Aʿmāl al-Kāmila* [Complete Works]. Beirut: Saʿādah Cultural Foundation, 2001.
Saʿadeh, Antun. *Mabādiʾ al-Ḥizb al-Sūrī al-Qawmī al-Ijtimāʿī wa Ghāyatu* [The Principles of the Syrian Social Nationalist Party and its Aims]. Beirut: Dār Fikr li-l-Abḥāth wa-l-Nashr, 2011.
Saʿadeh, Antun. *al-Ṣirāʿ al-Fikrī fī al-Adab al-Sūrī, 12th ed* [The Intellectual Struggle in Syrian Literature]. Beirut: Saʿādah Cultural Foundation, 2013.
Samné, Georges. *La Syrie* [Syria]. Paris: Éditions Bossard, 1921.
Schumann, Christoph. *Radikalnationalismus in Syrien und Libanon. Politische Sozialisation und Elitenbildung 1930–1958* [Radical Nationalism in Syria and Lebanon: Political Socialization and Elite Building 1930–1958]. Hamburg: Deutsches Orient Institut, 2001.
Schumann, Christoph. "Symbolische Aneignungen. Antun Saʿadas Radikalnationalismus in der Epoche des Faschismus [Symbolic Appropriations: Antun Saʿadeh's Radical Nationalism in the Era of Fascism]." In *Blind für die Geschichte? Arabische Begegnungen mit dem Nationalsozialismus* [Blind to the History? Arab Encounters with National Socialism], edited by G. Höpp/P. Wien/R. Wildangel, pp. 155–189. Berlin: Klaus Schwarz Verlag, 2004.
Tabet, Jacques. *La Syrie* [Syria]. Paris, 1920.
Taqi al-Din, Munir. *Wilādat al-Istiqlāl* [The Birth of Independence]. Beirut: Dar al-Nahār li-l-Nashr, 1997.
Tlass, Mustafa. *Mirāt Hayātī, Vol. 1* [Mirror of My Life, Vol. 1]. Damascus: Dār Ṭlāss, n.d.
Wizārat al-Iʿlā al-Lubnāniyya. *Qaḍīyat al-Ḥizb al-Qawmī* [The Case of the National Party]. Beirut, 1949.
Yammut, Ibrahim. *al-Ḥaṣād al-Murr – Qiṣṣat Tafattut Qiyādat Ḥizb wa Tamāsuk ʿAqīda* [Bitter Harvest: The Story of the Fragmentation of the Party Leadership and Ideological Cohesion]. Beirut: Dār al-Rukn, 1993.

Published Books, Articles and Other Material in English

Allawi, Ali. *Faisal I of Iraq*. New Haven: Yale University Press, 2014.

Anonymous. "The Intractable Roots of Assad-Makhlouf Drama in Syria." *Center for Global Policy*, 15 May 2020, accessed 25 August 2020: https://cgpolicy.org/articles/the-intractable-roots-of-assad-makhlouf-drama-in-syria/.

Arielli, Nir. *Fascist Italy and the Middle East, 1933–1940*. New York: Palgrave Macmillan, 2010.

Asseily, Youmna and Ahmad Asfahani, (eds.). *A Face in the Crowd: The Secret Papers of Emir Farid Chehab, 1942–1972*. London: Stacey International, 2007.

Atassi, Karim. *Syria – The Strength of an Idea: The Constitutional Architectures of Its Political Regimes*. Cambridge: Cambridge University Press, 2018.

Attié, Caroline. *Struggle in the Levant: Lebanon in the 1950s*. London: The Centre for Lebanese Studies, Oxford, and I.B. Tauris, 2004.

Bailony, Reem. "Transnationalism and the Syrian Migrant Public: The Case of the 1925 Syrian Revolt." *Mashriq & Mahjar* 1, no. 1 (2013): 8–29.

Barakat, Halim. *Lebanon in Strife: Student Preludes to the Civil War*. Austin: University of Texas Press, 1977.

Barr, James. *A Line in the Sand: The Anglo-French Struggle for the Middle East, 1914–1948*. New York: W.W. Norton & Company, 2012.

Batatu, Hanna. *Syria's Peasantry, the Descendants of Its Lesser Rural Notables, and Their Politics*. Princeton: Princeton University Press, 1999.

Baun, Dylan. "The Gemmayzeh Incident of 1949: Conflict Over Physical and Symbolic Space in Beirut." *Arab Studies Journal* 25, no. 1 (Spring 2017): pp. 92–122.

Bawardi, Hani J. *The Making of Arab Americans: From Syrian Nationalism to U.S. Citizenship*. Austin: University of Texas Press, 2015.

Beshara, Adel. *Antun Sa'adeh: The Man and His Thought: An Anthology*. Reading: Ithaca Press, 2007.

Beshara, Adel. *Outright Assassination: The Trial and Execution of Antun Sa'adeh, 1949*. Reading: Ithaca Press, 2010.

Beshara, Adel. *Lebanon: The Politics of Frustration – The Failed Coup of 1961*. New York: Routledge, 2011.

Beshara, Adel. *Syrian Nationalism: An Inquiry into the Political Thought of Antun Sa'adeh, Second Edition*. Melbourne: IPhoenix Publishing, 2011.

Beshara, Adel. *Khalil Sa'adeh: Many Men in One Man*. Beirut-Melbourne: al-Furat/IPhoenix Publishing, 2015.

Beshara, Adel. *Fayez Sayegh: The Party Years, 1938–1947*. London: Black House Publishing, 2019.

Browne, Walter L., *Lebanon's Struggle for Independence, 1944–1947 – Part II*. North Carolina: Documentary Publications, 1980.

Creswell, Robyn. *City of Beginnings: Poetic Modernism in Beirut*. Princeton: Princeton University Press, 2019.

De Wailly, Henri. *Invasion Syria 1941: Churchill and De Gaulle's Forgotten War*. London: I.B. Tauris, 2016.

Entelis, John P. "Party Transformation in Lebanon: Al-Kata'ib as a Case Study." *Middle Eastern Studies* 9, no. 3 (October 1973): pp. 325–340.

Entelis, John P. *Pluralism and Party Transformation in Lebanon: Al-Kata'ib, 1936–1970.* Leiden: Brill, 1974.

El-Solh, Raghid. *Lebanon and Arabism: National Identity and State Formation.* London: I.B. Tauris, 2004.

Firro, Kais. *Inventing Lebanon: Nationalism and the State under the Mandate.* London: I.B. Tauris, 2002.

Foreign Relations of the United States (FRUS): Diplomatic Papers, 1936–1960.

Fry, Michael G., and Itamar Rabinovich (eds.). *Despatches from Damascus: Gilbert MacKereth and British Policy in the Levant.* Tel Aviv: Dayan Center, 1985.

Gelvin, James L. "The 'Politics of Notables' Forty Years After." *Middle East Studies Association Bulletin* 40, no. 1 (June 2006): pp. 19–29.

Goodman, James. "Nationalism as a Social Movement." *Oxford Research Encyclopedia of international Studies*, 22 December 2017, accessed 24 October 2020: https://oxfordre.com/internationalstudies/view/10.1093/acrefore/9780190846626.001.0001/acrefore-9780190846626-e-267.

Hourani, Albert. *Syria and Lebanon: A Political Essay.* London: Oxford University Press, 1946.

Hourani, Albert. "Ottoman Reform and the Politics of Notables." In *Beginnings of Modernization in the Middle East: The Nineteenth Century*, ed. William R. Polk and Richard L. Chambers, pp. 41–68. Chicago: University of Chicago Press, 1968.

Hudson, Michael. *The Precarious Republic: Political Modernization in Lebanon.* Boulder: Westview Press, 1985.

Itani, Faysal, and Bassam Barabandi. "The Makhlouf Incident and the Infighting Within the Syrian Regime." *Center for Global Policy*, 4 May 2020, accessed 25 August 2020: https://cgpolicy.org/articles/the-makhlouf-incident-and-the-infighting-within-the-syrian-regime/.

Jankowski, James. *Nasser's Egypt, Arab Nationalism, and the United Arab Republic.* Boulder: Lynne Rienner Publishers Inc, 2002.

Kaufman, Asher. *Reviving Phoenicia: The Search for Identity in Lebanon.* London: I.B. Tauris, 2004.

Kaufman, Asher. "Henri Lammens and Syrian nationalism." In *The Origins of Syrian Nationhood: Histories, Pioneers and Identity*, edited by Adel Beshara, pp. 108–122. New York: Routledge, 2011.

Kader, Haytham A. *The Syrian Social Nationalist Party: Its Ideology and Early History.* Beirut, 1990.

Katibah, Habib. "Syria for the Syrians under the Guardianship of the United States," *Bulletin of the Syrian National Society* (Boston) 1, no. 9 (28 February 1919).

Katibah, Habib. *The New Spirit in Arab Lands.* New York: 1940.

Khalaf, Samir. *Civil and Uncivil Violence in Lebanon: A History of the Internationalization of Communal Conflict.* New York: Columbia University Press, 2002.

Khoury, Philip S. "Factionalism among Syrian Nationalists during the French Mandate." *International Journal of Middle East Studies* 13, no. 4 (November 1981): pp. 441–469.

Khoury, Philip S. *Urban Notables and Arab Nationalism: The Politics of Damascus 1860–1920.* Cambridge: Cambridge University Press, 1983.

Khoury, Philip S. *Syria and the French Mandate: The Politics of Arab Nationalism, 1920–1945.* Princeton: Princeton University Press, 1987.

Longrigg, Stephen Hemsley. *Syria and Lebanon under French Mandate.* London: Oxford University Press, 1958.
Maddy-Weitzman, Bruce. *The Crystallization of the Arab State System, 1945–1954.* Syracuse, New York: Syracuse University Press, 1993.
Makdisi, Nadim K. "The Syrian National Party: A Case Study of the First Inroads of National Socialism in the Arab World," Ph.D. Dissertation, American University of Beirut, 1960.
Maoz, Moshe. *Asad: The Sphinx of Damascus.* New York: Weidenfeld & Nicolson, 1988.
Ma'tuq, Muhammad. "A Critical Study of Antun Saada and his impact on politics, the history of ideas, and literature in the Middle East," Ph.D. Dissertation, University of London, 1992.
Martin, Kevin W. *Syria's Democratic Years: Citizens, Experts, and Media in the 1950s.* Bloomington: Indiana University Press, 2015.
McNamara, Vincent J. "Some Basic Notions of the Personalism of Nicolas Berdyaev." *Laval théologique et philosophique* 16, no. 2 (1960): pp. 279–280.
Micallef, Roberta. "Hatay Joins the Motherland." In *State Frontiers: Borders and Boundaries in the Middle East*, edited by Inga Brandell, pp. 141–158. London: I.B. Tauris, 2006.
Moubayed, Sami. *Steel and Silk: Men and Women Who Shaped Syria, 1900–2000.* Seattle: Cune Press, 2006.
Moubayed, Sami. *The Makers of Modern Syria: The Rise and Fall of Syrian Democracy, 1918–1958.* London: I.B. Tauris, 2018.
Mufti, Malik. *Sovereign Creations: Pan-Arabism and Political Order in Syria and Iraq.* Ithaca: Cornell University Press, 1996.
Mujais, Salim. *Antoun Saadeh, A Biography – Volume I: The Youth Years.* Beirut: Kutub, 2004.
Mujais, Salim. *Antoun Saadeh, A Biography – Volume II: Years of the French Mandate.* Beirut: Kutub, 2009.
Mujais, Salim. *Antoun Saadeh, A Biography – Volume III: Years of Exile.* Beirut: Kutub, 2018.
Mujais, Salim. *The Syrian Social Nationalist Party: Its Ideology and History.* London: Black House Publishing, 2019.
Narbona, Maria del Mar Logroña. "Development of Nationalist Identities in French Syria and Lebanon: A Transnational Dialogue with Arab Immigrants to Argentina and Brazil." Ph.D. diss., University of California-Santa Barbara, 2007.
Nordbruch, Götz. *Nazism in Syria and Lebanon: The Ambivalence of the German Option, 1933–1945.* New York: Routledge, 2009.
Nordbuch, Götz. "A Challenge to the Local Order: Reactions to Nazism in the Syrian and Lebanese Press." In *Arab Responses to Fascism and Nazism: Attraction*, edited by Israel Gershoni, pp. 35–54. Austin: University of Texas Press, 2014.
Pipes, Daniel. "Radical Politics and the Syrian Social Nationalist Party." *International Journal of Middle East Studies* 20, no. 3 (August 1988): pp. 303–324.
Pipes, Daniel. *Greater Syria: The History of Ambition.* New York: Oxford University Press, 1990.
Provence, Michael. *The Great Syrian Revolt and the Rise of Arab Nationalism.* Austin: University of Texas Press, 2005.
Rabinovich, Itamar. *The View from Damascus: State, Political Community and Foreign Relations in Modern and Contemporary Syria.* London: Vallentine Mitchell, 2011.

Rathmell, Andrew. *Secret War in the Middle East: The Covert Struggle for Syria, 1949–1961.* London: I.B. Tauris, 2014.

Rogan, Eugene. *The Arabs: A History.* London: Allen Lane, 2009.

Salameh, Franck. *Language, Memory, and Identity in the Middle East: The Case for Lebanon.* Lanham: Lexington Books, 2010.

Salem, Paul. *Bitter Legacy: Ideology and Politics in the Arab World.* Syracuse: Syracuse University Press, 1994.

Salibi, Kamal. *A House of Many Mansions: The History of Lebanon Reconsidered.* London: I.B. Tauris, 2002.

Schumann, Christoph. "The Generation of Broad Expectations: Nationalism, Education, and Autobiography in Syria and Lebanon, 1930–1958." *Die Welt des Islams* 41, no. 2 (July 2001): pp. 174–205.

Schumann, Christoph. "The experience of organized nationalism: radical discourse and political socialization in Syria and Lebanon, 1930–1958." In *From the Syrian Land to the States of Syria and Lebanon*, edited by Thomas Philipp and Christoph Schumann, pp. 343–358. Beirut: Orient-Institute, 2004.

Schumann, Christoph. "Nationalism, diaspora and '*civilisational mission*': the case of Syrian nationalism in Latin America between World War I and World War II." *Nations and Nationalism* 10, no. 4 (October 2004): pp. 599–617.

Seale, Patrick. *The Struggle for Syria: A Study of Post-War Arab Politics, 1945–1958.* London: I.B. Tauris, 1986.

Seale, Patrick. *The Struggle for Arab Independence: Riad el-Solh and the Makers of the Modern Middle East.* Cambridge: Cambridge University Press, 2010.

Sethian, R.D. "The Syrian National Party," Ph.D. Dissertation, University of Michigan, 1946.

Sharabi, Hisham. *Embers and Ashes: Memoirs of an Arab Intellectual.* Northampton: Olive Branch Press, 2008.

Solomon, Chris, Jesse McDonald, and Nick Grinstead. "Eagles riding the storm of war: The role of the Syrian Social Nationalist Party." *CRU Policy Brief* (January 2019).

Suleiman, Michael W. *Political Parties in Lebanon: The Challenge of a Fragmented Political Culture.* Ithaca: Cornell University Press, 1967.

Tauber, Eliezer. *The Emergence of the Arab Movements.* London: Frank Cass, 1993.

Tauber, Eliezer. *The Arab Movements in World War I.* London: Frank Cass, 1993.

Tauber, Eliezer. *The Formation of Modern Iraq and* Syria. London: Frank Cass, 1995.

The Black Book of the Lebanese Elections of May 25, 1947. New York: Phoenicia Press, 1947.

Tilly, Charles, and Sidney Tarrow. *Contentious Politics, 2nd Ed.* Oxford: Oxford University Press, 2015.

Watenpaugh, Keith D. "Middle-Class Modernity and the Persistence of the Politics of Notables in Inter-War Syria." *International Journal for Middle East Studies* 35, no. 2 (May 2003): pp. 257–286.

Wiktorowicz, Quintan, ed. *Islamic Activism: A Social Movement Theory Approach.* Bloomington: Indiana University Press, 2004.

Wien, Peter. "Arabs and Fascism: Empirical and Theoretical Perspectives." *Die Welt des Islams* 52, no. 1 (January 2012): pp. 331–350.

Yamak, Labib Zuwiyya. *The Syrian Social Nationalist Party: An Ideological Analysis.* Cambridge: Harvard University Press, 1966.

Zamir, Meir. *Lebanon's Quest: The Road to Statehood, 1926–1939.* London: I.B. Tauris, 1997.

Zisser, Eyal. *Lebanon: The Challenge of Independence.* London: I.B. Tauris, 2000.

Zisser, Eyal. “Who’s Afraid of Syrian Nationalism? National and State Identity in Syria.” *Middle Eastern Studies* 42, no. 2 (March 2006): pp. 179–198.

Zisser, Eyal. “The Syrian Phoenix – The Revival of the Syrian Social National Party in Syria.” *Die Welt des Islams* 47, no. 2 (January 2007): pp. 188–206.

Zisser, Eyal. “Memoirs Do Not Deceive: Syrians Confront Fascism and Nazism—as Reflected in the Memoirs of Syrian Political Leaders and Intellectuals.” In *Arab Responses to Fascism and Nazism: Attraction and Repulsion*, edited by Israel Gershoni, pp. 73–98. Austin: University of Texas Press, 2014.

Index

https://doi.org/10.1515/9783110729092-017

www.ingramcontent.com/pod-product-compliance
Lightning Source LLC
Chambersburg PA
CBHW050645270326
41927CB00012B/2876
* 9 7 8 3 1 1 1 1 2 1 7 4 1 *